2833

D1612427

The Eighteenth Centuries

The Eighteenth Centuries

GLOBAL NETWORKS
OF ENLIGHTENMENT

Edited by

DAVID T. GIES AND CYNTHIA WALL

University of Virginia Press

CHARLOTTESVILLE AND LONDON

University of Virginia Press
© 2018 by the Rector and Visitors of the University of Virginia
All rights reserved
Printed in the United States of America on acid-free paper

ISBN 978-0-8139-4075-5 (cloth)
ISBN 978-0-8139-4076-2 (e-book)

First published 2018

1 3 5 7 9 8 6 4 2

Library of Congress Cataloging-in-Publication Data
is available for this title.

Cover art: Reproduction of a 1745 globe by Robert de Vaugondy; *Pilgrimage to the Island of Cythera,* Jean Antoine Watteau, 1717, oil on canvas (Musée du Louvre, © RMN–Grand Palais/Art Resource, NY; photo: Stéphane Maréchalle)

Contents

Acknowledgments

Any book is a collaborative effort, but a book that draws on the intellectual talents of scholars from multiple disciplines suggests that the traditional thank-yous will fall short of the mark. This book is no exception, since from its beginning it has been the product of deep thinking, serious research, disciplined writing and—dare we confess it—much fun. The Eighteenth-Century Study Group (ECSG) at the University of Virginia has hosted discussions and lectures on eighteenth-century topics for more than fourteen years. The ECSG is a living organism: members come and go, move in and move on. Yet each meeting generates a host of comments, questions, and challenges that benefit the entire group. The numerous meetings of these scholars became the genesis of this book. A two-day conference organized in 2013 suggested the need for a more permanent record of our considerations of what we call "the eighteenth centuries." Our sincere thanks go to each and every member of the group; to S. Max Edelson, James Ambuske, and Carol Guarnieri, who created the MapScholar website that accompanies this volume; to Angie Hogan, who was there from the start and who helped shepherd the book through the University of Virginia Press; to the scholars and friends at the Jefferson Library and at Monticello; to the College of Arts and Sciences at the University of Virginia; and, of course, to the students in all the disciplines who are discovering how rich, entertaining, and challenging these eighteenth centuries can be.

During the production of this book, Mary D. Sheriff passed away. We deeply mourn her loss. We want especially to thank her husband, Professor Keith Luria, who carefully shepherded her essay through the final stages of the press.

The Eighteenth Centuries

Introduction

Why the eighteenth *centuries,* and not—if we insist on the pluralization of
the concept—*Enlightenments?* After all, scholars in the last twenty years
have realized that the Enlightenment (in the singular, as it had been known
for nearly two centuries) is a multifaceted, richly textured, and often contradictory phenomenon, not easily molded into a single concept or located
in a single geographical space. And it is precisely those eighteenth-century
spaces, both physical and conceptual, that concern us here.

This volume was born, we might say, in the heart of American Enlightenment: at Thomas Jefferson's university. To enter Monticello, Jefferson's magnificent—yet humble—residence in central Virginia, is to penetrate a space
at once imposing and intimate, crammed with well-chosen objects that recount, and perhaps reflect, the owner's catholic interests. Objects large and
small hang side by side in exuberant defiance of any predetermined coherence. Their unity surges from their individual differences. The eye discerns
a color, a shape, a texture, and a spatiality that fuse together into an original
and distinctive view of American and European history and culture. Enlightenment history and culture, of course. It is this image that governs the
collection. The March 2013 symposium at the University of Virginia that
inspired our volume—"The Eighteenth Centuries: An Interdisciplinary
Symposium"—marked the ten-year celebration of the still proudly ongoing
Eighteenth-Century Study Group at the University of Virginia. Faculty from
the Departments of American Studies, Anthropology, Architecture, Art History, Chinese, Economics, English, French, German, History, Italian, Jefferson Studies, Music, Philosophy, Politics, Religious Studies, and Spanish,
along with representatives from the Albert and Shirley Small Special Collections Library and the University of Virginia Press, meet once in the fall
and once in the spring, over wine and cheese, to share current work. We
have had presentations on (and discussed at length) common sense, Harle-
quin theater, Spanish American hierarchy, edges of empire, Orientalism on
the Italian stage, becoming a man in eighteenth-century France, exorcism
and Enlightenment, the prose of things, British art and national revival,
voice machines and the castrati, rococo eroticism in Spanish poetry, Kant
and organizing Enlightenment, enigmas and obscurity in French literature,

Fichte's inner life, metaphors of mind, Locke's moral man, Haydn's invention of Scotland, poetry on the page, the men who lost America, literature incorporated, material forms of judicial authority, Virginia and the American slave trade in art, colonial science, and the biblical foundations of radical thought. Different sizes, different textures, different tones, different takes. Our common and divergent interdisciplinary and intercontinental interests have ignited a localized globalization of sorts that now expands out into the texts and maps—print and digital—of this collection.

Contemplating the Western world in the post-1680 period, one realizes that the sugar produced in Jamaica (Nelson) found its way into the coffee served at the inn owned by Goldoni's *locandiera* in Venice (Ward), whose struggle for independence as a businesswoman also reverberated in Mozart's Viennese operas during the American War of Independence (Polzonetti). That same sugar sweetened the rum imbibed by John Greenwood's inebriated sailors in his painting *Sea Captains Carousing in Surinam* (Crawford) and was served in drinks by Jefferson's mixed-race slaves to guests at Monticello (Hill). Patrons reading the local press in Germany (Pasanek and Wellmon) collected and connected ideas in new, sometimes alarming ways. Artists, whether grappling with marriage, sex, and morality in the novels they were producing (Spacks), with subversive eroticism and utopian thought in their paintings (Sheriff), or with suffering and sympathy in their plays (Reed) struggled to understand how new knowledge and the new sciences informed daily life and marked the path into the future. Those sciences found their way into numerous works in the form of linguistic play in Spanish rococo (Eriksen) and book publishing, book collecting, and bibliographical taxonomies (Pickard). Jefferson himself drew on new scientific knowledge to buy, trade, and breed his horses (Douglass); the new breeding practices informed the scientific theories of race in the Spanish and North Americas (Hill). Many of these ideas circulated in books published in London or Paris ("I cannot live without books," wrote Jefferson), although the eighteenth century also privileged other modes of intellectual exchange, as will become clear to the readers of this collection.

So, why the eighteenth *centuries?*

During the chronological eighteenth century learning and knowledge were intimately connected across disciplinary and geographical boundaries, and it was precisely during this period that those connections became revealed in ways previously understudied. The present book looks at numerous issues from multiple interdisciplinary perspectives in an attempt to weave together some of the many threads that form the historical tapestry generally known as the Enlightenment.

The eighteenth-century Enlightenment has been seen by many as "the source of everything that is progressive about the modern world," although it is still the "subject of bitter debate."[1] Now more than ever, in a world that speaks frequently of "globalization," we turn back to the eighteenth century and witness the inherent globalization of its desires (and, at times, its accomplishments). And yet, the "eighteenth century" is much more than its arbitrary temporal boundaries of 1700–1799. We currently write of the "long" eighteenth century,[2] the "deep" eighteenth century,[3] or the "wide" eighteenth century.[4] Scholars began two decades ago to talk about "Enlightenments" rather than "Enlightenment."[5] Former categories that had shaped (and indeed limited) our thinking about the phenomenon called the Enlightenment no longer seem suitable.

All too often, we labor in academic silos. That is, we become experts in one ever-narrowing and ever-deepening aspect of the individual discipline to which we "belong." Historians move from the world to a continent, then to a country and a time period, and then to a topic or movement or individual. The same arc frequently describes the work of literary scholars, art or music historians, bibliographers, or historians of science. Such specialization (some would say overspecialization) is logical, necessary, and, perhaps inevitable, but in today's globalized environment it is energizing to revisit that perceived narrowness and challenge the practitioners of academic work to make connections beyond the boundaries of their individual disciplines.

What is more, scholars within each discipline often disagree about the nature of that discipline, the reach and approach of their "silo," and the way said discipline interprets the Enlightenment. The eighteenth century lends itself uniquely to such broadened views, since the polymaths of that period embraced fully the possibility of studying science along with history, philosophy, literature, and the arts. It was during the eighteenth century that the concept "citizen of the world" became part of what we understand both *citizen* and *world* to mean; cultured individuals aspired to be worldly citizens. In Anthony Pagden's words, "It is to the Enlightenment that we also owe the modern conception of the global society," although during the eighteenth century "the claim to be a 'citizen of the world' acquired quite different meanings."[6] Take, for example, Thomas Jefferson's friend Philip Mazzei. Mazzei (b. 1730), a native of Italy, worked as a surgeon in Smyrna, on the Aegean coast, before he became a merchant in London. When he moved to Albemarle County, Virginia, just before the American Revolution, he transformed himself into a farmer and winemaker. During the war, he served the state of Virginia as an agent in Paris. In Warsaw, he was privy councilor to King Stanislaus II. He never returned to America, and Jefferson took charge of selling his property there.

Maps, mapping, and space become, therefore, crucial indicators of globalization, as we see in Felicity Nussbaum's collection of essays, which attempt to "challenge the cultural dominant"[7] and range—as do many of the essays in our book—from Europe (including, importantly, the Spanish-speaking eighteenth century) to the Caribbean to the Americas to the Far East. The digital map that accompanies this collection (Ambuske, Guarnieri) helps visualize the global and temporal concentrations of these essays: the multimedia map includes additional images that represent particular physical locations mentioned in the chapters; title pages of contemporary texts; works of art; YouTube clips; strains of music; and links to external websites.

As did Mr. Jefferson, in this book we cross geographical and disciplinary boundaries. We bring together twenty-one scholars, all deeply knowledgeable in their disciplines, and charge each with opening a discussion about the eighteenth century, beginning with one angle of the world as his or her discipline sees it, and then connecting that view with those of other scholars; hence the cross-, trans-, and interdisciplinary nature of the collection. The members of the Eighteenth-Century Study Group who participated in the symposium were joined by eminent scholars from other lands (Chapel Hill, Notre Dame, Stanford, Vanderbilt) as well as by rising star graduate students. The original collection of presentations has been altered in some instances by authors choosing to expand or modify their original investigation. For various reasons, not all participants were able to contribute to this volume, but they enriched our discussions and informed the overall shape of the volume. These include a look at Lamarck's "more dangerous ideas" (Jessica Riskin, English, Stanford University), a study of Isaac Watts in the United States (David Vander Meulen, English, University of Virginia), a consideration of Jeremy Belknap, Isaiah Thomas and the American Antiquarian Society (David Whitesell, University of Virginia Library), the sound of eighteenth-century music (Downing Thomas, Music, University of Notre Dame), and a balancing of "good" and "bad" taste (Jennifer Tsien, French, University of Virginia). Here, our vision encompasses those different sizes, different textures, different tones, and different takes mentioned previously. The eighteenth century. The eighteenth centuries.

The volume is divided into four overlapping parts, each introduced by an eminent scholar of a different discipline, individuals who are or were members of the Eighteenth-Century Study Group, were privy to our conversations and participated in the symposium. Part I, "Knowledge and the Lives of Books," opens with the historian Sophia Rosenfeld, of the University of Pennsylvania, surveying the Enlightenment questions "How do we know what we know? Why are we so often deluded or downright wrong? And more practically, what can be done about this state of affairs?" She traces connections between the essays on Kant, on the London printer William Strahan, and on the romantic and historical novelist Eliza Haywood. Andrew O'Shaughnessy, professor of history at the University of Virginia, introduces part II, "Human Economies," and the dark side of the landscape: from the breeding of horses and the gift economy of the First Families of Virginia, to degeneration as *blanqueamiento* (whitening) in the Americas, to the economies of the Jamaican slave plantations. Part III, "Artists' Geographies," introduced by professor of music Richard Will, gives us visual representations of "the dissolute behavior fostered by the spoils of empire" in the Dutch West Indies and the "jarring images" suggested by the French figurations of Cythera, the "isle of love as an amusement park of decidedly perilous attractions," including the possibility of deportation to Louisiana. Part IV, "Dramatic Politics," as professor of music Bonnie Gordon puts it, encapsulates the resonances across time and space, genre and politics, high art and folk tradition, in the spirit of John Gay's 1728 *The Beggar's Opera:* the essays cover "a Spanish novelist's satire of preaching, an Italian marriage drama, the resonances of the American Revolution in a famous Mozart opera, and the spatial metaphors of sympathy." All the essays in this collection, while looking in different directions, at different objects—at different colors, shapes, textures, spatialities—at the same time contribute to our understanding of the interconnectedness of the "eighteenth centuries."

We have subtitled this book "Global Networks of Enlightenment," a phrase we think captures connections and crossovers better than something with *interdisciplinary* in it (as in the original subtitle of the conference that inspired the book), since our concepts of the disciplines of knowledge stem from nineteenth-century academic changes rather than from eighteenth-century practices. While, as Robin Valenza has shown, in the late seventeenth and eighteenth centuries the sciences and the humanities evolved their own technical languages, they also created others for popular consumption.[8] The essays in this volume reflect those kinds of popular engagements—networks—as well as scientific investigations across international borders into the seemingly limitless possibilities for both knowledge and representation.

The recovery of the eighteenth centuries has been a slow but meaningful process. By this we mean that other centuries and other isms have often captured the attention of scholars, some of whom viewed the eighteenth century as too regulated, too scientific, too mechanical, too "neoclassical," or too philosophical. But just as chemicals produce more intense results when compounded and combined with other ingredients, so too these eighteenth centuries take on new hues and new synergies when viewed together and from different angles. We aim for pluralism. These connections are not automatic. They need to be teased out of each discipline in a very conscious manner. Anthony Pagden worries about the "struggle over the legacy of the Enlightenment" and claims that the Enlightenment "still matters." With this collection, we hope to confirm that view and invite our readers to reflect on how that "matter" reveals itself across disciplines.[9] When the history of science is juxtaposed to philosophical concerns and then inserted into a discussion of literature and the arts, the individual disciplines are all revealed to be something slightly different—and significantly more—than they were before.

Notes

1. Keith Thomas, "The Great Fight over the Enlightenment," *New York Review of Books,* 3 April 2014, 68.

2. Frank O'Gorman, *The Long Eighteenth Century: British Political and Social History 1688–1832* (London: Bloomsbury Academic, 1997).

3. Joseph Roach, *It* (Ann Arbor: University of Michigan Press, 2007).

4. "Unstable Geographies: Global Transfer in the Long, Deep, and Wide Eighteenth Century," seminar, University of California at Davis, 2012, http://dhi.ucdavis.edu/?page_id=6444.

5. See Henry Kunneman and Hent de Vries, eds., *Enlightenments: Encounters between Critical Theory and Contemporary French Thought* (Kampen, The Netherlands: Kok Pharos, 1993); Douglas Anderson, *The Radical Enlightenments of Benjamin Franklin* (Baltimore: Johns Hopkins University Press, 1997); Ian Hunter, *Rival Enlightenments: Civil and Metaphysical Philosophy in Early Modern Germany* (Cambridge: Cambridge University Press, 2001); Gertrude Himmelfarb, *The Roads to Modernity: The British, French, and American Enlightenments* (New York: Knopf, 2004); Graeme Garrard, *Counter-Enlightenments: From the Eighteenth Century to the Present* (New York: Routledge, 2006); and László Kontler, *Translations, Histories, Enlightenments: William Robertson in Germany, 1760–1795* (New York: Palgrave Macmillan, 2014), among others.

6. Anthony Pagden, *The Enlightenment and Why it Still Matters* (New York: Random House, 2013), xi.

7. Betty Joseph, "Proxies of Power. Woman in the Colonial Archive," in *The Global Eighteenth Century,* ed. Felicity Nussbaum (Baltimore: Johns Hopkins University Press, 2003), 123.

8. See Robin Valenza, *Literature, Language, and the Rise of the Intellectual Disciplines in Britain, 1680–1820* (Cambridge: Cambridge University Press, 2009).

9. Pagden, *Enlightenment and Why it Still Matters,* ix.

PART I

Knowledge and the Lives of Books

Introduction

SOPHIA ROSENFELD

Knowledge, it might be said, was both the great subject and the great object of the Enlightenment. Of course, the use of the term *Enlightenment* to designate the rich intellectual and cultural life of eighteenth-century Europe and its New World outposts remains controversial, in part because of the great diversity of opinion and practice that it seems to erase. But a fascination with knowledge as simultaneously a field of inquiry and a collective goal constitutes one common denominator. Writers and thinkers of all stripes were animated in the eighteenth century by the kinds of questions that we now relegate primarily to psychologists and the occasional philosopher: How do we know what we know? Why are we so often deluded or downright wrong? And more practically, what can be done about this state of affairs?

In the first essay in the following section, Brad Pasanek and Chad Wellmon take up the largely theoretical answer to these questions provided by one of the towering figures of the era, the German philosopher Immanuel Kant. They do so, however, by drawing our attention to the significance of one, particularly important eighteenth-century technology and means of communication: the printed book. Specifically, Kant, in his effort to understand the nature of understanding, found it necessary to wrestle with the key Enlightenment conundrum whether books were better considered a means or an obstacle to truth.

As Pasanek and Wellmon explain, for most Enlightenment thinkers the key to genuine knowledge seemed to lie in the autonomous use of human reason and the senses quite apart from received ideas. At the same time, an exploding print culture centered on the book was essential both to generating and to organizing the public, or the network of readers and writers, that "enlightenment" required. Pasanek and Wellmon expose this dualism, and the worries it triggered, not only by scrutinizing the terms of the argument in Kant's great essay "What is Enlightenment?" but also by taking seriously the web of (often ignored) citations and footnotes that situate Kant's reply in a complex set of collective social and textual practices. We see here a novel Enlightenment marked by uncertainty and ambivalence about the real path to knowledge.

For as Pasanek and Wellmon's account of Kant makes clear, eighteenth-century thinkers were also well aware that new, improved ideas—even new, improved ideas about ideas—did not simply emerge full blown in individual minds and make their way seamlessly into the general consciousness. Knowledge development and transfer involved a good many more agents and steps, not to mention potential roadblocks. Picking up on such clues as changing citational practices, contemporary historians of science and scholarship, of books and reading and censorship, and of intellectual history more generally have become increasingly convinced that we need ask not only how knowledge (and error) was conceptualized in the past but also how, in practice, knowledge was produced, controlled, diffused, acquired, overturned, and transformed, and by whom. That is, the history of Enlightenment epistemology is insufficient on its own; we need also to pay attention to the subfield known as the social history of knowledge and, especially, the lives of books within it.

The next two essays in this section take up people, spaces, and institutional, book-based practices that played vital intermediary roles in the transmission and, ultimately, the shaping of ideas in this period and beyond. Michael Pickard concentrates on the printing sector. Focusing on the ledger books of William Strahan, one of the major compositors of mid-eighteenth-century London, Pickard demonstrates that much of what was—and also was not—disseminated to booksellers, libraries, and private living rooms and studies via Strahan's presses was a matter of business fundamentals above all else. The message here is that if we want to understand anything about knowledge circuits in the eighteenth century, the history of ideas cannot be separated either from the history of print and bibliography or from economic and commercial history. So, too, do we need to think further about the function of professional types like Strahan, who made a living out of concretizing enlightened knowledge production and then trading internationally in it. The book was always also a commodity.

Finally, Patricia Meyer Spacks wants us to think about how books, and their meanings, travel through time—especially from the eighteenth century to today. She draws our attention to Eliza Haywood's heavily historical (and currently not widely read) novel *The Fortunate Foundlings* (1744). Rather than insisting on one reading, Spacks demonstrates with great flair various possible modes of exegesis—moral, historical, literary. But Spacks does not try to reconcile them all with a paean to a murky kind of "inter-disciplinarity." Instead, she urges us to think clearly about "different ways of knowing" that shape not only what we see in texts like *The Fortunate Found-lings* but also what we read them to answer in the first place. She then asks all of us, across our distinctive disciplines and reading strategies, to talk to one another.

Which is to say, there is nothing actually antiquarian about any of these inquiries. The real reason we should be interested in eighteenth-century knowledge and books now, as all of these twenty-first-century scholars and authors demonstrate, is not simply that such inquiries add to what we know about the Enlightenment or even give the label its coherence. Rather, it is precisely because we continue to live with the fallout of the Enlightenment preoccupation with epistemology in theory and practice, whether we are contemplating the explosion of new knowledge made possible by further technological advance or engaging in the business of scholarship, from con-sulting manuscripts in archives to, indeed, working with publishers to pro-duce printed consumer goods such as the book you are holding in your hand. The following pages are intended to add to contemporary readers' knowledge about knowledge and books as imagined, debated, and lived in the past and—it is hoped—to stimulate new thinking about the conditions of knowledge production, consumption, and conceptualization today.

Enlightenment, Some Assembly Required

BRAD PASANEK AND CHAD WELLMON

The main figures that populate accounts of the Enlightenment are human, be they enemies of the Enlightenment, such as the priest or the tyrant; defenders such as the *philosophe* or *Aufklärer;* or intellectuals socially assembled in coffeehouses or salons, exercising opinion in rational, critical debate.[1] But in his 1784 essay "What is Enlightenment?," the first figure Immanuel Kant identifies as an antagonist of the Enlightenment is the book, *das Buch:* "It is so easy to be immature if I have a book that has understanding for me [*das für mich Verstand hat*]."[2] Personified books and other forms of print dispossess humans of their rational capacities; they alienate thought, just as priests or doctors serve as guardians for those who have yet to emerge from their "self-incurred immaturity." Kant's triplet—the book that has understanding for me, the pastor who has a conscience for me, and the doctor who judges my diet for me—shadows his three major critical works of philosophy. But the book, ranked first and aligned with the problem of understanding (with the *Critique of Pure Reason*), poses a special threat to enlightenment because it appears as an agent or knower in its own right. Standing between its human authors and readers, a book is not simply an inert container of human thoughts. It could, worried Kant, displace or supplant human understanding.

Kant's claims are complicated, of course, by their medium. For the Enlightenment to make progress, what was needed, as Kant put it, was "the freedom to make public use of one's reason," that is, "that use which anyone makes of it as a scholar [*Gelehrter*] before the entire public of the reading world."[3] For late-eighteenth-century German scholars intent on addressing this "reading world," print was the primary way of using their reason publicly. As a medium of exchange, the printed page separated author and reader even as it put them in contact. Even in the lecture hall, contact between a scholar and his audience was hardly immediate: the intimate tête-à-têtes contrasts sharply with broadcasts and publicity. In Jürgen Habermas's reconstruction of the bourgeois public sphere, an ideal type, an "audience-oriented subjectivity" nurtured in private, animates the *Gelehrter,* "whose writings speak to his public, the world."[4] Departing from Habermas and further simplifying for the sake of argument, we might say that to make public use of one's reason was to do so in print.

So Kant relied on books—his metaphor is significant—to help him "think out loud."[5] But books and other print products posed a threat to the activity of thinking (making use of one's own understanding without guidance) by which humans might free themselves from their immaturity. Or again, the Enlightenment came to depend on the circulation of printed texts, even as these same printed texts threatened to disorder the process of enlightenment. Kant's late-eighteenth-century moment witnessed an astonishing expansion of book-based knowledge, in Paul Keen's words, an "endlessly accelerating, self-regenerating inflation of print" that "threatened to exceed any strategy for its assimilation."[6] This ready availability of printed texts represented a challenge to the core of what Kant claimed was true enlightenment: "thinking for oneself [*Selbstdenken*]."[7] "Thinking for oneself," wrote Kant, "means seeking the highest touchstone of truth in oneself, that is, in one's own reason. And the maxim to think for oneself at all times is enlightenment."[8] An overreliance on books threatened the very disposition of the Enlightenment: "*Sapere aude!* Have courage to make use of your own understanding!"[9] Shun books and do one's thinking oneself. The philosopher Rüdiger Bittner drily remarks, "Booksellers at any rate would find such a maxim of enlightenment uncongenial," before he bends the Enlightenment imperative to think back on itself in order to cancel it. How could such a maxim even be applied? "You cannot fail to obey the injunction."[10]

By invoking "the book," then, in "What is Enlightenment?," Kant recasts the question so that his answer must specify what form autonomous thinking will take in an age beset by print. In this essay, we characterize Kant's media environment by looking to the reading public facilitated and produced by one of the late German Enlightenment's most important periodicals, the *Berlinische Monatsschrift*—the site for the original publication of Kant's essay on enlightenment. In reading the *Monatsschrift,* one of our broader aims is to revisit the concepts of "the public" and "publicness" as first articulated by Jürgen Habermas and then critiqued and complicated by English-language scholars over the past two decades.[11] In light of the revisions and challenges to Habermas's initial thesis, our point is rather simple: the eighteenth-century public, *das Publikum,* insofar as it can be said to have existed, had to be assembled. The "public" did not simply emerge as some ineluctable product of modernity, supervenient on rational subjects and informed citizens, but was a function of particular and contingent decisions facilitated by print technologies. The way the *Monatsschrift* assembled itself and its readership will therefore be described as a bibliographical and literary, as well as a political and ethical, undertaking.

Historians of the book have debated the term *print culture* for some time now, many asking whether it obscures more than it clarifies.[12] But the oxymoron serves the purposes of this essay quite well, because it captures the sense in which technology and the cultivation of the human are conjoined. The phrase aptly describes an eighteenth-century situation in which books were readily personified, while readers, publishers, hacks, and philosophers were all understood to be creatures of print. James Schmidt recently suggested that "one of the chief reasons why the Enlightenment has remained controversial is that it has never been entirely clear what the process of enlightenment involves."[13] In this essay, which is much informed by Schmidt's work on the Enlightenment, we detail a key element of this process, namely, the assembly of the Enlightenment in and as a print culture.

Thinking of reading publics as assembled enables us to see just how multiple, contingent, and particular they were. Doing so also helps us understand the Enlightenment as not simply a particular historical period or liberating philosophical activity but also a particular process bound up with print, that is, enlightenment.[14] To ask, as a great many German intellectuals did in the 1780s, "what is enlightenment?" was to consider the limits, boundaries, and conditions within which thought could be made public, or to put it more precisely, to consider what it meant to think with and through print technologies. The question of enlightenment concerned not a set of dates, 1784 or 1750, a national context (France, England, Germany?), or a list of thinkers (was it Diderot and Voltaire or Mendelssohn and Kant?) but rather the possibilities and limitations of thinking, communicating, and living together in an age of print.[15] This question, as the eighteenth-century Berlin pastor Johann Friedrich Zöllner noted, was almost as important as "what is truth?"[16]

Locating the Enlightenment in Kant's Essay

We begin with the first page of Kant's 1784 essay, entitled "An Answer to the Question: What is Enlightenment?" (fig. 1). As an answer, Kant's essay is not a response to a general question about a cultural moment floating around in some vague discursive field; instead, it is a specific response to a question posed in a particular footnote, namely, the question "what is Enlighten-

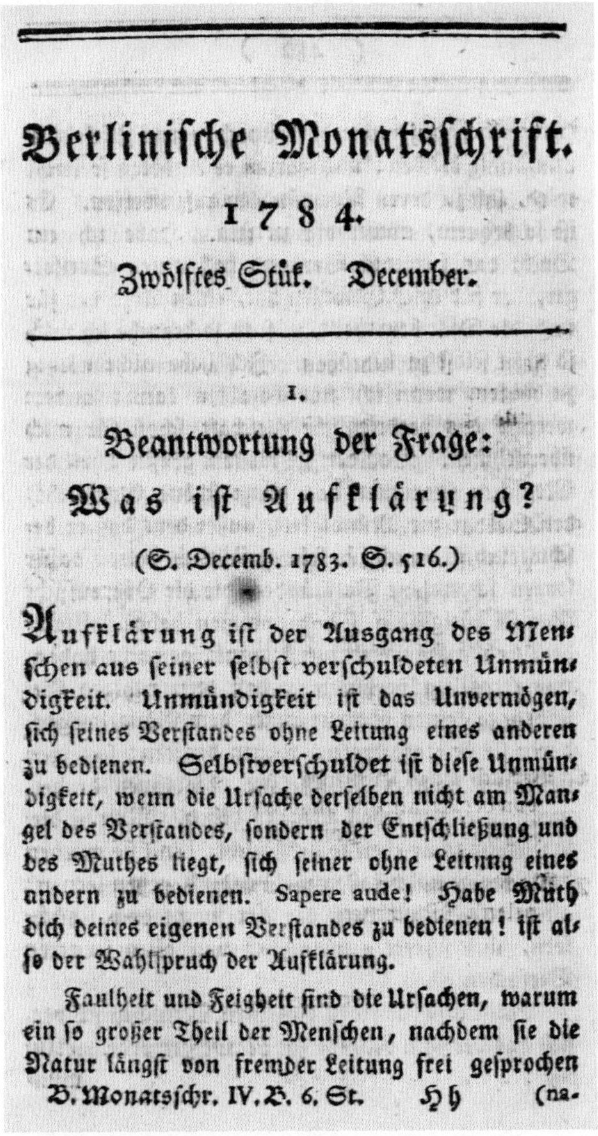

Berlinische Monatsschrift.

1784.

Zwölftes Stük. December.

I.

Beantwortung der Frage:

Was ist Aufklärung?

(S. Decemb. 1783. S. 516.)

Aufklärung ist der Ausgang des Menschen aus seiner selbst verschuldeten Unmündigkeit. Unmündigkeit ist das Unvermögen, sich seines Verstandes ohne Leitung eines anderen zu bedienen. Selbstverschuldet ist diese Unmündigkeit, wenn die Ursache derselben nicht am Mangel des Verstandes, sondern der Entschließung und des Muthes liegt, sich seiner ohne Leitung eines andern zu bedienen. Sapere aude! Habe Muth dich deines eigenen Verstandes zu bedienen! ist also der Wahlspruch der Aufklärung.

Faulheit und Feigheit sind die Ursachen, warum ein so großer Theil der Menschen, nachdem sie die Natur längst von fremder Leitung frei gesprochen

B. Monatsschr. IV.B. 6. St.   Hh   (na-

Figure 1. Parenthetical directive *away* from Kant's essay—"S. Decemb. 1783. S. 516" (See December 1783, p. 516)—in *Berlinische Monatsschrift*, 1784. (Courtesy of Zentral- und Landesbibliothek Berlin)

ment?," which had been posed by Zöllner in the same journal of the year before. The title of Kant's famous essay on the Enlightenment, originally printed as the lead essay in the December issue of *Berlinische Monatsschrift*, is immediately followed by a citation: "S. Decemb. 1783. S. 516" (See December 1783, p. 516). This parenthetical directive—to look for the Enlightenment on a page in the December 1783 issue of the *Berlinische Monatsschrift*—exhorts the reader, before he or she even engages with what has ever since been regarded as the *content* of Kant's essay, to look elsewhere, to look back to Zöllner's essay and into its footnotes. The graphic design and paratextual elements of Kant's essay are key elements of interpretation.[17]

In reading this way, the question posed in the title is, in effect, answered by the page's design and layout. The citation at once belongs to the title but, because put in parentheses and set in a smaller typeface, is distinct. It coordinates two pages in two different volumes of the same journal. Looking into the *Berlinische Monatsschrift*, we locate it not *here* on page 481 of the magazine in front of us (volume 4 from December 1784) nor even *there* on page 516 of another one (volume 2, from December 1783) but in the act and moment of cross-reference. The answer to the question of the Enlightenment is thus bifurcated: we can read Kant's essay, or we can stand back and locate it in the larger structure of reference and citation.[18] Following references, as we will in this study, serves to reassemble the networks of communication that constituted a "reading public," or trace what James Schmidt calls the "chain of questions and answers" that is the process of enlightenment.[19]

In fact, if we follow Kant's citation and look to page 516, where Zöllner's famous footnote is to be found (fig. 2), we find ourselves in the middle of an essay by Zöllner, who published several sermons in the *Berlinische Monatsschrift*. Zöllner's essay, like Kant's, is titled with a question: "Is it wise to no longer sanction marriage through religion?"; that is, Zöllner asks whether the removal of clergy from wedding ceremonies would be "enlightened." And his essay was, in turn, a response to another essay in the *Berlinische Monatsschrift*, from September 1783, Johann Biester's "A Proposal No Longer to Bring Clergy into the Execution of Marriages." The chain of questions and answers carries us from one issue to another, from question to proposal. Kant's essay refers to an essay by Zöllner that references an essay by Biester, editor of the journal.

Despite this linking of essay to essay, scholars have long read Kant's essay in isolation, as *Kant's* essay, an autonomous piece of thinking.[20] Dislocated from its position in the Enlightenment network of citation, it has been re-

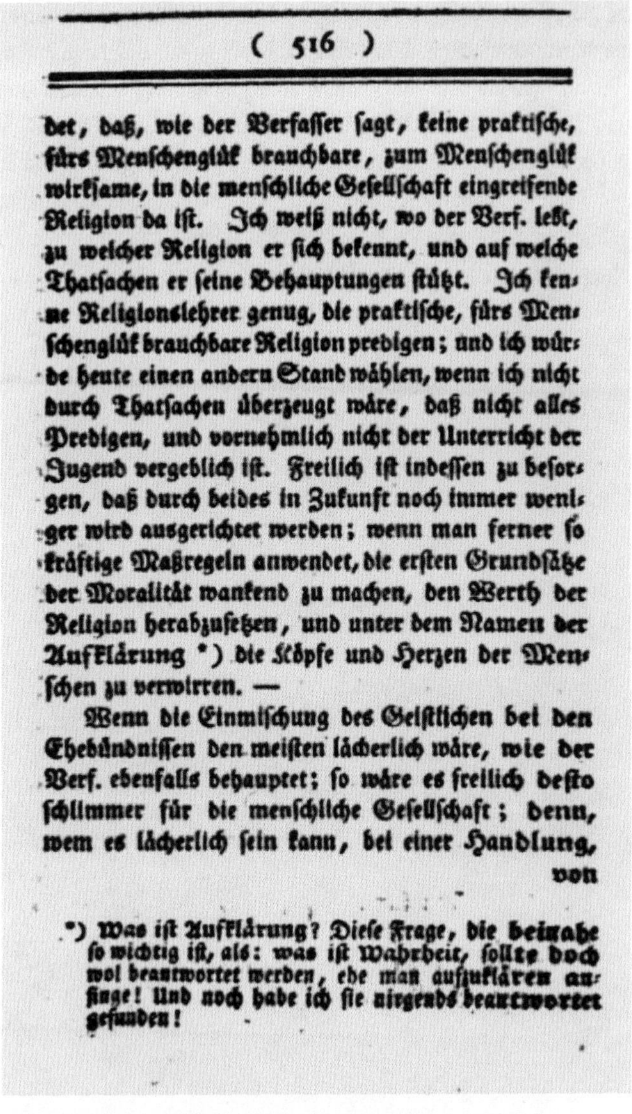

(516)

det, daß, wie der Verfaſſer ſagt, keine praktiſche, fürs Menſchenglük brauchbare, zum Menſchenglük wirkſame, in die menſchliche Geſellſchaft eingreifende Religion da iſt. Ich weiß nicht, wo der Verf. lebt, zu welcher Religion er ſich bekennt, und auf welche Thatſachen er ſeine Behauptungen ſtützt. Ich kenne Religionslehrer genug, die praktiſche, fürs Menſchenglük brauchbare Religion predigen; und ich würde heute einen andern Stand wählen, wenn ich nicht durch Thatſachen überzeugt wäre, daß nicht alles Predigen, und vornehmlich nicht der Unterricht der Jugend vergeblich iſt. Freilich iſt indeſſen zu beſorgen, daß durch beides in Zukunft noch immer weniger wird ausgerichtet werden; wenn man ferner ſo kräftige Maßregeln anwendet, die erſten Grundſätze der Moralität wankend zu machen, den Werth der Religion herabzuſetzen, und unter dem Namen der Aufklärung *) die Köpfe und Herzen der Menſchen zu verwirren. —

Wenn die Einmiſchung des Geiſtlichen bei den Ehebündniſſen den meiſten lächerlich wäre, wie der Verf. ebenfalls behauptet; ſo wäre es freilich deſto ſchlimmer für die menſchliche Geſellſchaft; denn, wem es lächerlich ſein kann, bei einer Handlung, von

---

*) Was iſt Aufklärung? Dieſe Frage, die beinahe ſo wichtig iſt, als: was iſt Wahrheit, ſollte doch wol beantwortet werden, ehe man aufzuklären anfinge! Und noch habe ich ſie nirgends beantwortet gefunden!

Figure 2. Biester's original footnote in which he asks, "What is Enlightenment?," *Berlinische Monatsschrift*, 1783. (Courtesy of Zentral- und Landesbibliothek Berlin)

duced to its ostensible *philosophical* content and arguments. This sundering of the essay from its print context was codified by the Akademie Ausgabe, which did not print the parenthetical citation "Siehe," but already in a 1799 edition of Kant's *Vermischte Schriften* (fig. 3) the essay was reprinted without the citation and effectively dehistoricized in its own moment. As Cliff

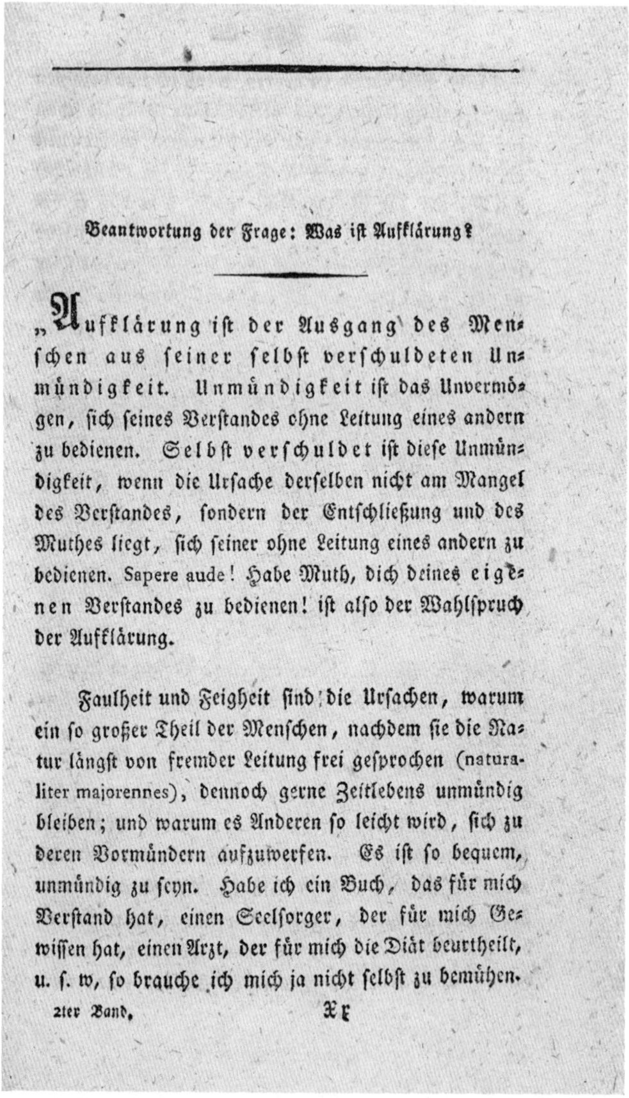

Beantwortung der Frage: Was ist Aufklärung?

„Aufklärung ist der Ausgang des Menschen aus seiner selbst verschuldeten Unmündigkeit. Unmündigkeit ist das Unvermögen, sich seines Verstandes ohne Leitung eines andern zu bedienen. Selbst verschuldet ist diese Unmündigkeit, wenn die Ursache derselben nicht am Mangel des Verstandes, sondern der Entschließung und des Muthes liegt, sich seiner ohne Leitung eines andern zu bedienen. Sapere aude! Habe Muth, dich deines eigenen Verstandes zu bedienen! ist also der Wahlspruch der Aufklärung.

Faulheit und Feigheit sind die Ursachen, warum ein so großer Theil der Menschen, nachdem sie die Natur längst von fremder Leitung frei gesprochen (naturaliter majorennes), dennoch gerne Zeitlebens unmündig bleiben; und warum es Anderen so leicht wird, sich zu deren Vormündern aufzuwerfen. Es ist so bequem, unmündig zu seyn. Habe ich ein Buch, das für mich Verstand hat, einen Seelsorger, der für mich Gewissen hat, einen Arzt, der für mich die Diät beurtheilt, u. s. w, so brauche ich mich ja nicht selbst zu bemühen.

2ter Band,   X r

Figure 3. Kant's *Vermischte Schriften*, 1799. (Courtesy of the University of Virginia)

Siskin and William Warner observe, later editions bold the word *eigenen* (own), as if further enforcing Kant's authority and ownership.[21] When editors of the essay excise the opening cross-reference, they obscure the dynamic structure of citation as the main process of the Enlightenment. That is, the editorial decision erases what the Enlightenment entailed, namely, a broad confidence in a bibliographical system, what Novalis termed the Enlightenment's *Bildungskette,* in which the Great Chain of Being was transfigured as a Great Chain of Books. This confidence was most simply the assumption that the system of print was robust and stable enough that the reference "S. 516" could be easily followed. It presumed that printed objects were bound together in a chain of relations that constituted a realm of print—standardized, ordered, fixed, and simultaneous.[22]

At the bottom of page 516 in Zöllner's essay there is an extended remark on the phrase "Unter dem Namen Aufklärung" in which the question "Was ist Aufklärung?" is posed. Eighteenth-century intellectuals had long expressed a widespread confidence that the expansion of print and literacy was proportional to the spread of enlightenment. But Zöllner's query, like Kant's thinking books, also signals an anxiety about the Enlightenment's increasing reliance *on* print. To ask, as Zöllner does, "what is enlightenment?" was a sign of an oversaturated semantics: a newly proliferating terminology (*Erklärung, Aufklärung, Bildung*) had to be fixed and defined.

Neither Zöllner nor Kant was saying anything radically new in his essay, but they were further circulating ideas already in print. They shared in the general eighteenth-century sense that print and enlightenment were not only compatible but necessarily related. Asking candidly and suddenly "what is enlightenment?" in medias res, Zöllner interrupts debate and exchange in order to fix the process of enlightenment and gain conceptual clarity. To nominalize the Enlightenment is to objectify it, but in our account the Enlightenment was neither fixed nor abstract; it was an activity. "I have yet to see [the question about the Enlightenment] answered!" writes Zöllner. Of course not, because every answer to the question extends the process of enlightenment. To engage with the Enlightenment was to assemble printed publics, to make connections and form networks in print. It is only the process of posing the question and debating the limits of distribution that gives content to the term. By the time Zöllner asked, "What is enlightenment?" there were already too many footnotes, too many journals, too much print clamoring in and under the name of the Enlightenment. Once the question about the Enlightenment had to be posed, it was too late to fix upon a single answer.

Herr Mendelssohn's Answer to the Same

Kant's "An Answer to the Question: 'What is Enlightenment?'" opens and closes with references that frame the essay. The first, the citation of Zöllner's question, has been discussed above; the final, a footnote shown below, follows Kant's signature and date stamp as a supplement (fig. 4) and points to another answer: "In the Büsching's *Weekly News* from the 13th of September, I read today the 30th of the same [month], the advertisement for the *Berlinische Monatsschrift* from this month, in which Herr Mendelssohn's answer to this same question is printed." Kant refers to a weekly newspaper that in turn refers to an essay in the *Berlinische Monatsschrift* by Mendelssohn that is a response, as Kant's is, to the question posed in Zöllner's footnote. Having read the weekly, Kant learns that Mendelssohn's essay exists (it was published in the September 1784 issue of the *Berlinische Monatsschrift*) but cannot know what it says.

The bifurcation of the Enlightenment is starkly illustrated in this closing note: "Knowledge is of two kinds," as Samuel Johnson put it, "We know a subject ourselves, or we know where we can find information upon it."[23] Knowing where to locate Mendelssohn, Kant saturates his footnote with deictic markers, words and phrases that without context, place, time, or topic would make little sense: "the 13th of September," "the 30th of the same," "today," "this month," "this same question." But the note is overloaded, as if Kant is unsure whether he is pointing his reader to the correct *pages* in the broader network of print or to a (to another) correct *answer*. Unlike the confidence displayed in the first parenthetical citation—look exactly *here* on page 516 of the December 1783 issue—Kant's final footnote is composed of a series of citational phrases all intended to locate his answer in relation to Mendelssohn's. The hyperindexical language dramatizes both the network's sentience (the Büsching's *Wochentliche Nachrichtung* and the *Berlinische Monatsschrift* have knowledge for us) and the fragile and contingent nature of the public. The Enlightenment was always being assembled and, at the same time, ever on the verge of dissolution.

What is revealed in these citations is a print system that was not in fact always simultaneous and smooth. Rational consensus and communication among deliberating publics were, in part at least, subject to the contingencies of print technologies, both their efficiencies and their failures. Kant's prose highlights, for example, the delays in the communication of information from his home in Königsberg, in east Prussia, to Berlin. Interruptions and delays were normal; the print network was neither homogenous nor complete but full of blockages and gaps.[24] Writing that he has not been able to "get his hands on" Mendelssohn's essay, Kant decided to go ahead and publish his own. The entire endeavor, he continued, would be an experiment to see if "chance" could bring about "unanimity of thoughts"—as if one type

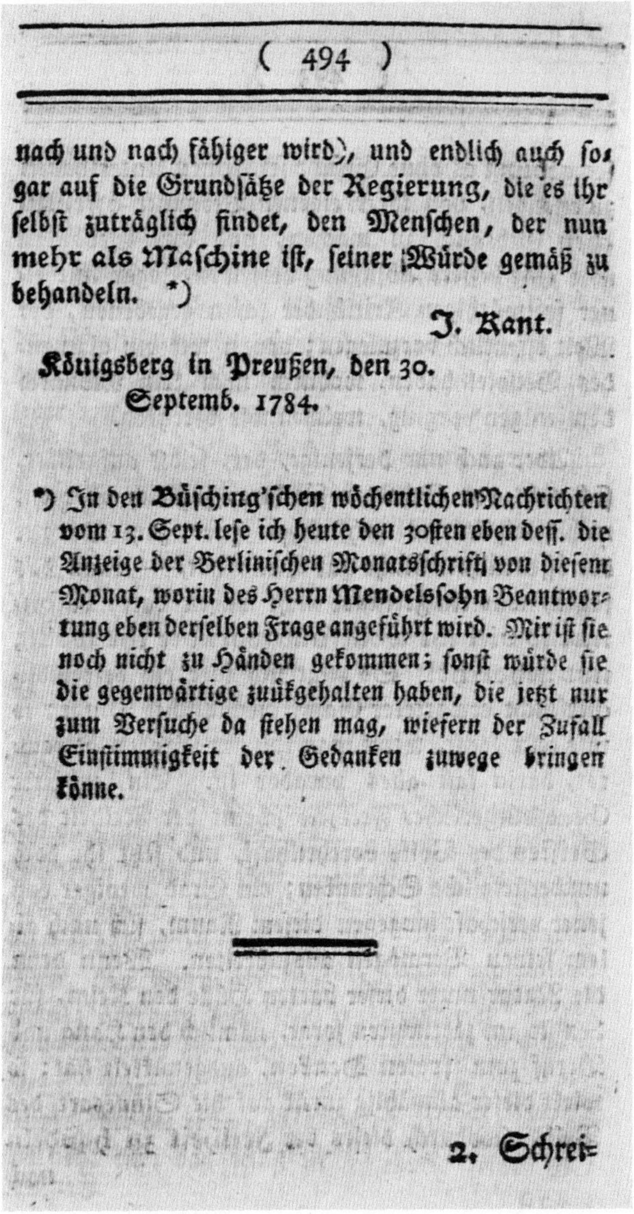

nach und nach fähiger wird), und endlich auch so,
gar auf die Grundsätze der Regierung, die es ihr
selbst zuträglich findet, den Menschen, der nun
mehr als Maschine ist, seiner Würde gemäß zu
behandeln. *)

J. Kant.

Königsberg in Preußen, den 30.
Septemb. 1784.

*) In den Büsching'schen wöchentlichen Nachrichten
vom 13. Sept. lese ich heute den 30sten eben deß. die
Anzeige der Berlinischen Monatsschrift von diesem
Monat, worin des Herrn Mendelssohn Beantwortung eben derselben Frage angeführt wird. Mir ist sie
noch nicht zu Händen gekommen; sonst würde sie
die gegenwärtige zurückgehalten haben, die jetzt nur
zum Versuche da stehen mag, wiefern der Zufall
Einstimmigkeit der Gedanken zuwege bringen
könne.

2. Schrei-

Figure 4. Final footnote in Kant's essay in the *Berlinische Monatsschrift*, 1784, pointing to Mendelssohn's essay. (Courtesy of Zentral- und Landesbibliothek Berlin)

of knowledge (knowing where to find information) might be reconciled with the other (knowing the subject ourselves).

Assembling *the* Berlinische Monatsschrift

The *Berlinische Monatsschrift,* which provided the network in which Zöllner's, Mendelssohn's, and Kant's essays appeared, ranks as one of the most important journals of the German Enlightenment.[25] Published from January 1783 to December 1811, the journal was closely associated with the Berlin Mittwochsgesellschaft, or Wednesday Society. The society was made up of twenty-four members, a combination of Prussian bureaucrats and cultural elites, who met twice a month in the winter and once a month in the summer in the home of one of their members.[26] Meetings began promptly at 6:00 p.m. with a dinner and ended at 8:00 p.m. After the meeting's host read a prepared manuscript, society members commented on the lecture one after the other in a set order. After the meeting, Johann Erich Biester, the society's secretary and coeditor with Friedrich Gedike of the *Monatsschrift,* would enclose the lecture manuscript in a capsule that would circulate among the society's members, each of whom had his own key.[27] Before passing the capsule on, each member would place written comments, referred to as *Vota,* in the capsule and lock it. After the capsule had been passed among all the members, Biester would have it delivered, now full of commentaries on the original lecture, to whoever had delivered the lecture. The commentaries would refer to the original manuscript as well as to the previous comments. The circulating manuscripts and commentaries reproduced the society's in-person interactions in written form and produced a lasting record of members' debates and questions.[28]

The same month that Zöllner's essay was published in the *Berlinische Monatsschrift,* Johann Karl Wilhelm Möhsen delivered a lecture to the society on 17 December 1783 entitled "What Is to Be Done toward the Enlightenment of the Citizenry?" Möhsen opened his lecture by suggesting that he and his Wednesday Society colleagues determine precisely "what is enlightenment?"[29] The society's interactions and procedures can be pieced together from archival material that was later edited and published.[30] In their individual *Vota,* members commented not only on Möhsen's original oral lecture but also on their colleagues' commentaries, each of which was dated. In this instance, the capsule seems to have circulated quickly at first. Half of the society's twenty-four members commented on the lecture between December 18 and January 2. But circulation among the remaining members took almost two months, not concluding until February 22. One member even asked his colleagues to forgive him for holding up the capsule. "Because my servant was not immediately available," he wrote, he had put the capsule in his desk drawer and "forgotten about it."[31] In this complex practice of oral presentation and discussion and circulation of written notes, we can observe how the society's protocols for interaction were deliberate, well organized, and designed to facilitate a certain type of interaction among a particular public.

Many of the oral lectures delivered for the society were eventually edited and published by Gedike and Biester in the *Monatsschrift*. But in addition to lectures delivered in the society, the journal also published excerpts and fragments from previously printed material or work that was just about to be published, including translations and travelogues. It recirculated items previously printed elsewhere. Looking back on the journal's run, Biester described the practice of republishing printed material of well-known authors as one of the journal's central feature, and thus what made it part of the larger system of print, which he termed the "multiplication industry."[32] The key feature of print, for Biester at least, was not the creation of something new but the circulation and reassembly of what already was.

In the preface to the first volume of the *Berlinische Monatsschrift*, Gedike and Biester laid out their plans for keeping the *Monatsschrift* from succumbing to the exigencies of ephemeral production, in particular what some intellectuals were by the 1780s calling the "journal flood." Regular subscribers, they explained, would be provided with all the necessary elements to collect their issues and then have them bound so as to ensure their longevity. Individual issues would be published on a monthly basis, and in addition every sixth issue would come with a title page and table of contents that organized the previous six issues. Every sixth issue would also come with a frontispiece, a copperplate engraving of, as the editors put it, "a remarkable, deserving man whose image is not yet well known."[33] These frontispieces, assured Biester and Gedike, would be included "at no additional price."

The images were generally not of Wednesday Society members but of other Prussian bureaucrats or of well-known men of the day. Shown in figure 5 are engravings of the heads, in profile, of Karl A. Freiherr von Zedlitz, a Prussian minister for ecclesiastical and educational affairs, and Benjamin Franklin, for volumes 1 and 2; and of Joachim Wichard von Möllendorff, a Prussian general field officer, and Stephan and Joseph Montgolfier, the

Fig. 5. Frontispieces appearing in the *Berlinische Monatsschrift* in 1783 and 1784 showing Karl A. Freiherr von Zedlitz, Benjamin Franklin, Joachim Wichard von Möllendorff, and Stephan and Joseph Montgolfier. (Courtesy of Zentral- und Landesbibliothek Berlin)

brothers of hot-air-balloon fame, for volumes 3 and 4. The frontispieces were engraved copper portraits that included a circular frame. Most of them also had an image of a nail or hook with a thin ribbon from which the portrait hung, emphasizing the portrait effect. The portrait-style frontispieces put a head on the body of the book, and they stood in for the physical bodies of the society's members and the authors of the various essays and contributions in each volume. They sought to remind readers that not just printed texts but also actual people participated in the process of enlightenment. The contradictions of print culture abide: the *Aufklärer* are remediated and printed as pages.

By including front matter at the end of the six-issue run, Biester and Gedike encouraged readers to have the individual issues bound together in a single volume. The readers then participated in the Enlightenment not least by converting their periodicals into bound books; the serialized *Monatsschrift* provided a kind of kit that a reader could use (in cooperation with a bookbinder) to collect the individual pieces of the journal into a volume, *ein Band,* that would lend the journal the printed book's greater sense of stability and heft. Within bound volumes monthly issues could be brought together and consolidated—physically gathered together, stab-stitched, and bound.[34] As each *Band* represents something like Kant's "unanimity of thought," each individual part was separated only by a thin printed line and a title introducing the issue.

In the pages of the journal, Biester and Gedike consistently exhorted readers to contribute essays, reports, translations, and poems. They worked hard to assemble a print public and to represent the public so assembled in conversation. That is, they called upon the journal's readers to assemble, physically, the *Monatsschrift* as a book while also participating in the exchange of ideas. The notion of what constituted a work of the Enlightenment was thus altered. A bound volume of periodical papers was produced through a variety of interactions—editorial, compositional, and bibliographical. All this assembly was necessary, noted Biester and Gedike, because the *Monatsschrift* was entering a print market that was not only "enriched" but also "drowning" and "infested" by printed material.[35] The best way to distinguish the *Berlinische Monatsschrift* was to cultivate a readership that would interact with it and make it their own. In the language of Silicon Valley, Biester and Gedike were recruiting readers by including user-generated content.

Assembling a Network of References

The contemporary book historian who bends back the pages of a bound volume of the *Monatsschrift* and peers into its gutter may discover the threads that, stitched through the individual issues, bind the *Band* together.[36] But the *Monatsschrift* was assembled in another, less obvious sense as well. The articles contributed by readers and authors prepared a citation network that Kant's exemplary essay on enlightenment joined in 1784 and that was further articulated in the issues that followed. The authors and the articles reference each other as part of a manifold and interactive whole.

Figure 6 is a graphic representation of this interaction as a map of references. Reading through the first four volumes of the *Monatsschrift*, we collected every footnote or citation and produced a directed graph of the cross-references internal to the magazine. That is, our visualization maps a structure of footnotes and citations that point from one article to another article published in the *Monatsschrift*. That the graph is "directed" means that the arrows point from one article to another article published in a previous issue (a few references internal to a single issue and a few to the "following issue" are not shown in our graph). As with any visualization, the graph sacrifices some detail: We analyzed hundreds of footnotes and in-text citations in order to isolate the seventy-eight cross-references shown. And because we wanted to emphasize links between issues, articles in the same issue are included together and not otherwise made visible. Each of the four vertical ranks corresponds to a *Band*, or volume, collecting six monthly issues (the issues are abbreviated thus: April 1783 is rendered "Apr (83)"). The "edges," or lines, connecting the nodes of the graph identify cross-references between articles in the issues. Notice that within each rank the monthly issues of the journal are not ordered chronologically: we allowed the graphing software (called Graphviz) to reorganize the nodes of the network so as to improve the legibility of the graph as a whole. Therefore, the issues in a given volume, although locked on their rank, do not appear in chronological order but are scrambled and spaced so as to minimize the crossing of lines. Readers new to network analysis learn that such matters of layout are not in themselves meaningful; it is the structure of the nodes and links (which nodes are linked and by how many edges) that is significant.

The graph shows the development of a network of citations from the first, to the second, to the third, and then the fourth volume. Read from left to right, it shows how increasingly interlinked the *Berlinische Monatsschrift* became over time as its new articles pointed more and more to previous

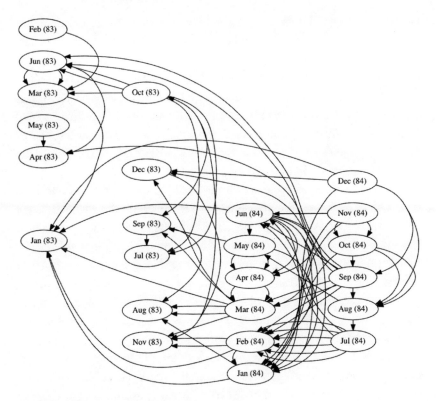

Fig. 6. Network graph. (Brad Pasanek)

articles. It visualizes the process of enlightenment with a web of links; and the visibly increasing number of references figure an Enlightenment that becomes aware of itself as distinct and self-perpetuating. With each new issue, more and more references, more lines, are filiated in the graph. We discover that by the December 1784 issue, in which Kant's essay on the Enlightenment appeared, a complex network had been assembled. Up to that December moment, the four-volume run of the *Berlinische Monatsschrift* is fully assembled, but the criss-crossed saturation of references betrays Kant's original anxiety that books "have understanding for us" and that the Enlightenment has become overly dependent on print mediations. Already by the third volume the structure of reference is too complicated to be easily described, and in order to comprehend it, we must draw it as a graph or set it out in a table.

Anxiety was the motor that produced links and the ground for editorial intervention. Throughout the *Monatsschrift*, footnotes appear signed "A. d. H." These are *Anmerkungen der Herausgeber*, the notes of the editors,

Gedike and Biester. For example, in an essay on deism the editors claim not to take sides: "an diesen oder ähnlichen Streitigkeiten."[37] But they do. They do not stand idly by; they intervene to train and cultivate their readers in the proper participation in the Enlightenment, encouraging diversity of opinion and repeatedly invoking the "deutschen Publikum"[38] even as they solicit "contributions from distant places."[39] In one footnote they lament that so many readers still cannot distinguish the publisher from the author.[40] They even collect citations of the *Monatsschrift* by other journals, recording the expanded conversation in new footnotes.

The cross-references, whether authorial or editorial, are sinews, threads that seem to proliferate spontaneously and stitch together the whole. As the *Monatsschrift* began to include more and more reflexive citations and editorial comments, its pages, as Christina Lupton puts it in a different context, "quicken[ed] with sentience."[41] One of the busiest nodes in the *Monatsschrift* was an article by the physicist Pierre Prévost entitled "On the Inventor of the Flying Air Machines," printed in the February 1784 issue. Prévost was trying to determine the validity of various reports on flying machines coming out of France and Italy. Citing reports and articles from a range of periodicals and newspapers, both German and French, Prévost points to particular pages in particular journals, using the reports to evaluate the new experiments. Immediately after Prévost's article, the editors printed what they termed a "Zusatz," in which Martin Heinrich Klaproth, a chemist who among other things had discovered uranium, identified calculation errors in Prévost's article. Immediately after Klaproth's "Zusatz," the editors included another short piece in which Prévost disputed Klaproth's arguments. In the July and September issues, articles, one written by Prévost, continue the debate by pointing back to Prévost's original article. This series of citations makes up one of the most complex and interlinked set of nodes in our graph. In the concluding article of the June 1784 issue, the editors report on articles in other periodicals in which the *Berlinische Monatsschrift* was mentioned; that is, they point to exact pages in other journals—in the *Der Teutsche Merkur*, for example—that cited the *Monatsschrift*. And they express their satisfaction: "The *Berlinische Monatsschrift* achieves its ultimate purpose when through the ideas that it reports, it provides an opportunity for further discussion."[42] The entire point of the journal was to circulate and link ideas.

In Dan Edelstein's influential genealogical account, the Enlightenment was both a self-aware narrative and a collection of texts and practices, yet he gives precedence to narrative and mentions only in passing its material embodiment in print.[43] This "narrative of the Enlightenment," however, was inextricable from its dissemination in print; or to put it more forcefully, this narrative was printed, and its self-awareness constituted as an interconnected and interacting set of print artifacts. Readers, scholars, writers, and publishers were increasingly aware that they were participating in something called the Enlightenment, because they were assembling it. The story of the Enlightenment is not one of epistemic shift but rather one of intensified self-awareness that brought both a new confidence in the potential of print to structure a cosmopolitan republic of letters and a related anxiety.

Kant claimed that he and his fellow contributors to the *Monatsschrift* lived in an age of small-*e* enlightenment, and not *die Aufklärung* (capital-*E* Enlightenment). By assembling cross-references and visualizing them as network graphs, we offer a synoptic view of the Enlightenment not available to Kant and his contemporaries. The graph captures a process and undercuts the common notion that the Enlightenment is primarily a period or a pure philosophical process of learning to think for one's self. It matters that each issue, or *Stück*—the German means literally "bit, piece, part"—is associated with a moment. The journal is published monthly; the cross-references point from month to month. The pieces only become a whole in and over time.

By describing the Enlightenment as a process, we want to suggest that the Enlightenment was or could only ever exist at a particular moment, in a particular arrangement. This is what our graph illustrates. The concern of Kant and his Berlin colleagues in the Wednesday Society was not simply with enlightenment as a philosophical process or activity of self-transformation but with what could be printed and assembled *now*. To ask about the limits and boundaries of the Enlightenment was to consider the legal, conceptual, and technological limits of the process of enlightenment. To consider the limits of the Enlightenment was to consider what could or should be made public, that is, what could be entered into the network of citation and print relations. Such considerations presupposed that not everything should necessarily be put into the print system. Some texts, manuscripts, and ideas were better left unprinted and thus kept out of circulation. These types of decisions undercut the notion that print culture was one, singular homogenous public open to all.

Private Association, Public Citation

When the members of the Wednesday Society posed and reposed the question of enlightenment, they were asking more broadly about the possibility of "thinking for oneself." The imperative "to use your *own* understanding!"—

what Kant calls the "motto" of the Enlightenment—follows uncomfortably after a quotation from Horace (*"Sapere aude!"*) and the opening reference to Zöllner's question.[44] That the motto for thinking on one's own is borrowed seems to involve it in a performative contradiction. But importantly, we believe, Kant quotes from but does not cite Horace, dramatizing again the distinction between knowing where and knowing that. Seeing the Latin, hearing an allusion, the reader is expected to supply his or her own annotation.

In the final decades of the eighteenth century, concerns about the feasibility of "thinking for oneself" led to the emergence of numerous secret societies to cultivate "thinking for oneself" as a program.[45] Both Biester and Zöllner were members of secret societies, and the *Berlinische Monatsschrift* published several articles debating their propriety and role in enlightenment. In this context, it is important to recall that the Wednesday Society was the public name for the secret society the Friends of Enlightenment.[46] Members of the Friends of Enlightenment were sworn to keep all conversations secret and "not to speak much" about the society.[47] According to the society's statutes, a member was accepted only when it was clear that he would not "be easily offended by unrestrained and unusual ways of thinking about things that touched on religion and morals."[48] The founders also preferred, as their statutes phrased it, that members not be of the same "views and ways of thinking, or in the private systems, doctrines, or opinions."[49] The guidelines were in large part designed, or so thought the founders, to facilitate a careful consideration of the limits and conditions of enlightenment in an age of easily accessible information, that is, in an age of print.

But why all the secrecy? For the society's founding members, concerns about the limits and conditions of enlightenment were inextricable from worries about, as Birgit Nehren puts it, the effect an "unenlightened public" could have on the discussions and interactions of society members.[50] Many society members worried that the quality and openness of the conversations would suffer if their comments were made public. Not "each and every bit of enlightenment is immediately useful and necessary for the general masses," argued one member.[51] The process of enlightenment was highly differentiated. Discussions concerning religion, morals, or politics should not be indiscriminately cast about. The social, intellectual, and moral situation of those who might encounter such knowledge had to be taken into consideration. The ideas and questions to which a citizen should be exposed, insisted Möhsen in his lecture before the Wednesday Society entitled "What Is to Be Done toward the Enlightenment of the Citizenry?," had to be determined according to his "degree of enlightenment." One's exposure to the process of enlightenment, the circulation of ideas, should be in proportion to his intellectual and practical capacities.[52]

In response to Möhsen, Moses Mendelssohn asked whether the limits and boundaries of certain ideas should be "determined through laws and censors" or based on "opinions of each individual."[53] Mendelssohn concluded that because ideas were so varied and dynamic, laws, fixed as they were, would not be adequate to determine how such limits should be set. The actual censorship and control of ideas would inevitably depend on the "judgment" of the individual censor. He concluded, therefore, that the only option was an "unrestricted freedom." By this Mendelssohn meant freedom from Prussian censors. Other members wondered if such freedom should be as "unrestricted" as Mendelssohn argued or, if there were to be limits, who should determine them? Who would make the actual decisions concerning what would be filtered and what would not?

The members of the Wednesday Society were not simply debating how best to maintain their cultural privilege and power and enforce a system of state-sponsored censorship. They were also struggling to understand the new flows in information and knowledge. Were authors responsible for their ideas once in print? While all "truths" might in the abstract seem worth distributing as broadly as possible, were some ideas pernicious or dangerous? Was an absolutely unrestricted dissemination of information, whatever the source or quality, *obviously* the best option? These were questions about the dissemination of knowledge and information in an age in which distribution could operate at increasingly greater scales.

The irony of such arguments and the secrecy of the society more broadly was the implicit assumption that even though enlightenment relied on the publicity of print, and thus the circulation of ideas, the ends of enlightenment—freedom, the capacity to think for oneself—could be undercut by the process of enlightenment. "The public" or "publicity" (*Öffentlichkeit*) was fragile, and so too was the capacity to participate in it. Not everyone, thought the founders and many society members, could handle the process of giving and exchanging reasons without a filter. All of these concerns about the limits, boundaries, extent, forms, and scope of enlightenment were questions about how the Enlightenment and its multiple, often incongruous publics should and could be assembled.[54]

These types of questions and concerns are not easily accounted for by more established conceptions of the public sphere and reading publics. For Habermas, the *publicum*, "the abstract counterpart of public authority," developed into the "public," the *subjectum* into "the [reasoning] subject, the receiver of regulations from above into the ruling authorities' adversary."[55] The "public" is the structural analogue of the critical human subject, who participates in rational and open debate. Such a public developed from the social sphere of the state's exercise of authority into a social sphere in which opinions were expressed and judgments made. In his original formulations, Habermas was interested in the conditions under which "rational, critical, and genuinely open discussion of public issues" became possible.[56] *Öffentlichkeit* was the sphere in which private people came together as a public, and the medium of this coming together was, as he writes, "the people's use of their reason [*öffentliches Räsonnement*]."[57]

Habermas, of course, emphasized the role that moral weeklies and other forms of print played in the emergence of such a public, but in his view these print objects were simply "instruments" that the frequenters of coffeehouses used to communicate. They were extensions of rational subjects, mere tools that could be manipulated as intended by human subjects. They simply served the ends of an emerging public. On occasion, Habermas acknowledges this distinction, as when he suggests that "the periodical articles were not only made the object of discussion by the public of the coffee houses but were viewed as integral parts of the discussions."[58] But these journals were not simply a "mirror" by which the public could recognize itself and become conscious of what had already been there. They were constitutive elements of that public, not readily distinguished from it. The language of "subject" implies that the public existed prior to and independent of its technological extensions, but this division is impossible. When reading and debating about journals like the *Berlinische Monatsschrift* or the *Spectator,* the public was reflexively constituting itself, assembling itself in print.

As we have tried to show, these conditions involved not only the development of a "political consciousness" on the model of the modern, rational subject but more particularly the actual mechanisms and technologies of print. The norms that guided the "public" concerned not only expectations governing rational, open debate but also bibliographical norms for interacting with print technologies, which determined how this debate might be assembled in the first place. By conceiving of enlightenment as a process of assembly and conceiving of the public as that which is assembled, we better observe how contingent these assemblies were and evaluate how differentiated the process of enlightenment was. We make better sense of the debates surrounding the question of the Enlightenment. Beyond its bound print artifacts (seemingly legible, standard, and reproducible), enlightenment was not a singular, homogenizing process in which a single public emerged. "Enlightenment is," as

Gedike put it, "just as much a relative concept as is truth."[59] Enlightenment, he continued, "varies, and so it must according to differences in place, time, estate, and gender and other not merely subjective but also objective conditions. Thorough homogeneity of enlightenment is just as undesirable as complete homogeneity of classes and, fortunately, just as impossible."[60] Here the politics of the Enlightenment come into sharp focus: an entire population cannot be enlightened all at once. The truths of enlightenment, concluded Gedike, should not be put into the "hands of a person who has not yet been sufficiently enlightened."[61] This discriminating process of enlightenment, nurtured in secret societies and shaped by its editors, is hardly revolutionary. Neither is it merely complicit with laissez-faire capitalism: the public sphere is not another commodity looking for more efficient distribution.[62] Varying according to national, class, and gender differences, the practice of critical debate promoted competing discourses of publicity even as it aimed to rationalize politics and unite public opinion. By proceeding one link, one citation, at a time, the Enlightenment process aspired to unanimity from this contingency. But its inclusions proved halting, and the structure of the whole was always subject to the disruptions of time and space and the vicissitudes of the networks that marked its boundaries, limits, and meaning.

Notes

1. Pasanek and Wellmon, "Enlightenment Index."

2. Kant, "What is Enlightenment?," in *Gesammelte Schriften,* 8:35. With occasional emendations, translations are our own.

3. Ibid., 8:37.

4. See Habermas, *Structural Transformation of the Public Sphere,* 28, 106. The second quotation is drawn from Kant's essay and quoted in Habermas's main discussion of Kant, 102–17. *Gelehrter* is rendered in Burger's English translation as "publicist."

5. Kant, "On the Common Saying," *Gesammelte Schriften,* 8:304.

6. Keen, *Crisis of Literature in the 1790s,* 107, quoted in Sher, *Enlightenment and the Book,* 597–98.

7. Kant, "What Does It Mean to Orient Oneself in Thought?," *Gesammelte Schriften,* 8:146.

8. Ibid.

9. Kant, "What is Enlightenment?," *Gesammelte Schriften,* 8:35.

10. See Bittner, "What is Enlightenment," 347, 348.

11. For an overview of the reception of Habermas in American academic circles, see Zammito, "Second Life of the 'Public Sphere.'" See also Calhoun, *Habermas and the Public Sphere.*

12. For an overview of these debates, see Baron, Lindquist, and Schevlin, *Agent of Change.*

13. Schmidt, "Question of Enlightenment," 5.

14. On the Enlightenment as a reaction to changes in print technologies and for an account to which we are indebted, see Siskin and Warner, introduction.

15. James Schmidt comes close to our concern: "Since neither Mendelssohn nor Kant are offering an account of an historical period, the demarcations they will be deploying in their definition of 'enlightenment' cannot take the form of dates (e.g., 'The Enlightenment began in the 1680s'), places (e.g., 'It's French'), or lists of names (e.g., 'Voltaire was part of the Enlightenment, but Rousseau wasn't'). Their concern is with how far a process can be allowed to proceed: do we set limits to what can be printed and discussed and, if so, what limits do we set?" Schmidt, "What Counts as an Answer," 7.

16. Johann Friedrich Zöllner, "Ist es rathsam, das Ehebündniss nicht ferner durch die Religion zu sanciren?," *Berlinische Monatsschrift* 2 (December 1783): 516n.

17. For an example of sustained reading in this mode, see Barchas, *Graphic Design, Print Culture.*

18. We can, to speak with Michel Foucault, consider enlightenment either "as a process in which men participate collectively" or as an "act of courage to be accomplished personally." In Foucault's rewriting of Kant, "Men are at once elements and agents of a single process." See Foucault, "What is Enlightenment?," 35.

19. Schmidt, "What Counts as an Answer," 2.

20. Schmidt, "Misunderstanding the Question," 2–3.

21. Siskin and Warner, introduction, 3.

22. We borrow the adjectives from Eisenstein, *Printing Revolution in Early Modern Europe.*

23. Boswell, *Life of Samuel Johnson,* 1:487.

24. See Jordheim, "Present of Enlightenment."

25. See Hess, *Reconstituting the Body Politic,* esp. chap. 1.

26. For more on the society, see Birtsch, "Berlin Wednesday Society."

27. See Hellmuth, "Aufklärung und Pressefreiheit," 316n. See also Adolf Stölzel, "Die Berliner Mittwochsgesellschaft," 201.

28. For a clear example of this interaction, see the *Vota* on Johann Carl Wilhelm Möhsen's lecture "Was ist zu thun zur Aufklärung der Mitbürger?," reprinted and edited in Keller, "Die Berliner Mittwochs-Gesellschaft."

29. Möhsen, "What Is to Be Done," 49.

30. See Keller, "Die Berliner Mittwochs-Gesellschaft," for a reproduction of the materials.

31. Ibid., 68–69.

32. *Berlinische Monatsschrift* 2 (1811): iv.

33. Ibid. 1 (1781), preface, unpaginated.

34. We draw inspiration from Matthew Garrett's reading of the Federalist Papers. See Garrett, *Episodic Poetics,* 23–59.

35. *Berlinische Monatsschrift* 1 (1783), preface, unpaginated.

36. Garrett, *Episodic Poetics,* 30.

37. *Berlinische Monatsschrift* 4 (1784):175n.

38. Ibid., 231n.

39. Ibid., 201n.

40. Ibid., 202n. See also ibid., 3 (1784): 571–72: The *Monatsschrift* "erreicht ihren Endzweck, wenn sie durch die Gedanken, die sie vorgeträgt, Gelegenheit zu deren weiterer Erörterung giebt."

41. Lupton, *Knowing Books*, 5–6.

42. Gedike and Biester, in *Berlinische Monatsschrift* 1 (1784): 571.

43. Edelstein argues, for example, that "to partake in the Enlightenment" it was not enough to write a particular type of philosophical treatise or visit a salon; instead, "it took an awareness, by oneself and others, that a particular action belonged to a set of practices considered enlightened." Edelstein, *Enlightenment*, 13.

44. See Horace, *Epistles* 1.2.40–41: "Dimidium facti qui coepit habet: sapere aude: Incipe." Others have remarked on the irony that clings to the use of a commonplace. See Siskin and Warner, introduction, 2–3. The phrase has its own citational history: it was chosen for a medal for Leibniz and Wolff and in several German engravings; also, Johann Georg Hamann used it in a 1759 letter to Kant. See Venturi, *Utopia and Reform*, 5–9. See also Schmidt, "Misunderstanding the Question."

45. On this issue, see Nehren, "Selbstdenken und gesunde Vernunft."

46. For a broader discussion, see Schmidt, "Question of Enlightenment."

47. Biester, as quoted in Nehren, "Selbstdenken und gesunde Vernunft," 92. Note that in "On the Common Saying: This May be True in Theory but it Does not Apply in Practice," Kant argues that the restriction of the public sphere ("Obedience without the spirit of freedom") is the *cause* of secret societies. Cited in Habermas, *Structural Transformation of the Public Sphere*, 107; see also 35.

48. Society statutes as quoted in Nehren, "Selbstdenken und gesunde Vernunft," 93.

49. Ibid.

50. Ibid., 92. For a further discussion of these concerns, see Hellmuth, "Aufklärung und Pressefreiheit," 321–25.

51. Möhsen, quoted in Hellmuth, "Aufklärung und Pressefreiheit," 324.

52. Möhsen, "What Is to Be Done," 49.

53. Mendelssohn, quoted in Keller, "Die Berliner Mittwochs-Gesellschaft," 81.

54. See Schmidt, "What Counts as an Answer."

55. Habermas, *Structural Transformation of the Public Sphere*, 26.

56. Melton, *Rise of the Public*, 4.

57. Habermas, *Structural Transformation of the Public Sphere*, 27.

58. Ibid., 42.

59. Gedike, quoted in Keller, "Die Berliner Mittwochs-Gesellschaft," 85.

60. Ibid. For a discussion of these comments, see Birtsch, "Berlin Wednesday Society," 242–43.

61. Gedike, quoted in Keller, "Die Berliner Mittwochs-Gesellschaft," 85.

62. Fraser, "Rethinking the Public Sphere," 74–75.

Works Cited

Barchas, Janine. *Graphic Design, Print Culture, and the Eighteenth-Century Novel.* Cambridge: Cambridge University Press, 2003.

Baron, Sabrina Alcorn, Eric Lindquist, and Eleanor F. Schevlin, eds. *Agent of Change: Print Culture Studies after Elizabeth Eisenstein.* Amherst: University of Massachusetts Press, 2007.

Birtsch, Günter. "The Berlin Wednesday Society." In *What is Enlightenment?*, ed. James Schmidt, 235–53. Berkeley: University of California Press, 1996.

Bittner, Rüdiger. "What is Enlightenment." In *What is Enlightenment?*, ed. James Schmidt, 345–58. Berkeley: University of California Press, 1996.

Boswell, James. *The Life of Samuel Johnson.* 2 vols. London: Henry Baldwin for Charles Dilly, 1791.

Calhoun, Craig, ed. *Habermas and the Public Sphere.* Cambridge, MA: MIT Press, 1992.

Edelstein, Dan. *The Enlightenment: A Genealogy.* Chicago: University of Chicago Press, 2010.

Eisenstein, Elizabeth. *The Printing Revolution in Early Modern Europe.* Cambridge: Cambridge University Press, 2012.

Foucault, Michel. "What is Enlightenment?" In *The Foucault Reader,* ed. Paul Rabinow, 32–50. New York: Pantheon, 1984.

Fraser, Nancy. "Rethinking the Public Sphere: A Contribution to the Critique of Actually Existing Democracy." In *The Phantom Public Sphere,* ed. Bruce Robbins, 1–32. Minneapolis: University of Minnesota Press, 1993.

Garrett, Matthew. *Episodic Poetics: Politics and Literary Form after the Constitution.* Oxford: Oxford University Press, 2014.

Habermas, Jürgen. *The Structural Transformation of the Public Sphere: An Inquiry into a Category of Bourgeois Society.* Trans. Thomas Burger. Cambridge, MA: MIT Press, 1999.

Hellmuth, Eckhart. "Aufklärung und Pressefreiheit: Zur Debatte der Berliner Mittwochsgesellschaft während der Jahre 1783 und 1784." *Zeitschrift für historische Forschung* 9 (1982): 315–45.

Hess, Jonathan M. *Reconstituting the Body Politic: Enlightenment, Public Culture, and the Invention of Aesthetic Autonomy.* Detroit: Wayne State University Press, 1999.

Jordheim, Helge. "The Present of the Enlightenment." In *This Is Enlightenment,* ed. Clifford Siskin and William Warner, 189–208. Chicago: University of Chicago Press, 2010.

Kant, Immanuel. *Gesammelte Schriften.* Ed. Königliche-preußischen Akademie der Wissenschaften. 29 vols. to date. Berlin: Walter de Gruyter, 1902–.

Keen, Paul. *Crisis of Literature in the 1790s.* Cambridge: Cambridge University Press, 1999.

Keller, Ludwig. "Die Berliner Mittwochs-Gesellschaft: Ein Beitrag zur Geschichte der Geistesentwicklung Preussens am Ausgange des 18. Jahrhunderts." *Monatshefte der Comenius-Gesellschaft* 5 (1896): 67–94.

Lupton, Christina. *Knowing Books: The Consciousness of Mediation in Eighteenth-Century Britain.* Philadelphia: University of Pennsylvania Press, 2011.

Melton, James Van Horn. *The Rise of the Public in Enlightenment Europe.* Cambridge: Cambridge University Press, 2001.

Möhsen, Johann Carl Wilhelm. "Was ist zu thun zur Aufklärung der Mitbürger?" In "Die Berliner Mittwochsgesellschaft. Ein Beitrag zur Geschichte der Geistesentwicklung

Preussens am Ausgange des 18. Jahrhunderts," ed. Ludwig Keller, 67–94. Special issue, *Monatshefte der Comenius-Gesellschaft* 5 (1896).

Nehren, Birgit. "Selbstdenken und gesunde Vernunft: Über eine wiederaufgefundene Quelle zur Berliner Mittwochsgesellschaft." *Aufklärung* 1, no. 1 (1986): 87–101.

Pasanek, Brad, and Chad Wellmon. "The Enlightenment Index." *The Eighteenth-Century: Theory and Interpretation* 56, no. 3 (2015): 357–80.

Schmidt, James. "Misunderstanding the Question: What is Enlightenment? Venturi, Habermas, Foucault." *History of European Ideas* 37, no. 1 (2011): 43–52.

———. "The Question of Enlightenment: Kant, Mendelssohn." *Journal of the History of Ideas* 50, no. 2 (1989): 269–91.

———. "What Counts as an Answer to the Question 'What is Enlightenment?'" Talk delivered at Boston University, 5 April 2011.

Sher, Richard B. *The Enlightenment and the Book.* Chicago: University of Chicago Press, 2006.

Siskin, Clifford, and William Warner. Introduction to *This is Enlightenment,* ed. Siskin and Warner. Chicago: University of Chicago Press, 2010.

Stölzel, Adolf. "Die Berliner Mittwochsgesellschaft über Aufhebung oder Reform der Universitäten (1795)." *Forschungen zur brandenburgischen und preußischen Geschichte* 2 (1889): 201–22.

Venturi, Franco. *Utopia and Reform in the Enlightenment.* Cambridge: Cambridge University Press, 1971.

Zammito, John H. "The Second Life of the 'Public Sphere': On Charisma and Routinization in the History of a Concept." In *Changing Perceptions of the Public Sphere,* ed. Christian J. Emden and David Midgley, 90–117. New York: Berghan Books, 2012.

An Inventory of the Estate of William Strahan in 1759

MICHAEL PICKARD

What do books as physical objects teach us about the cultures that produced them? How do they inform us about those who wrote them, those whose business it was to make them, the individuals and firms that distributed them? What do they tell us about the people who bought, borrowed, gave, or stole them and their aims and motivations? What can we learn from individual books about the conditions of book production at large and how those conditions mediate the transmission of texts from author to audience?

Most bibliographers agree that we should be asking these kinds of questions. G. Thomas Tanselle writes, for example, that "the artifacts carrying verbal texts constitute an enormous reservoir of information about the past, quite apart from the meanings of the words themselves."[1] D. F. McKenzie observes that "the book as a physical object . . . is in fact alive with the judgments of its makers."[2] McKenzie and Tanselle see bibliography as a humanistic discipline whose aim is to access that reservoir, the recovery of those judgments. Within the field, however, they have come to represent differing and at times opposed bibliographical methods. The debate between them turns on questions of knowledge. Are books alone sufficient for the purposes of reconstructing historical processes (the composition, or typesetting, of text, for example, or the movement of various parts of a text through the press)? Should we instead privilege information that comes to us from the few archives of printing and publishing records that remain?

The difference will seem less abstract if we focus on a single example: that of the compositor, whose job it was in the early modern printing houses to set in type each page of text, letter by letter. Among other reasons, compositors are worth studying because they exercised a degree of control over the final text of a printed book. In the absence of standardized spelling and punctuation, they were mostly free to put words and sentences together as they wished. In many cases, they also possessed the liberty to alter both spelling and punctuation where necessary to stretch or condense a line of type. They served, in other words, as intermediaries between author and audience in measurable ways.

The Albert and Shirley Small Special Collections Library at the University of Virginia includes in its holdings a Hinman collator, designed for just this kind of measurement. Developed by Charlton K. Hinman, this instrument enables minute collations between pages from two different copies of the same book. Hinman used this instrument to submit fifty-five copies of the Shakespeare First Folio to exceedingly close study. In addition to studying variations in the running titles, Hinman traced spelling patterns and even the progress of pieces of individual type throughout the book as it was composed, printed, and published in 1623. His analysis enabled him to overturn the prevalent theory of how the First Folio had been composed.

Traditionally, scholars argued that two compositors, A and B, set the entirety of Shakespeare's text. Although establishing how many compositors worked on the First Folio may seem mundane, it has significant implications. Editors who want to produce a scholarly edition based on the First Folio need to know what kinds of mistakes each compositor was likely to make—if the goal is to render Shakespeare's text as accurately as possible. Using the collator, Hinman was able to show that no fewer than nine compositors set at least a page of type and that some were far more error prone than others. For Tanselle, Hinman's book, *The Printing and Proof-Reading of the First Folio of William Shakespeare,* is a "monument of the flourishing post-war period of bibliographical analysis."[3]

McKenzie's approach to bibliography aims, by contrast, "to give some philosophical dignity to disbelief."[4] This is not the same thing as waiting with Thomas Hardy in "unhope,"[5] but it does mean playing a "doubting game"[6]—not with Hinman directly but with the school of analysis that he and Bowers pioneered. In "Stretching a Point: Or, the Case of the Spaced-Out Comps," first published in *Studies in Bibliography* in 1984, McKenzie examines 13,777 commas—more or less—in Joseph Beaumont's *Psyche,* printed by the Cambridge University Press from 1700 to 1701. Sometimes the compositors of this text put a space before commas, and sometimes they did not. Careful study of the data reveals a discernible pattern. It would be reasonable, McKenzie argues, to infer from this pattern that there were two main compositors, each with a different way of setting commas. As it turns out, however, Cambridge University Press possesses a ledger that identifies the compositors of Beaumont's *Psyche,* six in all, and the specific sections of the poem for which they were responsible. There is, in other words, no logical relationship between the pattern that emerges from examination of the book and what the historical record tells us about its production. In "Stretching a Point" and throughout his writings, McKenzie sought to challenge the assumption that we can move from correlation to causation, evidence to inference, based solely on the study of the book as physical object. The workflows of printing establishments, especially early modern ones, are likely to be messier and more driven by exigency than most of us would guess.

One might object to McKenzie's essay on the grounds that he set out, from the moment that he counted his first comma, to produce the reductio that it became. Tanselle also observes, rightly, that evidence from the archive is not necessarily less ambiguous, and no less conditioned by our assumptions, than evidence found within a book. Plainly, however, we should make use of archives where possible. As David Vander Meulen writes, "Each [kind of evidence] is valuable, each has limitations, each does things that the other cannot."[7] The trouble is that most scholars still find archival material "virtually inaccessible."[8]

Students of the eighteenth century have the advantage of consulting McKenzie's *Cambridge University Press, 1696–1712: A Bibliographical Study* and *A Ledger of Charles Ackers, printer of The London Magazine* and *The Bowyer Ledgers: The Printing Accounts of William Bowyer Father and Son*, edited by Keith I. D. Maslen with the help of John Lancaster. Spanning much of the eighteenth century, the Bowyer ledgers document the production of thousands of eighteenth-century books. As a reviewer of the volume observes, they provide "a treasure trove of material concerning specifically the Bowyer printing house but inferentially the operation and trade practices of other printers in London and beyond during the period."[9]

On the other hand, the reviewer implies the main problem when he suggests that we can use the Bowyer ledgers to infer the practices of other printing operations. We simply do not have data for the bulk of those operations, the hundreds of individuals and firms who made, published, and sold books during the eighteenth century. This makes it all the more lamentable that the ledgers of William Strahan, "equal in historical value to the Bowyer hoard," still remain inaccessible to most scholars.[10] From 1737 through 1785, Strahan built what Samuel Johnson was to call "the greatest printing house in London."[11] Johnson's compliment is all the more impressive when one considers that over the course of the eighteenth century London grew from an outpost into "a first-ranking book trades centre" of Europe.[12]

Strahan's ledgers provide a record of unprecedented thoroughness. They attest to the materials he used in printing, the supply chains he required to sustain productive capacity, the size of the print runs, and the prices he charged his customers. Valuable in itself, such information acquires greater significance in light of Strahan's clientele and status in the trade. Johnson, for example, had good reason to compliment Strahan's house. Strahan printed and/or helped finance nearly every major book that Johnson wrote: *A Dictionary of the English Language* (1755 and subsequent editions), *The Rambler, Rasselas, A Journey to the Western Islands of Scotland,* and *The Lives of the English Poets.*

Johnson was not Strahan's only famous author. Strahan was a friend, a literary executor, and the preferred printer of David Hume, and he printed Tobias Smollett's *Roderick Random* and *Peregrine Pickle,* Adam Smith's *Wealth of Nations,* Edward Gibbon's *The Decline and Fall of the Roman Empire,* and Hugh Blair's *Sermons.* During the mid-eighteenth century Strahan was at the center of a business network that included such booksellers and publishers as Thomas Cadell, the Dodsleys, William Johnston, Thomas Longman, Andrew Millar, John Newbery, and the Rivingtons.

Strahan chose printing as his profession, but he rose to prominence in part because he expanded his business beyond the traditional boundaries of his office. Most eighteenth-century printers worked by contract, taking finite jobs for definite but limited profits. Strahan understood that the more speculative branches of the book trade turned the higher profits:

> I quickly saw, that if I confined myself to mere *printing for Booksellers* I might be able to live, but very little more than live, I therefore soon determined to launch out into other Branches in Connection with my own, in which I have happily succeeded, to the Astonishment of the rest of the Trade here, who never dreamt of going out of the old beaten Track. Thus I have made Name of *Printer* more respectable than ever it was before, and taught them to emancipate themselves from the Slavery in which the Booksellers held them.[13]

Rather than entering into direct competition with the booksellers, Strahan respected the established branches of trade even as he transgressed them. His major customers were colonists, such as his longtime friends Benjamin Franklin and David Hall. As publisher or owner of copies, he left his name off the imprint, preferring (especially early on) to remain a "silent partner."[14]

Strahan's tact and entrepreneurism served him well. At his death in 1785, his estate was valued at ninety-five thousand pounds (the equivalent, at a conservative estimate, of more than 10 million pounds in 2016).[15] He was elected Master of the Stationers' Company in 1774 and served as member of Parliament for Malmesbury and Wootton Bassett from 1774 to 1784. In the years leading up to the American Revolutionary War, Strahan became a de facto political correspondent for Franklin and Hall, passing along both his own commentary and "copies of the proceedings of important debates closed to the public."[16] With Strahan's approval, Hall published much of this material in the *Pennsylvania Gazette.*[17]

On account of this connection with Franklin and Hall, the American Philosophical Society in Philadelphia (APS) purchased four Strahan notebooks in 1958. A small but salient complement to the main deposit of Strahan's papers at the British Library, these notebooks combine inventory and itinerary. They document Strahan's trips to his native Scotland over three decades, including a meeting with Franklin in Edinburgh in 1759, and contain a handful of records pertinent to Strahan's printing operations.

Of these records, several inventories of Strahan's estate have the greatest interest for historians of printing. They capture Strahan's workflow at distinct historical moments, each offering a horizontal look at the works in production, his accounts with customers, the number of copies he held at any one time, and his debts to his suppliers. As such, and especially until a comprehensive edition of Strahan's ledgers appears,[18] these inventories form an important index of the mid-eighteenth-century book trade. They also have value as encapsulations of diverse human presences—some recognizable, others unknown—and trade networks. Together, they constitute a nontrivial part of that "reservoir of information about the past" that Tanselle identifies as the object of bibliographical analysis.

The inventory of January 1, 1759, for example, shows Strahan presiding over a robust printing business. He possessed large and active wholesale accounts with retail booksellers elsewhere in England and in the American colonies, and he also owned a number of valuable copies. Strahan's inventory begins with works concurrently in production in his firm, moves to his accounts with customers of various kinds, delineates the copies that he owns, itemizes his other assets, lists his own debts, and concludes with a balance of more than ten thousand pounds.

Of the books under production, several, such as Paul de Rapin de Thoyras's *The History of England,* were staples of the London trade, underwritten by multiple booksellers through the share-book system.[19] Others, like the anonymous novel *The mother; or the happy distress,* reflect individual ventures. In this case, the author was William Guthrie, a fellow Scot. Guthrie's own *History of England from the invasion of Julius Caesar to 1688* (1744–51) "made unprecedented use of parliamentary papers for the later period," but the reception of his novel must have been mixed at best.[20] The English Short Title Catalogue lists only one other edition, also "printed for the author," from 1761.

The data in this section shed light on at least two questions about the economies of book production. First, how many copies of a book, in general, was it thought profitable to print at one time? If one printed too few, one would likely have to incur the expense (and further risk) of setting the type all over again for a second edition. If one printed too many, one was left, of course, with overstock. What demand did publishers, whose business it was to know, anticipate for different kinds of books during this period?

On this matter, the evidence from the Bowyer ledgers as well as from Patricia Hernlund's extensive study of Strahan's ledgers has led scholars to favor conservative estimates.[21] As Suarez writes, "A press run of 500–750 copies may be considered typical, with 500 being more common."[22] Strahan's 1759 inventory, which may represent an anomaly or a peak in the level of production, exceeds these calculations. Of the eleven unfinished works entered in the notebook, only three have print runs of less than 1,000, with none lower than 750. They range as follows: 2,000 (3), 1,500 (1), 1,000 (4), 750 (3). With respect to Strahan's firm, in other words, scholars may need to revise their estimates upward.[23] Of course, Strahan's printing office was the largest in London, so it stands to reason that with more presses at his disposal, he had the productive capacity to take on more large jobs than other firms.

As a holder of copies, Strahan himself had an interest in accurate calculation of print runs, but inventories such as this one do not tell us to what extent he aided customers in identifying plausible demand. Most likely, of course, he printed as many copies of a work as its owner wanted or could afford. In another way, however, Strahan's inventories place his own judgment as a businessman front and center. Strahan followed the traditional practice of taking the printed sheet as the unit of sale. For each of the unfinished works in the 1759 inventory, he lists the price per sheet that he charged his customer. Thus, for example, he billed £1 2s. per sheet for the first volume of Hume's *Essays*, £1 9s. per sheet for William Burkitt's *Expository Notes*, and £2 6s. for Ferdinando Altieri's *Dizionario italiano ed inglese*. How—this is the second question—did he determine how much to charge?[24]

By themselves, the inventories in the APS notebooks do not disclose the key to this question. Writing for himself, Strahan felt no need to explain the price per sheet for the works listed as under production in January 1759. A list of eleven works, a fraction of those Strahan printed over his fifty years in business, warrants few generalizations. One notes, nevertheless, that Strahan charged the same price per sheet for only two of this number. The works range in price per sheet from 15s. (for a "Descrip. of France") to £2 6s. (Altieri's *Dizionario* and "Military Dict.," possibly *The complete militia-man, or a compendium of military knowledge,* published by Ralph Griffiths in 1760). As a whole, Strahan values the works under production in January 1759 at almost £600, approximately 5 percent of the credit side of his estate.

Next, Strahan lists accounts with more than ninety customers, organizing them by their appearance in one of three ledgers: the "Folio Book," the "Octavo Book," and the "Quarto Book." Like many eighteenth-century printers, Strahan did a mixture of bookwork and jobbing printing. When printing books, he contracted either with booksellers or groups of booksellers, who paid authors for the rights to publish their works, or with the authors themselves, who paid out of pocket for their books or financed them through subscription.[25] Strahan took on all kinds of small, occasional jobs, including summons, bills, receipts, forms, and pamphlets.

The 1759 inventory records each kind of work. London booksellers, Strahan's core business network, make up more than half of the accounts. Thomas Osborne (£43 15s.), Ralph Griffiths (£363 16s.), Andrew Millar (£840 11s.), the Dodsleys (£33 10s.), Jacob Tonson the younger (£93 10s., £109 7s.), James Buckland (£35), William Owen (£47 5s.), John Knapton (£26 15s.), and John Newbery (£11 1s.), among many others, all owed Strahan for work performed. Individuals commissioning their own work include Saunders Welch, Esq. (£10 16s., presumably for *An Essay on the Office of the Constable*), and the preacher Dr. Ferdinando Warner (£136, presumably for *The Ecclesiastical History of England, to the eighteenth century*).

The 1759 inventory indicates similar debts from various persons, many no doubt identifiable. It does far less than the printing ledgers themselves to indicate the frequency and kinds of jobbing printing that Strahan undertook, for the simple reason that he would have expected ready money from these customers. Nevertheless, Strahan put the Goldsmith's Company, which "required only 'job work,'" down for £5 15s.[26]

The inventory also testifies to Strahan's efforts to free himself from the purely contractual work of printing. Here, one finds records of Strahan's dealings, as wholesale bookseller, with Benjamin Collins of Salisbury (£72 3s.);[27] his friend and fellow Scot David Hall, who left England for Philadelphia and rose through Franklin's firm from journeyman to partner (£457 10s.); and the Charleston Library, the third oldest subscription library in America (£112 9s.). Not all Strahan's ventures as wholesaler paid off. In 1759

he registers a debt, never to be repaid, of £333 15s. for books sold to Benjamin Mecom. Mecom's printing business in Antigua, which he founded with
the help of Franklin, his uncle, failed in 1756.[28]

In 1759, Strahan records ownership of copies (rights to publish) for
twenty-eight books. As Suarez observes, "Owning 'copies' . . . was, when
those works proved to be steady sellers over many years, the key to many
a bookseller's long-term financial success."[29] Strahan's holdings at this date
include a third share in Johnson's *Rasselas,* a ninth share in the lucrative
London Chronicle, a sixteenth share in Rapin's *History,* half of Tobias Smollett's *Peregrine Pickle* and a third share in *Count Fathom,* and a half share
in William Smellie's *Treatise on the Theory and Practice of Midwifery.* In
addition, Strahan lists himself as sole owner of three books: *A New estimate
of human life,* by Sir John Hill; *The polite philosopher: or, an essay on that
art, which makes a man happy in himself, and agreeable to others,* published
anonymously, but by John Forrester; and John Douglas's *Treatise on the Hydrocele.*

Strahan's involvement with the *Treatise on the Hydrocele,* which he
printed for David Wilson and Thomas Durham in 1755, exemplified his
foresight, generosity, and unique ability to consolidate the branches of the
book trade for personal gain. Terry Belanger provides relevant background:
"Strahan imported Thomas Durham from Edinburgh and set him to work
for Wilson; when Durham later opened his own shop . . . silent partner
Strahan apprenticed his son George to him."[30] As copy owner and printer of
the *Hydrocele,* Strahan profited twice by this book. He was also supporting
a business, in the firm of Wilson and Durham, in whose success he had a
special interest. By helping Durham establish himself in the London trade,
Strahan was paying forward the assistance he himself had received when he
arrived in London as a journeyman compositor in the 1730s. His generosity
was, at the same time, entwined with his own longer-term aspirations, in
this case for his son.

In January 1759 Strahan could tally his credits to more than ten thousand pounds. He records debts totaling less than eight hundred pounds.
His presses were busy with unfinished work, and he had established himself
as a wholesale bookseller as well as an owner of copies and a participant in
the London share-book system. To this much the 1759 inventory attests, yet
so much information about his firm remains in need of wider scholarly research. Even this brief inventory contains many data points that need both
clarification and further context. The list of works in production at this time
tells us how much Strahan charged per sheet, for example, but not how

much he paid his employees. Of Strahan's own creditors—the type founders, ink makers, "musick masters," tallow chandlers, and vendors of small beer to whose existence the inventory bears (perhaps the sole) witness—only a few can be traced at present. A comprehensive edition of Strahan's business records would enable bibliographers and literary scholars to study individual books within the historical context of their production. It would allow historians to examine the minute details of Strahan's highly successful business and track its progress over half a century. Equally important, such an edition would cast light on the judgments of one of eighteenth-century London's preeminent bookmakers, bringing Strahan back, in McKenzie's sense, to life.

Notes

I am indebted to the Bibliographical Society of the University of Virginia and the Buckner Clay Endowment of the University of Virginia for support that enabled me to research Strahan's ledgers and consult the William Strahan Collection at the American Philosophical Society.

1. Tanselle, *Bibliographical Analysis*, 30.
2. McKenzie, "Sociology of a Text," 335.
3. Tanselle, *Bibliographical Analysis*, 25.
4. McKenzie, "Stretching a Point," 92.
5. Hardy, "In Tenbris, I."
6. Elbow, *Writing without Teachers*, 148.
7. Quoted in Tanselle, *Bibliographical Analysis*, 56.
8. Brack, "Ledgers of William Strahan," 62.
9. Silver, review of *The Bowyer Ledgers*, 216.
10. Suarez, "Mining the Archive," 852.
11. Quoted in Austen-Leigh, *Story of a Printing House*, 26.
12. Raven, "Book Distribution Networks," 591.
13. Quoted in Austen-Leigh, *Story of a Printing House*, 15–16.
14. Harlan, "William Strahan," 115.
15. Hernlund, "Strahan, William (1715–1785)"; Officer and Williamson, "Five Ways to Compute."
16. Harlan, *William Strahan*, 48.
17. Ibid.
18. That larger project was proposed by Michael F. Suarez, SJ, in a January 2012 address to the American Printing History Association. Specifically, Suarez would like to see a collective, international effort by scholars to transcribe the British Library's collection of Strahan ledgers, making them available as a web resource.
19. Harlan, "William Strahan," 73–74.
20. Allan, "Guthrie, William (1708?–1770)."
21. Hernlund, "William Strahan's Ledgers," 104. Hernlund writes that "from 1738 to

1785, the most frequently ordered press run" in Strahan's house "was 500 copies, and . . . a run of 1000 was second in frequency" (ibid.).

22. Suarez, "Book Trade," 137.

23. Another entry in the same notebook, a statement of the work in the Strahan house for July 1759, supports the idea that Strahan was, at this time at least, frequently printing on this scale.

24. In her dissertation, completed at the University of Chicago in 1965, and in a series of articles published in *Studies in Bibliography,* Hernlund identified "a pattern which Strahan followed in charging his customers for printing." Few have spent as much time with the Strahan ledgers as Hernlund, and one does not doubt her observation of "the consistency of the prices he charged." Still, the idea that Strahan went so far as to develop "a standard scale of prices" that he could present to customers has struck other bibliographers, including some with equal or greater experience with eighteenth-century printing ledgers, as anachronistic, of "doubtful validity." Maslen, "Printing Charges," 92.

25. On this topic, see Maslen, "Printing for the Author."

26. Hernlund, "William Strahan's Ledgers," 95.

27. For another discussion of Strahan's relationship with Collins, see Ferdinand, *Benjamin Collins,* 27–60.

28. Harlan, "William Strahan," 45.

29. Suarez, "Book Trade," 138.

30. Belanger, "Directory of the London Book Trade," 14.

Works Cited

Allan, David. "Guthrie, William (1708?–1770)." In *Oxford Dictionary of National Biography,* online ed., ed. David Cannadine. Oxford: Oxford University Press, 2004. Accessed 14 May 2017. http://www.oxforddnb.com/view/article/11792.

Austen-Leigh, Richard Arthur. *The Story of a Printing House: Being a Short Account of the Strahans and Spottiswoodes.* London: Spottiswoode, 1912.

Belanger, Terry. "A Directory of the London Book Trade, 1766." *Publishing History* 1 (1977): 7–48.

Brack, O. M. "The Ledgers of William Strahan." In *Editing Eighteenth-Century Texts,* ed. D. I. B. Smith, 59–77. Toronto: University of Toronto Press, 1968.

Elbow, Peter. *Writing without Teachers.* New York: Oxford University Press, 1998.

Ferdinand, Christine Y. *Benjamin Collins and the Provincial Newspaper Trade in the Eighteenth Century.* Oxford: Clarendon, 1997.

Hardy, Thomas. "In Tenebris, I." In *The Complete Poems of Thomas Hardy,* ed. James Gibson, 167. New York: Macmillan, 1978.

Harlan, Robert Dale. "William Strahan: Eighteenth-Century London Printer and Publisher." PhD diss., University of Michigan, 1960.

Hernlund, Patricia. "Strahan, William (1715–1785)." In *Oxford Dictionary of National Biography,* online ed., ed. David Cannadine. Oxford: Oxford University Press, 2004. Accessed 17 November 2015. http://www.oxforddnb.com.proxy.its.virginia.edu/view/article/26631.

———. "William Strahan's Ledgers: Standard Charges for Printing, 1738–1785." *Studies in Bibliography* 20 (1967): 89–111.

Maslen, Keith I. D. "Printing Charges: Inference and Evidence." *Studies in Bibliography* 24 (1971): 91–98.

———. "Printing for the Author: From the Bowyer Printing Ledgers, 1710–1775." *Library,* 5th ser., 27, no. 4 (1972): 302–9.

McKenzie, D. F. "The Sociology of a Text: Orality, Literacy and Print in Early New Zealand." *Library,* 6th ser., 6, no. 4 (1984): 333–65.

———. "Stretching a Point: Or, The Case of the Spaced-out Comps." In *Making Meaning: "Printers of the Mind" and Other Essays,* ed. Peter D. McDonald and Michael F. Suarez, SJ, 91–106. Amherst: University of Massachusetts Press, 2002.

Officer, Lawrence H., and Samuel H. Williamson. "Five Ways to Compute the Relative Value of a UK Pound Amount, 1270 to Present." MeasuringWorth, 2017. https://www.measuringworth.com/ukcompare/result.php?year_source=1785&amount=95000&year_result=2017.

Raven, James. "Book Distribution Networks in Early Modern Europe: The Case of the Western Fringe (La rete distributiva del libro)." In *Produzione e commercio della carta e del libro secc. XIII–XVIII, Istituto Internazionale de Storia Economica F. Datini Prato* 23 (1991): 583–630.

Silver, Joel. Review of *The Bowyer Ledgers: The Printing Accounts of William Bowyer Father and Son Reproduced on Microfiche with a Checklist of Bowyer Printing, 1699–1777, a Commentary, Indexes, and Appendices,* ed. Keith Maslen and John Lancaster. *Library Quarterly: Information, Community, Policy* 63, no. 2 (1993): 216–17.

Suarez, Michael F., SJ. "Book Trade." In *Samuel Johnson in Context,* ed. Jack Lynch, 134–42. Cambridge: Cambridge University Press, 2012.

———. "Mining the Archive: A Guide to Present and Future Book-Historical Research Resources." In *The Cambridge History of the Book in Britain,* vol. 5, ed. Michael F. Suarez, SJ, and Michael L. Turner, 849–59. Cambridge: Cambridge University Press, 2009.

Tanselle, G. Thomas. *Bibliographical Analysis: A Historical Introduction.* Cambridge: Cambridge University Press, 2009.

Understanding an Obscure Text

The Fortunate Foundlings and the
Limits of Interdisciplinarity

PATRICIA MEYER SPACKS

Eliza Haywood's enormous literary production includes many works that have received little or no recent critical attention. Although such works readily lend themselves to various critical agendas, they often prove challenging to assess in their own terms. *The Fortunate Foundlings* (1744) provides a case in point: an elaborately plotted double narrative, alternately focused on a male and a female twin, that achieves a romance resolution but incorporates extensive historical references along the way. James Stuart, the "Old Pretender" to the British throne, and Charles XII of Sweden figure among its characters. Why does Haywood need them? What do they contribute to the text?

Any attempt to answer these ostensibly simple questions may embroil us in dilemmas about interdisciplinarity. A novel that employs historical fact as part of its raw material invites an interdisciplinary reading that makes use of historical insight. Yet the idea of an interdisciplinary reading is hardly transparent. How does one perform interdisciplinarity? What does the term really mean? How, exactly, does it relate to disciplinarity—and what, for that matter, does *that* mean?

The Fortunate Foundlings provides a pretext for pondering such questions. Although it was mildly successful at its first appearance, critics since the eighteenth century have largely ignored it. It offers abundant opportunity for exegesis, both literary and historical. I propose to attempt such exegesis and then to reflect on the implications of my procedures.

Like many of Haywood's other fictions, this one explores social and psychological problems of women. It differs from many of the others, though, in giving equal emphasis to male difficulties. The title's twin foundlings, a boy and a girl, are discovered as infants by a wealthy aristocrat, Dorilaus, under a tree on his estate. He provides them with good educations and ample opportunities, rearing them as though they were his own. In due time, both leave home to prove themselves as adults. The young man, Horatio, sixteen years old, with his guardian's consent seeks his fortune on the field of battle, fighting in European wars. His sister, Louisa, at the same age departs surreptitiously, with no financial help from her foster father. She must therefore find her own resources for survival. The remainder of the event-filled narrative focuses alternately on the adventures of each sibling, which do not intersect until everyone finally meets in Paris.

Both foundlings worry about "honor." As Horatio puts the point in a letter to Dorilaus, "My honour, my reputation, must survive when I am no more; it was the first, and will be the last of my desires."[1] The novel initially seems to endorse the conventional view of male and female honor: for women, honor equals chastity; for men, it depends on courage. Throughout their multifarious adventures, Louisa consistently (and successfully) defends her chastity against serious threats, and Horatio displays manly virtues on battlefields. Many eighteenth-century novels of the kind we now call "minor" seek no further for a plot. In such novels, heroes and heroines display honor in trying situations and are rewarded for their virtue. Haywood, however, in *The Fortunate Foundlings* seeks a good deal more, raising questions about the sufficiency of preserved chastity as a female achievement and of battlefield courage as a male one. Her protagonists' experiences cause them gradually to expand their views. Louisa comes to believe in self-sustained action as her mode of female integrity, and Horatio, although he never reaches a clear conclusion, keeps finding himself puzzled about how much he owes to love compared with what he owes to his reputation and to his commanders.

In addition to feeling urgent needs to defend their honor, the protagonists face immediate and long-range problems about money and social status. When they fall in love, as both predictably do, such problems become pressing. Horatio has proved himself to the father of his beloved by successfully defending the older man against would-be assassins, without knowing his identity. The Baron de Palfoy feels lastingly grateful. He admires and values Horatio, professing willingness to do anything for his savior and to give him anything he asks—anything, that is, except his daughter. Horatio, an Englishman of unknown parentage and limited financial resources, cannot qualify as a son-in-law.

Louisa ostensibly faces a less daunting situation. The Frenchman of wealth and family whom she reciprocally loves insists that he cares not at all about her dubious origins and her poverty. If she lacks family and riches, that fact only makes more obvious his devotion to her for herself alone.

Louisa, however, cannot accept his reassurances, having internalized values identical to the baron's. With no hope of acquiring wealth or status by her own endeavors, she comes close to despair. As she puts the point in her private reflections, "I have [no parents],—none to own me;—I am a nothing;—a kind of reptile in humanity, and have been shewn in a genteel way of life only to make my native misery more conspicuous" (178). The statement could hardly be more emphatic: without a family of enough distinction to live in a "genteel" way, a woman becomes worse than nothing, reptilian, disgusting, set apart from all humanity. For Louisa, everything seems at stake in the question of her birth. In other words, all depends on something over which she has no control. The generosity of the man who wishes to marry her cannot help her, nor can she help herself. She understands herself as having been "shewn" to the world, displayed in the marriage market, but under the circumstances no display can matter.

Although a great many eighteenth-century novels, such as *Tom Jones*, *Humphry Clinker*, and *Evelina*, turn on questions of birth, few provide such intense explicit commentary on the issue. For both siblings, *The Fortunate Foundlings* resolves the problem of family, as *Tom Jones* does: by the fortuitous discovery of true, and wealthy, parentage. As it turns out, Dorilaus literally fathered Horatio and Louisa, although he did not earlier himself know this fact. A youthful liaison with a lady "of very good family," already engaged to another man but captivated by Dorilaus, produced the infants after the couple separated. Their mother conceals the fact of their birth, living a virtuous and benevolent married life thereafter. Only on her deathbed does she impart her secret. Dorilaus thereupon hastens to Paris to seek his children, with whom he has lost touch. His wealth and social position facilitate the desired marital arrangements.

Horatio, unable to remedy his ambiguous birth, has concluded that money—a lot of money—will nonetheless make him an eligible husband for the baron's daughter. In his first conversation with Dorilaus about his desire to become a soldier, the elder man comments about "glory" and "profits" as rewards of the military life, without distinguishing their relative values (8). Horatio, in his first experience of battle, covers himself with glory. Old officers tell him that rich plunder is available, but he declines the opportunity, saying that he has come "to fight for the honour of his country, and not to rob for its disgrace." The Duke of Marlborough, his patron, when told of the episode, smiles and comments that Horatio "was yet too young to know the value of money" (55).

If so, he soon learns better, as he comes to connect possession of wealth with the possibility of fulfilling his love. Moreover, the novel's narrator assumes the identity of money and value. The dense record of Horatio's military career repeatedly specifies the financial rewards that the young man accrues, with considerable vagueness, often, about the precise sources of these rewards. The matter of "plunder" gets elided, as do all other morally dubious aspects of a soldier's activities. As Dorilaus earlier suggested, glory and profit go together; one need not think too much about how that happens.

But the narrative has introduced, casually and in passing, the matter of plunder and the possibility of considering it robbery and judging it disgraceful. Although *The Fortunate Foundlings* never again overtly considers the moral ambiguity of military life, it has alerted the reader to an uncomfortable fact that remains uncomfortably in the background.

In the foreground, another source of discomfort arises. Horatio, in his constant search for "honor," increasingly desires to fight for and with Charles XII of Sweden, who has conquered every army that opposed him and is known throughout Europe for his courage. Horatio travels to Poland to join Charles's forces, hearing everywhere of the king's achievements and regretting his own absence from the scenes of battle, since he thinks that honor would have accrued to him by association. His admiration of Charles only intensifies as he fights along with him, winning more honor and more wealth. Indeed, the narrative specifies that his riches become sufficient to make him a likely suitor for Baron de Palfoy's daughter. He does not, however, cease fighting, since his feeling for Charles joins with his "ambition of desiring still more than he had received" (227)—more money, that is.

Horatio's yearning for Charlotta helps motivate his commitment to the king of Sweden, not only because he wants to amass money partly for her sake but also because he believes that martial honor will make him more attractive to her. Yet a conflict between love and desire for honor repeatedly troubles the text. It occurs to Horatio in relation to his own situation, as over and over he rationalizes his choice of continuing to fight rather than returning to his beloved. He notes it in Charles XII, whose cheeks redden when Horatio transmits to him a message from his fiancée, the Old Pretender's sister, Princess Louisa. Subsequently, the young man observes that the king often looks at Louisa's picture; yet "he would on a sudden snatch his eyes away, as fearing to be too much softened" (224). Even though the beautiful princess is waiting for him, Charles gratuitously decides to invade Russia. He seems unable to stop. Horatio, although described as "no less fond of glory" than the conquering monarch himself, "had a softness in his nature, which made him languish for the sight of his dear Charlotta" (238).

He consequently faces difficulty in making necessary decisions. When he receives an unexpected letter from Dorilaus, summoning him back to Paris, he endures intense conflict. On the one hand, he believes that Charlotta, the baron, and Dorilaus would condemn him if he left the prince to whom he has sworn loyalty, given their high notions of honor, generosity, and gratitude. On the other hand, he owes everything to Dorilaus and, in another sense, to Charlotta. Love, friendship, and duty in specific forms call him back. A generalized notion of honor forbids.

He decides in favor of honor, writing Dorilaus that he would be branded with everlasting infamy if he left his post. The fiction punishes him by throwing him into a Russian prison, where interludes of help from a beautiful but chaste local princess alleviate his misery. King Charles, meanwhile, having likewise chosen honor, suffers a serious wound. Because the king will perhaps never fight again, Horatio feels little compunction about abandoning his own martial career. Love and prosperity await him in Paris, where his father, his sister, his beloved, and her father all shower praise upon him. Apparently he has now made the right choice. The narrative, however, emphasizes the ambivalence with which he makes it, reporting in full the letters Horatio writes to Charlotta, the baron, and Dorilaus, each recording perplexity about love versus duty, all calling attention to the fact that "honor" is by no means a transparent value.

Louisa suffers too, but not from ambivalence. Much of her pain derives directly from the social situation of women. If they belong to ranks superior to that of the working class, women exist, as Louisa suggests in a passage quoted above, to be "shewn" to the world and selected for marriage. Failing success in that passive role, they find few acceptable possibilities for action. Louisa nonetheless sets out to earn her own living. Although she cannot know what social class she belongs to by birth, she has been reared in lavish circumstances. Unlike her brother, though, she does not leave her guardian's home with his permission and support. On the contrary, she flees because of his undesired sexual overtures. She fears that he will rape her. She knows that he will continue to appeal to her sense of obligation, but she feels ungovernable horror at the idea of trying to convert her love for him as a father figure into love for a sexual partner.

Sexual persecution also marks her subsequent travels. After abandoning employment with a London milliner because of the sexual threats associated with such work, she acquires a position as paid companion to a rich woman, Melanthe, who treats her as a friend. With this woman, she, like her brother, travels to the European continent. Melanthe, however, dismisses her companion, abruptly and harshly, when she comes to believe that Louisa is trying to entice the man who has engaged her employer's affections. (In fact, Louisa has already fallen in love with her wealthy Frenchman.)

With no preparation and little money, Louisa once more sets forth into the world. As the plot develops, she has little choice about what to do next. The man who has most recently seduced Melanthe claims to have fallen in love with Louisa, whom he pursues to an inn, gaining entrance to her bedroom there. He insists that she is his runaway wife, and despite her fierce denials, the innkeeper and others feel inclined to believe him. In the nick of time, Louisa's true love, du Plessis, arrives to defend her, but language difficulties and the perplexities of ascertaining the truth of the situation cause both Louisa and her suitor to be thrown into prison.

Like many of Louisa's problems, this one finds easy resolution. Soon after her release, she finally acknowledges her love to du Plessis and allows him to escort her to a presumably safe convent. But her virtue and beauty make the senior nuns think her a prize; they plot to lure her into taking vows. Although they have stolen her letters from du Plessis, so that she has no idea where he is (like Horatio, he is presumably fighting in some European war), she manages to escape the convent, traveling alone across the Continent in a pilgrim's habit, seeking her lover. Coincidence in Paris unites her with her true father, and further coincidence reveals du Plessis, miraculously intact after much fighting.

This truncated summary omits many events that further complicate the intricate plot. John Richetti, one of the few commentators on *The Fortunate Foundlings,* notes "the lip service paid to historical particularity, with Haywood's parade of real places, glamorous and famous persons, and actual events. Action-packed, bursting with passion, martial glory, gallantry, and sentimentality, *The Fortunate Foundlings* is an amalgam and extension of Haywood's earlier style, a narrative manner necessarily free of irony or moral analysis in its pursuit of glamour and excitement."[2] Richetti's description of the book's tone—passion, glory, gallantry, sentimentality—aptly suggests its narrative energy. Adventure piles on adventure with breakneck speed. Characters appear and disappear, with little or no attention paid to the inner lives of anyone except the protagonists and with scant care for plausibility. Yet I think Richetti wrong in concluding that the play of often fractured, glittering surfaces implies primary authorial concern with glamour and excitement. On the contrary, *The Fortunate Foundlings* employs its "parade" of real and fictional persons and events in the service of serious, if sometimes underdeveloped, moral investigation.

Haywood's juxtaposition of a male and a female character illustrates not only conventional differentiations (males have more choice, more opportunity, and fewer restrictions on action than females) but also less predictable conjunctions of value. *The Fortunate Foundlings* investigates the claims of love and of honor, for men and for women, within the context of a society primarily concerned with money and status. Horatio, who seeks wealth, worries far more about honor. He also, in his early remark about plunder, reveals a capacity (never further substantiated) to question conventional assumptions. He wins praise for his courage and his martial skill, but the narrative more strongly endorses what it designates as the "soft" side of his nature: his commitment to love. Louisa cares little about money, except inasmuch as its lack, which she cannot remedy, makes her unmarriageable in her own view. She displays conventional virtue, but her interest for readers surely centers on her independence of spirit and her determination to think things out for herself. Even Dorilaus is impressed when he hears of her intrepid journey on foot across Europe. He says that he will keep her pilgrim's habit as a relic for after ages: she will have the reputation for "honor" that Horatio aspires to, along with a husband's love.

I have thus far neglected what Richetti calls "the lip service paid to historical particularity." The first clause of the novel's opening sentence refers to "the ever memorable year 1688," without specifying what made the year memorable, and the cast of characters includes not only the Old Pretender and Charles XII but also a number of minor, named historical figures. Horatio and du Plessis fight in actual wars, with historically specific named battles. The historical situation, I believe, serves a more serious purpose than decoration.

Most obviously, *The Fortunate Foundlings,* like *Tom Jones,* makes inheritance a complicated issue. The sequence of national events that began in that "glorious year," 1688, turns on the inheritance of a kingdom. Haywood's novel reflects actualities of her own period, as well as the "historical particularities" she specifies. In 1744, the book's date of publication, activities of the Old Pretender, James, son of the deposed King James II, and his son, Charles Edward Stuart ("Bonnie Prince Charlie"), both living in French exile, focused much national concern; the subsequent year would see Charles's second invasion of Scotland, with his troops penetrating England. Many residents of Scotland, and a good many of England, retained sympathy for the Stuart cause and for the exiled royalty in France. As Frank McLynn points out, "Supporters of the House of Stuart can be found among both long-serving members and those who entered Parliament for the first time in

1741; among army officers, though rarely among naval officers; among industrialists, and above all among lawyers."[3] Another historian, Daniel Szechi, characterizes the Jacobites as "a self-sustaining, recognisable minority who rejected the social, political and religious order installed after 1688."[4] Unquestionably a minority, the Jacobites nonetheless were a significant presence.

King George II of England, on the throne when Haywood wrote, had proved more popular than his father, partly because of his martial courage and leadership. Unlike his predecessor, he had learned to speak English. Yet even a twenty-first-century historian defending his contributions uses such terms as *boor, rude, brutal,* and *dull* to characterize him.[5] Questions of inheritance—how important was preservation of the Stuart line?—readily merged with questions of worth. Who was more worthy to be king? To what extent did a line of descent in itself determine worth? Such issues thrive in *The Fortunate Foundlings,* not only because some of the action occurs in the Jacobite court, with the Old Pretender a character, but because Horatio has deliberately set out to prove himself individually worthy of the inheritance he expects; and Louisa, who also proves herself, believes herself of no worth to anyone else without the lineage that an inheritance suggests.

The novel does not allude to the fact that Louis XIV, king of France, had assigned to the Old Pretender the title James III of England after his father's death in 1701, thus upholding his claim to be lawful inheritor of the British throne. Nor does the book refer directly to any such claims. It emphasizes what the Stuart family has lost, not what it hopes to gain, and represents the court as comprising people noble both in character and in rank, in splendid settings. Like his father, the younger James inhabited the chateau of Saint-Germain-en-Laye, outside Paris, given by Louis to the Stuarts. Here he had a lavish establishment. In 1704, when Horatio sets forth on his military career, the Old Pretender, born in the same memorable year as Horatio, was likewise sixteen years old.

Haywood's narrative refers only vaguely to this fact, observing that the Pretender and his sister "had both of them a very serious air, which denoted they had reflections more befitting their condition than their years" (64). James, his sister, and indeed the entire establishment serve Horatio as moral exempla, illustrating the instability of all worldly conditions and the importance of virtue, which the royal family embodies. We are told that association with the court "gave Horatio a manly way of thinking much sooner than otherwise he might have had" (64–65). I'll return to that notion of a manly way of thinking.

Writing in the early 1740s, Eliza Haywood risked something by bringing her protagonist to the Stuart court in exile. To betray political sympathy with an English royal family other than that of the Hanoverian on the throne might endanger an author legally and economically, although to flirt with such sympathy would perhaps titillate readers. Horatio as a character strongly hints his own Jacobite allegiance, connecting it to a vague sense of the family's suffering at being flung from a high place. Allusions to the court consistently emphasize the instability of human greatness. Turning the royal family into moral exempla skirts the political and converts the Stuarts into mediators of Horatio's progress toward "manliness"—while also entertaining the reader with at least a faint illusion of inner knowledge about a forbidden subject.

The other royal character in the novel receives fuller attention. Charles XII (1682–1718) had already, when *The Fortunate Foundlings* appeared in 1744, been the subject of a book by Voltaire, first published in 1731; he had become a type of martial heroism. (A few years later, he would provide for Dr. Johnson a type of the vanity of human wishes.) He was also a conspicuous enemy of the Hanoverian kings, another fact ignored in Haywood's fiction, though presumably alive for her early readers.

Voltaire's brilliantly readable account stresses Charles's martial prowess, his single-minded determination, his ingenuity in fulfilling his purposes, and his lifelong abstinence from alcohol and women. The king had begun his triumphant military career while yet a teenager, defeating far larger opposing armies all over Europe. He made himself the stuff of legends, and legends promptly accumulated.

Robert Nisbet Bain, an early-twentieth-century historian, comments on "the many erroneous notions concerning [Charles XII] for which Voltaire's brilliant and attractive work, I had almost said romance . . . is mainly responsible."[6] The word that Bain professes himself unwilling to say may readily occur to the reader of many extant accounts concerning Charles, whether or not they claim factuality. Charles's careful twentieth-century biographer, R. M. Hatton, points out how many passionately held, conflicting views of the king's nature and accomplishments have emerged. Conflicting views, many of them partaking of romance, developed early.[7] When Haywood included Charles in her own romance, she contributed to a varied and complicated legend already formed less than a quarter century after his death. Voltaire had probably influenced her with his representation of the king as generous and forbearing, strategically brilliant, and unfailingly courageous; Haywood's version exhibits the same traits in the ruler. Before Horatio actually encounters him, the young man longs "to behold a prince who seemed to have all the virtues comprised in him, and whose very thoughts, as well as actions, might be looked upon as supernatural" (114). The baron, who tells Horatio about this virtuous prince, comments that Charles's fiancée might wish him "of a less martial disposition." Horatio interrupts to say that such a disposition will make the king all the more worthy of the princess he plans to marry, "and the immortal fame of his actions [will] be a sufficient atonement for all the years of expectation that may be its purchase" (114).

But Horatio still has much to learn about love and honor. Haywood converts Charles, too, into a moral exemplar—but a negative one. She passes over the king's cruelty and propensity for violence, which even Voltaire noted on occasion, to suggest that his failure to consider the interests of his fiancée reflects a moral weakness. When Horatio decides to return to Paris instead of seeking out his wounded leader, he demonstrates that he has grown beyond Charles's model.

Voltaire uses the king's attitudes toward women to bolster a story of self-discipline and almost superhuman control. "He was suspected of having had a passionate affair with a lady at court; whether this was true or not, it is certain that he gave up women forever, not only for fear of being dominated by them, but as an example for his soldiers, whom he wished to control by the strictest discipline, and perhaps also through the vanity of being the only king ever to overcome so ungovernable an inclination" (43). Charles's twentieth-century biographer, Hatton, suggests a different interpretation of his asceticism, pointing out that he "was by some contemporaries, and many historians," thought homosexual.[8] Haywood ignores the resolution of abstention altogether and suggests, by having Charles look repeatedly at the image of the princess to whom he is engaged only to turn resolutely back to battle, that he experiences romantic heterosexual love. Only six years older than Horatio, the leader is, by this telling, in a conflicted situation comparable to that of the novel's protagonist, who does not yet have a fiancée but who loves and longs for a woman left behind. When he rejects the life of battle to act on that longing, Horatio has finally attained the "manliness" to which he aspires. Although he has approached a manly way of thinking at the Old Pretender's court, the novel sets him the more demanding task of attaining a proper balance between love and ambition. Having proved his courage and fortitude and won wealth by his own efforts, having relinquished his fantasy that a woman's love can flourish solely on the basis of a man's martial achievement, Horatio can be rewarded with happy marriage. Thus Haywood finally subordinates her narrative's historical references to its personal story.

Yet the historical references remain important. Even Louisa, who, unlike Horatio, reveals no consciousness of living in history, lives with an awareness of distant battles that may determine her romantic fate. Her knowledge of that fact may remind us of other facts about women's lives that belong to the 1740s as well as to the early part of the century. In many ways, women of the period experienced their lack of control over matters that profoundly concerned them: not only their lovers' fates but their own. Louisa shows unusual vigor in taking her life into her own hands whenever such a course is conceivable. Dorilaus's faintly ludicrous determination to preserve her nun's habit for future ages reminds us—a message from the author—that self-determined female action bears historical importance.

Louisa's most significant action, or series of actions, is her journey on foot across the Continent. Like the battles in which Horatio participates, her travels remain undescribed except in summary terms. The narrator, after speaking of the girl's uncertainty about what course she should take, explicitly invokes the reader's emotional participation. "Let any one figure to themselves the condition she was in, and they will rather wonder she had courage to go on, than that she was sometimes daunted even to despair" (309). The journey takes eight months. As Louisa reaches its end, the narrator intervenes again, to remind us that her female hero has walked every day of those eight months except for the time she was on a ship in the final stage of her travels. Such fortitude is, the narrator concludes, "a thing almost incredible, and what perhaps no woman, but herself, would have had courage to undertake, or resolution to perform" (312).

Unlike Horatio's battles, this heroic journey derives from fantasy. As far as Haywood knows, as far as twenty-first-century readers know, no such journey has ever occurred. History supplies few models for such female enterprise and endurance. Nonetheless, the episode engages with history inasmuch as it comments on historically specific social restrictions of women. Women in actuality lacked opportunity not only for battlefield exploits but also for solitary travel. Pointing to Louisa's "courage" and "resolution," the narrator calls attention to the young woman's embodiment of precisely the virtues that Horatio, more conventionally, displays on the battlefield. As her original readers would emphatically know, only fantasy enables such female achievement beyond a domestic context.

One may doubt whether Haywood actually knew a great deal about the Jacobite court or about battles of the War of the Spanish Succession. Her narrative method encourages the reader to share Richetti's view of the historical allusions as window dressing, since speed and vagueness mark her accounts of both court and battlefield. "It would be needless to give any description of this famous battle," she writes of the Battle of Blenheim, "few of my readers but must be acquainted with it, so I shall only say, that among the number of those few prisoners the French had to boast of . . . was the young brave Horatio" (55). Primarily interested in Horatio, she takes no interest at all in details of how he came to be captured or how he experienced the battle.

But the speed and vagueness of narrative rhetoric derive not only from lack of interest. Haywood's method invariably depends upon notation rather than development, accumulation rather than analysis. "Nothing could be more truly moving than the scene between them," she writes of an encounter between lovers (204), but she describes the scene no more than she describes the battle. She does not clearly elucidate either her moral and psychological concerns or her sense of an earlier historical period's significance, although both inform the novel. Her characters, particularly Louisa, experience moral dilemmas, recorded only as hints. Important decisions pass in a flash, as do episodes in which Louisa defines and resolves a moral perplexity.

The sentences quoted above about the battle in which Horatio is captured and about the moving scene between the lovers, suggest a single explanation for this evasive technique. Haywood assumes her reader's knowledge and awareness and solicits that reader's involvement in the narrative's development. Assuming that the reader can and will fill in the substance she omits, she gives herself space for a plot crammed with events. Such density is calculated both to entertain readers and to suggest the multiplicity of pressures bearing on young people struggling to attain maturity. It relies on the reader's experience, of fiction and of life, and on the reader's at least rudimentary knowledge of recent history.

In imagining the early years of the eighteenth century, Haywood emphasizes aspects of the culture that remain salient in the 1740s, such as concern with money and social status, conventional restrictions on women, and what Paul Langford calls "obsession with the sexual vulnerability of unmarried women," which, as he points out, "only makes sense in the context of a society which invested high stakes in marriage as an institution."[9] Both the history that Haywood attempts to invoke and the history of the time she inhabited when she wrote the novel matter in *The Fortunate Foundlings*. To recapitulate: by contemplating earlier years of Jacobite activity, Haywood reminds readers of the Jacobite threat experienced in England during the early 1740s. By purposeful characterization of two important historical figures, the Old Pretender and Charles XII of Sweden, she provides perspective on the concerns and on the nature of her male protagonist, as well as on the very structure of her plot. By insisting on the importance of birth and inheritance, she alludes to the current national situation. By her account of Louisa's trials and triumphs, she comments on the social situation of women.

Further historical investigation would reveal in more detailed ways the importance of the chronological setting and of the period during which *The Fortunate Foundlings* was composed. Such investigation would contribute not only to understanding of Haywood's novel but also to reflection on the possibilities and difficulties of the historical novel as genre. No matter what historical facts I discovered, though, and no matter how I used them, I would be employing them in my role as literary critic. The historian's perspective would remain absent.

A brief digression in the form of a story from my own experience that may function as parable: I codirect a small postdoctoral fellowship program at the American Academy of Arts and Sciences. It is an interdisciplinary enterprise in the sense that its participants come from various disciplines of the humanities and social sciences. At one early meeting of a young scholars' group, when participants were describing their projects to one another, a woman announced that she was investigating modern poetry and brain science. She explained what aspects of brain science concerned her and which poets she planned to consider. After she finished, I inquired what the point of all this was—in other words, so what? Without hesitation, she responded, "To make the poems more beautiful." Subsequently, in a private conversation, I asked what she had meant. She said that she thought the point of literary criticism in all its varieties should be to enrich for its readers the experience of encountering a given literary work.

This is essentially what I believe too, although I might choose an adjective other than *beautiful*. I want to make literary works more rich, more enticing, more pleasurable to their readers. When I think about historical facts or historical interpretations in relation to a piece of fiction, I'm thinking about how I can use history to clarify or illuminate the fiction. In other words, I'm employing history for literary argument. The historian who uses *Pamela* to help explain how attitudes toward marriage changed in the eighteenth century similarly subordinates literature to history. Literary scholars may feel irritated by her procedures, thinking that she fails to understand how fiction works. I can readily imagine, and have sometimes heard, how much literary scholars' efforts to use history irritate historians.

Annoying though they may be to those who profess another discipline, the ways in which practitioners of one discipline employ the resources of others can prove valuable. If literature serves history's purposes, fine. It doesn't simultaneously have to fulfill the agenda of literary criticism or even that of literary history. But an activity that subordinates one discipline to another is dubiously interdisciplinary, although it may often be so designated.

Years ago, at an interdisciplinary think tank, I joined a small seminar on nature. It included a political scientist, a historian, a philosopher, a classicist, an American literature specialist, and me. We met weekly, taking turns choosing the texts from different fields—biology, philosophy, political science—we would study. One week, our text was Wordsworth's *Ode on Intimations of Immortality.* The American literature person and I started talking about how the language of doubt infused the poem. "Is it true?" the philosopher inquired. We were bewildered: is *what* true? "The doctrine suggested by the poem." We talked some more about doubt. The philosopher persisted. Finally we told him that his question was irrelevant. "It's the only question that's relevant," he responded.

That moment was instructive. It forced me to realize, to *experience,* a fundamental difference in assumptions between disciplines. The philosopher's question about a poem bore little relation to mine. He and I, in fact, could barely understand each other. Common courtesy and academic convention may protect us from recognizing the chasms that separate one discipline from another, yet such deep divisions, potential sources of illumination, when looked at directly can call useful attention to different ways of knowing. The account of *The Fortunate Foundlings* provided by this paper develops from my interest in how fiction both articulates and questions beliefs and social possibilities. My investigations of history serve to corroborate, not to alter, insights I have already derived from the novel's text. I think like a literary historian and critic; I do not ask the questions that historians ask.

The word *interdisciplinarity* currently carries considerable weight in colleges and universities. Administrators like the idea of "interdisciplinary" courses, which sound complex, interesting, up-to-date. Professors who write books that claim to be interdisciplinary thus lay claim also to vast authority. But the cost of single-handed interdisciplinarity frequently includes lost clarity about assumptions and procedures, a blurring rather than a true intersection of disciplines.

Often, not always. Raymond Williams, Ronald Paulson, and John Barrell—to mention a few accomplished interdisciplinary thinkers who touch on my discipline—work across intellectual fields in ways that not only clarify but also at least metaphorically beautify texts they consider, enriching them by revealing unexpected links and affinities. Less well equipped practitioners, however, far outnumber those who can genuinely incorporate multiple ways of understanding. It may prove relatively easy to pick up the vocabulary of art history or anthropology, but it's not so easy to grasp the meaning of evidence as an art historian or an anthropologist would. All too frequently, an essentially alien vocabulary provides more decoration than insight.

A more dependable manifestation of interdisciplinarity emerges from human conjunctions, from activities that bring together members of different disciplines to apply individual, discipline-informed perceptions to a common question—formal and informal faculty groups (such as my seminar on nature), interdisciplinary conferences, meetings at the National Humanities Center. Such activities, exhilarating and clarifying for the participants, draw equitably on the resources of different disciplines. Emphasis on the differences in how we see from various disciplinary points of view clarifies the value of what we individually bring to collective understanding. That is to say, interdisciplinarity depends on disciplinarity. The more clearly we understand our own disciplines, the more clearly we can see how others differ from them, in assumptions and methods as well as in material—and the more we can learn from other modes of thought. Disciplines, ways of perceiving, uncover hidden aspects of texts, objects, happenings. Multiple disciplines reveal multiple aspects, and collaborations—combinations of human beings with different training and assumptions—produce unpredictable insights. Economic historians, social historians, military historians might all shed fresh light on *The Fortunate Foundlings.* Put them together with literary critics of various theoretical persuasions, and the light could be dazzling. William Blake pointed out that everyone sees "all things thro' narrow chinks of his cavern."[10] Collective interdisciplinarity cleanses the doors of perception, opening up our caverns.

Notes

1. Haywood, *Fortunate Foundlings,* 251. Hereafter this source is cited parenthetically in the text.

2. Richetti, "Histories by Eliza Haywood and Henry Fielding," 244–45.

3. McLynn, *Jacobites,* 81.

4. Szechi, *Jacobites,* 12.

5. Black, *Hanoverians,* 49, 51, 82, 95.

6. Quoted in "Translator's Introduction," in Voltaire, *Lion of the North,* 11.

7. Hatton, *Charles XII of Sweden,* xii, 522.

8. Ibid., 15.

9. Langford, *Polite and Commercial People,* 115.
10. Blake, *Marriage of Heaven and Hell,* 154.

Works Cited

Black, Jeremy. *The Hanoverians: The History of a Dynasty.* London: Hambledon & London, 2004.

Blake, William. *The Marriage of Heaven and Hell.* In *The Poetry and Prose of William Blake,* ed. David V. Edman. Garden City, NY: Doubleday, 1965.

Hatton, R. M. *Charles XII of Sweden.* New York: Weybright & Talley, [1968].

Haywood, Eliza. *The Fortunate Foundlings, 1744.* New York: Garland, 1974. Facsimile of the first edition, *The Fortunate Foundlings: being the genuine history of Colonel M——rs, and his sister, Madam du P——y, the issue of the Hon. Ch——es M——rs, son of the late Duke of R——l——d. Containing Many wonderful Accidents that befel them in their Travels, and interspersed with the Characters and Adventures of Several Persons of Condition, in the most polite Courts of Europe. The Whole calculated for the Entertainment and Improvement of the Youth of both Sexes* (London: T. Gardner, 1744).

Langford, Paul. *A Polite and Commercial People: England, 1727–1783.* Oxford: Oxford University Press, 1992.

McLynn, Frank. *The Jacobites.* London: Routledge & Kegan Paul, 1985.

Richetti, John. "Histories by Eliza Haywood and Henry Fielding." In *The Passionate Fictions of Eliza Haywood: Essays on Her Life and Work,* ed. Kirsten T. Saxton and Rebecca P. Bocchicchio, 240–58. Lexington: University Press of Kentucky, [c. 2000].

Szechi, Daniel. *The Jacobites: Britain, and Europe, 1688–1788.* Manchester: Manchester University Press; New York: St. Martin's, 1993.

Voltaire. *The Lion of the North: Charles XII of Sweden.* Trans. M. F. O. Jenkins. Rutherford, NJ: Fairleigh Dickinson University Press; London: Associated University Presses, 1981.

PART II

Human Economies

Introduction

ANDREW O'SHAUGHNESSY

Thomas Carlyle was one of the first historians to write critically about the Enlightenment. He did not treat it as simply part of the history of progress but identified negative features that culminated in the French Revolution. The objections he raised and the values he espoused find little sympathy among modern audiences, but the questions and challenges that he posed have resonated among a new generation of historians, particularly in regard to the plantation world of the Atlantic, which is the primary focus of the three chapters that feature in the second section of this book.

Thomas Jefferson and his ideas about breeding are central to two of these chapters. Jefferson was very much a product of the Enlightenment. He thought beliefs should be based upon reason, he put great emphasis upon facts, he was interested in science, he was a wide reader, and he believed passionately in the freedom of the mind. Yet he was also a planter who owned more than six hundred slaves during the course of his life and who is thought to have fathered six children by his slave Sally Hemings. As Carrie Douglass and Ruth Hill show, Jefferson's economies of horse breeding and slave breeding grimly intersect. Douglass's argument about his interest in breeding and purchasing thoroughbred horses gives us a novel glimpse into the role of credit and debt in Virginia. Jefferson was not interested in horse racing but rather in purchasing horses that were comfortable to ride or that could draw his carriages. In ninety-two recorded instances of his buying a horse, only once did Jefferson pay the full amount. More typically, he entered into a debt agreement with the seller. It was a transitional time between a face-to-face personal economy and a more impersonal capitalist society. The planters were not able to deal in cash, which was often unavailable, nor did they have recourse to banks, so that they were reliant on personal credit networks.

The practice of breeding thoroughbreds would seem relatively innocuous until read in conjunction with Ruth Hill's essay on "breeding whites" in the eighteenth-century Americas. Hill also invokes Jefferson, who in an 1815 letter estimated the number of stages he believed were required for someone of mixed race to become white: three generations of pairings with a white person for someone of black ancestry. This thinking reflects an elaborate racial hierarchy in both the European empires in the Americas—the English and the Spanish. Various categories were invented to designate proportions of white blood, such as "octoroon" for someone with one-eighth white ancestry. Jefferson had made similar estimates for a crossbred native ram to become a pure Merino. There were parallel calculations for breeding dogs and plants in Spanish America. The same number of stages was mentioned by Spanish authorities for the Indians. The number of stages of transition from black to white was reduced from four to three by papal bulls, but by the end of the century the process was not recognized in Mexico.

These racial distinctions were more important in Jamaica, where some white ancestry conferred limited privileges even among enslaved people, in contrast to in the United States. The system of slavery in the British islands of the Caribbean was generally much harsher during the eighteenth century than in the United States, as Louis Nelson, a pioneer in the study of the architecture of eighteenth-century Jamaica, definitively argues. He has shown elsewhere that the houses of the Jamaican planters were far grander than those of the Americans. His chapter in this collection reveals the exploitive and even more brutal economy that made this possible, which was based largely upon sugar plantations and a society in which almost nine-tenths of the population was enslaved. Sugar cultivation was more labor intensive than tobacco and rice crops, while the high proportion of slaves made for a harsher and more coercive environment. Nelson builds on the recent work by Richard Dunn in *A Tale of Two Plantations: Slave Life and Labor in Virginia and Jamaica* (2014), which represents more than forty years of research comparing the lives of some two thousand slaves on two of the best-documented plantations, Mount Airy in Tidewater Virginia and Mesopotamia in Jamaica. Nelson underscores the differences between Jamaica and America and points to the particularly high mortality rates in Jamaica. The more repressive systems of the islands were to be repeated wherever there were high proportions of slaves, as in nineteenth-century Cuba, Louisiana, and Brazil. It would indeed be in the French islands that the second revolution in the Americas occurred (St. Domingue, Haiti).

The essays in this section are indeed testimony to the darker side of the Enlightenment, but they are critiques that are very different from that of Carlyle, a notorious racist who penned *An Occasional Discourse on the Nigger Question* (1851). They also demonstrate the parallels and interconnections between the different European powers in the Americas. Contrary to the popular idea that the Iberian countries and France were more enlightened in their treatment of race and slavery, the authors show that their racial hierarchies and attitudes to miscegenation were very similar to those of the British and North Americans. The differences that existed were owing more to demographics than to culture, whether because of the gender balance among whites, in which a predominantly male society was more likely to have interracial relationships, or because of the relative proportion of free whites to slaves, with much harsher slave codes in societies that contained particularly high proportions of slaves.

How Long Does Blood Last?

Degeneration as *Blanqueamiento* in the Americas

RUTH HILL

For more than a decade, I have been convinced that folk knowledge, espe-cially Spanish folk knowledge, about selectively breeding plants and brutes generated and structured the *blanqueamiento,* or whitening, equations for humans in the Americas that were to become systematized and well known during the long eighteenth century. I would ask you to keep in mind this Spanish proverb: "Raza de can, amor de cortesano y ropa de villano, no dura más que tres años" (Correas 433; A purebred race of dogs, a court-ier's love, and a peasant's clothes don't last for more than three years).[1] This old saw reveals a degeneration equation that would resurface in discussions of breeding white people and other animals—Spanish horses and Merino sheep were the envy of the world well into the nineteenth century—in the Old World and the New.

The former US president Thomas Jefferson, in an 1815 letter to his friend the Bostonian Francis C. Gray, a Harvard-trained lawyer, cited a 1792 Vir-ginia statute (originally passed in 1779) that defined the mulatto as a person with one-fourth or more of negro blood. Jefferson then offered Gray an al-gebra lesson on how black became white in Virginia: the first sexual union, of white with black, yielded the mulatto; the second union, of mulatto with white, produced the quadroon; and the third crossing, between quadroon and white or almost white, engendered the octoroon, who was legally white because he had less than one-fourth of black blood. It took three crossings for the descendants of a black ancestor in Virginia to clear their blood, or depart from their stock (*generatio*), approximating though not matching the Spanish maxim about canine degeneration.

Jefferson's algebra for whitening human animals was, he clarified, once removed from "natural history," or animal husbandry, which demanded four crossings to arrive at purity, his example being the selective breeding of Spanish Merino rams with "country," or Shenandoah, ewes (Jefferson). As noted above, Spanish proverbial wisdom held that a purebred canine race preserved itself through three crossings and was lost after four. After three seasons of being used to improve or create other races of dogs (*rehazer las razas*), a pureblood race experiences *degeneratio:* if one attempts a fourth crossing, the issue will wholly depart or deviate from its race, or *generatio.* Although the Spanish folk equation for dogs conveys a setback, it matches the number of crossings Jefferson attributed to animal husbandry.

The former president's juxtaposition of the two breeding equations (one for breeding whites and the other, more stringent, for breeding Merinos) implies that white men are analogous (not identical) to Spanish Merino rams, and black women analogous to country ewes, as he charts how it takes four crossings of Shenandoah and Merino to produce a purebred Merino. I say analogous because humans required fewer crossings to "clear" their origins, or blood. Referring to Jefferson's definition and comparison, Werner Sollors concluded that all of this was an animal story, perhaps echoing *Othello,* about incest and hypodescent (the so-called one-drop rule) (114). A cognitive-anthropological approach, in contrast, situates Jefferson's letter in a radically different landscape: the animal-plant-human continuum.

The cognitive anthropologist Scott Atran has reconstructed the significance of folkbiology to both modern botany and zoology into the eighteenth century. Folk taxonomy of plants and brutes is rooted in appearance and a presupposed essence, or inside, that causes that appearance. Folkbiological essentialism (shared by Aristotle and his followers on both sides of the Atlantic) differs crucially from the assumptions about biological essentialism held by scholars of race. It is a *constructionist essentialism,* which allows for perceptible physical change over time and place, in plants, brutes, and humans alike (Atran, *Cognitive Foundations*).[2] As Atran and Doug Medin explain, "Even when people do not have specific ideas about essences, they may nonetheless have a commitment to the idea that there is an underlying nature (i.e., they may have an 'essence placeholder')" (*Native Mind* 21; see also Medin and Ortony). Innate in humans or not, this folk thinking about brutes, plants, and humans was central to the development of the modern sciences.[3] Thus, Jefferson's comparison of white and black humans to Spanish Merino rams and country ewes was not in and of itself deviant, as Sollors claims: it was normative, if we adopt a cognitive-anthropological approach to human whitening that makes it *analogous,* in the human mind, to selectively breeding plants and brutes.

My overarching argument is that equations for breeding white persons in the late eighteenth and early nineteenth centuries—not the categories negotiated or contested on the ground, which informed my earlier work,

but instead the cognitive matrix and belief structures around human taxonomies—*originated* in folk and learned notions of degeneration in brutes
(horses, sheep, dogs) and plants (grains, vegetables). In the first third of
the eighteenth century, papal briefs and bulls concerning the conversion
of native peoples in Spanish and Portuguese colonial territories exerted a
considerable influence on those *blanqueamiento,* or whitening, equations
for Indians as well as for blacks. In the last third of the eighteenth century,
equations for breeding whites from blacks became increasingly exigent, con-
testing papal influence in some parts of Spanish America. This retrenchment was undoubtedly inspired by what the Mexican historian Gonzalo
Aguirre Beltrán labeled "demographic metabolism" (*metabolismo demográf-
ico*) in his seminal 1946 study of Afro-Mexicans in the colonial period. The
last chapter of his study, entitled "The Color Line," is devoted to the late-
eighteenth-century trend among human *castas* (groups or kinds of brutes,
plants, or humans) with varying degrees of African ancestry to move up the
whitening ladder directly, by recategorizing themselves as belonging to a
casta with less African heritage, or indirectly, by marrying Spaniards or persons of mixed Spanish and Indian parentage (see Aguirre Beltrán, chap. 14;
and Vinson). Let us first survey eighteenth-century *blanqueamiento* equations, then review some notions of degeneration in animals, before we turn
back to Monticello.

In the 1745 *Orinoco ilustrado y defendido: Historia natural, civil y
geográphica de este gran río y de sus caudalosas vertientes* (The Orinoco illustrated and defended: Natural, civil, and geographical history of this grand
river and its mighty tributaries), for instance, the Spanish Jesuit missionary
José Gumilla explained that *four* crossings were required to transform a
black into a white in what is today the region of Colombia and Venezuela:

> In sum, you can be certain that a mulatto woman by the fourth genera-
> tion also becomes white by the very degrees that a mestizo woman does,
> through the following series of unions:
>
> I. European male and black female produce mulatto female (two quar-
> ters of each side).
>
> II. European male and mulatto female produce quadroon female (one-
> quarter of mulatto).
>
> III. European male and quadroon female produce octoroon female
> (one-eighth of mulatto).
>
> IV. European male and octoroon female produce *puchuela* female (com-
> pletely white). (2:86)

Father Gumilla was familiar with the Dominican Jean-Baptiste Labat's *Nouveau voyage aux isles de l'Amérique,* of which the second volume (published in 1722, but based on his notes from 1694–95) records whitening equations for blacks and Indians. The union of a white man and a black woman, or vice versa, produced mulattoes. The progeny of a white man and a mulatta were quadroons (*quarterous*). The children of a white man and a quadroon were octoroons. Labat claimed that one could detect blackness in octoroons by the whites of their eyes, which were tinged with yellow. This "defect" was absent after the fourth crossing—of an octoroon with a white—meaning that persons with one-sixteenth of black ancestry (hexadecaroons) were whites, just as the Jesuit Gumilla was to affirm some thirty years after the French Dominican. Thus the human whitening equations of both historians were in agreement not only with each other but also with the Spanish proverb about deracination in purebred canine races. Blood lasts for three years only, according to Spanish folkbiology, for when the product of the third crossing (one-eighth) is used for a fourth season, the progeny have only one-sixteenth of the original prized breed, which blood quantum is considered none.

On the other hand, if human octoroons went with blacks, according to Father Labat, their descendants "would return to their original blackness within the same number of generations, because a color gets stronger to the degree that it joins a color of the same kind and gets weaker to the degree that it distances itself from the same"(2:127–28). Similarly, the Jesuit Gumilla warned his readers that whiteness would be lost in the next generation if the *puchuela* had a child with a mulatto or black man. Such a reversion to blackness or mulattoness constituted another process of degeneration—a deviation from her whiteness or Spanishness—and henceforth she would belong to the category *salta-atrás* (2:87). Gumilla does not explain how, but throughout he assumes that there is an essence that produces a kind with specific characteristics and behaviors, even if that essence is neither observed nor observable.

Other Spanish colonial whitening equations for the descendants of blacks demanded only three crossings to arrive at whiteness, as Jefferson had stipulated following Virginia law. Luis Joseph Peguero, a landowner from the Baní Valley in Santo Domingo, wrote his *Historia de la conquista de la isla española de Santo Domingo trasumptada el año de 1762* (History of the Spanish conquest of Santo Domingo continued up to the year 1762) in 1762–63. There, in his "Tratado de las naciones que se procedieron en esta Isla" (Treatise on the groups who have come about on this island, Peguero deploys such common terms as *mestizo, mulato, mulato cuarterón,* and *indio cuar-terón.* The Indian or black octoroon is admitted into the white category, in contrast to Gumilla's equation that treated the *ochavón* as nonwhite, and he is now called a *puchuela,* which in Gumilla's rendering signified a purely white person (one-sixteenth of black or Indian ancestry being the crucible). Writes Peguero: "When a Spaniard mixes with a quadroon of either of the mentioned kinds, their offspring are called *Puchuela[s]*, or Virtual Whites" (1:274–75).

Another historiographical account from roughly the same period, written by the exiled Italian Jesuit Mario Cicala in 1771, tells a similar tale of *blanqueamiento.* The result of Cicala's twenty-four years of travels and missioning throughout Quito (1743–67), his *Descripción histórico-topográfica de la Provincia de Quito* (Historical and topographical description of Quito Province) informs readers that "those who in the said crossing and propagation between Indians and Europeans have one-eighth of Indian ancestry are called *puchiveles,*" or whites ("Advertencias" 17). Writing of persons with some black ancestry, Father Cicala defines the mulatto as the offspring of a Spaniard and a black, and he repeats the same terms used in the foregoing discussion of transforming Indian descendants into whites (18). After only three crossings, then, Cicala's *puchivel* (a variant of *puchuela*) is a white because he or she has only one-eighth of black or Indian blood. For both the Italian Jesuit Cicala and the Dominican landowner Peguero, then, a white with only one-eighth of nonwhite blood is a *puchivel/puchuela,* whereas this term signified a white with one-sixteenth of Indian or black ancestry (a hexadecaroon) in the Jesuit Gumilla's *Orinoco ilustrado y defendido.* In other words, their *puchivel/puchuela* could have twice as much black or Indian blood as Father Gumilla's and still be categorized as white.[4] Moreover, this difference signals a similarity between Jefferson's equation for whitening the descendants of blacks in Virginia and Spanish colonial equations for whitening the descendants of blacks in Panama, Cartagena, Quito, and Spanish Santo Domingo: octoroons (persons with only one-eighth of black blood) are whites.

But where and how did these competing whitening equations for humans in the Americas come into being? There is convincing evidence, from a cognitive-anthropological standpoint, that the underlying origins of human whitening equations were degeneration equations for brutes and plants; as we saw earlier, the human mind reasoned analogically and essentially. The question then becomes, how did Enlightenment folk and educated persons alike move from animal and plant breeding to blood equations for arriving at whiteness or Spanishness? In his 1736 essay entitled "Color etiópico" (The color black), the Spanish Benedictine Benito Feijoo y Montenegro argued that skin color and other distinguishing features in human kinds were not caused by blood or sperm. Feijoo's work was renowned from England to Italy and supported by the Spanish Crown. Thoroughly steeped in the scientific and aesthetic theories of the cosmopolitan Enlightenment, as Dorinda Outram has defined it, the Spanish Benedictine often explicated the human body through recourse to mechanical metaphors such as machine or watch, hewing to arguments from design. And yet, the same Enlightenment icon reveals his adherence to folkbiological essentialism while attempting to explain how human beings might undergo perceptible and seemingly permanent changes without inheriting them:

> It is proven through analogy to brutes and vegetables, that with a change in terrain often change considerably in succeeding generations. You see left and right that livestock, once moved to another country, engender offspring of a different size, of a different hair or coat, etc. That with the seeds of plants sown in a location even slightly different from where they were born, their harvests deteriorate so much that they appear to be plants of a different kind. (86)

Feijoo uses an essence placeholder: some unknown quality in every country, perhaps the air, acts on the organic world to produce deracination (*degeneratio*) over time, in animals, plants, and humans. The Spanish monk reasons analogically about this degenerative process in relationship to essence and to features perceptible to our senses (taste, sight, touch):

> The seed of wheat planted in less fertile soil produces a grain very inferior in shape, color, flavor, etc., that they call rye. The seed of cabbage grown in good soil, planted in another that is less suitable, produces in the first generation cabbage not as good as that from which the seed was taken; in the second, it already produces wild cabbage; and in the third and fourth this same plant starts deteriorating so much that these wild cabbages, grandchildren and great-grandchildren of the cabbage, appear to be vegetables of a completely different type from their grandparent and great-grandparent. Why couldn't the same thing happen, in proportion, to men? (86)

Note here that *degeneration is complete*—a different kind has been produced in nature by sowing seeds in a nonnative soil—*by the third or fourth crossing*.

More than one hundred years earlier, strikingly similar claims about degeneration in plants had appeared in a popular book of secrets, Manuel Ramírez de Carrión's *Maravillas de naturaleza* (Marvels of nature). After asserting that wheat degenerates into oat, barley, or chaff after it is planted in wetlands, he fixes the temporality of wheat's essence: "In humid soil, wheat planted from the same germ seed for three years becomes rye in the third year" (135). This is an especially vivid example of folkbiological essentialism. On one hand, Ramírez de Carrión notes that a pedigree wheat will reproduce itself when the preceding generation's or harvest's seed is sown in the same soil; on the other, he warns that sowing that high-quality seed in a soil adverse to its original environment causes the wheat to lose its superior essence—to degenerate, to depart from its origins or nature. It becomes *in the third or fourth generation* a bastardized, or inferior, grain.

Selective dog breeding in the Spanish world generated similar equations. For breeding farm dogs or mutts, rather than hunting dogs, the Catalonian friar Miguel Agustín advised in his *Libro de los secretos de agricultura, casa de campo y pastoril* (Book of secrets of agriculture, country life, and husbandry), first published in 1617, that the male not mate with a female that was less than a year old nor with a female who was more than two years old (352). In sum, the blood of a female dog *without* pedigree survived only two crossings or mating seasons: one-quarter of the mutt's blood was the minimum required to preserve the breed. If one substituted for this undistinguished canine a female who ranked low in the social hierarchy of Spanish America, the equation would be three crossings for that female's blood to be cleared: the first crossing/mating season with a Spaniard yielded the *mestizo* or *mulato;* the second, the *cuarterón;* and the third, the *ochavón,* who was no longer Indian or black but instead white (per Peguero's and Cicala's shared definition of *puchuela*). Three crossings is the equation for degeneration, whether it is constructed ideologically as a benefit or as a setback, for in the progeny with only one-eighth of that Indian's or black woman's blood *the original essence* (Indianness or blackness) *has been replaced with Spanishness.* This certainly does not conform to Gumilla's *blanqueamiento* equation for blacks, but it does indeed conform with Jefferson's, Peguero's, and Cicala's.

Let us now recall the old saw about selective dog breeding that specifies that degeneration is completed in *four crossings:* "A purebred race of dogs, a courtier's love, and a peasant's clothes don't last for more than three years." Beyond three seasons of being used to improve or create other races of dogs, the essence (whatever it is presumed to be) of the pureblood canine is exhausted: the product of a fourth crossing will be of an entirely different race from the purebred race. Say, for instance, that a farmer decided to improve his native breed of dogs by breeding them with a pedigree dog. The product of the first crossing would be a half-breed (one-half purebred and one-half native). Now, if the same farmer were to perform a second crossing, between that half-breed and the native canine race, the result would be a quarter-breed, that is, a pedigree dog with one-fourth of the thoroughbred's blood. A third crossing, between that quarter-breed and the native breed, would yield a dog with one-eighth of purebred lineage, which is the minimum amount of blood required to preserve the prized dog's pedigree. This coordinates neatly with Gumilla's and Labat's blood equations for whitening blacks, in which the octoroon is still a black and the fourth crossing produces a white, but it is stricter than Jefferson's, Cicala's, and Peguero's whitening equations for blacks. In comparing Labat's and Peguero's whitening equations for blacks, I note in passing that I am comparing neighbors: French Saint Domingue and Spanish Santo Domingo. The French colonial equation was more restrictive than its Spanish counterpart.

It should by now be clear that like the majority of human whitening equations analyzed heretofore, the majority of degeneration equations for brutes and plants posit that *degeneration is complete*—a different kind (with its essence or essence placeholder) has been produced in nature—*by the third or fourth crossing.* In addition, however, and heeding Peter Wade's urgent call to study in tandem the respective positions of Indians and blacks in colonial Spanish America (Wade 25; see also Forbes; Vinson and Restall; Restall, *Beyond Black and Red;* Restall, *Black Middle*), canon law and scholastic moral theology must be brought into scholarly discussions of Portuguese and Spanish colonial situations and of the broader history of race, for they were the proximate cause of *blanqueamiento* equations for non-European peoples.

At the turn of the thirteenth century, canon law on consanguinity was explicitly rooted in the Fourth Lateran Council, which began in 1215, after which Catholic marriage would demand only four degrees of separation between spouses (Moritz Kalisch 1:368–69). Innocent III reasoned that it took only four crossings—four generations of mixing bloodlines—for the shared ancestry of potential spouses to be lost, because in each generation one of the four elements of the blood (air, fire, water, earth) was corrupted or lost. Paradoxically, debates over the concept "neophyte" in the late seventeenth century were to resort to that canon in order to wrestle with the mixture of bloods from different, biologically unrelated peoples. In brief, Alonso de la Peña Montenegro, bishop of Quito, interpreted the popes' *mixtim progeniti* or *mixtim geniti* (mixedly engendered) to mean that all persons of mixed parentage, up to and including the fourth degree of mixing, were eligible for the privileges accorded neophytes in Portuguese and Spanish settlements outside Europe. He explicitly referred to Spanish law, which since Alphonso X had been in consonance with Innocent III's ruling on consanguinity and affinity: "Cognation extends to the fourth degree inclusive, because blood and relation lasts up to that degree . . . ; therefore this Indian mixture should at least extend to the *puchuelas,* who are related in the third degree to the Indian great grandmother and have ⅛th of her blood" (403–4).

The bishop of Quito drew the line at *puchuelas,* then, excluding other percentages of mixed ancestry from the papal language of inclusion, on the basis of the canon of consanguinity and affinity. His interpretation would become the legal and moral basis of local practice in different parts of Spanish and Portuguese America until the end of the eighteenth century, roughly the period that covered the print history of his work (1668, 1726, 1771). Increasingly, his application of the canon on consanguinity to interpret papal bulls on conversion generated new theological interpretations and legal challenges; so much so, in fact, that popes were asked from 1668 onward to clarify what *neophyte* and *mixtim progeniti* or *mixtim geniti* meant.

The Jesuit Gumilla, after demonstrating the degrees by which Indians become whites after four crossings, added the following note: "But by the new bull of Pope Clement XI it is declared that by *neophytes* one can understand Indians and *mestizos* only; therefore, quadroons and octoroons are popularly known as, and must be legally considered, Whites" (2:85). According to royal decree no. 57, from 31 January 1703, "A los virreyes, audiencias, gobernadores, arzobispos y obispos de las Indias, remitiéndoles los trasuntos de los breves de su Santidad tocantes a los indios" (Muro Orejón 2:79–82), the Spanish Bourbon Philip V's predecessor, the Hapsburg Charles II, had requested from the Holy See the clarification of grave matters, including marriage dispensations granted to neophytes in all of the Spanish and Portuguese overseas territories. Three briefs from Clement XI were subsequently announced.[5] The question was "if the name *Indian neophytes* includes only newly converted Indians, or, rather, all of those who are natives on all four sides [even if they were baptized as infants], or those who have native ancestry from just one side, commonly known as Quadroons, and if those who have ⅛th ancestry from a great-grandfather or a great-grandmother, or some from one and from the other, whom we call *puchuelas,* are also included." One of Pope Clement XI's 1701 briefs determined that *neophyte* did not signify "quadroons, much less *puchuelas*" (Muro Orejón 2:80).

The French Dominican Labat's whitening equation for Indians in the

French Caribbean, unlike his whitening equation for blacks there, already reflected the papal innovation: the offspring of a white man and an Indian woman were called *méstis* (2:127–28), Labat reported in 1722. These half-breeds were typically as white as Europeans, but the whites of their eyes gave them away: "If a *méstisse* marries a White man, the children who come from them do not preserve anything of their first origins" (2:132). In the Dominican's equation, the Indian quadroon was not an Indian at all: he was white. Chroniclers such as Peguero and Cicala did not whiten Indians after only two crossings, as Gumilla suggested that Clement XI in 1701 (and Benedict XIII in 1729) had done by reducing the semantic field of *neophyte* to include only persons with at least one-half of non-Spanish origins, and as the French Jesuit Labat's whitening equation for Indians had stipulated. But the concept of *puchuela* as white in Peguero and Cicala's respective chronicles was the same one found in the aforementioned papal bulls and decisions: a person with one-eighth of non-Spanish ancestry—not one-sixteenth, as Gumilla had defined the same term.

Throughout the first two-thirds of the eighteenth century, popes insisted that their seventeenth-century predecessors had been correct in extending neophyte privileges to Ethiopians, Angolans, and natives in Asia, as well as to natives in the New World. This impelled the blood-quantum equations that defined persons with one-eighth of black ancestry as *puchuelas*, or whites. (This also matched the capacious interpretation of whiteness that was to appear in Virginia in 1779, as noted earlier.) The aforementioned bulls and briefs in fact signaled a shift that was recorded without pause by the polymath missionary Pedro Murillo Velarde (1696–1753), procurator for the Jesuit order in the Philippines, in his *Curso de derecho canónico hispano e indiano* (Course on canon, Spanish, and Indies law). First published in 1743, only two years before the definitive edition of Gumilla's *Orinoco ilustrado y defendido,* then republished in 1763 and 1791, his was the authoritative and most consulted manual of canon, Spanish, and Indies law in the eighteenth and nineteenth centuries. Murillo Velarde refers to Clement XI's 1701 brief, confirmed by Benedict XIII in 1729 and cited by Gumilla (*Curso* 3:263).[6] The dissemination of Murillo Velarde's manual throughout the government and church centers of Iberia's global empire ensured that educated historians and others would be aware of the conceptual shift. Hence, Peguero's and Cicala's understanding that black blood lasted for three crossings only.

Folkbiological essentialism, as the cognitive anthropologist Atran explains it, allowed for permanent changes in appearance, such as color, facial features, bodily structures, and so forth. In the Spanish world, I am convinced, it did not yield to (modern) biological essentialism, which underpins the modern race concept and biological racism (see Root), until the nineteenth century. Thus, in 1760, when the first of twenty-six legal petitions for whiteness was filed in Venezuela with the Spanish Crown, through 1808, when the last case for *gracias al sacar* was made, it was still a given that whiteness was achievable, as Ann Twinam has argued in different words ("Purchasing Whiteness" 141). In a 1788 case from Caracas, a man with some black ancestry petitioned the Crown to allow him to purchase whiteness for his son (153), arguing that the son's parents and grandparents were not *neophytes*. This would mean that the grandparents had had no more than one-fourth of black blood, if we apply eighteenth-century canon law, for only blacks and mulattoes would be neophytes. Thus, the parents too would have had no more black blood than did quadroons, since they were not neophytes either. At most, then, the parents and grandparents had one-fourth of black ancestry, and in all likelihood they had less, as did the son, or he would not have applied for a certificate of whiteness.[7] The language and the equation—the invocation of the neophyte standard—of this potential purchase of whiteness strengthens my hypothesis that papal efforts to clarify Church doctrine regarding neophyte privileges in Spanish and Portuguese Asia, America, and Africa decisively influenced whitening discussions around blacks and their descendants.

As the century wore on, however, the intertwined fates of Indians and blacks began to unravel in the preracial imaginary of Spaniards. It was believed to be easier to breed whites from Indians, and to be harder to breed whites from blacks, at the very same time that it became impossible in colonial reality to stop persons of African, or mixed African and Indian, or even mixed African and Spanish ancestry from whitening themselves socially and legally. In this respect, what can visual whitening equations—specifically, *casta* paintings from the eighteenth-century viceroyalties of New Spain, Peru, and New Granada—add to our understanding of *blanqueamiento* as a biological and religious construct? One series from either the Viceroyalty of Peru or the Viceroyalty of New Granada (García Sáiz 114–21) conveys that Indian blood is completely lost after four crossings with Spaniards, what today might be termed a racial retrenchment, for it hearkens back to more stringent *blanqueamiento* equations. In the first union, the Spaniard and the Indian engender a *mestizo* female. In the second crossing, the Spaniard and the *mestizo* female engender a *cuarterona de mestizo* (mestizo quadroon female). In the third crossing, the Spaniard and the *mestizo* quadroon female engender a *quinterona de mestizo* female, and this quintroon female was the equivalent of Gumilla's *ochavona*, or octoroon female. Finally, in the fourth and foundational crossing, the Spaniard and the Indian quintroon female produce a Spaniard, for the *requinterona de mestizo* (Indian hexadecaroon female) has only one-sixteenth of Indian ancestry, the crucible for entering whiteness according to Gumilla.

There is still another, more fundamental difference between the blood equations in this Viceroyalty of Peru or Viceroyalty of New Granada series and others analyzed earlier in this essay, one that signals the increasing strictness of blood equations for whitening persons descended from blacks in eighteenth-century Spanish America. Marking a departure from what we have seen before, this series of *casta* paintings demands an extra crossing for black blood to dissolve into whiteness. The first union, between the Spaniard and the black woman, produces the mulatto woman. The second crossing, between the Spaniard and the mulatto woman, engenders a *cuarterona de mulato,* or black quadroon female. In the third mixture, the Spaniard and the black quadroon female produce the *quinterona de mulato,* or black quin-troon female (i.e., octoroon). The fourth union, between the Spanish male and the black quintroon female, yields the *requinterona de mulato,* or black hexadecaroon female. She has only one-sixteenth of black ancestry, but she is not a Spaniard. The fifth and decisive union, between the Spanish male and the black hexadecaroon female, engenders "gente blanca" (white folk) (García Sáiz 119). Only after five crossings, then, can black blood be cleared from the human body.[8]

The deeper we go into the Spanish eighteenth century, the more the cognitive matrix and belief structures around breeding whites from blacks diverge from Jefferson's, becoming increasingly stringent. Whitening was foreclosed for blacks, according to the preracial imaginary that generated *casta* paintings for European clients (see Carrera, Katzew, Katzew and Dean, Martínez). "Sobre negro no hay tintura" (There's no dye that covers up black), as the Spanish saying goes,[9] and the cognitive matrix and be-lief structures that informed pictorial representations of blackness in late-eighteenth-century *casta* paintings bear this out. It is the norm for black blood to return atavistically in the fourth generation; that is, whitening is visually rendered as a biological impossibility for blackness. Even when it appears to be happening—in the extreme—with the *albino* produced by the third crossing, of Spaniard and *morisca* (black quadroon female), the residual essence of blackness overpowers the emerging essence of whiteness. Black blood lasts forever.

It is worth looking at this cul-de-sac of blackness more closely. In a series of *casta* paintings executed in New Spain probably in the 1760s (García Sáiz 90) by José Joaquín Magón, the whitening process for blacks is short-circuited by an evolutionary throwback that predates evolutionary theory: a folkbiologically essentialist *salta-atrás* (94–96). In the first crossing, between the Spaniard and the black woman, the mulatto woman is produced. The second crossing, between the Spaniard and the mulatto woman, engenders a *morisca,* or black quadroon female. Whitening starts to go wrong in the third crossing, as the portrait depicts the Spaniard and the black quadroon female engendering an albino octoroon male. In the fourth union, between the Spanish female and the albino octoroon male, the atavism appears: the offspring is a male *torna-atrás,* or throwback (96). What would have cleared Indian blood from the human body—a fourth crossing—has revealed the inexpungible essence of blackness: it cannot be cleared from the human body; whites cannot be bred from blacks.

Likewise, in a series of *casta* drawings found in *A Description of the Kingdom of New Spain* (O'Crouley, between pp. 18 and 19) the whitening process for blacks is rendered an impossibility that was unimaginable in Jefferson's Virginia (fig. 1). In the first crossing, between the Spaniard and the black woman, the mulatto woman is produced. The second crossing, between the Spaniard and the mulatto woman, engenders a *morisco,* or black male quadroon. Again, whitening goes awry in the third crossing, as the portrait depicts the Spaniard and the black quadroon female engendering an albino octoroon male. In the fourth union, between the Spanish female and the albino octoroon male, a fugitive blackness resurfaces in the male *torna-atrás.* The depth of Negrophobia in late-eighteenth-century Mexico can be more precisely gauged by comparing this black no-exit to the far more lenient whitening equation applied to Indians. Joaquín Antonio de Basarás wrote his *Origen, costumbres y estado presente de mexicanos y filipinos* (Origins, customs, and present state of the Mexican and Filipino native peoples) in 1763. The rhymed motto that accompanies the illustration of a *castiza* and an *español* in Mexico claims that after the third crossing, a Spaniard is born (Basarás 199); that is, the process of degeneration is complete. At the very same time, Basarás's account reconfirms the ideology of black atavism found in *casta* paintings: although blacks and their descendants hew to the whitening process, they never arrive at whiteness. The particulars of this blackness that never leaves, which Gumilla had dismissed as a popular myth, are worth examining.

First, the Spanish male has a mulatto child with a black woman. In the second crossing, a mulatto woman and a Spaniard engender the three-

Figure 1. Drawings from Pedro Alonso O'Couley, *A Description of the Kingdom of New Spain* (*from top left*): Spaniard and black > mulatto; Spaniard and mulatto > *morisco;* Spaniard and *morisco* > albino; Spaniard and albino > *torna-atrás.* (Courtesy of John Howell Books)

fourths Spanish and one-fourth black child, the *morisco.* This is considered an infelicitous result: an *argel* stallion ("que de español y mulata / produce Argel un morisco") (200). What did Spaniards associate with the *argel* stallion? In Spanish manuals of hippography, the *argel* always designated the horse with a white right foot; it was rejected as unlucky by nobles and commoners alike (Correas 96; García Conde 431; Ramírez de Carrión 34). As the Spanish proverb puts it, "Del hombre malo y del caballo argel, quien fuere cuerdo guárdese de él" (Whether it's a bad man or an *argel* stallion, avoid him if you're smart) (Jiménez 21). A morisco woman (three-fourths Spanish) and a Spanish male parent a black quadroon known as *albino* in New Spain (seven-eighths Spanish and one-eighth black). An *albino* woman and a Spanish male engender a black *torna-atrás* (Basarás 200). It becomes clear that the black blood can never be cleared from the body—"Menos se advierte salir / la sangre" (200)—even after four crossings, notwithstanding the fact that only one-sixteenth of black ancestry remains to resist whiteness. This black *torna-atrás* couples with a Spaniard and produces the *tente-*

en-el-aire (literally, "stay up in the air"), also known as *grifo* (literally, "griffon," a canine breed) (201), who has one-thirty-second of black ancestry and yet marks a very visible regression to blackness.

The aforementioned Magón provides a visual chronicle of the *blanqueamiento* process for Indians (García Sáiz 103–4), which requires only three crossings for Indians to clear their blood and become Spaniards. The first crossing is between a Spanish male and an Indian female, which produces a *mestizo* male (103). The second union joins a Spanish man and a *mestizo* female to bear a male *castizo* (literally, "purebred"); and the third and culminating commingling brings together a *castizo* male and a Spanish female to produce a Spanish male (104). After three crossings, then, the descendants of Indians are whites. Andrés de Islas too, in 1774, demonstrated that it required only three crossings for persons with native origins to completely clear their blood of Indian essence and be whites (125–26).

Three observations are in order. First, all of these *casta* paintings and illustrations suggest that the papal interventions of the first third of the eighteenth century, which influenced human whitening equations for Indians and blacks, did not hold sway over Mexican painters and historians of the late eighteenth century. Second, when mixed persons with Indian and Spanish ancestry *violate* the whitening process, *they regress to their Indian essence,* or nature, whereas mixed persons with black and Spanish ancestry who *follow* the whitening process *nonetheless regress to their black essence.* All descendants of the black *tente-en-el-aire,* or *grifo,* remain in that category no matter how many times they have children with Spaniards (Basarás 127). Third, it is not just that blacks cannot whiten at all, but that blackness grafted onto Amerindian ancestry also renders the latter impenetrable to whiteness. The crossing of a black woman and an Indian male results in someone who is a *lobo* (literally, "wolf"): half Indian, half black. If that *lobo* male and an Indian female have a child together, he or she is a *tente-en-el-aire.* The latter is three-fourths Indian, but that one-fourth of black blood renders becoming an Indian as impossible as becoming a Spaniard: no matter how many times the descendants have children with Indians, they will always and forever belong to the *tente-en-el-aire* category. This three-fourths Indian and one-fourth black *tente-en-el-aire* is ineluctably black: "if he crosses with one of his own kind, [the offspring] returns to the original Black issue" (128).

Moreover, and as if Negrophobia were not already relentless enough in Mexican *casta* paintings from the end of the eighteenth century, the 1793 census in the Viceroyalty of New Spain contained no category *negro,* as if blacks did not exist. The only category associated with black blood in Mexico City was that of *mulato* (Seed 577 and nn. 29 and 30), while *pardo* (meaning a free black or black-Indian mixture) and *moreno* (a free black or a free person with some African ancestry) were used in other parts of New Spain (see Aguirre Beltrán; Vinson; Von Germeten), as they were in New Granada during the same period.[10] Contradictorily, then, the ideology of whitening suggested via the 1793 census that *negros* had disappeared— that all blackness had whitened into mulattoness at least—but confirmed through *casta* paintings and illustrations from the last third of the eighteenth century that black always came back, when one least expected it, on the heels of the *albino*.

As Gonzalo Aguirre Beltrán confirms in his analysis of archival censuses and reports from various parts of New Spain in the 1770s, officials knew only too well that marginalized groups were passing as members of a "mejor casta" (276; better group). The taxonomies being abandoned by marginalized people living there were *negro, moreno, pardo, lobo,* and *mulato,* and those people were negotiating for new privileges and responsibilities by entering into categories such as *mestizo, castizo,* or *español* (Aguirre Beltrán 275). A census taker in Tlaxcala sarcastically remarked that "*morenos* and *pardos* are an extinct race in this head-count" (qtd. in Aguirre Beltrán 278). Another royal official, charged with conducting a census of Texcoco for military purposes, told the Viceroy of New Spain that distinguishing between the different groups would be temerity:

> This would be an odious process, and were it conducted rigorously, very dark stains erased over time would be revealed in the most distinguished of families, with this precision resulting in scandalous filings that, once bound over to the courts, would never end. I view the charge of conducting censuses for the establishment of militias as one of giving honor rather than taking it away. I have indicated the groups [*castas*] *español, castizo, mestizo, pardo,* etc., using the declarations of residents themselves as my guiding principle, although some have given me cause to suspect that they did not tell me the truth. In the census from Tepetlaoztoc, Your Honorable Viceroy will see a town full of Spaniards, but whether they are or aren't, they are certainly well-to-do, they live honorably, and if some abrogate for themselves a higher rank [*mejor casta*], they have valid legal titles to support it. (qtd. in Aguirre Beltrán 274)

The foregoing comparative analysis of blood equations in the Americas razes the hybridity-purity dyad of critical race studies of the Americas.

Since the late twentieth century, antiessentialist, constructionist scholars of race have not hesitated to harness the racial-hybridity paradigm to Latin America and the racial-purity paradigm to this one.[11] And yet, as the whitening equations from the eighteenth-century Americas prove, the colonial racial order in South America was far less forbearing toward blackness than that in the American South: breeding whites from blacks was by law far easier in Virginia than it was charted to be in the Orinoco region, Santo Domingo, Quito, and Mexico City. Current theorizing about whitening in the eighteenth-century Americas is reductive, then, because it not only ignores the degeneration equations of animal and plant breeding cultures that gestated human whitening equations but also denies the overlapping Anglo-American and Spanish American colonial histories of hybridity-within-whiteness. By probing further into Jefferson's analogy between breeding whites from blacks and breeding Merinos from Shenandoahs, it will become clear how notions of degeneration and improvement in brutes and plants traveled from Madrid and other points in the Hispanic world to the British and Spanish Atlantic.

The Duke of Newcastle, William Cavendish, was exiled in 1640 to Antwerp, where a protector introduced him to Don Juan José de Austria (King Philip IV's illegitimate son) and the rest of the Spanish court in Flanders. He opened an elaborate *manége* and riding school and in 1657–58 published his *New Method of Dressing Horses* in French (*La méthode nouvelle et invention extraordinaire de dresser les chevaux, les travallier selon la nature, et parfaire la nature par la subtilité de l'art*). In 1667, Cavendish published *A New Method and Extraordinary Invention to Dress Horses* in English. Jefferson the horse breeder was certainly familiar with these foundational works by Cavendish, who was the first to argue in print that horses should be improved by crossbreeding then inbreeding. Specifically, he recommended crossbreeding a native dam with a Spanish stallion, then breeding that half-breed (half indigenous, half Spanish) with her father, and thereafter the one-fourth native dam with her full-blooded Spanish grandfather, so that after three crossings (i.e., in the fourth generation) the blood of the country race would be cleared, or improved. Pure-blooded dogs, we will recall from the Spanish proverb, do not last for more than three years or crossings. Here in Cavendish's manual the full-blooded equine race is not a prized one, so the departure from the stock, or *generatio,* is an improvement: the native blood is cleared after three crossings, so that the fourth-generation filly or colt is a purebred. This is the same equation that was borrowed from Cavendish by sheep breeders in numerous manuals from the Enlightenment (Russell;

Wood and Orel). Jefferson the sheep breeder (see Stanton; *Thomas Jefferson Encyclopedia*) borrowed the "natural history" blood equation requiring four crossings to achieve purity from works on sheep breeding that he owned and that bear Cavendish's influence, as I have argued elsewhere.

At the same time, Cavendish warned that if you were to breed a hybrid dam (half Spanish, half native) with your native stallions (i.e., if you stopped injecting Spanish blood), the improving race would deviate from the Spanish, or better, race and revert eventually to indigeneity: "Besides, should the *Stallions* be of your Own Breed, in Three or Four *Generations* they would come to be Cart-horses; so Gross and ill-Favored would they be" (*New Method* 92). Again, this equation approximates the Spanish proverb about the degeneration of prized breeds of canines. Moreover, in colonial Spanish American discussions of whitening humans, the reversion to indigeneity (Native American or black stock) in so-called half-breeds (*mestizos* or *mulatos*) was, as noted above, called *salta-atrás*.

But where had Cavendish gotten them from? His 1667 *New Method and Extraordinary Invention to Dress Horses* details his preference for Spanish horses and his friendship with Don Juan José de Austria and the Spanish nobles loyal to him who had come "in above 20 coaches" to visit Cavendish's *manége* in Antwerp. The duke boasted of his horses and his fame among the Spanish nobles and among Spanish grooms in Antwerp: "Being returned to Don Juan, he'd ask them whether my horses were as rare as their reputation was great. To which they answer'd that my horses were such, that they wanted nothing of reasonable creatures, but speaking" ("To the Reader," in Cavendish, *New Method*). Cavendish picked up Spanish breeding practices while exiled in Antwerp, interacting not only with Spanish nobles but with Spanish grooms and other folk. Of course, he probably also studied books of secrets, veterinary treatises, and manuals on plant and animal breeding produced in the Spanish world.

The legal definition of whiteness in Jefferson's Virginia, which he rehearsed for Gray as he defined the category *mulato*, has allowed us to explore the gestation of *blanqueamiento*, or whitening, in the Americas. Writ large, those passages in the 1815 epistle have led us from Madrid to Monticello and from Spanish America to Antwerp, discovering along the way some Spanish folk notions of degeneration in plants and animals that generated whitening equations for humans in the eighteenth-century Americas. Additionally, a proximate cause of *blanqueamiento* equations for humans with non-European ancestry in Spanish and Portuguese America has been established. Canon law and moral theology on the inclusion of mixedly engendered persons (*mixtim progeniti*) within the category *neophyte* entailed the medieval revisal of the canon on consanguinity and affinity in order to grapple with the degeneration, or mixing, of different bloods or ancestries and the concomitant dissolution of categories such as black, Spanish, and Indian.

Notes

1. All English translations are my own.

2. This pre-Darwinian (or pretheoretical) essentialism doubtless encouraged adherence to theories of maternal impression, the Curse of Ham, the Mark of Cain, and combinations of these theories in the Spanish and British Atlantic world that I have discussed elsewhere. Moreover, constructionist essentialism quite possibly explains the popularity of Lamarck in nineteenth- and early-twentieth-century Latin American arts and sciences, beyond the reasons adduced by Nancy Stepan in her landmark study of eugenics in Latin America.

3. This piece of what Atran and the cognitive psychologist Doug Medin term the "cultural construction of nature" is universal: an *umwelt*, as the biologist Carol Kaesuk Yoon recently termed it. While Atran speculated that an analogical transfer from the animal and plant domains to the human domain might be the cause of racial essentialism, others, such as Susan Gelman and Lawrence Hirschfeld, argue that the human mind automatically essentializes human groups.

4. The category *puchuela* appears in *blanqueamiento* equations outside of the Viceroyalty of New Granada—in cities such as Montevideo, Santiago, and Buenos Aires—and is ubiquitous in Crown and church discussions of persons of mixed parentage and how canon law was to be applied to them. However, in the censuses archived for Gumilla's Viceroyalty of New Granada in the second half of the eighteenth century, a person with only one-sixteenth of Spanish ancestry is a *quinterón* (Solano D.), not a *puchuela*. The latter term is virtually nonexistent in the censuses from Enlightenment Mexico as well.

5. The decree refers to natives in the Spanish and Portuguese overseas territories. The papal briefs date from 2 April, 22 April, and 11 June 1701.

6. Again, in the volume devoted to the Americas from his monumental *Geographia histórica* (1752), Murillo Velarde reviews the taxa and recalls the rulings of Clement XI and Benedict XIII (51–52).

7. In her more recent work, Twinam defines *cuarterón* as an individual with one-fourth of black ancestry and *quinterón* as an individual with one-fifth of black ancestry. I can find no evidence of *quinterón* defined this way. In the Crown decree, *quinterón* is not defined. The cases that Twinam analyzes are from the Viceroyalty of New Granada, which then encompassed today's Ecuador, Venezuela, Colombia, and part of Peru. In New Granada, besides Gumilla's categories, the taxa for mixed persons with African ancestry were mulatto, *tercerón* (one-fourth of black ancestry), *cuarterón* (one-eighth), and *quinterón* (one-sixteenth). The offspring born to a *quinterón* and a white were whites (one-thirty-second). A *quinterón* who was applying for a Crown mercy or pardon of his black ancestry was purchasing a generation, so to speak—a certificate that attested

one-sixteenth or less of African blood—as if he were the *son of a quinterón* rather than a *quinterón*.

8. This matches the blood quantum required in New Granada. See the preceding note.

9. This old saw must have originated in husbandry and textiles, for it is omnipresent in agricultural discourses. Ramírez de Carrión, for instance, observes that white rams may produce black or multicolored sheep, but black rams never produce white sheep (33). However, genetics proves that primitive Spanish Merinos were black, not white, and that Spanish Romans began to crossbreed them with nondomestic sheep in order to whiten their wool (Fuentes García, Sánchez Sánchez, and Abascal 403). In light of this, not only Jefferson's analogical thinking but even Eurocentric comparisons of black African hair to wool may be understood as instantiations of folkbiology.

10. In fact, *pardos* were the other group who were allowed to petition for and purchase legal whiteness from the Spanish Crown. See Twinam, *Purchasing Whiteness*.

11. Linda Alcoff, for instance, writes: "The fact of the matter is that throughout Latin America and the Caribbean, a true melting pot of peoples, cultures, and races was created unlike anything north of the border. . . . In North America, . . . assimilationism and its heir apparent, cultural appreciation, have not led to a true mixing of races or cultures" (270–71).

Works Cited

Aguirre Beltrán, Gonzalo. *La población negra de México, 1519–1810: Estudio etnohistórico.* Mexico City: Ediciones Fuente Cultural, 1946.

Agustín, Miguel. *Libro de los secretos de agricultura, casa de campo y pastoril.* Facsimile ed. Valladolid, Spain: Editorial Maxtor, 2001.

Alcoff, Linda. *Visible Identities: Race, Gender, and the Self.* New York: Oxford University Press, 2006.

Atran, Scott. *Cognitive Foundations of Natural History: Towards an Anthropology of Science.* Cambridge: Cambridge University Press, 1996.

Atran, Scott, and Douglas Medin. *The Native Mind and the Cultural Construction of Nature.* Cambridge, MA: MIT Press, 2008.

Basarás, Joaquín Antonio de. *Origen, costumbres y estado presente de mexicanos y filipinos.* In *Una visión del Siglo de las Luces: La codificación de Joaquín Antonio de Basarás,* ed. Ilona Katzew. Mexico City: Landucci, 2006.

Bauer, Ralph. "The Hemispheric Genealogies of 'Race': Creolization and the Cultural Geography of Colonial Difference across the Eighteenth-Century Americas." In *Hemispheric American Studies,* ed. Robert Levine and Caroline Levander, 36–56. New Brunswick, NJ: Rutgers University Press, 2007.

Carrera, Magali. *Imagining Identity in New Spain: Race, Lineage, and the Colonial Body in Portraiture and Casta Paintings.* Austin: University of Texas Press, 2003.

Cavendish, William, Duke of Newcastle. *La méthode nouvelle et invention extraordinaire de dresser les chevaux, les travaller selon la nature, et parfaire la nature par la subtilité de l'art.* Antwerp: Jacques Van Meurs, 1657–58.

———. *A New Method and Extraordinary Invention to Dress Horses, Work Them Ac-*

cording to Nature, as Also to Perfect Nature by the Subtlety of Art. London: Thomas Milbourn, 1667.

Cicala, Mario. *Descripción histórico-topográfica de la Provincia de Quito.* Trans. Julián G. Bravo and Marcos Gándara Enríquez. Quito: Biblioteca Ecuatoriana "Aurelio Espinosa Pólit," 1994.

Correas, Gonzalo. *Vocabulario de refranes y frases proverbiales.* Prol. Miguel Mir, ed. Víctor Infantes. Madrid: Visor Libros, 1992.

De la Peña Montenegro, Alonso. *Itinerario para párrocos de indios en que se tratan las materias más particulares tocantes a ellos para su buena administración.* Madrid: Joseph Fernández de Buendía, 1668.

Feijoo y Montenegro, Benito Jerónimo. "Color etiópico." In *Teatro crítico universal,* 7: 66–93. Madrid: Real Compañía de Impresores y Libreros, 1778.

Fisher, Andrew B., and Matthew D. O'Hara, eds. *Imperial Subjects: Race and Identity in Colonial Latin America.* Foreword by Irene Silverblatt. Durham, NC: Duke University Press, 2009.

Forbes, Jack. *Black Africans and Native Americans: Color, Race and Caste in the Evolution of Red-Black Peoples.* Oxford: Basil Blackwell, 1988.

Fuentes García, Francisco C., José María Sánchez Sánchez, and Carlos Gonzalo Abascal. *Tratado de etnología animal: Razas de rumiantes y monogástricos.* Murcia, Spain: Librero-Editor Diego Marín, 2006.

García Conde, Pedro. *Verdadera albeitería.* Madrid: Antonio González de Reyes, 1707.

García Sáiz, María Concepción. *Las castas mexicanas: Un género pictórico americano.* Milan: Olivetti-Grafiche Milani, 1990.

Gelman, Susan A., and Lawrence A. Hirschfeld. "How Biological Is Essentialism?" In *Folkbiology,* ed. Douglas L. Medin and Scott Atran, 403–46. Cambridge, MA: MIT Press, 1999.

Gray, Francis C. "Francis C. Gray to Thomas Jefferson, March 24, 1815." Thomas Jefferson Papers at the Library of Congress, Series 1: General Correspondence, 1651–1827. http://hdl.loc.gov/loc.mss/mtj.mtjbib021987.

Gumilla, José. *El Orinoco ilustrado y defendido: Historia natural, civil y geográfica de este gran río y de sus caudalosas vertientes.* 2 vols. 2nd rev. and exp. ed. Madrid: Manuel Fernández, 1745.

Hill, Ruth. "Before Hypodescent: Whitening Equations in South America and the American South." In *The Oxford Handbook of the Literature of the U.S. South,* ed. Barbara Ladd and Fred Hobson, 33–54. Oxford: Oxford University Press, 2016.

Jefferson, Thomas. "Thomas Jefferson to Francis C. Gray, March 4, 1815." Thomas Jefferson Papers at the Library of Congress, Series 1: General Correspondence, 1651–1827. http://hdl.loc.gov/loc.mss/mtj.mtjbib021963.

Jiménez, Antonio. *Colección de refranes, adagios y locuciones proverbiales.* Madrid: Pierart Peralta, 1828.

Katzew, Ilona. *Casta Painting: Images of Race in Eighteenth-Century Mexico.* New Haven, CT: Yale University Press, 2004.

Katzew, Ilona, and Susan Deans. *Race and Classification: The Case of Mexican America.* Stanford, , CA: Stanford University Press, 2009.

Labat, Jean-Baptiste. *Nouveau voyage aux isles de l'Amérique.* 3 vols. Paris: Pierre-François Giffart, 1722.

Martínez, María Elena. *Genealogical Fictions: Limpieza de Sangre, Religion, and Gender in Colonial Mexico.* Stanford, CA: Stanford University Press, 2008.

Medin, Douglas L., and Scott Atran, eds. *Folkbiology.* Cambridge, MA: MIT Press, 1999.

Medin, Douglas L., and Andrew Ortony. "Psychological Essentialism." In *Similarity and Analogical Reasoning,* ed. Stella Vosniadou and Andrew Ortony, 179–95. New York: Cambridge University Press, 1989.

Moritz Kalisch, Marcus. *A Historical and Critical Commentary on the Old Testament with a New Translation: Leviticus.* 2 vols. London: Longmans, Green, Reader, & Dyer, 1867–72.

Murillo Velarde, Pedro. *Curso de derecho canónico, hispano e indiano (Cursus Iuris Canonici Hispani et Indici).* Trans. Alberto Carrillo Cázares, Pascual Guzmán de Alba, et al. 4 vols. Zamora, Michoacán, Mexico: El Colegio de Michoacán—Facultad de Derecho, UNAM, 2005.

———. *Geographia histórica.* Vol. 9, *De la América y de las islas adyacentes de las tierras árticas y antárcticas y islas de los Mares del Norte y Sur.* Madrid: Agustín de Gozdejuela y Sierra, 1752.

Muro Orejón, Antonio. *Cedulario americano del siglo XVIII: Colección de disposiciones legales indianas desde 1680 a 1800, contenidas en los cedularios del Archivo General de Indias.* 2 vols. Seville: Escuela de los Estudios Hispano-Americanos, 1956.

Naveda Chávez Hita, Adriana, ed. *Pardos, mulatos y libertos: Sexto Encuentro de Afromexicanistas.* Veracruz, Mexico: Universidad Veracruzana, 2001.

O'Crouley, Pedro Alonso. *A Description of the Kingdom of New Spain, 1774.* Trans. and ed. Seán Galvin. San Francisco: John Howell Books, 1972.

Outram, Dorinda. *The Enlightenment.* 3rd ed. Cambridge: Cambridge University Press, 2013.

Peguero, Luis Joseph. *Historia de la conquista de la isla española de Santo Domingo trasumptada el año de 1762.* Prol. Vicente Rubio, ed. and intro. Pedro J. Santiago. 2 vols. Santo Domingo: Publicaciones del Museo de las Casas Reales, 1975.

Ramírez de Carrión, Manuel. *Maravillas de naturaleza en que se contienen dos mil secretos de cosas naturales, dispuestos por abecedario a modo de Aforismos fáciles y breves de mucha curiosidad y provecho.* Monzilla: Juan Bautista de Morales, 1629.

Restall, Matthew, ed. *Beyond Black and Red: African-Native Relations in Colonial Latin America.* Albuquerque: University of New Mexico Press, 2005.

———. *The Black Middle: Africans, Mayas, and Spaniards in Colonial Yucatan.* Palo Alto, CA: Stanford University Press, 2009.

Root, Michael. "Race in the Social Sciences." In *Handbook of Philosophy of Science: Philosophy of Anthropology and Sociology,* ed. Stephen P. Turner and Mark W. Risjord, 735–53. Amsterdam: Elsevier/North Holland, 2007.

Russell, Nicholas. *Like Engend'ring Like: Heredity and Animal Breeding in Early Modern England.* London: Cambridge University Press, 2006.

Seed, Patricia. "Social Dimensions of Race. Mexico City, 1753." *Hispanic American Historical Review* 62 (November 1982): 569–606.

Solano D., Sergio Paolo. "Padrones de población e historiografía sobre la configuración socio-racial hispanoamericana del siglo XVIII." *El Taller de la Historia* 5, no. 5 (2013): 125–71.

Sollors, Werner. *Neither Black Nor White Yet Both: Thematic Explorations of Interracial Literature*. New York: Oxford University Press, 1997.

Stanton, Lucia C. "Sheep for the President." Talk at dinner in memory of Thomas Jefferson, Monticello, 3 November 2000. Charlottesville: Thomas Jefferson Memorial Foundation, 2000.

Stepan, Nancy. *The Hour of Eugenics: Race, Gender, and Nation in Latin America*. Ithaca, NY: Cornell University Press, 2001.

Thomas Jefferson Encyclopedia, s.v. "Sheep." Accessed February 2010. www.monticello.org /site/research-and-collections/tje.

Twinam, Ann. "Purchasing Whiteness: Conversations on the Essence of Pardo-ness and Mulatto-ness at the End of Empire." In *Imperial Subjects: Race and Identity in Colonial Latin America,* ed. Andrew B. Fisher and Matthew D. O'Hara, foreword by Irene Silverblatt, 141–65. Durham, NC: Duke University Press, 2009.

———. *Purchasing Whiteness: Pardos, Mulattos, and the Quest for Social Mobility in the Spanish Indies*. Stanford, CA: Stanford University Press, 2015.

Vinson, Ben, III. "La dinámica social de la raza: Los milicianos pardos de Puebla en el siglo VIII." In *Pardos, mulatos y libertos: Sexto Encuentro de Afromexicanistas,* ed. Adriana Naveda Chávez Hita, 61–78.Veracruz, Mexico: Universidad Veracruzana, 2001.

Vinson, Ben, III, and Matthew Restall, eds.. *Black Mexico: Race and Society from Colonial to Modern Times*. Albuquerque: University of New Mexico Press, 2009.

Von Germeten, Nicole. *Black Blood Brothers: Confraternities and Social Mobility for Afro-Mexicans*. Foreword by Stephen W. Angell and Anthony B. Pinn. Gainesville: University Press of Florida, 2006.

Wade, Peter. *Race and Ethnicity in Latin America*. London: Pluto, 1997.

Wood, Roger J., and Vítězslav Orel. *Genetic Prehistory in Selective Breeding: A Prelude to Mendel*. Oxford: Oxford University Press, 2001.

Yoon, Carol Kaesuk. *Naming Nature: The Clash between Instinct and Science*. New York: Norton, 2009.

Thomas Jefferson

Breeding and Buying Horses, Connecting Family, Friends, and Neighbors

CARRIE B. DOUGLASS

In eighteenth-century Virginia, newly imported English horses were among the many possessions that passed between family members and sealed relationships between friends. As a member of the Virginia planter elite, Thomas Jefferson moved in these horse-owning circles, in which horses were a "natural" medium of exchange. Like the exchange of plants and seeds, books and ideas, farming tips, architectural plans, even enslaved men and women, the trade, exchange, buying, and selling of horses often retraced lines of other social relationships. An important attribute of these horses was the carefully recorded pedigree that went with them as they passed from owner to owner or as offspring were "sold" to other members of the gentry.

However, when one wades into the documentation relating to Jefferson's domestic life, one constantly bumps up against disapproving accusations about Jefferson's personal debt, about his debt as one of his "moral failings." Scholars from various disciplines outside anthropology have asked me, in censorious tones, why Jefferson bought such expensive pedigreed horses when he was so deeply in debt and could not really "pay" for them. These questions may say more about our own preoccupations than they do about Jefferson.

Jefferson inherited much *debt* from his father-in-law, accrued much *debt*, continued to spend himself deeper in *debt*, failed to pay off his *debt*, "foolishly" guaranteed others' *debts*, died in *debt*, and then his house and, tragically, his slaves were sold to resolve his *debt*. Here I want to elucidate what Jefferson was doing when he "bought" expensive pedigreed horses on credit (the other side of *debt*) from the local "moral economy" of Virginia gentry and horsemen. For anthropologists (with nods to Evans-Pritchard, Graeber, Gregory, and Mauss), outside market capitalism and debt-based money, debt is a social promise, a form of communication, like the reciprocity Mauss says is owed a gift.

Marcel Mauss's work in *The Gift* and elsewhere helps illuminate the eighteenth-century Virginia rural gentry's relationship with "blood horses." The plantation-owning gentry in colonial Virginia were still immersed in an honor culture, caught in the intersection and disjunction between gift economies and an emerging capitalist economy. Although the gentry spoke about "buying and selling" the blooded horses to one another, this was a special sphere of exchange, and in many ways these horses functioned as gifts: they created social ties and group solidarity and were inalienable from previous owners. This was precisely what made them status objects. In the seemingly irrational behavior of accruing "debt," we can see the old forms of solidarity working within and through the newer mercantile capitalist world order (shortly to overtake the still rather provincial Virginia gentry). Yet the old colonial elite were soon to be challenged in post-Revolutionary Virginia by a new class of market-minded capitalists.

By drilling down on Jefferson's record and through thick description, to use Clifford Geertz's term, I show how the "buying" and "selling" of horses in eighteenth- and early-nineteenth-century Virginia gives insight into social aspects of the plantation economy. First, in many ways breeding and selling pedigreed horses in colonial Virginia mimicked marriage, in that it joined families and linked names of prestigious members of the gentry. Second, cash was rarely exchanged in a horse transaction between planters. Rather, hands were shaken, agreements were recorded in account books, money was owed, payments were postponed, later bonds were given, estates were credited, notes were passed, and debts were accumulated. Interest was not charged, years might go by, other horses were sold back, trades were made, and debts were voided or eventually paid off. The historian T. H. Breen wrote on the role of credit and debt in his book *Tobacco Culture* (1985). For the Tidewater planter society of eighteenth-century Virginia, credit and debt were a "form of communication,"[1] and owing money was a way of establishing and maintaining enduring social relations.[2] Horses were a conflation of that indissoluble social relation and bond with the original owner.[3]

The Horses

After the 1720s in Virginia, tobacco wealth and the emergence of a gracious lifestyle produced a spate of mansion building and many other symbols of elite status. One of the most important icons of elite status at the time was the new blooded horse imported from England into Virginia after the 1730s. These champions on the turf in England were imported to "improve

A VIRGINIA RACE HORSE.

Figure 1. "A Virginia Racehorse," from *The gentleman's new pocket farrier.* (Courtesy of HathiTrust)

the blood" of American horses, originally for long-distance course racing. Known as "blooded" or "high bred" horses, these animals later became the foundation stallions and mares of the American Thoroughbred "breed," the racehorse par excellence (fig. 1).

Originating in England, the Thoroughbred horse was the first true horse "breed" created.[4] All Thoroughbred horses trace back to three stallions imported into England from the "Orient" between 1690 and 1730. *Thoroughbred* was a term that meant "pure-bred" and was not attached to this "breed" of horse until late in the nineteenth century. The appearance in England in 1791 of the *General Stud Book,* with its pedigree data assuring "purity" of all the animals listed,[5] effectively sealed the breed from further outside influences[6] and led to official registration for recognition as a Thoroughbred. That is, for these race horses, the owner had to be able to prove that both sides of the horse's pedigree traced back to one of the originating three "Oriental" studs. In this sense, the English royalty and aristocracy, those in control of racing stables and breeding, projected their own marriage rules and rules about membership in the aristocracy onto the "high bred" blood horse.[7]

Importing a winning race horse from England to Virginia was extremely expensive; it could only be attempted by the most wealthy and successful members of the Virginia landed gentry. Fifty-nine blooded horses were imported from England to Virginia (and other states) between 1730 and 1776.[8] Course racing in Virginia soon became an important social event and form of entertainment for all social classes in colonial Virginia, although the race horses were owned and bred by a small number of upper-class planters. Race horses became another product (after tobacco) raised for profit on the extensive plantations of Tidewater Virginia. However, owning several blooded horses as saddle horses and carriage horses (and fox-hunting horses)—in other words, not just for racing—quickly became a symbol of the aristocratic-mimicking gentry classes in Virginia.

Before these horses soon to be called Thoroughbreds arrived to spread their "blood" (we would say genes), Virginia horses (like those in all the colonies) had been smallish, short, stocky beasts, used for riding but also for working the fields (fig. 2). They were crosses of the early imported Irish and Scottish horses, called Hobbies or Galways, with the offspring of Indian-traded Spanish Barbs (called Chickasaws). In general, these small horses were pacers, not trotters, which meant that they were comfortable to ride for long-distance trips from plantation to plantation, or from Albemarle

Figure 2. "A Cart Horse," from *The gentleman's new pocket farrier.* (Courtesy of the Albert and Shirley Small Special Collections Library, University of Virginia)

Figure 3. This nineteenth-century birth record includes a depiction of a quarter race. Judges stand at the end to decide the winner. *Birth Record for Samuel Asay,* Burlington County, New Jersey, ca. 1830, watercolor and ink on wove papers. (Accession # 1933.305.2, image # TC1982–1068; the Colonial Williamsburg Foundation, gift of Abby Aldrich Rockefeller)

County[9] to the capital in Williamsburg.[10] Until later in the century the lack of passable roads inhibited carriage use for long-distance travel; carriages were used only by an elite few in the government seats, such as by the governor in Williamsburg. Thus, most people rode their horses rather than traveled by carriage.

Some of these indigenous horses had blazing speeds at a quarter of a mile, which explains the popularity of quarter racing (matches between two horses down a straight trail or road, sometimes through the center of town, for a quarter of a mile) from early times in the colonies (fig. 3).The bigger English horses were imported precisely to increase the "bottom" (endurance) of the American horses and to be used in the newly popular long-distance course races (comprising several heats of three to four miles each) that were being promoted and developed by the royalty in England, soon to be known as the sport of kings (fig. 4).

The imports were taller, more elegant perhaps, and certainly faster for longer distances. As riding horses, however, most were probably less comfortable than the so-called quarter horses, because the "new" breed of horse was characterized by the jarring trot rather than the smooth pace (posting to the trot, i.e., rising to the trot, was a later riding style innovation). However, as a symbol, owning and riding these horses trumped comfort. All were infused with "Oriental" blood and held themselves in a more "aris-

Figure 4. Course races pitted several horses and their jockeys against each other on a mile-long oval track. *A Race Meeting at Jacksonville, Alabama,* W. S. Hedges, oil on canvas. (Birmingham Museum of Art; museum purchase with funds provided by Mr. Coleman Cooper; EBSCO Industries, Inc.; Mr. Henry S. Lynn Jr.; Mr. and Mrs. Jack McSpadden; the Regina and Harold E. Simon Fund; and Mary Arminda Mays in the memory of John Edward Mays, by exchange, 1985.278)

tocratic" way than did the smallish workhorses. These horses pranced and danced, holding their heads high; appropriately, they became the "high" horses of the elite, a kind of metaphor for the elite's own self-image. These blooded horses represented their (male) owners. Thomas Jefferson was said to ride or drive only highbred horses.[11]

Although only a few plantation owners were able financially to import these first horses, the planters soon recouped their monetary outlay by standing the stallions at stud or selling the offspring of the imported horses to others. Elites one rung down were eager to use the stud services of these horses, especially the most renowned horses, to produce their own Thoroughbred racing or riding horses in order to have their own symbol and verification of status. All of these imported horses oozed status, but inevitably some horses, such as Fearnought and Diomed, produced more offspring (get) or more valued offspring (race winners) than others. Thus, breeding was done for both profit and status.

Inalienability

Significantly, blooded horses in colonial Virginia were valued because they were not "alienable objects." Recording the pedigree of the horse, in which the name of the animal often included that of the previous "owner," underlines the connections, such as marriage connections, of these families. Thomas Jefferson, for example, as we can see from the pedigrees he carefully noted in his *Farm Book*, used horses to retrace kinship and marriage lines, as well as to cement other important social relationships with Virginia's eighteenth-century elite families (see fig. 5).

Like their elite owners, these horses were bred only to one another. Comments from contemporary observers underlined, sometimes in surprise, the identification and almost fetishization that the gentry men had with their horses. Planters would identify their horses with the same genealogical terminology as they would themselves. One visitor to the Carters' Nomini Hall plantation in 1774 noted in his journal the "loud disputes concerning the Excellence of each other's Colts—Concerning their Fathers, Mothers (for so they call the Dams), Brothers, Sisters, Uncles, Aunts, Nephews, Nieces, & Cousins to the fourth Degree!—"[12]

Virginia gentlemen spared no expense on their prized horses, and portraits of the successful racehorses and prolific stud, in gilded frames, adorned their walls alongside the portraits of family progenitors. The same visitor mentioned above, Philip Fithian, noted that in Colonel John Tayloe's dining room hung "twenty-four of the most celebrated among the English Race-Horses, Drawn masterly, & set in elegant gilt Frames."[13]

Anthropologists and historians have long recognized that marriages tie families and social classes together. We have long written about how marriage (and kinship) weaves the fabric of society. Certainly this was true in colonial Virginia. The FFVs (First Families of Virginia) originated from the first colonists from England, who settled along the James River and other Tidewater rivers in the seventeenth century. They were the leading families of Virginia, not necessarily the first chronologically. They were socially prominent and wealthy and overly represented on the colonial council. Many were "second sons" of aristocrats in England who were granted large tracts of land by the king and often transplanted family ties to the Virginia colony. Others rose from modest beginnings. In a society based on the possession of land and slaves, land was tightly controlled and often passed between families of corresponding social rank. Consequently, there was a tendency to marry with their social equals for generations, and certain surnames became common in the growing colony.[14] Marriage among FFVs helped seal their status and maintain a hierarchical society.

Like many planters in colonial Virginia, Thomas Jefferson kept detailed notebooks and account books in order to rationalize, organize, and document his farming activities. Jefferson's *Farm Book,* a bound manuscript volume, is a veritable gold mine of information on agriculture and husbandry at Monticello and Jefferson's other properties, as well as an example of the late-eighteenth- and early-nineteenth-century Piedmont Virginia plantation economy in general. The volume spans the years 1774–1824 and includes "Diary" (Jefferson's term) entries arranged by date on his plowing, sowing, planting, and cutting activities, inventories of his livestock and slaves, and a section titled "Aphorisms, Observations, Facts in Husbandry." Along with his *Garden Book* and *Memorandum Books* (or account books), Jefferson's *Farm Book* helps portray Jefferson's extrapolitical interests.

Conventionally it is said that the *Farm Book* begins with a list and location of Jefferson's slaves (his own, those inherited from his mother, and those inherited from his recently deceased father-in-law) as of January 1774. However, this is not literally true. Technically, inside the front cover of the *Farm Book* we find a hand-drawn pedigree of one of Jefferson's favorite saddle horses at the time, Caractacus (foaled in May 1775). The first page of the *Farm Book,* probably written before the graphic pedigree drawing, lists the horses in Jefferson's possession, possibly as of January 1774 (fig. 5).[15] These were his riding horses, carriage horses, and broodmares. The list does not contain his plantation horses, or workhorses, which are included in other inventories in the book (fig. 6). Most of the twenty-eight horses in the list are named, described by color, age (year foaled), and pedigree. Significantly, the previous owners of each horse's dam and sire are noted.

Here I offer two examples of Jefferson's horses to examine the various relationships that are conflated in each horse. If Jefferson recorded the names of a horse's owners in several generations of its pedigree, it was because the owners were in some way part of the horse. Their names "counted"; that is, those relationships give social value to the horse and were important to Jefferson and to others of his social class.

In his notes on the first horse listed in the *Farm Book,* Allycroker, Jefferson's most important broodmare,[16] we see an emphasis on the male line, which actually continues today in the way we record a Thoroughbred's lineage or genealogy. The dam, or the tail line, is considered weaker and must be justified more.[17] The sire is stated first. In Allycroker's case the sire was Silver-eye (grandson of the Godolphin Arabian, through Regulus)[18] (fig.

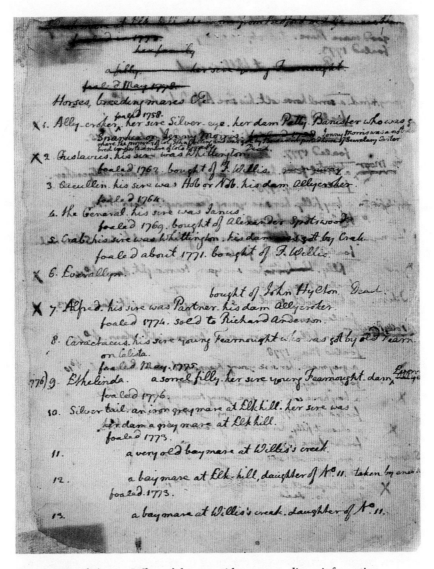

Figure 5. List of Thomas Jefferson's horses, with names, pedigree information, physical description, and previous owners, from Jefferson's *Farm Book,* 1774–1824. (Collection of the Massachusetts Historical Society)

7). Silver-eye was a pale sorrel horse with clear blue eyes, imported to the colonies in 1756 by Samuel Duvall, of Henrico County. Duvall was a member of the House of Burgesses and attended the first and second Virginia Conventions in 1774 and 1775. Duvall had a great deal of income-producing land (mines and coal) and built the first brick house in the town of Rich-

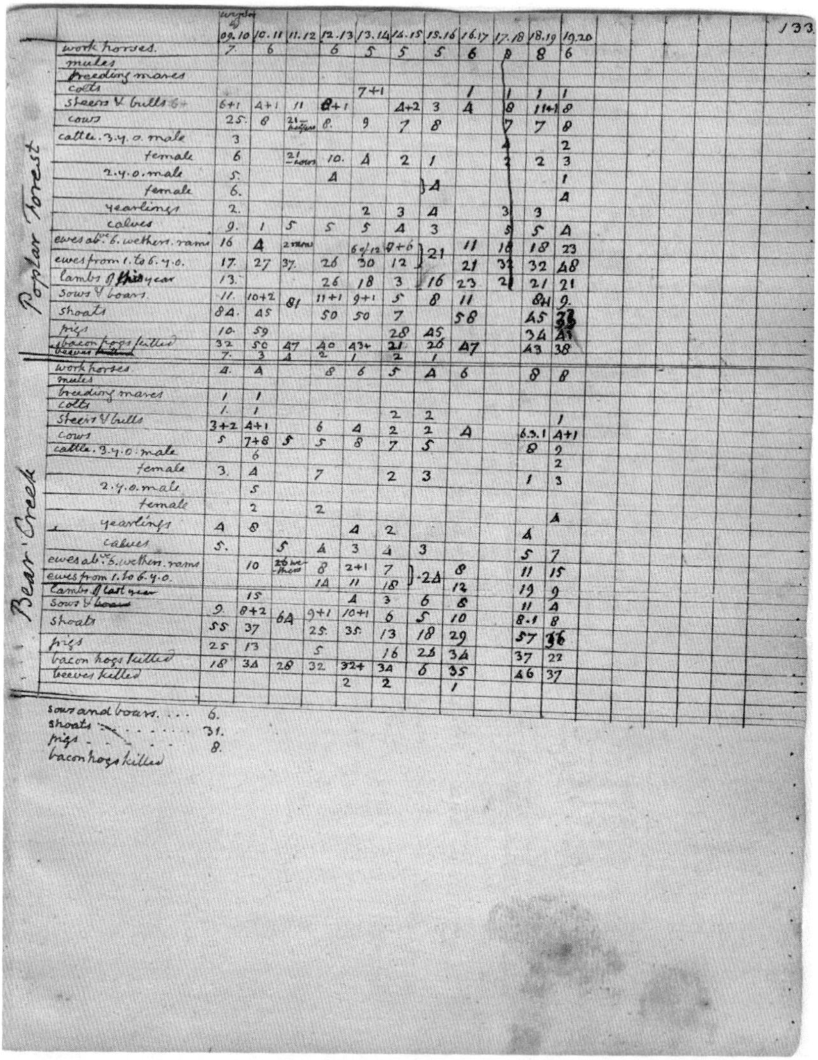

Figure 6. List of Thomas Jefferson's other stock, including "work horses" on his various quarter farms, from Jefferson's *Farm Book,* 1774–1824. (Collection of the Massachusetts Historical Society)

mond. Silver-eye's get (offspring or descendants) spread out to Kentucky, where they founded many "Matriarchal" pedigrees of the later American Thoroughbred breed.[19]

Allycroker's female line is much more articulated in the *Farm Book.* Although Jefferson claimed not to give much weight to human pedigrees, specifically casting doubt on the importance of his mother's Randolph connec-

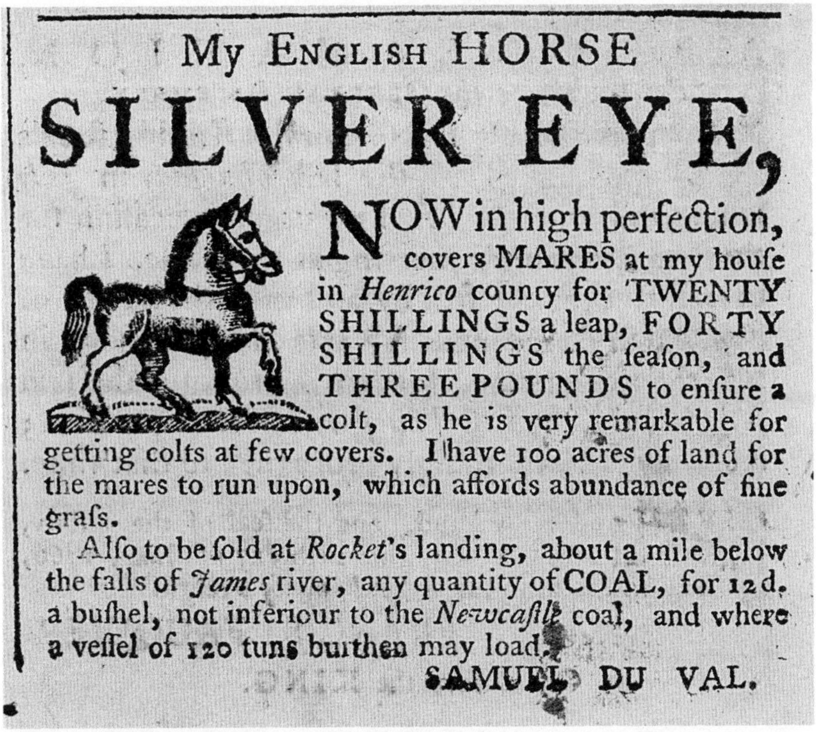

Figure 7. Advertisement for Silver-Eye's stud services, *Virginia Gazette,* June 13, 1766. (Virginia Historical Society)

tions,[20] it was precisely through his mother that Jefferson was intimately connected to the FFVs. Jefferson tells us in his *Farm Book* that Allycroker's dam was Patty Banister out of Spanker, an Andalusian horse owned by William Nelson of Yorktown.[21] William Nelson, an important planter, was governor of Virginia between royal governors (1770–71), and his son, Thomas, signed the Declaration of Independence. Spanker was imported from southern Spain in 1740. Patty Banister's dam was Jenny Morris. Jefferson continues in the *Farm Book:* "Jenny Morris was a noted mare, the property of Col. John Bolling, and was got by Bow an imported horse of Secretary Carter's, [and by] an imported mare of Col. Eppes's."[22] So Jenny Morris's owner was Colonel John Bolling of Cobbs, in Chesterfield near Petersburg, whose son had married Jefferson's sister Mary in 1760 (i.e., he was Thomas Jefferson's brother-in law). These Bollings were directly related to Thomas Rolfe and thus to Pocahontas. Jenny Morris's sire was Beau, imported from England by Secretary John Carter in 1740 to Shirley plantation on the James in Charles City County.[23]

Carter's horse Beau was crossed with an imported mare owned by Colonel Eppes of Eppington in Chesterfield (thus near Bolling). Colonel Eppes married a Bolling and was the father of Francis Eppes, Jefferson's brother-in-law through his wife, Martha Wayles (and her cousin). (Many years later, Jefferson's second daughter, Mary [Polly] married John Wayles Eppes, son of Francis Eppes and Elizabeth Wayles). Again, if Jefferson mentioned the names of the owners of the horses back several generations, it was because they "counted." They were part of the horse.

Allycroker was Jefferson's leading broodmare at the time because she had produced several prized foals, one of which, Caractacus, became Jefferson's favorite riding horse in the years before he went to Paris. So impressive was Caractacus in both conformation and performance that others requested his stud services, as we shall see later. Jefferson bred Allycroker and many mares to a stud called Dandridge's Young Fearnought. During the 1770s, Jefferson bred at least ten mares, including Allycroker, to the "blood" of the famous imported turf horse Fearnought (or "Imported" Fearnought) through William Dandridge's Young Fearnought. Jefferson also bought a mare that was pregnant with Dandridge's Young Fearnought's foal Everallin (foaled in 1774). Everallin later foaled another filly, Ethelinda (1776), with Fearnought blood, this time through a Fearnought offspring known as John Bolling's Young Fearnought.

Fearnought (or "Imported" Fearnought) was a bright bay colt foaled in 1755 in England standing 15 hands, 3 inches. His sire was Regulus, son of the Godolphin Arabian, one of the original three progenitors of the Thoroughbred. Fearnought "was a King's Plate winner, and won four mile heats under high weights and so was considered the most desirable of specimens for importation to improve the small, sprinting types prevalent at the time in the Virginia Colony."[24] The Virginian Colonel John Baylor of Newmarket in Caroline County, an important breeder and the chief importer of Thoroughbreds in the colony before the Revolution,[25] imported Fearnought to Virginia in 1764 at the age of nine. After Baylor's death Fearnought stood more seasons in southern Virginia, dying at age twenty-two.

All the early commentators on American turf horses lauded the value of this horse for the legacy of his "blood." One said: "Fearnought left the most numerous and valuable stock of any horse that was ever stood in Virginia and North Carolina before the days of old Diomed."[26] Fearnought's stud fee was five times the amount charged for other good sires. Many Fearnought mares were taken to Kentucky, and five are among the Matriarchs.

One of the leading sons in the get of Fearnought was William Dandridge's

Young Fearnought, a chestnut colt foaled in 1768.[27] His dam was an oft-cited mare called Calista, owned by William Byrd III at Westover in Charles City County.[28] Young Fearnought was acquired from the Byrd stud by William A. Dandridge II of Hanover County. Young Fearnought covered in Hanover and Cumberland Co. from 1775–82.

William Dandridge had a long relationship with Jefferson through horses. Dandridge married Ann Bolling of Cobbs in Chesterfield, whose father, the previously mentioned John Bolling, also had an offspring of old Fearnought. William Dandridge himself was a cousin of Martha Dandridge Curtis, the wife of George Washington (her second marriage). William knew Jefferson at the College of William and Mary, and he, Jefferson, and Patrick Henry once played the minuet at his father's house in Hanover County. Jefferson stopped often at the Dandridge place, which was on Allen's Creek in Hanover County, about twenty-five miles from Jefferson's Elk Hill, on his way back and forth from Williamsburg. Dandridge served in the Revolutionary War and was the commissary for troops in Yorktown.

During those early years at Monticello, Jefferson bred not only to Dandridge's Young Fearnought but also to other Fearnought colts owned by nearby friends and neighbors. The names of these offspring of Imported Fearnought advertised their owners' names as well as those of their sires, for example, John Bolling's Fearnought (Ethelinda) and Gay's Fearnought (Raleigh).

Old Fearnought was imported to America for his speed and racing victories; the hope was that he would pass his speed on to his offspring. It is important to emphasize, however, that Jefferson was breeding riding horses, not racing horses (fig. 8). Contemporaries all said he never raced a horse, nor is there any record of his doing so, although he often attended the races. Rather than merely speed, Jefferson was looking for horses with stamina, carriage, and a comfortable gait to carry him around his extensive farms and back and forth to the seats of government—Williamsburg, Philadelphia, and Richmond. Jefferson wanted a well-bred horse and the personal connections that came with that horse.

For the most part, Jefferson took his mares to the studs of other gentry to breed. In general we can say that in Virginia before the end of the Revolutionary War there was a hierarchical relationship between those wealthy members of the Tidewater gentry who imported and owned studs and those who took their mares to breed with imported stallions in hopes of bettering their American stock and also perhaps producing their own turf champions and, later, studs.[29] Only at the end of the ten years he devoted to horse breed-

Figure 8. "A Saddle Horse," from *The gentleman's new pocket farrier.* (Courtesy of the Albert and Shirley Small Special Collections Library, University of Virginia)

ing did Jefferson own a stallion that stood at stud. Only with one horse, Caractacus, did Jefferson reverse the social direction of breeding. Apparently Caractacus was impressive enough as a riding horse that many of Jefferson's neighbors in Albemarle County paid for their mares to have a leap (one time) or a season (several months' boarding at Monticello) with the horse between 1779 and 1782.

Gentlemen who paid for a leap or a season with Caractacus included Thomas Garth, Colonel John Harvie, Dr. Gilmer, James Jones, William Turner, Charles Goodman, James Powell Cocke, Benjamin Norell, Claudius Bustard, and Davy Watson. Garth, who owned thousands of acres along Ivy Creek, was a magistrate and later served as sheriff. Harvie, whose father had been one of Jefferson's guardians after his father died, owned the Barracks, Pen Park, and Belmont; he was a lawyer and member of the House of Burgesses and delegate to the Continental Congress. Gilmer, a physician, served as sheriff and was a member of the House of Delegates; he bought Pen Park from Harvie and made his home there. Jones had acreage on Old Lynchburg Road near Dudly's Mountain. Goodman had land on the south fork of the Rivanna River, west of the mouth of Ivy Creek. Cocke, a relative of John Hartwell Cocke of Bremo, had come to Albemarle sometime after 1770 and at least once supplied fish to stock the pond at Monticello. It is almost certain that Jefferson designed Cocke's house, Edgemont, built around 1797 between Keene and Scottsville. Bustard had three hundred acres on the north fork of the Hardware River and kept a tavern. Watson, a house joiner by trade who went to work for Jefferson in 1781 (after deserting from the British army), was a carriage maker at Monticello at the time. Although many of these friends and neighbors were members of the First Families of Albemarle, few were FFVs.

Soon after his wife's death in 1782, Jefferson left Monticello on various governmental assignments. He was sent to France in August 1784. After his return from France in 1790, Jefferson never again had the opportunity or the inclination to breed and raise his own horses. Rather, to satisfy his daily riding habit, Jefferson bought fully mature and trained horses from others. Nevertheless, despite his democratic leanings, all the riding horses Jefferson bought during his lifetime had connections, both equine and human, to FFVs. Horses still condensed human relationships.

Paying for Horses: Credit and Debt

In their own Virginia world of Tidewater planters, Jefferson and his fellow gentry competed not only for money and income but also, and more importantly, for honor and social reputation. Wealth, of course, becomes a measure of self and a means of obtaining a high standard of living, which is the symbol of honor, pride, and even masculinity. Without a doubt, the elite valued independence and autonomy as the ideal social conditions,[30] and the external trappings of independence and social status—the great houses, the blooded horses, the sumptuous carriages, and other finery—cost money. Yet, as symbols of status, these horses, and houses, and carriages seemed more like necessities than luxuries. However, in eighteenth-century Virginia, honor was bestowed by one's social equals, and so the values of honesty, generosity, hospitality, loyalty and the pretense of not caring about practical economical matters produced honor and reputation. Rather than pay for these luxuries with money, the gentry extended each other credit and accumulated long-term debt.

Moreover, extending credit and owing debts were two sides of the same coin in a local agrarian community. Planters were honor-bound to repay debts, especially to their social equals, but time was not of the essence.

Long-term debt merely kept the individuals mentally woven together and provided important personal links. "Indeed, beyond the members of one's own immediate family, credit offered a recognized means of structuring social relationships within the white community. Almost all the colony's freemen were involved in this vast, largely informal network of giving and receiving credit."[31] Credit was considered a personal favor. Locally, commercial relationships were personal relationships.

Furthermore, colonial Virginia was not a cash economy. Since colonial Virginia literally did not have circulating money (few coins and bills), the local economy ran on informal credit networks.[32] There were no banks in the colonies, so colonists depended on the sale of their crops (once a year), or even the exchange of their crops, for goods. When crops failed or prices declined, debts were carried over for years. However, "cooperation and competition were two sides of the same economic culture."[33] Since the community was tied together and mutually dependent, it was in no one's interest to call in debts precipitously. Better to bask in the web of relationships created by the debt culture, or as one historian called it, the "mesh of continuing loyalties."[34] Part of the "code of gentlemen's credit" was a "willingness to help a deserving planter restore his personal honor . . . even if that act placed one's own finances in jeopardy."[35] This was an expression of friendship in this agrarian economy. But in order to gain honor and show wealth, planters often plunged themselves deeper into debt. On the eve of the war in 1776 many of Virginia's great planters, fifty-five members of the House of Burgesses, as well as George Washington and Thomas Jefferson, had large debts.[36]

Of course, the early Virginia tobacco planter elites wanted to maximize their income (not just their honor). However, they were not quite yet agricultural capitalists on a par with the emerging British merchants with whom they were ultimately engaged in a global exchange.[37] Virginians had convinced themselves that credit was an advance (to bridge the gap until receipt for payment of a tobacco crop). Moreover, the Virginians projected their local values and mental categories onto their global commercial transactions and were confused when just before the Revolutionary War in the 1760s and 1770s they came out on the losing end as their debts were called in, their commercial "friendships" betrayed, and their (financial) independence lost. "They were dishonored."[38]

It is very difficult to follow the money trail of the horses that Thomas Jefferson bought from and sold to his friends, family, and acquaintances. This is because although "prices" were recorded in his account books, money rarely changed hands. Moreover, in Jefferson's account books we see that cash, much less full price, rarely directly passed hands in a horse transaction. Swift payment was not paramount; long-term relationships were.

Sometimes Jefferson obtained horses in a barter arrangement. In December 1813 Jefferson jotted down in his account book: "Bartered a gold watch with Sam Carr for a horse, got by Nosley, a red bay, 2 white hind feet, 6 years old."[39] At times the price was bartered in produce. In January 1775 Jefferson "bought" from his friend John Walker the horse Le Fleur for £35, "to be paid in wheat." However, we note in Jefferson's account book that the wheat did not yet exist. Jefferson went on to stipulate that the horse was to be paid in wheat "in Richmond at the current price in April 1776" (one year later). However, Jefferson further protected himself (and inadvertently revealed Walker's obvious overriding concern for their friendship rather than his payment) by writing, "If the stoppage of ports or other accident wheat does not sell tolerably, I am at liberty to withhold payment till it does only allowing 5 bushels percent ann. interest from that time" (*MB*, 390).

Occasionally the price was paid in labor. For example, in 1799 Jefferson sold the horse Darlington to Richard Richardson, a Monticello workman, for £60.[40] The £60 was due in two installments of work, "to wit £36 this year and £25 next year" (*MB*, 1001). Early in his career as a lawyer, Jefferson himself had been paid in horses for legal work done over a period of several years in the Shenandoah valley. His fee of £55 was "paid" by his two clients with a horse of William Waterson's worth £20 in September 1769 and with a horse of John Madison's worth £35 in January 1770 (*MB*, 94, 279, 299).

Supposedly, direct exchanges also took place but were almost always qualified so as to achieve true equity. Boot (extra) was paid if the quality of the animals was not equal. For example, in March 1773 Jefferson sold the horse Cuthona to Colonel Thomas Mann Randolph Sr. for a mule plus £15 boot (*MB*, 336). An exchange with boot was very common, and Jefferson bought at least ten horses this way, including his riding horse Jacobin in 1805, during his presidency. In 1774 Jefferson exchanged his black horse for a sorrel mare (later called Everallin) belonging to John Hylton.[41] However, Hylton thought the mare was with foal by young Fearnought, and if this was so, Jefferson was going to pay £3 "for putting her to horse" (*MB*, 368). In this case Jefferson seemed to have gotten the better part of the deal. Two days after the sale, Hylton came back and requested $40 more "to boot between our horses" because he was dissatisfied with their first bargain. There is no record that Everallin had a foal in 1774, but two years later, in December 1776, Jefferson paid off the £5 balance of the boot for Everallin to Hylton. In

1780 in Williamsburg Jefferson exchanged his three-year-old roan colt for his much-admired friend and mentor George Wythe's sorrel horse Thor. Nevertheless, the owners were sensitive to possible differences in value and agreed, in this case, to have the horses valued by Jerm. Baler "at the old prices" and to pay the difference. Moreover, Jefferson was to have his roan horse "broke & delivered next spring [1781] unless sooner called for" (*MB*, 494).[42]

Sometimes a complicated exchange would take place. In September 1783, Jefferson "received a horse" called Raleigh from Colonel Randolph in exchange for two horses, the General and Alfred, plus the promise to make the colonel a phaeton (a kind of carriage). Jefferson noted in his account book that he did not need to "find cushions or linings for the wings, etc., nor harness" for the phaeton (*MB*, 535). Moreover, in this exchange Jefferson was relieved of the "bond" he still owed on another horse, Sprightly, a blooded horse that he had bought from Randolph the previous May for £75 (the bond had not been due until May 1784) (*MB*, 531).

In one case we know of, Jefferson refused payment for a horse and gave a horse to his son-in-law Thomas Mann Randolph as a gift. The horse in question was the roan former race horse Tarquin, which Jefferson had bought from William Fitzhugh in Alexandria, Virginia, when Jefferson was on his way to be Washington's secretary of state in New York (and later in Philadelphia). Tarquin must have been a striking riding horse, because correspondents with Jefferson mentioned him more than a decade later (*PTJ*, 32: 400). However, upon making his plans for retirement to Monticello in 1793, Jefferson was at first reluctant to take the roan horse back to Monticello, saying that the horse's front feet were too tender for the rocky Albemarle trails: "I should not use him myself, because of his awkwardness in going down hill, that is to say half the time one is on him, as all is either up hill or down hill with us," he wrote to his son-in-law on 30 December 1793 (*PTJ*, 28:638). Jefferson offered to return the horse to Fitzhugh, who declined, saying he was no longer fit enough to ride such a horse. Although still looking for a buyer, Jefferson then made plans to send Tarquin back to Monticello. The horse was to be led to Georgetown on the Potomac and exchanged for a horse that his son-in-law Randolph had procured for him in Albemarle. There was an involved series of letters back and forth between Randolph and his father-in-law about the adequacy of the substitute horse. Nevertheless, on 4 September 1793 the horses were exchanged at Georgetown; Tarquin returned to Albemarle with a Monticello servant, and the substitute continued on to Philadelphia. Randolph took over the care of Tarquin and on 14 November wrote Jefferson that the horse had "mended so much that I must beg to have the preference at 120 Drs. if you are determined to part with him" (*PTJ*, 27:378). On 24 November, Jefferson answered Randolph, insisting that he keep the horse:

> I am happy that you think Tarquin will suit you, and insist on your accep-
> tance of him. This is no sacrifice to me, because my sole motive for having
> thought of parting with him was that he is unnecessary for me, as I must
> keep carriage horses, which will do to ride. I insist also as a condition,
> that you feel yourself perfectly free to part with him whenever he ceases
> to answer your end or you can by parting with him have your end better
> answered. From this moment then he is yours, and I am much happier in it
> than to have turned him over to any other person. (*PTJ*, 28:431)

Randolph again offered to pay for the horse, and a month later, on 30 December, Jefferson underlined that the horse was a gift: "I must repeat and insist that you take Tarquin, and on the express condition of making the most of him whenever you have good opportunity" (*PTJ*, 27:637).

When buying a horse, Jefferson rarely, if ever, handed over the full price when he took possession of the horse from a "seller." In fact, among ninety-two recorded instances in Jefferson's account books of an exchange or a transaction involving a horse, I found only one unambiguous instance in which the horse was completely paid for on the very day it was bought. This was when Jefferson purchased a handsome seven-year-old bay horse that he called Tecumseh from David Isaacs in Charlottesville.[43] Jefferson didn't pay in cash, of course, but drew a note on his account at Gibson and Jefferson (in Richmond) in favor of Isaacs for $125 on 14 June 1815, the day he recorded buying the horse. Jefferson noted, "paid in full for the sd. horse" (*MB*, 1311). Jefferson probably paid Isaacs in full because Isaacs was of a different social class than Jefferson's friends and neighbors, with whom he usually bought and sold horses. Isaacs was not a planter, nor did he belong to the Virginia elite. Rather, he was a Jewish merchant and shopkeeper with a general store on West Main Street in Charlottesville, married to a free woman of color, Ann West.[44] Jefferson kept running accounts at the store for goods and foodstuffs. Whatever the reason, this transaction with Isaacs was unique.

In the vast majority of cases, Jefferson negotiated a future date for payment, often explicitly dependent on the sale of his crops, and carefully recorded his obligations in his account book. Especially in the last twenty-five years of his life, Jefferson bought almost all of his horses on credit (rather than by barter or exchange).[45] Quite often Jefferson wrote in his account book, along with the description of the horse, the price agreed upon and when it was payable. For example, Jefferson bought Brimmer from Carter Braxton on 3 October 1790. As usual, Jefferson described the horse: "5 yrs old last spring, got by Brimmer, who was got by Eclipse." Jefferson then added: "Gave him my note 116.2/3 Doll., paiable at Philadelphia Dec. 31 or Richmond Jan.15" (*MB*, 762). On 12 January 1791 Jefferson sent Braxton a note from his bank, "remitted under cover of Dr. Currie" (*MB*, 809). Common future due dates were after three months, four months, six months, or a year. The money debt simply retraced the attachment of the horse to the previous owner.

In the case of Tarquin, however, the original seller, William Fitzhugh of Chatham, a fellow member of the gentry himself, pressed for cash, wrote Jefferson four months after having Tarquin delivered, requesting some immediate payment. Fitzhugh said he was anxious to know about Tarquin, having "never heard a Tittle respecting him" since Jefferson's letter confirming delivery:

> I must beg leave to request of you, when disengaged from more weighty Concerns, to inform me whether he has answered your Purpose. It is possible his lameness may have returned, and that he has not been equal to the Business, for which you intended him. If it shou'd be so, I am still willing that you shou'd dispose of him, on my Account, for any thing you may think him worth; but if on the contrary he has proved a good Horse, and you can, with the most perfect Conveniency to yourself, contrive me the seventy five Pounds, by some safe Conveyance, you will do me a singular Favour.—The loss of my tobacco and Corn last year, had thrown me so much in Arrears, that even a tolerable Crop of Wheat will not relieve me. (*PTJ*, 17:243)

Credit had advantages as well as disadvantages.

Jefferson never recorded "paying" for a horse using cash. Recall that during Jefferson's lifetime, Virginia agrarian society was not a cash economy. Usually Jefferson gave his bond (which was a promise of future payment) or simply waited and then wrote a note (like a check) on his account at his commercial accountant company. Sometimes payment went through a third party. For instance, in 1815 Jefferson bought a mare for $60 from a man called Cobb. Jefferson "drew on Archib. Robertson [his accountant] in favor of Jer. A. Goodman to be paid to Cobb" (*MB*, 1309).

Often Jefferson had to request an extension on his payment due date. The reaction of John Hartwell Cocke[46] to this request was typical: "I am sorry that you deemed it necessary to trouble yourself upon the subject of payment for the Horse, the understanding between us & the course of events prevents my expecting the money at this time, and be assured Sir, that I wish you to consult your convenience entirely about it in future."[47] As Breen noted, "It was the creditor, not the borrower, who made excuses."[48]

In most cases, at least with his horses, Jefferson did record final payment for those he bought on credit, albeit two or even three years later. In other cases, Jefferson arrived at another deal with the buyer before the amount was due. For example, Jefferson would "sell" the buyer a horse for the same price as the one he had contracted, thereby obviating his debt (it is not clear if money ever changed hands in these cases). For example, Jefferson sold a horse called Ryno to his brother Randolph for £35 on 19 February 1777. Six months later, on 31 August, Jefferson noted in his account book, "Bot Oroonoke of R. Jefferson & pd for him in full £36" (*MB*, 450). In another case, on 1 January 1815 Jefferson gave Pleasant German a note for $100 for a horse called Bedford, payable in a year, on 8 January 1816. Later, on 15 April 1815, Jefferson sold German a mare called Hyatilda for $100 and "received back my note for $100" (*MB*, 1306).

Most of the time we can assume that no interest was charged when Jefferson bought horses on credit. Once in awhile, however, Jefferson noted potential interest. On 9 October 1783, Jefferson "bought of" S. Carr's estate a sorrel mare and colt by giving his bond. Jefferson noted that the price was £40 10s. "if pd. by 1st of June 1784. If not, £41–16" (*MB*, 536). Interestingly, Jefferson's last overseer, Edmund Bacon, charged Jefferson interest on horses he sold him. For example, for Traveller, bought on 3 June 1817, the price was $120 with interest "from the first day of this month" (*MB*, 1334). Again, like Isaacs, Bacon, a paid workman and yeoman farmer, was not of the same social class as Jefferson and had no qualms about charging interest to Jefferson, to whom he lent money.

With these examples, I show that with horseflesh in Jefferson's time "buying" and "selling," "bartering" and "exchanging," "giving" and adjusting "boot," "credit" and "debt," "postponing payment" or "payment in full," "bonds" and "notes," were much more about social relationships than about just financial accounting. Horses bought became equated with people—neighbors, kin, sons-in-law, colleagues, mentors, and friends. Consequently, I think it is a misreading of the historical record to reduce "buying" and "selling" "blood horses" among eighteenth-century rural Virginia planters to mere market transactions. "Blood horses" were inalienable objects, and their carefully recorded pedigrees conflated many local ideas about class and other relationships of solidarity among the FFVs. The Virginia planter elite lived in a local economy that collapsed the moral and the material; commercial relationships were personal relationships. In the honor culture of the Tidewater planters, the flow of credit and debt still existed outside the capitalist market and could not be reduced to "economic rationality" or "self-maximization." A sale in which money was exchanged immediately avoided the enduring bond created through credit and debt. Examples show that Jefferson only paid cash when buying from men below gentry status. If we follow Mauss, buying (and selling) horses through credit and debt was like a gift exchange, because it led to a mutual interdependence over time between giver and receiver. So besides obtaining an animal (a condensed symbol of a class), when "buying" a horse, the Virginia gentleman reified a relationship with the animal's previous owner.

Thanks to Jefferson's habit of recording all his transactions assiduously in his *Farm Book,* account books, and letters, it is relatively easy to use the specifics of Thomas Jefferson's horse dealings in this special sphere of exchange in eighteenth-century Virginia. Following these trails also gives particular insight into this sometimes inscrutable man, who, although he lived twenty-six years into the nineteenth century,[49] remained in the grips of the eighteenth-century Virginia rural gentry's worldview all his life.

Others in Jefferson's planter's world (turfmen such as John Baylor) certainly bred horses to race and to stand at stud in a kind of entrepreneurial commodification of the animal. And other men in Jefferson's political world (such as Secretary of the Treasury Alexander Hamilton) were urbane cosmopolitans with a more economically liberal conception of debt. It was these men who actually led the United States into the economic future of the nineteenth century. In this way, Jefferson and his fellow Virginia planters were anachronisms. Nevertheless, to understand why Jefferson bought such expensive pedigreed horses when he was so deeply in debt, it is necessary to place Thomas Jefferson in the context of the earlier-eighteenth-century relational culture and gift society. Yes, Jefferson died "in debt"—and in this sense his world backfired on him—but during the first part of his life Jefferson knew the rules of his rural Virginia society, which were coherent and practical. Our accusatory questions are questions of a much later century.

Notes

1. Breen, 29.

2. As anthropological studies have shown, debt in many cultures advertises, even stands for, enduring social relations.

3. Gregory, 18.

4. In seventeenth-century Europe few true horse breeds existed. Rather we can talk about horse *types,* which were naturally selected groups of animals that shared certain physical characteristics (phenotype or appearance) or purpose. The animals had adapted to a specific and limited geographical location.

5. Both sire and dam must trace ancestry to the imported Oriental blood.

6. This is ironic given that the breed began by crossing three foreign horses with indigenous mares.

7. See Cassidy.

8. Harrison, *Early American Turf-stock,* 2:59.

9. Albemarle County, Virginia, is where Jefferson lived and built his home, Monticello.

10. George Washington once rode his Chincoteague pony, "Chinky," 147 miles from Mount Vernon to Williamsburg in a single day. Cavileer.

11. Bear, 60.

12. Quoted in Fithian, 233.

13. Fithian, 127. John Tayloe II (1721–79) was an important importer of English race horses. His plantation, Mt. Airy in Richmond County, was home to one of the largest studs in the state at the time, plus a one-mile racetrack.

14. In Virginia many FFVs were also proud of their relation to Pocahontas, the youngest daughter of Chief Powhatan, leader of the Native American peoples during the first ten years of English settlement, which began at Jamestown in 1607.

15. Jefferson's father-in-law, John Wayles, died in May 1773. After Wayles's will was probated, Jefferson, through his wife, Martha, inherited much wealth, doubling his landholdings and the number of his slaves. Many of the horses listed at the beginning of the *Farm Book* were inherited from Wayles.

16. Jefferson inherited this mare from his father-in-law upon his death in 1773.

17. Cassidy, 147.

18. The Godolphin Arabian was one of the three founding Oriental stallions of the Thoroughbred breed.

19. Harrison, *Early American Turf-stock,* 2:70. There are thirty-nine so-called American Foundation Mares, or Matriarchs, of the American Thoroughbred breed. These are the female taproot lines (from dam to grand dam, etc.) that produced the most racing winners. See http://www.tbheritage.com/HistoricDams/FamilyNumbers.html and http://www.stallionsoftware.com/amfam1.htm.

20. Jefferson, *Autobiography,* 1.

21. George Washington got his well-known bay war steed named Nelson from the same source.

22. Jefferson, *Garden and Farm Books,* 220.

23. Secretary John Carter (1689–1742), secretary of the colony from 1722 until his

death in 1743, was the oldest son of Robert "King" Carter (1663–1732), one of the wealthiest men and largest landholders of the colony. John Carter explored Albemarle County and owned almost the entire mountain known as Carter's Mountain. His son Edmund was a neighbor and friend of Jefferson's.

24. See Thoroughbred Heritage, "Fearnought."

25. At Baylor's death he had one hundred horses, including fifty Thoroughbreds.

26. Harrison, *Early American Turf-stock,* 2:117.

27. Another important son was Syme's Wildair, sire of Jefferson's horse while president, Wildair.

28. William Byrd III (1728–77) inherited the family land at Westover on the James. An inveterate gambler, Byrd lost the family fortune, made bad investments, and eventually, deep in debt, sold the family estate.

29. Cohen, 379, 381.

30. Breen, 85.

31. Ibid., 94; Sloan, 29, 41.

32. Sloan, 29.

33. Breen, 94.

34. Ibid., 96.

35. Ibid., 102.

36. Ibid., 128.

37. According to Breen, 73, economic historians have discovered that the planters were naive about international market procedures.

38. See ibid., 31.

39. Jefferson, *Jefferson's Memorandum Books,* 1296; hereafter cited as *MB.*

40. Darlington is another complicated case. Jefferson's son-in-law John Wayles Eppes bought Darlington for Jefferson in 1796 with money from the estate of Jefferson's deceased father-in-law, John Wayles (*MB,* 941). Jefferson was to credit Wayles's estate for £65, the debts of which Jefferson was responsible for. Jefferson never succeeded in repaying these debts in his lifetime. Nevertheless he "sold" Darlington to Richardson for labor in 1799.

41. Hylton was an importer of cattle and horses and the comptroller of the Port of the James River, Upper District. Jefferson, *Thomas Jefferson's Farm Book,* 519.

42. Also in Jefferson, *Papers of Thomas Jefferson,* 17:512; hereafter cited as *PTJ.*

43. Tecumseh became one of a team of four carriage horses for Jefferson's landau.

44. Isaacs's daughter Julia Ann married Eston Hemings, who was a son of Sally Hemings and Thomas Jefferson, in 1832.

45. This may point to the progressively commercial ethos of the times compared with the former mutual interdependence of the agrarian planter economy.

46. John Hartwell Cocke was a friend, intellectual colleague, political protégé, fellow planter, and neighbor (in the next county) of Jefferson's. However, Cocke was a generation younger than Jefferson.

47. Cocke to Jefferson, 27 August 1814, in Jefferson, *Thomas Jefferson's Farm Book,* 107.

48. Breen, 103.

49. Thomas Jefferson lived from 1743–1826.

Works Cited

Bear, James A. *Jefferson at Monticello: Recollections of a Monticello Slave and of a Monticello Overseer.* Charlottesville: University Press of Virginia, 1967.

Breen, T. H. *Tobacco Culture: The Mentality of the Great Tidewater Planters on the Eve of Revolution.* Princeton, NJ: Princeton University Press, 1985.

Cassidy, Rebecca. *The Sport of Kings: Kinship, Class and Thoroughbred Breeding in Newmarket.* Cambridge: Cambridge University Press, 2002.

Cavileer, Sharon. "George Washington's Horse." 2007. http://www.equisearch.com/horses _riding_training/travel/eqmtvernon2213/.

Cohen, Kenneth. "Well Calculated for the Farmer: Thoroughbreds in the Early National Chesapeake, 1790–1850." *Virginia Magazine of History and Biography* 115, no. 3 (2007): 370–411.

Evans-Pritchard, E. E. *Nuer Religion.* Oxford: Clarendon, 1956.

Fithian, Philip Vickers. *Journal and Letters of Philip Vickers Fithian, 1773–1774: A Plantation Tutor of the Old Dominion.* Ed. Hunter Dickenson Farish. Williamsburg, VA: Colonial Williamsburg, 1943.

Graeber, David. *Debt: The First Five Thousand Years.* Brooklyn, NY: Melville House, 2011.

Gregory, Chris. *Gifts and Commodities.* London: Academic, 1982.

Harrison, Fairfax. *Early American Turf-stock, 1730–1830.* 2 vols. Richmond, VA: Old Dominion, 1934–35.

———. *The Equine FFV's: A Study of the Evidence for the English Horses Imported into Virginia before the Revolution.* Richmond, VA: Old Dominion, 1928.

Jefferson, Thomas. *Autobiography.* Keswick, VA: Thomas Jefferson Society, 1821. http://libertyonline.hypermall.com/Jefferson/Autobiography.html#return.

———. *The Garden and Farm Books of Thomas Jefferson.* Ed. Robert C. Baron. Golden, CO: Fulcrum, 1987.

———. *Jefferson's Memorandum Books: Accounts, with Legal Records and Miscellany, 1767–1826.* Ed. James A. Bear and Lucia C. Stanton. Princeton, NJ: Princeton University Press, 1997.

———. *The Papers of Thomas Jefferson.* Ed. Julian Boyd et al. 60 vols. to date. Princeton, NJ: Princeton University Press, 1950–.

———. *Thomas Jefferson's Farm Book: With Commentary and Relevant Extracts from Other Writings.* Ed. Edwin Morris M. Betts. Charlottesville: Thomas Jefferson Memorial Foundation, 1999.

Mauss, Marcel. *The Gift: Forms and Functions of Exchange in Archaic Society.* 1954. Reprint, London: Routledge, 1990.

Sloan, Herbert E. *Principle and Interest: Thomas Jefferson and the Problem of Debt.* Charlottesville: University Press of Virginia, 1995.

Thoroughbred Heritage. "Fearnought." http://www.tbheritage.com/Portraits/Fearnought .html.

The Jamaican Plantation

Industrial, Global, Contested

LOUIS P. NELSON

A bumpy, twenty-minute drive south from the coastal highway takes you to Good Hope, John Tharp's late-eighteenth-century Jamaican plantation.[1] Passing the steep drive up to the great house, the road leads to a stone warehouse on the way to the rushing waters of the Martha Brae River. Just before the river, on a flat parcel to the right stands a substantial cut-stone building that now serves as an orange-packing plant (fig. 1). This was Good Hope's boiling house, where raw cane juice was purified, separating molasses and other residue from the thick cane syrup that would cure into crystalized sugar. When in production, the boiling house was the center of any plantation's sugar works, and the sugar works was the center of the sugar plantation.[2] I argue here that the boiling house on any Jamaican sugar plantation stood at the heart of an extraordinary landscape, simultaneously industrial, global, and contested.

Unlike the processing of tobacco or rice, the processing of sugar was a very complicated process that required careful synchronization of both labor and product. One late-eighteenth-century planter described the sugar plantation as "a well-constructed machine, compounded of various wheels, turning in different ways, and yet all contributing to the great end proposed."[3] Enslaved laborers planted acres of cane shoots in straight rows. Once the cane was cut, the sugar juice in the cane would begin to ferment within hours, so recently cut cane had to be quickly crushed in a mill, extracting the juice to be carried to the boiling house for reduction in a series of large boilers into molasses and purified cane juice. The press to refine the sugar before it spoiled, together with the financial investment of starting up the boiling process and the constant drive toward greater profits, meant that boiling houses often ran twenty-four hours a day for days or weeks at a time. The juice was then cured in a huge curing house, usually for weeks, before being packaged into hogsheads for exportation. The molasses by-product either was used as a calorie supplement for the enslaved or could be dis-

Figure 1. Good Hope boiling house, Trelawney Parish, Jamaica, built mid-eighteenth century, expanded c. 1802. (Photo by author)

tilled into rum, usually in another large building called a "distillery." A sugar works was a substantial capital investment; there was no such thing as a small sugar planter.

John Tharp's boiling house, as it stands today, is a late-eighteenth-century threefold expansion of an earlier boiling house that stood on the property through the eighteenth century (fig. 2). Careful examination of the building's plan reveals that the grander elevation of the building encased a mid-eighteenth-century boiling house that likely stood on the site when Tharp purchased the property in 1766. Measuring 37 feet long by 16 feet wide, the mid-eighteenth-century boiling house was already a fairly large, industrial-scale building. But Tharp substantially enlarged the building to 64 feet long by 34 feet wide. In the flush of refining, this boiling house disgorged smoke and heat, running continuously through night and day as teams of exhausted slaves ladled scalding-hot syrup from one cauldron to another. The boiling house was the epicenter of the plantation and the center of "clock time consciousness," to use Justin Roberts's phrase.[4] The boiling house was so central, in fact, that one overseer assured the plantation owner that "the Boiling House has been my constant residence all day as soon as light would permit work to be done."[5] And as at Good Hope, Jamaica's boiling houses were usually paired with equally large curing houses, where enslaved Afri-

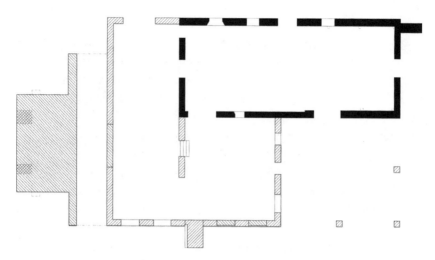

Figure 2. Plan of Good Hope boiling house, Trelawney Parish, Jamaica, mid-eighteenth-century boiling house in solid black, 1802 expansion hatched. (Plan by author)

cans poured the thick syrup into heavy clay molds to cure into crystal cones. In scale and complexity of form and process, these buildings were not agricultural but industrial.

The investment of a sugar works was in not only buildings but also machinery. One seventeenth-century writer warned that planters would want regularly to inspect "the Rollers, the Goudges, Sockets, Sweeps, Cogs, or Braytrees," because if any of these failed, "the whole work stands still." The same would be true of the equipment in the boiling house, where the brick platforms that carried the boilers might crack or break "by the violence of the heat from the Furnaces." Again, such a mishap meant "a stop in the work, till that be mended." In each case, the single failure would bring the entire process to a halt, "for all these depend on one another, as wheels in a Clock."[6] And bringing the process to a halt meant a significant loss, as all cut cane would be spoilt before the machinery was repaired. Replacing a burnt or cracked boiler, for example, would take at least fifteen days, and that if a replacement were on hand.[7] In preparation for a harvest to begin in five days' time, enslaved "Masons, Millwrights, and Coppersmiths" were all "busy repairing the works" on Colbeck, according to one early-nineteenth-century visitor.[8] In his comparison of the sugar works to a clock, Richard Ligon recognized not only the delicacy and interdependence of the machinery of a sugar plantation but also the time discipline required for fiscal success.[9] But it was also important to enlist slaves who knew how to operate the machinery, because mishaps were often fatal. As described by one planter, "If a stiller slip into a rum-cistern, it is sudden death; for it stifles in a moment. If a mill-feeder be catched by the finger, his whole body is drawn in, and he is squeezed to pieces. If a boiler gets any part into the scalding sugar, it sticks like glue, or birdlime, and 'tis hard to save either limb or life."[10] As a result, preserving the lives of the more skilled slaves working in the sugar works was important to a smooth and profitable operation. As the historian Justin Roberts has argued, planters "flinched more at the loss of labor than at the loss of life."[11]

The Jamaican sugar plantation was obviously agricultural, but it was also industrial.[12] While the traditional historical narrative identifies the third quarter of the eighteenth century as the time of the launch of Britain's famous industrial revolution, more recent scholarship has come to question the notion of a temporal threshold, arguing instead for a gradual emergence of industrialization over the course of the eighteenth century.[13] Additionally, industrialization has historically been located in the motherland. But a number of recent historians of the Caribbean have rightly noted that the sugar plantation, while agricultural in product, was decidedly industrial in process. That the boiling house was a major center of British industrialism was a point powerfully reinforced by the fact that boiling houses often burned in shifts through the night. The time and labor discipline central to the successful operation of a sugar plantation is one of the central features of industrialization. The complexity of the process required the organization of the labor force into "interchangeable units," another dimension of industrialization. Jamaica's sugar plantations were among the earliest and most economically important dimensions of Britain's nascent industrial revolution.

The sugar works, of course, depended entirely on the labor of those slaves that lived in the plantation village, the collection of houses used to shelter the enslaved inhabitants. The village at Good Hope appears to have comprised about fifty individual buildings, each positioned on its own small lot (fig. 3). The houses built for and by Africans in eighteenth-century Jamaica appear to have varied little in form or materials.[14] Usually containing two rooms, each measuring only 10 feet by 8 feet, the houses usually had mud walls and thatch roofs and were in form not unlike examples still found along the West African coast (fig. 4). Most accounts report that the houses were "composed of hard posts driven into the ground."[15] The whole of the house frame was lashed secure with vines, "which the wood[s] afford of various sizes in great abundance," and the interior and exterior of each wall was "plaistered smoothly with mud."[16] Some early-nineteenth-century

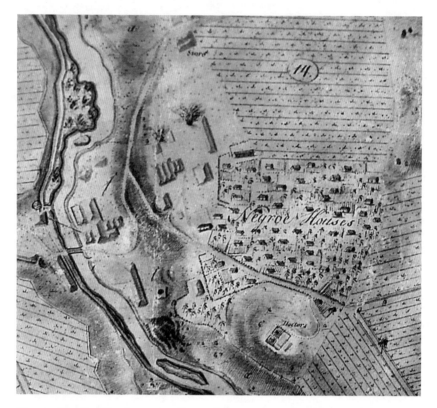

Figure 3. Detail of the plantation village site, Good Hope plantation plat. (Private collection)

accounts and sketches suggest that wattle houses also had what were de-scribed as foundations. But rather than foundations in the traditional sense, with a house frame resting on masonry, these were stones placed around the base of the exterior walls to offer support to the earthfast posts and to hinder erosion by rain.[17] The roofs were almost always made of palm or coconut thatch descending from either side of a horizontal ridge pole, with some bending from one side down to the opposite side of the roof "in such a man-ner as affords no admittance for the rain to penetrate."[18]

Critical to the house site was the yard garden, providing some provisions for those in the house to consume but also generating revenue (fig. 5).[19] As one writer argued, "With their surplus produce, and their pigs and poultry, they supply even to the distance of Anotto Bay, and from this traffic derive a very considerable profit." Africans commonly grew yams, cassava, corn, plantains, bananas, mangoes, oranges, and other fruit as well as pens for hogs and poultry.[20] "Being always intermingled with fruit-trees . . . the Ne-

Figure 4. Ewe House, vicinity of Cape Coast, Ghana. (Photo by author)

Figure 5. Sketch of a plantation village, artist unknown, from the Storer Sketchbook, c. 1820. (Private collection)

groes' own planting and property," these villages often included breadfruit, mangoes, oranges, plantains, cocoa, and pepper trees.[21] Interspersed with trees, slave villages were often described as picturesque by late-eighteenth-century British observers.

Comprising clusters of houses, each positioned on its own parcel and supported by an aggregate of smaller sheds and pens, the village was the site of a wide range of everyday activities. The activities animating life in the village that received the most commentary by white observers were music and dancing. As numerous scholars have made clear, music and dance played a critical role in West African life, and this persisted to Jamaica's shores. While most observers derided the dancing as grotesque, a few recognized its complexity. Wrote Matthew Lewis, "I am told there is a regular figure, and that the least mistake, or a single false step is immediately noticed by the rest."[22] Dancing was almost always supported by drumming. Because white planters knew the function of the drum as a vehicle for communication, drumming was outlawed in Jamaica, although it was practiced all the time regardless.[23]

The village was also, of course, the site of occasional events of great importance, specifically births and deaths within the community. A number of sources make clear that a newborn child was not considered viable until it had survived the first nine days, time spent entirely inside the mother's house.[24] As Edward Brathwaite has argued, the birth of a child was often followed by the burial of the placenta near the house of birth; often a small tree was planted over the site, establishing a connection between the child, the tree, and the house site. But the house site was also important at the time of death. A deceased enslaved African was occasionally buried in the immediate vicinity of his or her house and garden, sometimes even under the bed.[25] In this practice, the documentary record is substantiated by house-yard burials from the archaeological record.[26] Douglas Armstrong excavated four burials associated with early- to mid-eighteenth-century house-yard sites from Seville plantation, providing information about burial practices and the use of coffins and grave goods.[27] The village was typically the site of elaborate mourning practices. Thomas Thistlewood reported that on the death of one of his slaves, the slave's wife "killed a heifer, several hogs, &c. to entertain her company with." The company spent an entire day and night "singing &c. at the Negro houses," possibly encouraged by the eighty gallons of rum provided by their master.[28] Another account reports that "the body [is] put in the ground; all the while they are covering it with Earth, the Attendants scream out in a terrible manner, which is not the effect of Grief, but of Joy; they beat on their Wooden Drums and their Women with their Rattles make a hideous noise."[29] But the celebration of the death of a master was equally riotous. Thistlewood noted that upon the occasion of the death of his nephew, the slaves of the village blew on a shell, and "afterwards in the Night 2 guns fired with a loud huzza after each." The overt celebration of the death of an oppressor was noted by Thistlewood as only "Strange Impudence."[30]

The village was also the locus for the practice of Obeah, a complex belief system that involved spirits in the events of everyday life.[31] In one early-nineteenth-century account, a visitor reported on a conversation with an elderly slave who suggested that charms and talismans were common: "The old patriarch said, that 'formerly people minded the *puntees,* hung up in trees and grounds as charms to keep off thieves.'"[32] Individuals described as Obeah men or Obeah women would have a regional reputation and could wield significant authority over other slaves in their district.[33] Obeah was also enlisted in assaults on whites. According to one report, for example, a slave had thrown a headless fowl down a well in an effort to enact revenge on his master for sending his sister to work as a field slave.[34] In this common practice, the plantation well became a point of weakness in the machinery of the plantation, a point assaulted by particularly aggravated slaves. The practice of Obeah required numerous talismans and sacred objects, including "blood, feathers, Parrots Beaks, Dogs Teeth, Alligators Teeth, broken Bottles, Grave Dirt, Rum, Egg-shells," among others.[35] Such a range of objects meant that particularly active Obeah practitioners transformed their quarters into veritable markets of such sacred items, as was described by one Jamaican planter in a 1775 account from his own plantation:

Upon hearing [of the report of an Obeah woman] he repaired directly with Six White Servants to the old Woman's House, and forcing open the Door, observed the whole Inside of the Roof (which was thatch), and every Crevice of the Walls, stuck with the Implements of her Trade, consisting of Rags, Feathers, Bones of Cats, and a thousand other Articles. Examining further, a large earthen Pot or Jar, close covered, was found concealed under her Bed—It contained a prodigious Quantity of round Balls of Earth or Clay of various Dimensions, large and small, whitened on the Outside, and variously compounded, some with Hair or Rags or Feathers of all sorts, and strongly bound with Twine; other blended with the upper section of the skulls of Cats or stuck round with Cats Teeth and Claws, or with Human or Dogs Teeth, and some Glass Beads of Different colours.

Upon the discovery, the planter burned the house to the ground and sold the woman to slave traders from Cuba.[36]

Yet Jamaican planters knew that they needed not just a workforce but a compliant workforce, since the labor of slaves "is the foundation of [our] riches."[37] But if that workforce was central to the wealth of the planters and even the nation at large, it was also a potential tinderbox. Tacky's Rebellion in 1760 was only the most extraordinary and horrific of a series of slave insurrections on the island throughout the eighteenth and nineteenth centuries, reinforcing the baldly honest sentiment of one planter: "However they may disguise it, [slaves] hate their masters and wish them destroyed."[38] As a result, British planters enlisted the plantation as a landscape of control, exercising authority over the enslaved majority through fear, which Bryan Edwards suggested was "the leading principle upon which the government is supported."[39]

From their first encounter with Africans through to emancipation, Jamaican planters used corporal torture as a means of punishing those who resisted their slavery. One writer noted that if any slaves "committed robbery, prove sullen, or refuse to work," they were bound hand and foot to the whipping post, "which they have in all plantations." The whipping was followed by a salt rub, which proved so painful that it "forces 'em to their work againe." If their infraction was serious, however, planters and overseers substituted molasses for the salt and left the slave to "stand for some time for the wasps, merrywigs and other insects to torment."[40] The practice of securing an African to a post with rope or bilboes—iron wrist and ankle restraints—for whipping was common throughout the period of slavery, as was the practice of covering the bloody body of the victim with lime juice, pepper oil, molasses, salt, or anything else that might amplify the pain.[41] The overseer (later owner) Thistlewood also used human feces, which he rubbed on the faces of disciplined slaves.[42] On occasion he required one slave to urinate into the face and mouth of another.[43] His most extreme version of these practices, however, was "Derby's Dose," in which the flogging and salt-pickle rub was followed by the order of one slave to defecate in the open mouth of the victim. The African was then "immediately put in a gag whilst his mouth was full," and the gag was left in place for hours.[44] As recent historians have demonstrated, there was no limit to the punishments white planters and overseers in eighteenth-century Jamaica might exact.[45]

Jamaica was also a landscape of death. Many towns had places of public execution, and on occasion such executions extended also to the landscapes

Figure 6. Untitled Jamaican scene by Pierre Eugene D'Simitiere, c. 1760s. The gibbet is in the left of the image. (Library Company of Philadelphia)

of plantations. In May 1764, one diarist noted in passing, "A Negro wench hanged at Savannah la Mar today."[46] A few years later he noted that "Stompe, was burnt alive this evening, and his wife (Dr. Frazier's Polly, a mulatto) was hanged."[47] Just months later, he recorded that "as I was coming home [from Savannah la Mar] they were hanging two Rebel Negroes."[48] On another occasion, a "stout Negro man . . . is gibbetted alive in the [Savannah la Mar] Square," hanged in an iron cage from a post and left to die of thirst and exposure.[49] In the 1760s, one European traveler to Jamaica produced an astonishing sketch of a double gibbet, one empty, the other not (fig. 6). Among the most horrible executions recorded by Thomas Thistlewood was of the surviving rebellious Africans from Tacky's Rebellion in 1760. One slave, condemned to be burnt alive, was "made to sit on the ground, and his body being chained to an iron stake, the fire was applied to his feet." Thistlewood was amazed at the man's courage: "He uttered not a groan, and saw his legs reduced to ashes with the utmost firmness and composure." Other slaves were simply hanged.[50] These public executions had an afterlife that marked the plantation landscape. In 1774 Thistlewood noted that "the head of Gold, the Rebel, [was] carried to Leeward this evening, to be put up as a terror," a reminder to slaves of the consequences of rebellion.[51] In the early nineteenth century another sugar planter openly acknowledged "the necessity of terror to coerce . . . obedience."[52] Such terrors were not uncommon and were to be found along roadways and on plantations.[53] On one occasion, Lady Nugent reported that if she had not already promised her attendance at church, "I would not have gone, for we were obliged to pass close by the pole, on which was stuck the head of a black man who was executed a few days ago."[54] In another example, the head of one planter's slave—a thief and a persistent runaway—was put on a pole and "Stuck . . . in the home pasture."[55]

White male power over enslaved Africans was exacted in particular ways on enslaved women. The names of many of the female slaves at Good Hope suggest that their physical appearance was noticed by the white men who named them: Beauty, Grace, Venus, Plaything.[56] As Trevor Burnard has demonstrated, planters and overseers raped their female enslaved Africans as a mechanism of social control.[57] Thistlewood's journal records sexual activity with 138 women in his thirty-seven-year tenure on Jamaica, averaging 14 women a year. And while it is clear that Thistlewood had preferred sexual partners, he was never monogamous. On numerous occasions, Thistlewood raped women as punishment for transgressions.[58] While the extent to which Thistlewood's sexual predation was typical is uncertain, it is clear that he and many other men regularly preyed on enslaved women.[59] His most frequent victims were his own slaves; of the women he owned, only the very young and the very old escaped his advances.[60] But the fact that he raped 63 slaves who were owned by others is evidence enough that planters and overseers felt free to prey on women beyond those they owned for both pleasure and discipline.[61] The reality of consistent rape meant that for enslaved women the plantation became a landscape of fear in a way unknown by their male counterparts. Women fell victim to Thistlewood in the curing house, in the wash house, in cane fields, on the loading dock, on a hill overlooking the sea, on the garden bench, and in their own provision grounds.[62] In a 1751 account, Thistlewood reported having sex with Flora "among the canes." He likely happened upon her, as he indicated that "she [had] been for water cress."[63] He raped Ellin "in the garden," where just the day before she had been "weeding."[64] Thistlewood even raped women in the houses of other slaves.[65] Like his assaults on Flora and Ellin, the vast majority of these encounters were unanticipated by the women who bore the brunt of his desire. In response, enslaved women surely navigated the plantation in a way that attended to this fear. Many who had been raped on the garden bench— one of Thistlewood's favorite spots—would surely have avoided the garden when they thought he might present himself. Furthermore, those who undertook to leave their own plantation without permission risked likely rape if they were caught traveling illegally and alone.[66]

These realities of life on Jamaican plantations marked those landscapes with sites of terror that simply do not appear on plantation plats. Whipping posts were common and well-used sites of discipline. Numerous slaves, especially runaways and those caught otherwise avoiding labor, were punished first with whippings and then with extended agony through the application of various juices, oils, and syrups. The public display of these beatings mirrored the public executions taking place in most town squares. Executions were often followed by the public display of the victim's head, posted on roadways and on plantations as objects of terror. And for enslaved women, the plantation landscape was a landscape of rape, where white planters and overseers unleashed their desire and punishment on women in fields, on garden benches, in curing houses, and in their own homes.

Over the course of the eighteenth century, the explicit violence to black bodies came under question. In 1781, for example, the Jamaican Assembly outlawed mutilation and dismemberment as forms of discipline.[67] While the degree of amelioration remains in question, the late eighteenth century brought with it increasing moral anxiety about corporal and capital punishment.[68] In the context of gradual and uneven moral uncertainty about torture, planters added a second mechanism to suppress slave resistance and to support the smooth operations of the plantation: surveillance. The capacity to see was from the beginning focused on slaves' spaces of labor, not on their spaces of residence. The 1752 *Art of Making Sugar,* for example, makes clear that sugar should be planted in straight rows so as to better "inspect the negroes employed in weeding the canes, etc."[69] And slowly the person undertaking surveillance began to change. The vast majority of seventeenth- and early-eighteenth-century planters in Jamaica oversaw their own plantations. Yet by the middle decades of the century—not entirely disconnected from the rising numbers of Scots immigrants—more planters began hiring overseers rather than doing that work themselves. As a result, probate inventories of planters' houses from the first half of the century make occasional references to a room given over specifically for use by an overseer.[70] As their wealth increased, later eighteenth-century planters came to see themselves as country gentlemen, preferring to hire overseers to actually manage the day-to-day operations of the plantation. The increasing distinction between planter and overseer is evident in inventories of plantations from the second half of the century, which replace the overseer's room with an overseer's house.[71] The introduction of the person of the overseer over the course of the eighteenth century foregrounded oversight—or surveillance—as central to plantation management.[72] By extension the later-eighteenth-century overseer's house not only symbolized white authority—as did the planter's great house—but also offered easy surveillance over the plantation.

Overseers' houses were commonly outfitted with piazzas, and while these features surely helped to mediate the heat, they also served to facilitate surveillance. Thomas Thistlewood's recorded in his journal in 1754 that his newly built overseer's house boasted both front and back piazzas (fig. 7).[73] Upon traveling to another plantation's overseer's house some years later, he noted that the overseer was keen to show him the view from his piazza.[74] But the view in question was surely not just the picturesque landscape; as overseers these men had a particular interest in the ability to survey the activity of the plantation, especially the ongoing labors of the sugar works. William Beckford's description of an overseer's house presumed the presence of "a front and a back piazza," spaces for comfortable viewing of the works.[75] And the literal oversight and management of the plantation from the piazza was increasingly assisted by the use of timepieces and telescopes. In 1754, for example, Thistlewood had two of his slaves flogged for "meddling with my watch and telescope," both of which were kept on the piazza.[76] Overseers managed shifts by clock time as early as the early eighteenth century, well before similar regimes appeared in factories in England or on plantations in Virginia or South Carolina.[77] One visitor to a Jamaican sugar plantation recognized that the overseer kept meticulous accounts of hours and recorded daily in log books but that "he has no Clock, nothing but an Hour Glass to put the people to work by."[78] The absence of a watch or clock was remarkable. John Lord's 1788 probate inventory included an overseer's house on his plantation; the only object listed at the overseer's house was "a spyglass," an object provided by the owner to the overseer to more fully execute his responsibilities.[79] Telescopes, also called "spyglasses," appear commonly alongside hourglasses in probate inventories of the period; by the second half of the century they were ever present on piazzas and balconies.[80] On his tour through Jamaica in the early nineteenth century, Cynric Williams found himself sitting on a piazza disturbed by a commotion from the vicinity of the sugar works: "I looked through the spy glass (a very usual piece of furniture in every piazza) towards the quarter whence the noise of the whip appeared to come, and observed a black man laid on the ground, and two drivers flogging him."[81] If the telescope allowed the overseer supernatural views into the workings of the plantation, a watch or hourglass allowed the imposition of time discipline over a process that depended heavily on careful timing.[82] A third object found on overseers' piazzas was the plantation plat. An inventory of one overseer's house, for example, included "an old plan of the estate" recorded "on the front piazza."[83] As Barry Higman has argued, the plantation plat became a significant management tool allowing overseers to "see" the plantation in entirely new ways. Over the course of

Figure 7. North elevation of Mount Plenty plantation, St. Ann's Parish, Jamaica, built c. 1770. (Photo by author)

the eighteenth century, the piazza had become a convenient stage for surveillance.

One dimension of surveillance that played a critical role in control was the practice of ticketing and branding. Mid-eighteenth-century slaves, for example, were required to have a ticket of passage from their owners giving specific allowance for traveling beyond the bounds of their plantations.[84] Many planters enlisted the watchful eyes of their peers through slave branding.[85] Thomas Thistlewood, for example, was so frustrated with one slave who made a persistent practice of running away that he branded her on the forehead, forever marking his ownership of her and raising the probability of questioning by others when she was away from his plantation.[86] Early advertisements in the newspapers make clear that branding was fairly common: "Anthony, a Mandingo, RS on right shoulder," or "York, a Coromantee, to Mrs. Slack, at Falmouth, the brand marks on his shoulders are illegible," or "Jack, a Congo, marked BL left shoulder."[87] Through regular requests for tickets or through the visible markings of a brand, Jamaican planters enlisted the eyes of their peers in the collective surveillance of the enslaved.

As surveillance became an increasing concern in Jamaica, some planters worked to extend this control to the architecture and organization of the village, but with very limited success. As suggested by the plat of Good

Figure 8. Barracks quarters at Mount Plenty plantation, St. Ann's Parish, Jamaica. (Photo by author)

Hope, the slave village there was an aggregate of small plots of land each containing a single house and separated one from the next by a fence. There is no evidence of linear or orthogonal organization. Using plats as a data set, Higman has determined that only 22 percent of villages were organized in straight streets, with a concentration between 1790 and 1810.[88] In 1790 William Beckford noted the increasing tendency to build quarters in streets: "It is the custom now to have [quarters] built in straight lines, constructed with some degree of uniformity and strength, but totally divested of trees and shrubs."[89] The absence of trees and shrubs, so important to the slave yard gardens, allowed unobstructed sightlines. In his assessment of the slave village at Seville, Douglas Armstrong argues that the positioning of the street was oriented to "maximize planter surveillance and control."[90] John Baillie, of Roehampton, built a range of quarters in what he described as barracks "to distinguish them from houses with each of them ground around them; a barrack is a range of houses, or a row of houses, not detached."[91] Standing not far from the main house at Phoenix plantation is a longitudinal building that was once a row of four quarter chambers, each with a door opening onto the shallow stoop that faces toward the main house and a window opening through the rear wall into each room. Another example survives also at Mount Plenty plantation, this one fronted by a piazza (fig. 8).

The earliest reference to quartering in attached units appears in a 1774 description of a wattle-and-thatch row, but barracks-style housing did not become common in Jamaica and across the Caribbean until the 1790s.[92] In his examination of slave quartering in the Danish West Indies, William Chapman found abundant evidence for the construction of such barracks beginning in the 1790s and lasting well into the early nineteenth century.[93] In fact, he asserts that almost all of St. Croix's quartering was rebuilt sometime between the 1790s and the early 1830s. The architectural similarities between barracks on Jamaica and on St. Croix and their simultaneous appearance in the 1790s reinforce Chapman's claim that these new building forms derive from broader "improvements" to workers' housing across the British Empire.[94] Surviving 1790s examples from England include the rows of duplexes built by John Tharp for the laborers on his English country estate, Chippenham Village, in Cambridgeshire (fig. 9). These were likely inspired by conversations about agricultural improvement in England that first took visual expression in John Wood's 1781 publication of *A Series of Plans for Cottages or Habitations of the Laborer either in Husbandry or the Mechanic Arts* (fig. 10). In that volume, which was republished in 1792 and again in 1806, Wood not only offers designs for laborers' houses but also advocates for improved conditions. Interestingly, Tharp undertook purpose-built housing for his

Figure 9. Workers' housing, Chippenham Village, Cambridgeshire, England, late eighteenth century. (Photo by author)

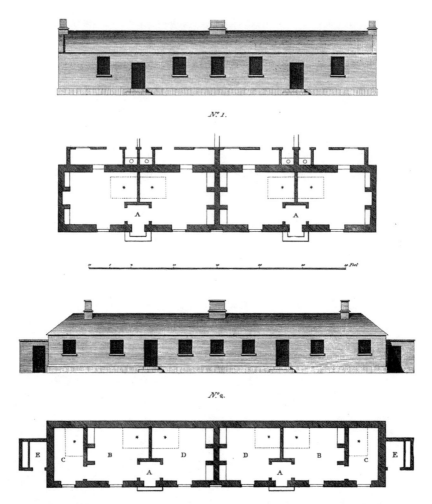

Figure 10. Cottages with One Room, plate 3 from John Wood, *A Series of Plans for Cottages or Habitations of the Laborer either in Husbandry or the Mechanic Arts,* 1781. (Harvard Library)

English laborers but not for his Jamaican laborers, who the plat suggests continued to live in individual houses.

Some documentary evidence suggests that slaves resisted their relocation from open villages to linearly aligned streets. John Baillie would write that although he built a slave village of houses uniform in size and shape, at first his slaves "refused to occupy them, stating, that they were so much exposed to their neighbors, they did not like to let them know what they were doing on all occasions."[95] Eventually, however, the Africans "got a fashion among them, and would not make fires in several of their houses; they spoiled my range by putting kitchens or outbuildings in front of some of them for themselves."[96] While planters might have directed the construction of streets or rows on sites devoid of large vegetation, allowing greater surveillance over those spaces, enslaved Africans fought back by building attendant buildings and sheds that restored their privacy. If British planters always exacted terror to reinforce their authority over Africans, they also eventually imposed surveillance over the landscape, although often with limited success.

John Tharp spent much of the 1790s rebuilding his plantation at Good Hope. The plantation he purchased in the 1760s was already marked by a great house and a sugar works standing amid cane fields. But in the closing years of the eighteenth century he drastically enlarged his boiling house, a transformation still visible in the landscape. However, he was not alone in rebuilding in the 1790s. The late eighteenth century was a time of substantial reconstruction of plantation landscapes across the island. As successful planters began to build sugar empires, they had the wealth and capacity to build increasingly sophisticated sugar works centrally positioned amid their fields. Planters provided peripheral and unproductive land to their enslaved Africans for the construction of villages, and unlike their counterparts in mainland America, Jamaican planters generally left their enslaved Africans to build their own houses, creating a space removed from the pulse of sugar processing. Thus, Jamaica's landscapes of sugar production were very near the forefront of the emergent British industrial revolution. With an intensive focus on time discipline, a compliant workforce, intensive capital investment in machinery, and interchangeable components, the island's sugar plantations undermine common misconceptions of Jamaica as both backwards and marginal, and they contest national histories of Britain that explode the empire's colonial holdings.

Jamaica's plantations were also intensively global. Most obviously, they were characterized by a European- or Jamaican-born white minority and a majority African population. These landscapes were often described as African in nature, with spaces for the enslaved imaged as little African villages. But these places were also global in their connectivity to international networks of productivity and commodity exchange. The continuous inflow of Africans depended on a very complex system of transatlantic investment, insurance schemes, and capital flows. The mechanisms for product transfer from Jamaica back to Britain—usually for final processing—expanded the global networks back to the places of capital origin. Most importantly, the Jamaican plantation was intensively contested; enslaved Africans were not

passive. Neither planter nor slave was ignorant of the fact that the plantation depended entirely on the coerced labor of the enslaved. This meant
that the plantation was also a landscape of terror, marked by heads of rebellion slaves, whipping posts, and sites of rape. Even trespassing had its
dangers. Thistlewood "set traps of nails in boards in the paths through the
thatch against the Lime-Kiln provision ground." In order to protect his own
slaves, he "acquainted all my Negroes of them."[97] Since slaves were rarely
provided with shoes, the unawares slave passing along that path was des-
tined to step on an upturned nail, certainly deterring future trespass. Later
planters erected houses for overseers that foregrounded the capacity of one
person to "oversee" the plantation—especially the works—through surveillance. A few planters strived to extend that surveillance into the spaces of
the village, but usually to no real effect. In turn, slaves resisted by stealing
their own labor as runaways, depending on the help of Obeah, sometimes
even assaulting whites individually or in small groups. Resistance surfaced
most clearly through outright rebellions, which consistently targeted the
architectures of oppression; during insurrections whites watched as great
houses burned.[98] Marked by massive masonry boiling houses, African-built
housing, and physical manifestations of violence and surveillance, the Jamaican plantation was industrial, global, and contested. In this respect it
was one of early modern Britain's most modern landscapes.

Notes

1. The best published history of Good Hope is Tenison, *Good Hope, Jamaica*. An
important, if unpublished, source on the history of the plantation is Hart, "Good Hope,
Jamaica, 1744–1994." Some of Hart's information and arguments have been incorporated
into Besson, *Martha Brae's Two Histories*. For more intensive studies of individual Jamaican plantations, see Armstrong, *Old Village and the Great House*; Craton and Walvin,
Jamaican Plantation; Higman, *Plantation Jamaica, 1750–1850*; and Satchell, *Hope Transformed*. For a broader overview of the concept of the plantation, see Curtin, *Rise and Fall
of the Plantation Complex*. For the most recent examination of the institution of slavery,
see Roberts, *Slavery and the Enlightenment*.

2. On sugar in the Caribbean, see Hagelberg, "Sugar in the Caribbean." For the power
of the boiling house as social metaphor in creole Jamaica, see Higman, *Plantation Jamaica*, 143.

3. Martin, *Essay upon Plantership*, 9, 30.

4. Roberts, *Slavery and the Enlightenment*, 72.

5. Quoted in ibid., 233.

6. Buisseret, *Jamaica in 1687*, 79.

7. *Art of Making Sugar*, 12.

8. Jamaica Journal of _____ of Loanhead near Rathven, Banffshire, 1823–34, National Library of Scotland, Edinburgh. Available on microfilm in the West Indies Collection of the University of the West Indies Library, reel 3518, p. 20.

9. Ligon, *History of the Island of Barbados*, 79. For a detailed discussion of time discipline on the sugar plantation, see Roberts, *Slavery and the Enlightenment*, 26–79.

10. Quoted in Amussen, *Caribbean Exchanges*, 98.

11. Roberts, *Slavery and the Enlightenment*, 200.

12. Mintz, *Sweetness and Power*, 47–52. See also Dunn, *Sugar and Slaves*, 189, 198; Higman, *Plantation Jamaica*, 8–10, 15, 180, 18; Fogel *Without Consent or Contract*, 23–26; Watts, *West Indies*, 385; and Pritchard, *In Search of Empire*, 171.

13. For the older view, see Hobsbawm, *Age of Revolution*. For a summary of the gradualist view, see Berg and Hudson, "Rehabilitating the Industrial Revolution."

14. For archaeological evidence of comparable examples from eighteenth-century South Carolina, see Ferguson, *Uncommon Ground*, 63–82.

15. Edwards, *History*, 164. Evidence from South Carolina suggests that early-eighteenth-century African builders laid their posts in line in a single trench, while builders later in the century dug an individual hole for each post. No such differentiation has surfaced in the Jamaican evidence. See Ferguson, *Uncommon Ground*, 65–66.

16. *Columbian Magazine or Monthly Miscellany*, April 1797.

17. Higman, *Montpelier, Jamaica*, 158.

18. Edwards, *History*, 164; *Columbian Magazine or Monthly Miscellany*, April 1797.

19. Burnard, *Mastery, Tyranny, and Desire*, 153–54.

20. Brathwaite, *Creole Society in Jamaica*, 133; Armstrong, *Drax Hall*, 98–99; Hall, *In Miserable Slavery*, 238.

21. Edwards, *History*, 163; Lewis, *Journal*, 10 January 1816, 56.

22. Quoted in Brathwaite, *Creole Society in Jamaica*, 221.

23. Brathwaite, *Creole Society in Jamaica*, 220–22.

24. Ibid., 213–14.

25. Ibid., 216.

26. Armstrong, "Reflections on Seville," 95–97.

27. Ibid. See also Hall, *In Miserable Slavery*, 185.

28. Hall, *In Miserable Slavery*, 145.

29. Quoted in Brathwaite, *Creole Society in Jamaica*, 217.

30. Burnard, *Mastery, Tyranny, and Desire*, 138.

31. Bilby and Handler, "Obeah."

32. Williams, *Tour through the Island*, 19.

33. Brathwaite, *Creole Society in Jamaica*, 162.

34. Lambert, "Account of David Henderson," 219.

35. Brathwaite, *Creole Society in Jamaica*, 162.

36. Lambert, "Account of David Henderson," 218.

37. Long, *History*, 2:269.

38. Burnard, *Mastery, Tyranny, and Desire*, 138.

39. Edwards, *History*, 13.

40. Buisseret, *Jamaica in 1687*, 269.

41. Hall, *In Miserable Slavery*, 73.

42. Ibid., 192.

43. Ibid., 73.

44. Burnard, *Mastery, Tyranny and Desire,* 104.

45. Ibid., 96–97, 183–84.

46. Hall, *In Miserable Slavery,* 133.

47. Ibid., 161.

48. Ibid., 165.

49. Ibid., 142.

50. Ibid., 97.

51. Ibid., 235.

52. Delle, "Habitus of Jamaican Plantation Landscapes," 128.

53. Higman, *Plantation Jamaica,* 198.

54. Nugent, *Lady Nugent's Journal,* 165.

55. Burnard, *Mastery, Tyranny and Desire,* 3, 7.

56. 1829 Inventory of Good Hope, fols. 154–57, Archives of Jamaica.

57. See Burnard, *Mastery, Tyranny, and Desire,* 160–62, 219.

58. Ibid., 160. On Thistlewood and rape, see 219.

59. Ibid., 156.

60. Ibid., 210.

61. Ibid., 157.

62. Ibid., 159.

63. Hall, *In Miserable Slavery,* 20.

64. Ibid., 122.

65. Ibid., 155.

66. Burnard, *Mastery, Tyranny, and Desire,* 167.

67. Brathwaite, *Creole Society in Jamaica,* 292.

68. Roberts, *Slavery and the Enlightenment,* 44–56.

69. *Art of Making Sugar,* 6.

70. For an overseer's room on plantations, see 1719 probate inventory of Thomas Belchkin, Archives of Jamaica.

71. For an overseer's house, see 1750 probate inventory of Mathias Pilpsale, ibid.

72. See Ligon, *History of the Island of Barbados,* 79; and Higman, *Plantation Jamaica,* 18.

73. Hall, *In Miserable Slavery,* 64.

74. Ibid., 264.

75. Beckford, *Island of Jamaica,* 2:136.

76. Hall, *In Miserable Slavery,* 140.

77. Roberts, *Slavery and the Enlightenment,* 30, 72.

78. Quoted in ibid., 27.

79. See 1788 probate inventory of John Lord, Archives of Jamaica.

80. 1750 probate inventory of John Vere, telescope in counting house; 1761 probate inventory of John Robert, spyglass in the hall; 1767 probate inventory of Sarah Houghton, 2 hourglasses in overseer's house; 1769 probate inventory of William Matthews, spyglass; 1769 probate inventory of Beecher Fleming, spyglass and 2 hourglasses in hall; 1768 probate inventory of Robert Dellap, spyglass on piazza. See also *Short Journey in the West Indies,* 2:26; and Williams, *Island of Jamaica,* 154.

81. Williams, *Island of Jamaica*, 239.

82. On time discipline and plantations, see Smith, *Mastered by the Clock*.

83. Higman, *Jamaica Surveyed*, 242.

84. Hall, *In Miserable Slavery*, 101, 151, 197. For the legislation, see MS 60, Jamaica Council Minutes, 26:132, National Library of Jamaica.

85. Hall, *In Miserable Slavery*, 124, 150, 191.

86. Burnard, *Mastery, Tyranny and Desire*, 217.

87. *Cornwall Chronicle*, 5 November 1781, 28 March 1810, 21 March 1811.

88. Higman, *Jamaica Surveyed*, 244.

89. Quoted in Higman, *Montpelier, Jamaica*, 130.

90. Armstrong, "Reflections on Seville," 87.

91. Quoted in Higman, *Montpelier, Jamaica*, 147.

92. See ibid., 148; Chappell, "Accommodating Slavery in Bermuda"; and Farnsworth, "Negroe Houses."

93. Chapman, "Slave Villages in the Danish West Indies."

94. See Mingay, *Agricultural Revolution*.

95. Quoted in Higman, *Montpelier, Jamaica*, 147.

96. Quoted in ibid., 128.

97. Hall, *In Miserable Slavery*, 174.

98. Ibid., 54–55.

Works Cited

Amussen, Susan Dwyer. *Caribbean Exchanges: Slavery and the Transformation of English Society, 1640–1700*. Chapel Hill: University of North Carolina Press, 2007.

Armstrong, Douglas V. *The Old Village and the Great House: An Archaeological and Historical Examination of Drax Hall Plantation, St. Ann's Bay, Jamaica*. Urbana: University of Illinois Press, 1990.

———. "Reflections on Seville: Rediscovering the African Jamaican Settlements at Seville Plantation, St. Ann's Bay." In *Out of Many, One People: The Historical Archaeology of Colonial Jamaica*, edited by James A. Delle, Mark Hauser, and Douglas V. Armstrong, 77–101. Tuscaloosa: University of Alabama Press, 2011.

Art of Making Sugar. London, 1752.

Beckford, William. *A Descriptive Account of the Island of Jamaica*. 2 vols. London, 1790.

Berg, Maxine, and Pat Hudson. "Rehabilitating the Industrial Revolution." *Economic History Review* 45, no. 1 (February 1992): 24–50.

Besson, Jean. *Martha Brae's Two Histories: European Expansion and Caribbean Culture-Building in Jamaica*. Chapel Hill: University of North Carolina Press, 2002.

Bilby, Kenneth, and Jerome Handler. "Obeah: Healing and Protection in West Indian Slave Life." *Journal of Caribbean History* 38, no. 2 (2004): 154–83.

Brathwaite, Edward. *The Development of Creole Society in Jamaica, 1770–1820*. Oxford: Clarendon, 1971.

Buisseret, David. *Jamaica in 1687: The Taylor Manuscript at the National Library of Jamaica*. Kingston: University of the West Indies Press, 2008.

Burnard, Trevor. *Mastery, Tyranny, and Desire: Thomas Thistlewood and His Slaves in the Anglo-Jamaican World.* Chapel Hill: University of North Carolina Press, 2004.

Chapman, William. "Slave Villages in the Danish West Indies: Changes of the Late Eighteenth and Early Nineteenth Century." In *Perspectives in Vernacular Architecture, IV,* edited by Thomas Carter and Bernard Herman, 108–20. Columbia: University of Missouri Press for the Vernacular Architecture Forum, 1991.

Chappell, Edward. "Accommodating Slavery in Bermuda." In *Cabin, Quarter, Plantation: Architecture and Landscapes of North American Slavery,* edited by Clifton Ellis and Rebecca Ginsburg. New Haven, CT: Yale University Press, 2010.

Craton, Michael, and James Walvin. *A Jamaican Plantation: The History of Worthy Park, 1670–1970.* Toronto: University of Toronto Press, 1970.

Curtin, Philip D. *The Rise and Fall of the Plantation Complex: Essays in Atlantic History.* Cambridge: Cambridge University Press, 1990.

Delle, James A. "The Habitus of Jamaican Plantation Landscapes." In *Out of Many, One People: The Historical Archaeology of Colonial Jamaica,* edited by James A. Delle, Mark Hauser, and Douglas V. Armstrong, 122–43. Tuscaloosa: University of Alabama Press, 2011.

Dunn, Richard S. *Sugar and Slaves: The Rise of the Planter Class in the English West Indies, 1624–1713.* Chapel Hill: University of North Carolina Press for the Institute of Early American History and Culture at Williamsburg, Virginia, 1972.

Edwards, Bryan. *A History, Civil and Commercial, of the British Colonies in the West Indies.* 2nd ed. Dublin, 1793.

Farnsworth, Paul. "Negroe Houses Built of Stone Besides other Watl'd and Plaistered." In *Island Lives: Historical Archaeologies of the Caribbean,* edited by Paul Farnsworth, 234–71. Tuscaloosa: University of Alabama Press, 2001.

Ferguson, Leland. *Uncommon Ground: Archaeology and Early African America, 1650–1800.* Washington, DC: Smithsonian Institution Press, 1992.

Fogel, Robert. *Without Consent or Contract: The Rise and Fall of American Slavery.* New York: Norton, 1989.

Hagelberg, G. B. "Sugar in the Caribbean: Turning Sunshine into Money." In *Caribbean Contours,* edited by Sally Price and Sidney Wilfred Mintz, 85–126. Baltimore: Johns Hopkins University Press, 1985.

Hall, Douglas. *In Miserable Slavery: Thomas Thistlewood in Jamaica, 1750–86.* London: Macmillan, 1989.

Hart, Richard. "Good Hope, Jamaica, 1744–1994." Institute of Jamaica, Kingston.

Higman, Barry W. *Jamaica Surveyed: Plantation Maps and Plans of the Eighteenth and Nineteenth Centuries.* San Francisco: Institute of Jamaica Publications, 1988.

———. *Montpelier, Jamaica: A Plantation Community in Slavery and Freedom, 1739–1912.* Kingston: University of the West Indies Press, 1998.

———. *Plantation Jamaica, 1750–1850: Capital and Control in a Colonial Economy.* Kingston: University of the West Indies Press, 2005.

Hobsbawm, Eric. *Age of Revolution: 1789–1848.* London: Abacus, 1962.

Lambert, Sheila, ed. "Account of David Henderson." In *House of Commons Sessional Papers of the Eighteenth Century, 1714–1805,* vol. 69. Wilmington, DE: Scholarly Resources, 1975.

Lewis, Matthew Gregory. *Journal of a West India Proprietor, kept during a residence in the island of Jamaica*. London: J. Murray, 1834.

Ligon, Richard. *A True and Exact History of the Island of Barbados, 1657*. Edited by J. Edward Hutson. Bridgetown: Barbados National Trust, 2000.

Long, Edward. *The History of Jamaica: or, General survey of the antient and modern state of that island: with reflections on its situation, settlements, inhabitants, climate, products, commerce, laws and government*. 3 vols. London: T. Lownudes, 1774.

Martin, Samuel. *An Essay upon Plantership*. St. John's, Antigua, 1765.

Mingay, G. E. *The Agricultural Revolution: Changes in Agriculture, 1750–1880*. London: A. and C. Black, 1977.

Mintz, Sidney. *Sweetness and Power: The Place of Sugar in Modern History*. New York: Penguin, 1985.

Nugent, Maria. *Lady Nugent's Journal of Her Residence in Jamaica from 1801 to 1805*. Edited by Philip Wright. Kingston: Institute of Jamaica, 1966.

Pritchard, James. *In Search of Empire: The French in the Americas, 1670–1730*. Cambridge: Cambridge University Press, 2004.

Roberts, Justin. *Slavery and the Enlightenment in the British Atlantic, 1750–1807*. Cambridge: Cambridge University Press, 2013.

Satchell, Veront. *Hope Transformed: A Historical Sketch of the Hope Landscape, St. Andrew, Jamaica, 1660–1960*. Kingston: University of the West Indies Press, 2012.

Short Journey in the West Indies, A. 2 vols. London, 1790.

Smith, Mark. *Mastered by the Clock: Time, Slavery, and Freedom in the American South*. Chapel Hill: University of North Carolina Press, 1997.

Tenison, Patrick J. *Good Hope, Jamaica: A Short History*. Kingston, Jamaica, 1971.

Watts, David. *The West Indies: Patterns of Development, Culture, and Environmental Change since 1492*. Cambridge: Cambridge University Press, 1987.

Williams, Cynric. *A Tour through the Island of Jamaica*. London, 1827.

Wood, John. *A Series of Plans for Cottages or Habitations of the Laborer either in Husbandry or the Mechanic Arts*. London, 1781.

III

Artists' Geographies

Introduction

RICHARD WILL

The Enlightenment always had a dark side. This is not news; after two centuries of critique, no one would claim that its big thinkers were infallibly progressive, nor that the societies they inhabited lacked injustice and human misery. Reminders are everywhere, not least at the University of Virginia, where this volume originated. A neoclassical temple of learning conceived by a quintessentially fallible thinker, the university was built with slave labor and long open only to white men. The essays in this section examine some comparably discomfiting subjects, as captured in visual representations of the Enlightenment's global effects.

Katelyn Crawford focuses on *Sea Captains Carousing in Surinam,* painted by the Bostonian John Greenwood during a midcentury sojourn in the Dutch West Indies. A tavern scene in the vein of Hogarth's *Midnight Modern Conversation,* the painting has been interpreted along similar lines, as a critique of the dissolute behavior fostered by the spoils of empire. Greenwood puts those spoils on display, chief among them African slaves who serve the card-playing, drinking, and puking captains. But Crawford demonstrates that he also conveys the formidable subtleties of the eighteenth-century transatlantic world. Like the painter himself, the sea captains hail from New England, and one of them evidently commissioned the work to illustrate his success on the trade routes between New World ports. Meanwhile, Greenwood capitalized on another trade route, between Surinam and Holland, to collect prints by Rembrandt and other Dutch artists that were readily available in the colony. Their painterly technique and long-standing traditions of tavern scenes exert their own influence on his work. In Crawford's account, *Sea Captains* is as much commercial promotion and aesthetic experiment as social critique, reminding us that no two points in the imperial nexus were the same.

The focus of Sheriff's essay, Watteau's *Pèlerinage à l'île de Cythère,* would seem to be anything but social criticism. In my own field of music history, the painting has long been used to reference a world of frivolous escapism,

aristocratic and amorous, that shaped the development of opera and domestic chamber music. The connection runs both ways: as Sheriff notes,
many art historians regard the painting as itself indebted to contemporary
trends in opera and the fair theaters. She proposes a new reading in light of
different sources, namely, earlier French representations of Cythera, from a
figurative map to Fénelon's popular *Aventures de Télémaque*. They depict the
isle of love as an amusement park of decidedly perilous attractions, among
them debauchery, a village called Inquiétude, ill-intentioned satyrs, and
boredom. "The realm of Cythera," writes Sheriff, "was not always the happy
land of happy endings represented on stage." Reviewing several versions of
Watteau's painting, she spots some jarring images amid all the rococo pret-
tiness: a damaged sculpture of Venus, a siren, figures who seem trapped in
pointless stasis, even a potential love child. The last suggests an even more
disquieting connection, to a second painting by Watteau depicting France's
notorious practice of deporting social undesirables to Louisiana. At the
head of the departure queue stands a pregnant woman being bid adieu by
her *galant* lover. No less than Greenwood's *Sea Captains,* Watteau's *Pèlerinage* registers the moral price of the privilege it represents—not to mention
the looming presence of the transatlantic network, which left no corner of
eighteenth-century life untouched. Even in paradise, shadows lurked.

Emotional Geographies

Watteau and the Fate of Women

MARY D. SHERIFF

> Car la peinture doit être regardée comme un long pèlerinage où l'on voit
> dans le cours du voyage plusieurs chose capables d'entretenir agréable-
> ment notre esprit pour quelque temps.
> —Roger de Piles, *Cours de peinture par principes*, 1709

Nowhere has the representation of love been seen as more ubiquitous than
in eighteenth-century French art. Venus and Cupid have long been hailed as
the titular deities of the rococo, with Cythera as their favored site. Whether
it be the loves of the gods, the seductions of gallant suitors, the clumsy
grappling of country boys, or the king's infatuation with his mistress, the
visual arts of eighteenth-century France seem to celebrate love with neither
nuance nor shadow. Yet this is hardly the case. Take, for example, Nicolas
Vleughels's image of Love's kingdom, which introduced canto 9 of Voltaire's
Henriade in the 1728 first edition (fig. 1). When Voltaire dictated what the
illustration was to show, he prescribed: "L'amour sur un trône couché entre
des fleurs; des nymphes et des furies autour de lui, la discorde tenant dans
ses mains; deux flambeaux; la tête couverte de serpents parlant à l'amour,
qui l'écoute en souriant. Plus loin un jardin où l'on voit deux amants couchés
sous un berceau; derrière eux un guerrier qui paraît plein d'indignation."[1]
Despite Voltaire's explicit instructions, the artist did not follow directions
exactly. We see the Age of Gold represented in the landscape visible through
an archway that divides it from the foreground scene, and there he places
both the couple and the warrior gesticulating his scorn. But Vleughels em-
bellishes the scene of Cupid's lair, adding elements from the larger description the text offers. In the immediate foreground we see a group of figures,
including those made languorous by the music of love and the mistresses
celebrating their shame and vaunting their weakness. Behind them is the
throne of Love surrounded by negative emotions and approached by Discord: "Quel spectacle funeste épouvante des yeux! / . . . / Les plaintes, les
dégouts; l'impudence; la peur; / Font de ce beau séjour un séjour plein

Figure 1. Canto 9, *Discord descending into the Realm of Love,* Edmé Jeaurat after Nicolas Vleughels, 1728, etching and engraving. (Museum of Fine Arts, Boston, William A. Sargent Collection, bequest of William A. Sargent, 37.2398; photograph © 2017 Museum of Fine Arts)

d'horreur. / La sombre jalousie, au teinte pâle & livide; / Suit d'un pied chancelant le soupçon qui la guide: / La haine, & le couroux répandant leur venin, Marchent devant ses pas un poignard à la main."[2]

This vision of love was certainly known to the artists of eighteenth-century France. In his 1721 *Discours prononcez dans les Conferences de l'Académie Royale,* Antoine Coypel took up the question of representing the passions. His commentary on love is as much a warning as a lesson in how best to represent the emotion. The love that grabs his attention is concupiscence, that is, lust, love's most dangerous form. He first describes how "un amant passionné aux pieds de sa Maîtresse, dans une idolâtrie qui l'attache à elle, oublie le Ciel & les Terres, & s'oublie dans ce moment lui-même," and observes that "le Coeur toujours ingénieux à se tromper, trouve de faux pretexts pour s'affaiblir lui-même & refuse d'entendre la voix importune de la raison. . . . La première blessure que l'amour fait naître dans une âme est presqu'incroyable, l'on se flatte quelquefois que la raison pourra la combattre, & c'est dans ce même instant qu'il sçait vaincre & triompher sans même qu'on s'en appercoive."[3] Love, he admits, is accompanied by the Graces, Amusements, Laughter, Enjoyment, and Pleasure. But continuing, Coypel reminds students that love can lead them to

> les précipices les plus dangereux. Il faut encore ajouter que si l'amour dans sa naissance paraît n'avoir rien que d'aimable, à mesure qu'il croît & qu'il s'aggrandit, il abuse de ses forces; non-seulement il règne dans les coeurs en superbe Tyran, mais il y entretient encore des guerres cruelles & secrètes; son aveuglement furieux le porte même jusqu'à troubler son empire par toutes les passions qui le suivent & qui l'environnent, les désirs inquiet, la crainte, les soupçons, les tristes fureurs de la jalousie, la haine & la colère qu'un rival inspire, &c. Il est d'autant plus dangereux, que sous les apparences les plus aimables, il sait vaincre dès qu'il attaque, & triumphant des plus grands coeurs & des Maîtres de la terre, il renverse les États, produit les plus sanglantes guerres, & rend souvent un people entier victime d'un seul homme, dont l'aveugle passion l'entraîne avec lui dans les malheurs le plus affreux. (174)

Love was indeed a force to be feared, as Bernard Picart showed in *Allegory of Love,* a work mingling the different aspects of love in a single image. Here Cupid takes to the air, a happy infant hurling a barrage of arrows. The results of his assault are represented through figures arranged and posed as if enjoying a *fête galante,* the party-scene genre indebted to Picart but now identified with Antoine Watteau. Prominent couples are seated in the foreground, with others dispersed in the distance. One woman caresses her lover's face, while another turns from a pleading beau. A third couple would be out of place in a party scene, for the kneeling man threatens to plunge a sword into his breast. Nearby, a standing pair seem absorbed with each other, but the woman is surreptitiously slipping her servant a note. Behind

them, a woman grieves over a fallen man as a duel progresses, but farther
still three courting couples suggest love's pleasures in poses that recall those
of the *fêtes galantes*. Yet their courtship is framed with tragedy: on one side
a man has hung himself from a tree, while on the other a poor soul has
jumped from a window. Above it all, the happy infant laughs, while a poem
delivers its warning:

> En Amour comme au Jeu la fortune est diverse;
> L'un gagne, l'autre perd; l'une à tromper s'exerce,
> L'autre à favoriser à la fois deux Amans;
> L'un tâche en vain de paraître sincère;
> L'un est heureux l'autre se désespère;
> Et les plus fortunés ne sont jamais contents.

Neither Coypel nor Voltaire nor Vleughels nor Picart invented this
doubled vision of love that considered both positive and negative emotions
within its domain. In mapping that domain, I suggest how attending to
love's contradictions and uncertainties as well as to its pleasures and satis-
factions opens paintings to unexpected interpretations. Artists had at their
disposal a range of cultural materials that offered differing conceptions of
Love's empire, in the sense of an emotion dominating an individual and in
the sense of a fictive realm, such as that of Cythera, ruled by the gods of love.
One painting that has fixed in our minds a particular image of that empire
is Antoine Watteau's 1717 *Pèlerinage à l'île de Cythère* (fig. 2).

Watteau painted *Cythère* as his reception piece for final admission into
the Académie royale de la peinture et de la sculpture, and the Academy's
minutes record that he submitted a work representing a "pèlerinage à l'isle
de Cythère." But the record was changed: the specific title was crossed out
and replaced with the generic "fête galante." Although we know nothing of
the group's deliberations, scholars have understood the change as representing the Academy's bafflement as to how the painting should be categorized.[4]
Yet the Louvre canvas diverges significantly from the typical *fêtes galantes*
both in having an overt mythological theme and in representing those little
flocks of cupids that eventually spread the dust of their butterfly wings on
the whole of rococo art.[5] Thrown in the eyes of the Goncourts, who wrote so
famously about the rococo, Watteau's magic dust made them see the artist
through a haze of nostalgia. For many contemporary interpreters, it has left
a trail leading to the fair theaters and operas, a straight and narrow path that
has seemed more promising than those complicated routes whose twists and
turns encourage us to wander more widely.[6]

Figure 2. Pèlerinage à l'île de Cythère, Jean Antoine Watteau, 1717, oil on canvas. (Musée du Louvre, © RMN–Grand Palais/Art Resource, NY; photo: Stéphane Maréchalle)

François Moureau has argued, for example, that the Cythera theme was born at the fair theater and given body in Fuzelier's *Les Pèlerins de Cythère,* which appeared at the Foire Saint Laurent in 1713. In this play the lovers' departure for the mythical island is compared to a trip down the Seine to the park at Saint-Cloud, a place where one could enjoy many pleasures, including those of the adulterous sort. Moureau asks what light these productions shed on Watteau's painting and concludes that they explain his choice of theme and tie his paintings to both actual stage plays and real social practices, even though they directly represent neither.[7] Although with Moureau nearly every commentator cites the fair theaters as precedents for Watteau's *Pèlerinage,* it has proved difficult to say how these account for the ambiguous, allusive, and complex painting that for three centuries has inspired artists, poets, and musicians.

To suggest that there are other routes to Watteau's Cythera is to point out that the artist's range of subjects is broader than those typically associated with his name, and his cultural milieu wider, more complex, and more contested. It is not to deny the theatricalization of life that so many have commented on so convincingly in relation to Watteau's works.[8] Nor is it to deny the influence of the theater and opera on many of his paintings.

Rather it is to see that the tradition of representing Cythera in France is older, more complicated, and more multivalent than either Picart's image or the fair theaters suggest. In mapping out a path to love's empire, Watteau's celebrated image embeds conceptions of love beyond those represented in the fair theaters, vaudevilles, and comic operas that today form a privileged frame for viewing his work. Ambiguity remains central to the *Pèlerinage,* for little is certain about this illusive, allusive painting.

Mapping Cythera

Ancient mythologies made the Ionian island Cythera a place sacred to Venus. By the mid-seventeenth century, the diverse images of Venus's realm produced in France created a contradictory Cythera, an enchanted and enchanting island prone to disenchantment and open to parody. The story of love's progress often began with an ocean voyage that brought pilgrims to Cythera; sometimes Cythera was the planned destination, at other times a storm pushed travelers there. No matter how they arrived, once in Cythera they were detached from everyday life, for the island evinced the physical aspects of the golden age: a perfect climate, an abundantly fertile earth, and an atmosphere conducive to sensual pleasure. In this idyllic locale, love's progress through time was imagined as travel through space, with changing emotional states represented as the island's physical and social sites. Love's progress, however, was rarely smooth; the path could be dangerous both morally and emotionally, and the final goal of perfect happiness a cruel mirage.

A map is indispensable for navigating the complex terrain of this Cythera, and I have found a useful one in Jacques Defreveaulx's *Royaume d'Amour en l'isle de Cythère* (fig. 3). The engraving, which appeared in 1650, refers to a short story by the poet Tristan L'Hermite.[9] Like so many other emotional geographies, it became linked to Madeleine de Scudéry's immensely popular *Carte de Tendre,* which first appeared in her 1654 novel *Clélie* and was associated with the group of literary women known as the Précieuses.[10] The map complements a long textual description of the possible paths to Tenderness, and these are explained to the male suitors, whom we see in the right corner. Scudéry's *Carte de Tendre* thus describes ideal courtship from a woman's point of view. Interest in emotional geographies ran well into the eighteenth century, and references to them appear, for example, in Fuzelier's *La Mode* of 1719, in which an editor announces publication of a "nouvel Itinéraire de l'Ile d'Amour."[11]

Figure 3. Reproduction of the original engraving *Royaume d'Amour en l'isle de Cythère, Carte descripte par le Sieur Tril'Hermite, 1650,* Jacques Defreveaulx. (Courtesy of University of Victoria Legacy Art Galleries, gift of Pat Martin Bates and Al Bates)

On one side of Defreveaulx's map the island of love is bound by a Mer des Précieuses emblematized in a siren, and at the top it is edged by the Mer d'Inclination, recalling the main river traversing the Royaume de Tendresse. Cythera is set off from its surroundings, but despite the island's border, the darkened blue that represents the sea flows into the lighter blue of the sky that reigns over the vignette on which the map is superimposed. There is a similar play with the ambiguities of visual representation on the left side, where we see a "Table et description des villes, bourgades et aussi le chemin qu'il faut tenir pour y fair voyage." At the top, this "Table" appears to be inscribed on the side of an architectural element, denoted by the red entablature and the female caryatid. Yet as the eye moves down the "Table" the architectural form disappears, and we see a flat strip of writing affixed to the map's left side. This is a playful image, and its playfulness is emphasized in the cartouche that encloses the title of the piece, whose form is that of a jester's hat turned upside down.

Woman is pictured on Defreveaulx's map as siren, caryatid and goddess, but the tour of the island is not presented from her vantage, and it is not tenderness but physical love that reigns, symbolized by Venus, goddess of pleasure, and the amours who serve her. The "Table" describes the principal locations of the realm, starting with the Grande Plaine d'Indifférence, where the route begins with the Inclination nouvelle. In contrast to the multiple choices of the *Carte de Tendre,* here we have a single route illustrated as a path circling the island and punctuated with woods, inns, and towns each representing a different pleasure, emotional state, or stage of seduction. Some are suggestive of activities associated with the *fêtes galantes:* in the Bois de Belle Assemblée, for example, there are lute concerts, singing, and often a comedy or a ball. At the Hôtellerie Doux-Regard, one can sip a nice glass of wine, but passing on to the small village of Inquiétude, one doesn't sleep so well. There the anxiety associated with vicissitudes of love is represented wittily as the sleeplessness that comes from a lumpy mattress. Further along the path there is the large and famous town of Soins-sur-Complaisance, whose university boasts professors in the little nothings of love poetry. From there it is a short hop to Feu Declaré, and then through several villages before arriving at Entreprendre, marked by the ruins of a fortified castle called Résistance, which wars had devastated. From there the lovers move on to Jouissance, with its beautiful gardens and labyrinths in which couples can lose themselves, and then on to a rose-strewn path leading to Satiété. Satisfied to the point of losing their appetite, the lovers then find themselves at the town of Faible Amitié, and then on to the forest of Inclination Nouvelle. Thus the circuit begins again with a new lover. On this Cythera, physical satisfaction rather than tenderness is journey's goal, and it leads to boredom, so the circuit must begin again with a new object of desire. Here lovemaking is repetitive, predictable, and ultimately unsatisfying.

Thus far the map seems entirely amusing, yet below the map the scene changes. On first glance it appears that we see simply what one could expect to find on the island of love: a group making music; a feast with jugs of wine; an amorous couple clutched in the bushes. Alongside this merrymaking we see a rustic village, perhaps one of those suggested in the narrative. Yet who is the figure in the cloud seeming to communicate with someone kneeling on the ground? We would be mistaken to think that the relation between the island and the vignette is one of simple illustration. The vignette copies plate 9 of Jan Sadeler the elder and Maarten de Vos's *The Story of the Family of Seth* (1586), which depicts the perniciousness of man given to sins of the flesh (fig. 4). It is a pendant to plate 10, which shows wickedness on earth represented as violence. Plate 11 depicts God appearing to Noah in a cloud, pre-

Figure 4. The Story of the Family of Seth, plate 9, *The Perniciousness of Man,* Maarten de Vos, engraving by Jan Sadeler, 1586. (British Museum, © Trustees of the British Museum/Art Resource, NY)

cisely the scene that is rendered in a reduced version in the background of plate 9 and below the map of Cythera. Once we recognize the source of the background image, the figure embracing the woman as she plays the guitar now looks suspiciously like a debauched satyr rather than a gallant suitor.

If we stop to contemplate this figure and the critique of debauchery he embodies, our thoughts might wander to a print series in which satyrs take a starring role. The work of Watteau's close associate Claude Gillot, *Passions Represented by Satyrs* includes four passions, which divide into pairs of two: the passions of love and war belong only to male satyrs, while those of gambling and riches affect both sexes. Love and war are of particular interest because they reconstitute the excesses represented in *The Story of the Family of Seth*. In *The Passion for Love,* nubile young women, whom the satyrs adore from below, surround an animated statue of Cupid (fig. 5). These devotees of Love have brought flowers, floral crowns, and money as offerings, and among the group on the left is one satyr dressed as a high priest. On the right a satyr raises the torch of desire, another dares to touch the foot of a nymph, while a third, positioned with dagger in hand, thrusts his hips forward and pushes his genitals toward the nymphs in a display rare

Figure 5. The Passion for Love, Claude Gillot, engraved by Jean Audran, etching. (Elisha Whittelsey Collection, Elisha Whittelsey Fund, 1957, Metropolitan Museum of Art, New York; image © Metropolitan Museum of Art; image source: Art Resource, NY)

Figure 6. Preliminary drawing for *The Passion for Love,* Claude Gillot, red chalk on paper. (British Museum, © Trustees of the British Museum/Art Resource, NY)

in the visual arts, and more exaggerated in Gillot's preliminary drawing (fig. 6). Lest these satyrs, traditional representatives of the animal passions, get too rowdy, cloaked enforcers are there to push them away. The moralizing legend warns against the poisonous influence of love and the pleasure that attracts and enchants the voluptuaries:

> Volupteux, moderéz vos transports
> Fuyez ces vains Objets s'ils sont doux au-dehors
> Un fond des plus amers tromperez vôtre attente

Ces Plaisirs, dont l'attrait follement vous enchante.
Vous les déstesterez un jour
Malheur à qui se livre au Poison de l'amour
Jeunesse, on vous l'a dit mais vous se serez sage
Qu'après avoir cent fois pleuré, votre Naufrage.

But Gillot's image overstates the case; overcharges it. The visual language of Cythera's map, however, is more complicated in its levels of ambiguity.

Notice how different is the handling between the figures taken from *The Story of the Family of Seth* and those on the map of Cythera. The first are rendered in the language of the high arts; the second seem more naïvely drawn. The handling of even the naked Venus differs from that of the figures in the scene below: although nude, she is more schematically depicted, her body less sensual than those drawn from the print. A sort of innocence is suggested in the playful cupids making music, showing the route, and planting flowers. The work offers contradictory images of Cythera, on the one hand placing it within a moral critique and on the other, offering the pleasures of a trip through Venus's domain rendered amusing through wordplay.

The cartouche that recalls a jester's hat locates the image in the realm of travesty, and of course, the map has several targets. One is the *Carte de Tendre* and the realm of the Précieuses, to which it also pays homage. Another is the monastic life. Notice the capital city, at the center of the map, set on a mountain elevated above the clouds. That city is inaccessible; one can only get there on foot via an arduous path. Serious authors called the city Amour Celeste, but moderns have named it Sainteté Monastique. The inhabitants are happy, because their minds are always at peace, although their bodies are often in pain: they eat little, scarcely sleep, and often say the rosary, praying that the rest of the inhabitants of this province will convert and make themselves worthy of living in this beautiful place. The map thus takes aim at both libertinage and abstinence, and neither leads to true happiness. It is both devotion to the pleasures of physical love and devotion to physical deprivation in the name of love that are the objects of this satire. Yet the visual juxtaposition of *The Story of the Family of Seth* with the map of Cythera does not make clear which image is satirizing the other. Does the map drawn in all its innocence and offering us the scene of pleasure mock the moralizing story that presents such pleasures as evil and perfidious, or does the moralizing story show that the innocence of the map is simply a cover for sinful and dangerous behavior? Or does the viewer take delight in her suspension between these two possibilities, in an image that plays at the right distance between them?[12]

Defreveaulx's map offers something that the works set on Cythera and staged at the fair theaters often do not: it suggests that from early on in French art and literature, the realm of Cythera was not always the happy land of happy endings represented on the stage. The quest for the physical pleasures of love is repetitious, and lovers end up bored with one another. This is libertine love, sequential love, love Don Juan style. In this Cythera the passion for love is never sated; it continuously seeks new objects of desire. This thematic was reiterated in 1713, the same year as the Cythera plays at the fair theaters. That year saw a new edition of Paul Tallemant's *Voyage de l'isle d'amour* and *Le second voyage de l'isle d'amour,* originally published in 1663 and 1664, respectively. And these texts would be reprinted again in 1788 in the collection *Voyages imaginaires.*[13] Tallemant's text has often been cited as a source for Watteau, but oddly enough there is little discussion of either its contents or its relation to the emotional geographies.

The story is presented overtly from a man's point of view and unfolds in two letters from a traveler, Tyrcis, describing his experiences on the Island of Love. This realm has many of the same villages as that of Tristan l'Hermite, as well as emotional sites based on the *Carte de Tendre,* but Tallemant adds many more, and in each case the emotional state is instantiated in a town ruled by a titular deity, an allegorical figure bearing the same name as the town and described in such a way as to reinforce the emotion she represents. On this island emotional storms and bitter disappointments mark love's progress, even as the island is punctuated with sites of pleasure, such as the town of Petit Soins, where one finds "parties de galanterie," dancing, and music-making. There the narrator wins the object of his desire, Amyte, with whom he travels through a series of places representing the stages, or emotions, associated with love. Pleasure turns to distress at the Antre de la Cruauté and the Lac du Désespoir, but the couple finally arrive at the town of Confiance, where lovers rendezvous in small *bosquets* set in secret paths where one is not interrupted. This happy trysting is only temporary, however, for Rivaux and Jalousie enter the picture and have to be endured before the couple arrive at the capital of Amour, from where they make their way to a *maison de campagne* that is the site of sexual fulfillment and the Palais du Vrai Plaisir. But sexual satisfaction does not endure, and even in this paradise they meet an ugly woman who "fait la précieuse," a shrew called Tiédeur, who cools the ardors of sexual attraction and tends to lovers who want to leave the island, taking them to the Lac du Dégoût. The narrator ignores her, but an even more powerful figure arrives: Destin, who takes lovers to the Désert de l'Affliction, where they are tormented by the memory of love. It is in this torment that the narrator closes his first letter.

If in the first *Voyage* the narrator seeks sexual pleasure, in the second he travels to that portion of the island dedicated to gallantry. Learning that Amyte has taken a new lover, he comes out of the Désert du Souvenir, where he experiences a profound sadness, and eventually makes his way to the village of Mépris and then to that of Indifférence, where he meets up with Galanterie, who invites him to her kingdom, also named Galanterie. In the kingdom, there is a perpetual *fête galante* with a thousand divertissements, including music, balls, serenades, and theater. Day in and day out the narrator is called on to participate in these pleasures, but this life tires him. Still, there he has met two women who particularly attract him—Sylvie and Iris—and with them he leaves Galanterie for the realm of a queen called Coquetterie, who holds that if love is all the happiness of life, the more one loves, the happier one will be. She advises him not to choose between Sylvie and Iris but to enjoy both. The narrator, however, eventually believes he must choose, which drives him to the village of Irrésolution, where the woman who will resolve his dilemma appears. She is Gloire, and he describes her as of incomparable beauty. She advises him that love enlivens life but that to continue to dwell in love's realm is folly; love never brings the honor sought by fine minds. Following Gloire he arrives at the departure point and sees Raison in the crowd; going to her, he begs her pardon. In the end, he concludes that on the island he paid for his "few sweet moments" with "much unhappiness."[14] Thus the sojourn on the island of love ends with a celebration of reason and glory; love is cast as unreasonable, emotional, filled with uncertainty and caprice, as well as unlimited in desires that are never fulfilled. In the realm of love, he concludes, there is evil in the greatest delights and abuse in the greatest pleasures:

> Je prends congé de vous, ô belles, dont les traits
> Soumettent tant de coeurs sous leur injuste empire,
> Vous pour qui, sans raison, tant de monde soupire,
> Je prends congé de vous, je n'aimerai jamais.
> Je connais bien l'Amour, & je hais ses caprices,
> L'on n'y trouve jamais de borne à ses délices,
> Et j'en ai vu l'abus dans ses plus grands plaisirs.[15]

If both Defreveaulx and Tallement present an ambiguous illusory island of love, we find a completely unnuanced vision of Venus's realm in the most widely read text of eighteenth-century France, François de Salignac de La Motte Fénelon's *Avantures de Télémaque,* which first appeared in a 1699 pirated edition. When Telemachus arrives in Cythera, he finds that he is struck with a weakness for debauchery. His guide, Mentor, arrives to reveal the true nature of the island: "Fuyez, me dit-il d'un ton terrible; fuyez, hâtez-vous de fuir. Ici la terre ne porte pour fruit que du poison; l'air qu'on respire est empesté; les hommes contagieux ne se parlent que pour se communiquer un venin mortel. La volupté lâche & infame, qui est de plus horrible des maux sortie de la boîte de Pandore, amollit les coeurs, & ne souffre ici aucune vertu. Fuyez, que tardez-vous?"[16] Throughout Fénelon's *Télémaque,* seductive women and the pleasures they offer are forces of corruption; sexuality does not simply provide the illusion of happiness, it is morally dangerous and transforms manly men into effeminate voluptuaries worshipping at the altar of Venus.

Watteau's reception piece, then, entered into a cultural field that included not only vaudevilles and comic operas but also moralizing texts and images as well as emotional geographies. Together these cultural forms painted a more ambiguous picture of Cythera; they questioned both the illusions and the passions of love and pointed to its disruptions, dangers, and disappointments. It is in the intersection of these cultural forms that I want to reposition the Cythera Watteau represented as his reception piece.

A Pilgrimage to Cythera

In the tradition of Tallement, I begin my pilgrimage to Cythera with the titular goddess of the realm. Venus marks the 1717 *Pèlerinage* not as a voluptuous full-bodied figure but as a *terme,* a statue of a man or a woman whose lower parts end in a sheath. *Termes* were usually placed as boundary markers in gardens at the end of *allées,* and *terme* comes from the Latin *termini,* referring to the stones Romans used to mark the limits of their lands and to which they added sculpted heads. In Watteau's work the *terme* of Venus placed at the far right of the composition marks several boundaries, but most prominently that between the clearing at the top of the hillock and the woods behind, between the spaces open to view and the more secluded areas to which lovers inevitably fled. Were it not for the pink roses that stand out from the green foliage, the *terme* would merge more fully into the nature that surrounds her. Yet she is posed on the edge of nature and culture; she recedes into the landscape but remains a work of artifice, a sculpted figure, a sign of demarcation, and the representation of a titular deity. Katie Scott's analysis of Watteau's arabesques demonstrates how the symbolic aspects of the work typically reside in its borders and edges. I propose that we find a similar effect in the *Pèlerinage*.[17]

The *terme* is far from the happy, maternal, and fully sculpted Venus we see in the later Berlin version of the pilgrimage. In the Louvre painting Venus is not only a *terme*, but she is also a fragmented body. Although some *termes* were born with neither arms nor legs, many of them created in antiquity, as well as those sculptured for the gardens of Versailles, had fully functional upper limbs. We can see from Watteau's image that his Venus once bore arms: notice the rough surface indicating the place where they were broken off. Watteau's Venus is a fragment of antiquity that persists still; here the stumps of the severed limbs appear as the wounds of abandonment not yet smoothed over by the passage of time. Watteau represents Venus as disarmed, wounded, and outliving her time, even though there is still a residual belief in her efficacy suggested by the offerings left at her base and the rose garlands that adorn her. The roses are the titular flower of Venus, but they represent love not only because of their beauty and sweet smell but also because of the thorns whose pricks are the wounds of love.

The *terme* of Venus marks another important boundary, for it terminates the figural composition. And terminating the figural elements on the other side of the canvas is another character loosely associated with Venus: a siren pinned on what appears to be the back of a boat, and situated just below a shell, an emblem of Venus, on which she rests her head. What, we may ask, is a siren doing on an invisible love boat bound for Cythera? This is not the first instance of a siren appearing near the island, for one inhabited the waters of the Mer de Précieuse on Defreveaulx's map. Sirens were among those monsters popular as decorative motifs on everything from ewers to sleds. In Watteau's *Allegory of Spring* we see a small garden boat quite clearly rendered with a siren affixed to its stern, but the siren's presence is justified by the singing woman, the siren's playful double, whom we see riding under the boat's canopy.[18] Knowing their ancient literature, Watteau's audience would have recognized the sirens from Ulysses's encounter with them in the *Odyssey*; to avoid the consequences of their seductive song, the hero lashes himself to a mast and fills the ears of his crew with wax. Bernard de Montfaucon mentions this encounter with the sirens in his *Antiquité expliquée* (1719), where he describes the sirens as enchantresses who enchanted so well that their prey no longer thought of returning home, and becoming entirely "ensorcellé," they forgot to drink and eat and died for want of nourishment. Following Alciati's emblems, Montfaucon's commentary also points out that for moralists the sirens represented "femmes de mauvaise vie" who seduced men with their charms, leading them to perish in debauchery.[19]

Watteau's figural composition thus spreads out horizontally between the poles marked by a disarmed Venus and an immobilized siren. Between these two poles lies the activity of several couples, the play of many amours, and the work of two boatmen. One boatman rests on his oar, while his companion actively pushes his down as if to maneuver the boat. It is not clear on what the oars rest, and we cannot see the boat that their efforts might propel. The first boatman seems merely to watch the crowd, while the other is working to no visible effect. We might imagine that their job in the painting is to direct our attention to the figures approaching the boat. Yet if we notice the pilgrims, not one of them pays the boatmen the slightest bit of attention. But well they might be interested, for these are not the usual sailors who bring pilgrims to Cythera: that has long been the job of those small, winged infantile amours seen, for example, in Watteau's 1709 *L'île de Cythère,* now in Frankfort. In that work they steer the ship of love, but in the Louvre *Pèlerinage* they are released to more playful antics. These boatmen seem less cupids and more rococo versions of Charon, who conveyed the souls of the dead to the other world. Subleyras's image of Charon (fig. 7), which shows the back view of a beautiful, muscled figure, might be a good comparison were it not for the diminutive scale of Watteau's fleshy and sensuous male nudes. One might easily believe that in a reception piece the artist felt compelled to include some nude male bodies just to show that he could do it. Yet, perhaps they do carry out something like the duties of Charon. These oarsmen, I propose, convey pilgrims back to the place where Voltaire located the realm of Love, back to the place where the Age of Gold was said still to exist, the Elysian Fields, a specific place antiquity located in the underworld, a place where the virtuous dead never die, where its denizens enjoyed not only sensual pleasures but also innocent sexuality. This Age of Gold was, of course, a beautiful fantasy, a metaphor for a better time and place that could be summoned to contrast with the actual present.

Going or gone to such a place are two groups of couples bracketed between siren and *terme.* Neither group is securely located in either the foreground or the background; rather, they inhabit some middle ground caught between the materiality of the landscape that runs horizontally across the lower quadrant of the composition and the magical landscape, the ethereal view that extends across the upper half of the canvas. And if we look to this distant landscape, we might notice that it sings its seductive song through spectacular effects of color, light, movement, and brushwork.[20]

Figure 7. Charon Crossing the Styx, Pierre Hubert Subleyras, oil on canvas. (Musée du Louvre, © RMN–Grand Palais/Art Resource, NY; photo: Hervé Lewandowski)

In the fiction of the painting, we might understand this distant landscape as holding out the promise of some locale even more conducive to love, seduction, and gallantry than the one in which the figures are currently situated. Indeed, the difference between these two locales provoked some interpreters to ask whether these pilgrims stand on the ground of Cythera or are readying themselves to sail there?[21] There are many reasons why this question cannot and should not be resolved. What I want to notice here is that not a single one of the figures pays the landscape the slightest attention. Comprising the majority of the picture space, the landscape is laid out to seduce the spectator's eye, to draw the viewer into Watteau's imaginary world. I use the phrase *seduce the eye* purposefully, to invoke the theorist Roger de Piles, who consistently defined the purpose of art as giving pleasure and the aim of painting as seducing the eye. He imagines painting as a siren calling to viewers, stopping them in their tracks and substituting—if only momentarily—the pleasures of artistic illusion for the demands of reality.[22] Part of this pleasure comes from the way the artist has painted the landscape, what de Piles calls the *légèreté du pinceau,* which endows the scene with soul and vivacity.[23] Execution also enters into de Piles's discussion of the *style ferme* and the *style poli;* whereas the highly finished *style poli* leaves nothing to the imagination of the spectator, the *style ferme* gives life to the work and engages the viewer whose imagination is pleased to find and finish things. Some beautiful landscapes, he argues, are very lightly worked, a technique he praises when it is "spiritual," that is, responding to the quality of the terrain.[24]

This *légèreté* of brush is evident in Watteau's landscape, in which the finishing of the forms—of the foliage in the foreground and the mountains behind—is indeed left to the spectators' imagination, pulling them into the landscape, involving them in its very making. Some scholars have noted that Watteau painted the *Pilgrimage* quickly; others have considered it a sketch, citing, for example, the rapidity of execution in the left part of the sky. But all agree that it is painted with a virtuosity of execution that uses to advantage a thin paint layer consisting almost entirely of glazes.[25] This technique produces the terrain as imaginary and dreamlike, evanescent and fleeting. And here is where the watery reflections, vaporous clouds, trailing smoke, shimmering leaves and fading mountains gain their metaphoric value. But the painting also indicates the unreal quality of the environment in other ways. Notice the dark and heavy log of blasted tree protruding in the left foreground, which elides foreground and midground to touch the curving edge of the boat. This fragment of landscape points to the emptiness, the absence of anything that resembles an actual boat's body under the siren's wing. Thus, if the absence of the real marks every representation, here that absence is made present to the eyes of the viewer.

But what of the figures and their relation to this dreamlike, imaginary vista? De Piles noted: "Le peintre en composant son paysage peut avoir dans la pensée d'y imprimer une caractère conforme au sujet qu'il pourrait avoir choisi, et que les figures doivent représenter. Il se peut faire aussi (et c'est ce qui arrive ordinairement) qu'il ne songe à ses figures qu'après que son paysage est tout à fait terminé. . . . Je suis persuadé que le meilleur moyen de faire valoir les figures est de les accorder tellement au caractère du paysage qu'il semble que le paysage n'ait été fait que pour les figures."[26] These comments invite us to consider the *Pèlerinage* as a landscape in which the character of the figures accords with that of the surroundings in significant ways.

Indeed, the unreality of the landscape is underscored by the impossible placement of the figures within it. The couples on the hillock have no path by which to join the couples below. Rather than sloping down, the hillock falls off as a rather sharp edge. And the distribution of the figures provides no visible entry points for the group gathered at the base of the hillock, and so these couples appear to just be there. This improbable lower group is entirely involved with its own interactions, and while their attentions to one another may seem real enough, little else ties them to the actual—not the space in which they operate and not their theatricalized costumes, which here mix rustic garb with more elegant dress. Adding to the unreality of the scene, as well as to its *légèreté,* are the amours, winged and naked, who are dispersed in the composition. Some mingle with the couples, urging them along even as the lovers go on about their business as if the cupids were not there. Others enact the emotional transport, the ecstasy anticipated or remembered: they cavort in the air playing with a lighted torch, rising, falling, and diving into the flames. While emotional transport is depicted through the amours, real transport seems impossible in an insubstantial boat rendered unseen.

For de Piles, however, the figures had a purpose beyond their accord with the landscape. "Je voudrais qu'elles ne fussent ni insipides ni indifférentes, mais qu'elles représentassent quelque petit sujet pour réveiller l'attention du spectateur."[27] But once awakened, to what should attention attend? On this point de Piles does not specify. It is through attention to the relation of figures to landscape that we notice the extent to which Watteau's *Pèlerinage* keeps viewers from too close an identification with the represented figures. We find enjoyment in the beckoning landscape, with its subtle color harmonies and atmospheric effects, while the pilgrims take their pleasure only in their engagement with one another. They never join us in gazing upon the fantasy dreamscape that surrounds them, nor are we invited through look or gesture to enter into their exchanges. Intentionally or not, the different relations that viewers and pilgrims have with the landscape separates them one from the other and thus, intentionally or not, generates meaning.

On the one hand, viewers are invited to escape the real, to lose themselves in the visual pleasure of the fantasy landscape and yield to its seductive handling. On the other, noticing the relation between the figures and the landscape shakes viewers awake and offers them an opportunity to see that the pilgrims operate in a fantasy world of love and gallantry, that they have totally succumbed to the call of the siren and the rule of Venus that frames them. As spectators we can be seduced and immobilized before the landscape, but our attention—and with it our critical faculties—can also be aroused. Although viewers might momentarily be in the same entranced state as those who inhabit this fantasy world, they can escape the enchantments of art in meditating on the relation between figures and landscape.

There is another sense in which the pilgrims—and in particular those on the hill—belong to the landscape of Cythera, for they are enacting love's circuit. By their varied costumes we can identify the three couples on the knoll as different couples, but they could also represent the same couple, as their movements create a sense of continuous progression. But *progression* is not the right word, for while the couples appear to be progressing, by which I mean readying themselves to move down the hill to the next "stage" of love, whatever that might be, they are also going nowhere. Or at least that's how Watteau shows them, for a compositional movement backward counterbalances any sense of their moving forward. This dynamic suggests the repetitiveness of the process, couples going through the same routines time after time. Looking at the couple nearest the *terme* of Venus, we see that the man seems to be both rising up and coaxing the seated woman. The gentleman in the next couple is helping his lady up, apparently having persuaded her to go—somewhere. In the third couple, both figures are standing and appear ready to descend toward the boat. But wait. They are looking back to the couples behind and leading us back to the beginning of the circuit. It is in this effort that the little dog turns at the edge of the hill, blocking the last couple's forward movement. Even as the pilgrim in pink stretches his arm forward and steps onto his right foot, even as he seems to coax his lady to move forward, he simultaneously leans backward. The staff he holds is tilted slightly back, and an implied diagonal leads the eye from his right shoulder down his arm to where it meets up with the more definitely backward tilt of his lady's staff. This backward movement is more definite in his partner, who looks at the couple behind her, holding her staff at a diagonal that leads in their direction. Were it not for the landscape beckoning us, the eye might be perpetually caught in the back and forth of the figural composition, which reminds us that love in Cythera is a circuit that continually leads back to the same point.

Yet these figures are doing more than enacting a circuit, and here the couple nearest Venus also awakens my attention and urges me to contemplate the particular relation to the landscape. Although Mary Vidal was quite right to locate conversation as a significant element of Watteau's *fêtes galantes,* what conversation do we see here?[28] I ask this question since the man seems to be talking, and the woman listening. Here we do not find two people engaged in a lively exchange of wits, but rather one who seems to be persuading, or even seducing, the other. The woman is firmly seated on something, but beside this stable pose, notice her partner's awkward position, made pronouncedly odd by the shadow indicating that he has raised his knees from the ground. With his feet planted and his knees raised, to maintain this precarious pose he would have to balance his weight entirely against this partner. But this is not what the image shows us. Rather than exerting any effort, he seems nearly to be levitating, filled with *légèreté,* both literally and metaphorically. Like the sweet nothings he whispers in his partner's ear, his impossible pose hovers on the edge of true; he nearly convinces us that it is possible, just as he hovers on the edge of convincing her of something. This couple, moreover, is made more prominent by two inclusions that are easy to overlook and that Watteau has eliminated in two other versions of the scene.[29] First, there is a pile of clothes on a bench between the woman and Venus. But whose clothes are they? Are these the clothes the woman was wearing, her more formal outer dress, taken off for the purposes of Cythera? Or do these abandoned garments suggest another couple hidden in the woods who have yet to conclude their lovemaking? Somewhat less cryptic is the child seated near to the woman. Although rendered quite differently from the rest of the amours, we can recognize this child as a disguised cupid by the quiver of arrows on which he sits. He pretends to be just another pilgrim of love, dressed as he is in the pilgrim's cape, yet we notice he seems naked beneath it. And why does this cupid tug at the woman's skirt? If he is trying to get her attention, is he in the service of the man and thus may be seen as encouraging her to rise up? Is the amour the lover's rival, competing with the man for her attention? Or is he shown as a human child because he is warning her about the outcome of sexual intercourse, and that is why he sits on his arrows rather than using them to ignite ardor? Or is he both an amour and a love child, a reminder that making babies is the natural outcome of making love, an outcome that in Regency France might not bode well for the woman if she were seduced and abandoned.

Embarking for Cythera, Arriving in the Islands

If this interpretation seems far-fetched, it is not only because we have for-gotten the larger tradition of representing Cythera. We have also not looked to some of Watteau's other island images. Take, for example, *Départ pour les isles,* engraved for the Recueil Julienne after a lost painting by Watteau (fig. 8).[30] Rendered in a satiric mode, this *Départ* recalls in its manner an earlier leave-taking that Watteau painted: *Départ des comediens Italiens en 1697,* also known through an engraving. And like the earlier work, *Départ pour les isles* comments on a particular history, which suggests that the painting was created around the same time as the *Pèlerinage;* most likely, it was made shortly thereafter. Represented there is a scene that was becoming frequent in Regency France, when it was policy to deport undesirables to Louisi-ana, where they would land not on the mainland but on l'Île Dauphine. Yet some may have conceived of Louisiana, and especially Nouvelle Orléans, as an island—a pestilential island surrounded by marshes where settlers died of yellow fever. It is also possible that the title, most likely chosen by the engraver, was calculated to refer to Watteau's other embarkations, cast-ing a different light on those images. It is likely that the engraver chose the poem at the bottom, and although it does not record Watteau's intention, it is a contemporaneous interpretation that casts all the women as prostitutes: "Allons, il faut partir sans vous faire prier / Mignones, renforcés s'il vous plait vos courages. / Si vos Matrones étaient sages / Elle vous auraient dit que le galant métier / Oblige à de fréquents voyages." The idea of a prosti-tute making frequent voyages reminds us that in the slang of the day, "voy-age to Cythera" referred to sexual intercourse.[31] Yet as we shall see, not all the women depicted in Watteau's *Départ* are prostitutes, and the women actually deported included a range of undesirables: beggars, vagabonds, poor women, women who practiced prostitution only when necessary, and women of "questionable morals." The latter case fit the fictional deportee the Abbé Prévost imagined some years later in his 1731 novel *Manon Lescot,* a deportee who died of an illness contracted in New France. Manon was not a prostitute per se but a gold digger who duped the lovers she seduced and who was in turn punished for her misdeeds.

The story of the deportations actually began in 1712, when Louis XIV granted a monopoly on trade in Louisiana to the wealthy Antoine Crozat, brother to Pierre Crozat, one of Watteau's significant patrons. The depar-tures began in 1716 with the deportation of salt smugglers and girls from poorhouses. At that time Crozat was an advocate of deportations, which

Figure 8. Engraving by Dupin, 1921, after *Départ pour les isles,* Jean Antoine Watteau, c. 1718. (© Musée du Louvre, dist. RMN–Grand Palais/Angèle Dequier/Art Resource, NY; photo: Angèle Dequier)

were relatively popular because the homeless population on the streets had become a public nuisance. Along with the deportations, there was also a propaganda campaign that tried to seduce poor French citizens into volun- tary emigration; that campaign depicted the colony as an idyllic land with miraculously fertile soil, a mild climate, and a territory filled with riches such as gems and gold that could be had for a minimum of effort.[32] It was by any measure a campaign that seduced the vulnerable with false prom- ises. And just as Watteau's Cythera represented an impossible land of love, Crozat's Louisiana lured settlers with visions of the golden age.

Crozat held his monopoly on trade until August 1717, when it was given over to John Law, who set up the Company of the Occident. From that time on, the Regency government pursued the most aggressive emigration policy in the history of settlement in North America. From 1717 to 1720 so many men and women were deported to Louisiana that there were riots and pro- tests throughout the kingdom, especially after the regent sanctioned whole- sale arrests that increased the numbers of deportees. Yet at the same time, demands from middle-class families to send young relatives judged to be "libertine" to Louisiana poured into police stations.[33] In light of this history, I want to consider the *Départ* as a kind of pendant to the Louvre pilgrimage, even a rethinking of it from another point of view, for intentionally or not, this work is in dialogue not only with the *Pèlerinage* but with all those images by Watteau that focus on love and gallantry. The main male figure of the *Départ* is a parody, a caricature of the gallant lover as he makes an exaggerated bow and doffs his hat to the woman who is being sent away.

The *Dictionnaire de l'Académie française* (1694) offers a range of meanings for *galant* and *galanterie,* the first of which for *galant* is entirely positive: "Honnête, civil, sociable, de bonne compagnie, de conversation agréable." A bit further down we find that the term also has a meaning particular to the male sex: "Un homme qui cherche à plaire aux Dames."[34] Yet the terms *galant* and *galanterie* were derived from the old French *galer,* "to play tricks," and before the seventeenth century these terms were associated with cunning and deceit.[35] A shadow of this definition clung to their newer significations, and despite the positive connotations, a less desirable notion lurked below. The *Dictionnaire* of 1694 also tells us that if used as a noun, *galant* signified a male lover, usually one who made love to a married woman or to a girl he had no plans to marry: "Il est aussi substantif, & signifie Amant, amoureux. . . . Mais il se dit plus ordinairement de celuy qui fait l'amour à une femme mariée, ou à une fille qu'il n'a pas dessein d'épouser."[36] Gallantry here slides into seduction, which in the legal code referred to the deflowering of a woman through a false promise of marriage. In the course of the eighteenth century, the term *galant* was tipped back toward the earlier notion of *galer* and associated with seduction. To seduce was to fool or abuse or lead into error. It also signified to corrupt or debauche, with this example: "cette fille se laissa séduire sous prétexte de mariage."[37]

Despite the poem's first stanza, Watteau's image does not depict all the women as prostitutes. Looking at the image, we see three different sorts of women deportees, each led to or by a different type of man and each in a different emotional state. From both the way she carries herself and her protruding belly, which pushes out her dress, we can recognize that the woman at the head of the line is pregnant. She wears the most elegant costume; in fact, it is of a type that we often find in Watteau's images. This is the *robe volante,* or *robe battante,* the earliest form of the sack-back dress, a loose-fitting garment that many moralists complained was worn specifically to hide pregnancy.[38] With its striped fabric and bow at the neckline, it seems to be finer than the dresses worn by the other two deportees. The distraught woman handing her over to the authorities looks less like a hard madam and more like a distressed but determined relative urging the pregnant girl to go along so the family can avoid disgrace. Indeed, in a later text, Bernardin de Saint-Pierre's 1788 *Paul et Virginie,* Marianne voluntarily goes into exile on an island because she has been impregnated by a man who seduced her with promises of marriage. Notice that the pregnant young woman is being given over to the man in the group who feigns gallantry, who is a parody of gallant lover in the deep bow he makes.

The second woman is drawn as a sorrowing Magdalen, wiping her tears with her veil. The figure is reminiscent of Jacques Sarazin's sculpture of the Magdalen, but here she is the prostitute who will be exiled rather than converted. Next to this woman is a soldier, perhaps of the sort who once made up her clientele, and he holds high a pike tipped with an arrowhead, not simply a phallic symbol but also a parody of the staff held by the pilgrims of love, a staff often crowned with the arrow of cupid. And finally we come to the third girl, with the little hat, kneeling and accompanied by what appears to be an *avocat*—a lawyer or perhaps some other judicial representative—recognizable by his black robes, white collar, and long wig. She seems younger than the other women, her costume perhaps that of a servant. That she has fallen on her knees might associate her with religious practices of repentance, but at the same time it suggests an act of passive resistance. As she resists, the representative of the law seems to be encouraging her to move along. Here we have three types of women and three types of men distributed in couples—the young woman of some status and wealth with the parodic gallant; the prostitute with the soldier; and the poor girl with a representative of the law. All six of these types were implicated in the deportations.

I note that the image is quite readable, composed very differently from the *Pèlerinage à l'île de Cythère*. Firmly located in the real, the departure for the islands is a reflection on the practices of love, gallantry, and seduction from a quite different point of view, one that in an image both mocking and tragic reveals not only the dangers of love but also the foolishness (and tragedy) of the women who fall for its ruse. In this light, notice how the first woman, the one who is pregnant and in the center of the composition, has a bland, gullible expression on her face, while the other two women express emotions of sorrow and resistance. Hers may be a stupefaction caused by surprise at finding herself forced to make a voyage to somewhere other than Cythera, or it may be one of simple trust in the man to whom she is being delivered.

To turn from this image back to the *Pèlerinage à Cythère* is to experience the sort of dislocations of theme and style offered in Defreveaulx's map of Cythera. Yet the turning from one Watteau to the other also offers two other forms of dislocation: from the illusory nature of Cythera to the actual situation of French women as they are forcibly deported, and from an image that offers no discernible narrative to one that has a clear reference to contemporary events. But even without imagining the *Départ* as a pendant, within itself Watteau's *Pèlerinage* makes visible more than desire expressed through the codes of *galanterie*, more than the pleasures of love represented through a mythology that no longer commanded belief. Whether or not Watteau intended it to be the case, his reception piece incorporates a more complex image of Cythera than the vaudevilles and comedies alone could offer, bringing to the island residues of emotional geographies and moralizing texts as well as the tradition of seeing Cythera as a site of pleasure and unfettered love. Complexity emerges not only through the two main groups of figures but also in the amours, the oarsmen, the invisible boat, the discarded clothing, the disguised cupid, all arrayed between an immobilized siren and a wounded goddess of love. Complexity emerges as well in a phantasmatic landscape, emblematic of an unattainable Shangrila, that the enchanted figures inhabit even as they remain blind to their surroundings and hence to their immersion in a fantasy of love. Like the woman in the sack-back dress on her way to La Louisiane, they are oblivious to the dangers of their voyage and to the risks of seduction. But as viewers awakened, we can separate ourselves, escape the bewitchment of art, and by meditating on pilgrims imbedded in their fantasies we can be reminded of a larger discourse that seeks to break the illusions of love and to present the voyage to Cythera as uncertain, repetitive, and fundamentally unsatisfying, a voyage that could leave us abandoned in the deserts of bitter remembrance. In making captivation evident, Watteau's dreamscape might also bring our attention back to the real world in which gallantry, seduction, and love can have sorrowful and even tragic consequences.

Notes

1. As quoted in Menges-Mironneau, "De l'épopée au théâtre galant," 84.
2. Voltaire, *La Henriade*, 165. On the violence of desire that Eros represents, see Sheriff, "Aux prises avec le désir."
3. Coypel, *Discours prononcez*, 173.
4. For a discussion of this problem see Plax, *Watteau*, 108–9.
5. Goncourt and Goncourt, *L'Art du dix-huitième siècle*, 2:288: "Voyez-vous dans *l'Embarquement de Cythère*, en haut du ciel, à demi perdus, tous ces petits culs nus d'Amour;

effrontés, polissonants? Où vont-ils? Ils vont jouer chez Fragonard, et mettre sur sa palette la poussière de leurs ailes de papillon."

6. The notable exception to this trend is found in Plax, *Watteau*, 143–49, which teases out some of the more ominous aspects of Watteau's famous image.

7. Moureau, "Watteau in His Time," 493–501.

8. On this point see Pucci, "Watteau and the Theater."

9. See, e.g., Bruno, *Atlas of Emotions*, 227–28; and Lestringant, *Le livre des îles*, 315–16.

10. In addition to Bruno and Lestringant, see, Collinet, "Allégorie et préciosité"; and esp. DeJean, *Tender Geographies*, 78–93.

11. Tomlinson, *La fête galante*, 112. See also Reitinger, "Mapping Relationships."

12. Viala, *"Les Signes Galants,"* 23.

13. Hélène Adhémar was among the first to mention Tallemant, in "Watteau, les romans et l'imagerie de son temps," 165–68.

14. Tallemant, "Voyages de l'isle d'amour," 305.

15. Ibid., 306.

16. Fénelon, *Les avantures de Télémaque*, 1:77.

17. Scott, *Rococo Interior*, 154–55.

18. Known from an engraving in the Recueil Julienne titled *Le Printemps*.

19. Montfaucon, *L'Antiquité expliquée*, 1:390.

20. This analysis of landscape was inspired by Démoris, "Watteau, le paysage et ses figures."

21. This issue was first raised in Levey, "Watteau's *Embarkation for Cythera*."

22. De Piles, *Cours de peinture par principes*, 19. De Piles defines the goal of painting as "séduire nos yeux." He characterizes true painting as that which "nous appelle (pour ainsi dire) en nous surprenant" (20), and he claims that the essence of painting is "de surprendre les yeux et de les tromper." We also find the following: "Ainsi, l'obligation de la peinture étant d'appeler et de plaire, quand elle a attiré son spectateur, ce devoir ne la dispense pas de l'entretenir des différentes beautés qu'elle renferme" (26).

23. Ibid., 122.

24. Ibid.,123–24.

25. Bergeon and Faillant-Dumas, "Restoration of the *Pilgrimage*." The formal qualities of the work are interrogated in exhaustive detail in Vinçon, *Cythère de Watteau*.

26. De Piles, *Cours de peinture par principes*, 112–13.

27. Ibid., 113.

28. See Vidal, "Style as Subject."

29. The two works are the Berlin version, often titled *Embarcation to Cythera*, and an engraving after a lost, smaller version of the Berlin *Cythera* that is focused on this couple.

30. On the importance of the Recueil Julienne, see Plax, "Interpreting Watteau across the Centuries," 28–30.

31. Moureau, "Watteau in His Time," 500.

32. *Le Nouveau Mercure*, September 1717, 130–34. On the deportations, see Conrad, *"Emigration Forcée."* For an earlier work, see Guilmoto, *Louisiane sous le Compagnie des Indes*, 1off.

33. Conrad, *"Emigration Forcée,"* 131.

34. *Dictionnaire de l'Académie française*, s.v. "galant."

35. Viala, *"Les Signes Galants,"* 19.
36. *Dictionnaire de l'Académie française,* s.v. "galant."
37. Ibid., s.v. "séduire." See also Nicholas Mirzoeff's excellent analysis of seduction in Watteau's work, "Flickers of Seduction."
38. On the *robe volante,* see Benhamou, "Clothing in the Age of Watteau," 134.

Works Cited

Adhémar, Hélène. "Watteau, les romans et l'imagerie de son temps." *Gazette des Beaux-Arts* 90 (1977): 165–72.

Benhamou, Reed. "Clothing in the Age of Watteau." In Sheriff, *Antoine Watteau,* 133–49.

Bergeon, Ségolene, and Lola Faillant-Dumas. "The Restoration of the *Pilgrimage to the Island of Cythera.*" In *Watteau, 1684–1721,* ed. Margaret Morgan Grasselli and Pierre Rosenberg, 460–64. Washington, DC: National Gallery of Art, 1984.

Bruno, Giuliana. *Atlas of Emotion: Journeys in Art, Architecture, and Film.* London: Verso, 2002.

Collinet, Jean-Pierre. "Allégorie et préciosité." *Cahiers de L'Association internationale des études françaises,* no. 28 (1976): 103–16.

Conrad, Glenn R. *"Emigration Forcée:* A French Attempt to Populate Louisiana, 1716–1720." In Conrad, *French Experience in Louisiana,* 125–35.

———, ed. *The French Experience in Louisiana.* Lafayette: Center for Louisiana Studies, University of Southwestern Louisiana, 1995.

Coypel, Antoine. *Discours prononcez dans les conferences de l'Académie Royale.* Paris: J. Collombat, 1721.

DeJean, Joan. *Tender Geographies: Women and the Origins of the Novel in France.* New York: Columbia University Press, 1991.

Démoris, René. "Watteau, le paysage et ses figures." In *Antoine Watteau (1684–1721): The Painter, His Age, and His Legend,* ed. François Moureau and Margaret Grasselli, 157–63. Paris: Champion-Slatkine, 1987.

De Piles, Roger. *Cours de peinture par principes.* Paris: Jacques Estienne, 1708.

Dictionnaire de l'Académie française. Paris: J. B. Coignard, 1694.

Fénelon, François de Salignac de la Motte. *Les avantures de Télémaque fils d'Ulysse.* 2 vols. Paris: Florentin Delaulne, 1717.

Goncourt, Jules de, and Edmond de Goncourt. *L'Art du dix-huitième siècle.* 2 vols. Paris: A. Quantin, 1873–74.

Guilmoto, E. *Louisiane sous le Compagnie des Indes, 1717–1731.* Paris: Librairie Orientale et Américaine, 1908.

Lestringant, Frank. *Le livre des îles: Atlas et récits insulaires de la Genèse à Jules Verne.* Geneva: Librairie Droz, 2002.

Levey, Michael. "The Real Theme of Watteau's *Embarkation for Cythera.*" *Burlington Magazine,* May 1961, 180–85.

Menges-Mironneau, Claude. "De l'épopée au théâtre galant vu par quelques peintres et graveurs du XVIIIe siècle." *Revue Voltaire* 2 (2002): 81–92.

Mirzoeff, Nicholas. "The Flickers of Seduction: The Ambivalent and Surprising Painting of Watteau." In Sheriff, *Antoine Watteau,* 123–32.

Montfaucon, Bernard de. *L'Antiquité expliquée et représentée en figures.* 5 vols. Paris: Florentin Delaulne, 1719.

Moureau, François. "Watteau in His Time." In *Antoine Watteau (1684–1721): The Painter, His Age, and His Legend,* ed. François Moureau and Margaret Grasselli, 469–506. Paris: Champion-Slatkine, 1987.

Plax, Julie-Anne. "Interpreting Watteau across the Centuries." In Sheriff, *Antoine Watteau,* 27–40.

———. *Watteau and the Cultural Politics of Eighteenth-Century France.* Cambridge: Cambridge University Press, 2000.

Pucci, Suzanne R. "Watteau and the Theater: Movable Fêtes." In Sheriff, *Antoine Watteau,* 106–22.

Reitinger, Franz. "Mapping Relationships: Allegory, Gender and the Cartographical Image in Eighteenth-Century France and England." *Imago Mundi* 51 (1999): 106–30.

Scott, Katie. *The Rococo Interior: Decoration and Social Spaces in Early Eighteenth-Century Paris.* New Haven, CT: Yale University Press, 1995.

Sheriff, Mary D., ed. *Antoine Watteau: Perspectives on the Artist and the Culture of His Time.* Newark: University of Delaware Press, 2006.

———. "Aux prises avec le désir." In *Fragonard amoureux,* 41–48. Paris: Réunion des musées nationaux, 2015.

Tallemant, Paul. "Voyages de l'isle d'amour, à Licidas." In *Voyages imaginaires, romanesques, merveilleux, allégoriques, amusans, comiques et critiques, suivis des songes et visions, et des romans cabalistiques,* 26:235–306. 39 vols. Amsterdam and Paris: Rue et Hotel Serpente, 1788.

Tomlinson, Robert. *La fête galante: Watteau et Marivaux.* Geneva: Droz, 1981.

Viala, Alain. "*Les Signes Galants:* A Historical Reevaluation of *Galanterie.*" *Yale French Studies* 92 (1997): 11–29.

Vidal, Mary. "Style as Subject in Watteau's Images of Conversation." In Sheriff, *Antoine Watteau,* 76–93.

Vinçon, René. *Cythère de Watteau: Suspension et coloris.* Paris: L'Harmattan, 1996.

Voltaire. *La Henriade de M. de Voltaire, avec des remarques et les différences qui se trouvent dans les diverses éditions de ce poème.* London, 1728.

Painting New England in
the Dutch West Indies

John Greenwood's *Sea Captains Carousing in Surinam*

KATELYN D. CRAWFORD

On 16 December 1752 the Boston-born portrait painter John Greenwood arrived in Paramaribo, the capital of the Dutch colony of Surinam, on the northeast coast of South America. Sailing from Boston, the twenty-five-year-old did not know that he would never again set foot in his hometown. Likely seeking patrons for his portraits, he set about documenting every English vessel arriving at the port and its point of origin.[1] Though his listing of boats lasted only one month, he persisted in studying his surroundings, accounting for the flora and fauna, slavery and plantation systems, English and Dutch mercantile networks, and linguistic intersections of the colony. He reported on his time in Surinam in two memoranda books. His final entry in the second book is a twenty-page narrative in the style of better-known chroniclers of travel, considering the colony's geography, natural resources, and inhabitants.

Throughout Greenwood's text, however, his work as a portraitist receives no direct attention beyond a list of portraits he painted and their prices; instead it is mentioned only in scrawled asides like that on the inside cover of the volume, specifying three sizes for six frames the artist supplied to one Surinam resident. Just one among many clues about the scale of Greenwood's business and social connections while in the colony, this note indicates the sale of six frames to "Tarton," a planter holding five hundred acres on a tributary of the Commowiene River. Tarton's plantation is among the first Greenwood mentions visiting. Yet while Greenwood sold this planter frames and may even have provided the works filling those frames, his Surinam memorandum book never indicates that he painted Tarton's portrait. Greenwood's visits to plantations around Paramaribo did result in commissions, however, as in the case of "J. Scherping," whose coffee plantation, Rasten Lust, was located near the mouth of the Suriname River, downstream and on the opposite bank from Paramaribo. A short trip from the port city, Rasten Lust was the second plantation Greenwood listed visiting, and this relationship later led to the artist's painting a half-length portrait of Scherping for one hundred gilders. Greenwood not only painted portraits but also sold pictures and frames while residing in Paramaribo; however, his list of portraits is the only steady source of income he tracks in his Surinam memorandum book. The majority of the canvases he painted were kit-kat, quarter-, half-, or whole-length representations of merchant-captains or planters living near or passing through the port city.[2]

Greenwood reported painting 113 portraits, or about 23 a year during his six-year stay in the colony from 1752 to 1758. These canvases were not painted in a continuous stream of work or on a single price scale, however. Greenwood's earliest Surinam portrait, a whole-length painting of "C. Macknich" for 200 gilders, was among the most expensive canvases commissioned from the artist during his residence. The portraits he painted earlier in his time in the colony were similarly priced and equally opulent, as he painted families and their children primarily in half- and whole-length formats. A notable drop in his prices occurs at a midpoint in the list, when Greenwood charges "Miss V: Coper" not 200 gilders for a whole-length portrait but instead 140. Though Greenwood painted almost two-thirds of his total Surinam canvases after this picture, the later canvases were rarely on the scale of his earliest Surinam portraits or painted for similar amounts. This precipitous drop in the prices he was charging for portraits never recovered before his departure from the colony for Amsterdam in 1758. For an artist who likely traveled seeking new patrons for his portraits, Greenwood's time in Surinam appears easily attributable to supply and demand. Leaving Boston as the population of portrait painters increased and competed for a small pool of patrons, the artist visited another colonial port city until his business slowed and another opportunity presented itself.[3]

Yet this essay argues that Greenwood's visit to Surinam was not simply the early wandering of a developing itinerant portraitist. It was the product of Greenwood's following established trade routes between New England and Surinam that were well traveled by the sea captains whose portraits he painted in both locales. While art historians have considered the formal aspects and local histories of early American portraits, scholars of American art have only recently connected the work of one of these artists, John Singleton Copley, to study of the eighteenth-century Atlantic world.[4] Himself the son of a sea captain living in a port city in the mid-eighteenth century, Greenwood was familiar with maritime Britain's opportunities for travel throughout the Atlantic. This essay moves beyond geographical subspecialty to take an Atlantic perspective on early American artists like Greenwood, the importance of oceanic travel, and burgeoning mobility both within and proximal to British imperial spaces. At a time when visual representation was exploding throughout the British Atlantic, in his journey to Surinam Greenwood followed the example of previous portraitists whom he had seen moving to Boston from England. Through his travel, his list of patrons in Surinam, and one surviving canvas from his time in the South American colony, Greenwood demonstrated his attention to and reliance on transatlantic shipping networks for patrons, materials, and visual sources. His careful records of both shipping networks and local events while residing in Paramaribo further reveal him to have been an aware colonial agent, operating at the intersection of the British and Dutch empires.

The whereabouts of none of the portraits Greenwood documented having painted in Surinam are known today; the only surviving painting from his time in the colony is *Sea Captains Carousing in Surinam,* painted with oil on bed ticking between 1755 and 1758 and signed by the artist (fig. 1). It is the only group picture on this large scale from colonial America. In the painting, twenty punch-fueled figures play cards, drink, sleep, or fall victim to their inebriation (including one unlucky gentleman who vomits in a companion's pocket while setting fire to his coattails), while four African slaves either serve beverages or sleep. These activities are confined to a second-floor barroom in a Paramaribo tavern, the most common type of nondomestic building in America in the eighteenth century. *Sea Captains Carous-*

Figure 1. *Sea Captains Carousing in Surinam,* John Greenwood, c. 1755–58, oil on bed ticking, 37¾″ × 75″. (Saint Louis Art Museum, Museum Purchase 256:1948)

ing in Surinam reveals the impact Greenwood's surrounding influences had on his painting. Within this picture, the artist deftly and purposely navigates his role as a commissioned portraitist, painting for his merchant clients, while deploying pictorial devices that locate the scene within an Atlantic world of intersecting empires—in particular British and Dutch—characterized by the movement of people, goods, and ideas. In the canvas the artist depicts primarily Rhode Island sea captains but also integrates Dutch and enslaved figures into his drama.

To represent these figures, Greenwood relied not only on English visual precedent, with which he had familiarized himself while developing his portrait practice in Boston, but also on formal and thematic concepts he discovered in Dutch sources, to which he was exposed through prints and original canvases imported to Surinam. These metropolitan visual structures organize colonial subjects as Greenwood represents Paramaribo's drinking and tavern culture. As Greenwood traveled to Surinam, these myriad visual influences also moved throughout the Atlantic world. Connecting in Paramaribo, these cross-cultural visual and material influences enabled the production of a canvas that depicts the porousness and mobility of Caribbean colonies and port cities.

When Greenwood arrived at the end of 1752, Paramaribo was a bustling port city situated in a well-established and profitable colony. Described by the eighteenth-century natural historian Edward Bancroft as "the most ancient and considerable of all the *Dutch* Colonies in *Guiana*," Surinam had been established by the English but then surrendered to the Dutch during the Second Anglo-Dutch War in 1667.[5] Over the course of the eighteenth century, Surinam grew into a prosperous plantation society, producing sugar, coffee, cotton, and cacao for the province of Holland. According to Dr. David Nassy, another visitor to Surinam in the mid-eighteenth century, the colony was producing more revenue for the Dutch Empire and consuming more imported manufactured goods than any other Caribbean colony of any nationality.[6] The lavish, opulent living that accompanied the wealth of the colony was described in detail by the Englishman John Gabriel Stedman in his 1790 account of his residence in the colony. Steadman was an artist himself, and paintings are among the first features he notes in Surinam's domestic ornament: "The houses in general at Paramaribo are elegantly furnished, with paintings, gilding, crystal chandeliers, jars of china &c. The rooms are never papered or plastered but beautifully wainscoted and stocked with the neatest joinery of cedar, brazil wood, and mahogany."[7]

The wealth Stedman encountered is further emphasized in his description of the sartorial leanings of the occupants of Paramaribo, both long-term residents and those like the captains in Greenwood's group picture, who were passing through the city: "profuseness in dress, which is truly magnificent—silk, embroidery, Genoa velvets, diamonds, gold- and silver-lace being daily wear—not so much as a captain of a trading ship appearing in solid gold buckles to his socks, breeches, &c, nor are they less refined at their tables, where everything that can be called delicate is produced at any price, and served up in the newest fashioned silver plate and Japan china."[8] Stedman's account of life in Paramaribo describes not only the wealth Greenwood sought when traveling to the colony but also the opulent lifestyle that accompanied this wealth, which the artist encountered upon arrival.

While Stedman was at times awed by the richness of the occupants of Paramaribo, he also found himself periodically distraught at their manner of living. Both Stedman and Greenwood recount excessive bouts of drinking of the type Greenwood painted in *Sea Captains*. These events were visible in the city's streets as much as in the city's taverns, buildings that melded public and private realms, serving as inns for travelers in need of a place to rest and coffeehouses for information seekers interested in local news and news from abroad. Though according to his memoir Stedman occasionally participated in drinking bouts, he was not inured to their excess. The Englishman judged Surinamers harshly, writing that "luxury and dissipation in this country are carried to the extreme and, in my opinion, must send thousands to the grave. The men are generally a set of poor, withered mortals, as dry and sapless as a squeezed lemon, owing to their intemperate way of living—such late hours [and] hard drinking."[9] The subjects of *Sea Captains* lack moderation, partaking in the late hours and hard drinking Stedman condemns, and this lure of intemperance was compounded by the threat of violence for residents of Surinam.

For Stedman, the prominence of slavery within the colony also spoke to the wealth of the colony. Greenwood also knew Surinam as a slave society wracked with tension and violence, exploding both between masters and slaves and between masters and escaped slaves who had formed independent inland communities, called Maroons. News of volatility in Surinam traveled as far as the Boston: just before Greenwood's departure in May 1752, excerpts from a letter were published in the *Boston Evening Post*: "A few days ago the Plantation of Mr. Cardava was over-run and destroyed by the wild negroes, who murdered him in a barbarous Manner, cutting him into pound Pieces; they then took his wife, and a child at her breast, and after stripping her stark naked, set her up as a Mark to shoot at, with the Child in her arms, but one of the Chiefs relenting, he entreated the rest for her, and she was again set at Liberty."[10] The colony's ratio of African to European occupants was among the highest in the West Indies, with an average of twenty-five enslaved Africans to each white colonist, but jumping to as many as sixty-five to one in the plantation districts. In addition to the tension surrounding this extreme ratio, Maroon communities waged war on planters, leading one mid-eighteenth-century commentator to state that "the colony had become a theater of perpetual war."[11] Greenwood arrived just as fighting between the colonial government, planters, and Maroons had subsided with a peace treaty signed by the colonial governor and the Maroon leaders in 1749. Yet work by the anthropologist and historian Richard Price indicates that attacks and conflict persisted throughout the 1750s. Although the threat of violence between blacks and whites is not clearly presented in *Sea Captains,* the inescapable presence of slavery in the colony is foregrounded in the canvas.

Traces of slavery are almost entirely absent from eighteenth-century British North American colonial portraiture, but Greenwood includes multiple enslaved figures in two possible roles. The barman and the server were likely enslaved by the tavern keeper for service labor, but the two additional figures who sleep on the floor may have been enslaved by participants in the evening's events, tasked with accompanying their slaveholders as body men but not participating in the entertainment.[12] Here Greenwood constructs a somewhat edited account of colonial slavery, a view of his daily experience as he resided in the colony. Like the mirror on the rear wall reflecting the drunken sea captains' behavior onto themselves, this canvas presents an edited refraction of Paramaribo painted from life.

We do not know with certainty the patron of *Sea Captains Carousing in Surinam,* and no firm evidence documents the identity of the figures in the canvas. However, while acting as an agent for the sale of the painting, Edward A. Wild described the traditional identifications of the figures, including "Mr. Wanton of Newport, fat, round faced, asleep, and just being baptized" and "Capt. Hopkins, with a broad hat."[13] These men were likely William Wanton and Esek Hopkins, both painted by Greenwood in quarter-length individual portraits around 1754 in Paramaribo. In his list of portraits painted in Surinam, the artist noted painting "W Wanton" and "K Hopkins" shortly before the *New-York Mercury*'s shipping news ran a notice placing both men in the colony in late June and July.[14] While some traders stopped in Paramaribo for only a few days before continuing on to other West Indian ports, the average layover for a North American ship was ten weeks.[15] Hopkins and Wanton were again placed in Surinam with a critical mass of New England merchants in 1757 by a shipping announcement in the *New-York Mercury*.[16] We can believe that either of the Rhode Island sea captains previously painted by Greenwood wished to have a record of his working excursion at the edge of the British and Dutch empires painted during this second visit. With at least fifteen captains on layover in Paramaribo from Rhode Island, Massachusetts, and Connecticut, the three colonies most economically invested in trade to Surinam, the commissioner placed himself within a maritime fraternity.

British North American ships were commonplace in mid-eighteenth-century Surinam, as one of the three lines to Atlantic markets on which the colony relied. Supplies, tools, food, European settlers, administrators, and soldiers arrived through the bilateral shuttle trade between Surinam and the Dutch Republic. Surinam's tropical products returned to the Dutch Republic in these ships. A second necessary trade route connected the colony to both the Dutch Republic and Africa, with the triangle trade transporting slave labor to the colony to cultivate tropical products. The third circuit included British North American colonials transporting horses, flour, fish, and other meat products to Surinam, primarily from New England. According to the historian Johannes Postma, of the 4,478 ships participating in the intra-Caribbean trade that were documented anchoring at Paramaribo in the eighteenth century, about 4,000 of them, or almost 90 percent, were American ships from New England.[17]

Although it was an unusual commission for a New England merchant in the 1750s, this picture would have served its owner as an amusement but also as an advertisement of his skills as a mariner. Represented in the company of notable Rhode Island traders in Surinam, Wanton, Hopkins, and the other captains participate in an informal gentlemanly club of misbehavior during their voyage to the West Indies. They are also shown as having completed successful trading voyages, exchanging the horses, flour, fish, and meat provided to the colony by New England for the molasses that was distilled into rum in British North America. For merchant-captains like Wanton and Hopkins, in Newport this image became a document attesting to their seafaring skill as much as to their consumerist sophistication, allowing them to pursue even more lucrative voyages. William Wanton and his brother and business partner Joseph aspired to compete for the most lucrative routes departing Newport, beginning to work as traders in the transatlantic slave trade in the early 1760s. Writing to another Newport firm, Nicholas Brown & Company, in 1764, Joseph Wanton offered to captain a slave-trading vessel to the coast of Africa after a competing captain had declined the post: "I am at present out of Business and [if] you have a mind to fit that Voyage I offer my Service to you and Fllatter my self that I can give you satisfaction in the execution of the same being well acquainted and well experienced in the Ginea Trade all Down the Coasts."[18] Ultimately, Nicholas Brown & Company gave this voyage on the ship *Sally,* not to Wanton, but to Hopkins, who the Wanton brothers insisted was not experienced enough for the post.[19] All three men affirmed their professional identities through their presence in this scene even as they aspired to captain the most profitable voyages departing from Newport, those of the slave-trading vessels sailing the Guinea coast.

Greenwood's services were also endorsed by having a patron like Wanton or Hopkins display this uncommon image, advantageous because while working in Surinam he did not know that he would never return to Boston. Even when he wrote to his fellow Boston artist John Singleton Copley fifteen years later, in 1770, to commission a portrait of his aging mother, Greenwood still appeared to intend a return trip: "I have of late enter'd into connections, that may probably keep me longer in London than I coud wish."[20] By painting and signing a novel picture in a fashionable style that would be seen by Rhode Island merchants—wealthy men capable of commissioning pairs or suites of family pictures—Greenwood promoted his ability as a painter and his worldliness as an artist, showcasing his personal travel and influences and positioning himself to reenter a market recently saturated with both local portraitists and those arriving from London.

While its subject was unusual, the scale and scope of *Sea Captains Carousing in Surinam* was also exceptional among canvases produced in the mid-eighteenth-century American colonies. Scholars have emphasized, however, that the work is not without precedent, citing the painting's similarity to William Hogarth's 1733 engraving *A Midnight Modern Conversation,* printed after the painting of the same title he created from 1729 to 1732 (fig. 2). Historians of American art have understood Hogarth's model to be a moralizing critique of an empirewide culture of overindulgence, and Greenwood's work is often cited as early criticism of the merchants portrayed and of Surinam's slave system.[21] Unlike Hogarth's work, however, this painting was commissioned from Greenwood by its subjects, evidenced by its quick return to Rhode Island and corroborated by traditional accounts of the identity of the sitters depicted, discussed above. And while the canvas was painted to satisfy Greenwood's patrons, the artist also constructed an aesthetic experiment within this composition. In the painting, Greenwood

Katelyn D. Crawford

Figure 2. A Midnight Modern Conversation, William Hogarth, 1733, engraving.
(Yale Center for British Art, Paul Mellon Collection, B1981.25.1409)

explores the model Hogarth established not only in his print of *A Midnight Modern Conversation* but also in many of his "busy" pictures. The viewer is led through the canvas, in which the distinction between portrait and genre scene is blurred, by the dynamic action of the scene's participants. Greenwood uses Hogarthian precedent as much for his thematic and compositional exploration as for an exemplar of moralizing commentary.[22]

Fleeting scholarly attention to Greenwood's canvas has argued that Greenwood imitates Hogarth in order to critique his misbehaving Rhode Island sea-captain subjects—for their outright behavior, their place within the slave trade, or both. Linking Greenwood's critique to that presented in *A Midnight Modern Conversation,* historians of American art have viewed Greenwood's work through Hogarth's moralizing lens. Interpreting Hogarth's project as singularly moralizing, however, forecloses the ambiguity present in both pictures.

Turning the conversation piece on its head, *A Midnight Modern Conversation* takes the conventions of an emerging genre that Hogarth helped to develop, defined by genteel politeness, and twists them into a satiric image. Hogarth repeatedly destabilized the conversation piece during this period, painting the inversion of a society that believed itself to be "well and balanced," according to the art historian Frédéric Ogée. Ogée argues that Hogarth "invites the beholder to a visual experience of limits," painting works like *A Midnight Modern Conversation* as foils to pictures presenting the polite conversation of gentlemen, such as *Captain Lord George Graham in his Cabin,* in the National Maritime Museum, London.[23]

For Hogarth, the polite and impolite are intertwined, both within the conversation piece genre and beyond; the impolite and excessive exist within the polite. Hogarth's dense, dynamic compositions lead the viewer through the depicted scene, with the narrative relying on and dominated by its visual presentation. This reading of Hogarth's work reopens possibilities for Greenwood's, encouraging us to read *Sea Captains Carousing in Surinam* as a venue for aesthetic experimentation, created as a counterpoint to the artist's formulaic portraits, following the model of *A Midnight Modern Conversation.* As with Hogarth, any moral commentary by Greenwood is ambiguous and subsumed within a composition centered on aesthetic experimentation.

Greenwood's composition is undeniably inspired by Hogarth's print, with similar paneling framing both interior scenes and analogous tall case clocks striking late evening hours as a plenitude of drinking equipment surrounds inebriated participants. Yet Greenwood's subtle departures from Hogarth's model are significant. Hogarth's shallow picture plane forces the viewer of his print into the sullied room where the urine from the overflowing chamber pot seeps across the foreground, forcing the audience into the realm of social excess. Alternately, Greenwood paints a panoramic picture plane, with a centrally hung mirror on the rear wall of the tavern reflecting the excessive realities of life in 1750s Surinam while simultaneously providing the viewer options for escape, either through the exterior door at the right—admittedly made unappealing by the spewing participant—or deeper into the punch through the continued service at the left of the canvas.

Sea Captains Carousing in Surinam lingers within Greenwood's memorandum book from his time in the colony. Although the artist never explicitly discusses a multifigure composition, he recounts not only painting portraits of the scene's participants but also witnessing the type of behavior engaged in by the sea captains as being common on the streets of Paramaribo, including one incident in October 1757: "Holscher & Vander Gogh [were] up all night Drinking—saw 'em at 1 o'clock as I came from the watch. Dinker was very Drunk & told me that a very holy & Religious Dispute had kept 'em together all night & that was not yet settled—that is they were to Have another drinking match."[24] It is a visual clue, however, that reiterates

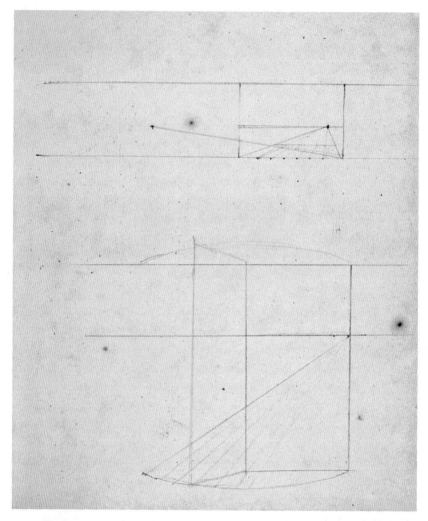

Figure 3. Page 80 from *Memorandum Book No. 2,* John Greenwood, c. 1752–58, graphite on paper. (New-York Historical Society)

the interpretation that Greenwood approached this canvas as an aesthetic experiment. Situated in his Surinam memorandum book between technical descriptions and drawings of fireworks at Fort Zeelandia in Paramaribo and Greenwood's narrative description of Surinam are two sketch studies for *Sea Captains,* each suggesting one of the two light sources around which the final canvas is constructed (fig. 3). The perspectival study at the top of the page fixes one point at the right of the study, possibly where an open door leads to the balcony in the final canvas. From this point lines cascade down to a lower edge bounding the space. A second line stretches from the lower right corner of the top study, reaching into unstructured space, perhaps to the bar window, a second fixed light source for the composition. The study at the bottom of the page suggests the balcony's open door, sweeping into the interior.

For Greenwood this attention to light and the construction of space within his canvases came not from Hogarth but from genre scenes by seventeenth-century Dutch artists. Greenwood collected the works of and information about Dutch artists while residing in Surinam, amassing a diverse group of prints, drawings, and art and architecture books. Among these volumes, which he valued at 361 guilders, were a "Folio—No. 1—Cont[aining] 172 Capital Drawings by Different Masters & Prints of Rembrants, Ostade, &c.," "a Fine Print of Ostade," and "an Addition of 46 prints to [the folio]—6 of Ostade."[25] In his collection of twenty-six art and architecture books and more than three hundred drawings and prints, Greenwood identifies only two artists by name: Rembrandt van Rijn and Adriaen van Ostade.

It is not surprising to find prints after Rembrandt and Ostade amid the wealth and excessive imports from the Netherlands in Surinam. Both artists grew popular in the Netherlands over the course of their careers and the seventeenth century. Ostade was regarded as highly as Rembrandt by eighteenth-century collectors, who were eager to possess scenes of contented Dutch peasants who even while drinking excessively and brawling among themselves did not threaten the civility or stability of their refined neighbors. This type of painting by Rembrandt and Ostade was collected widely in both England and the Netherlands. As evidenced by Greenwood's collection, prints after these artists and other seventeenth-century Dutch painters circulated throughout the Dutch Atlantic, just as Hogarth's prints made their way throughout the British Empire.

In the 1640s and 1650s, the Dutch artist Adriaen van Ostade painted scenes of figures boozing or brawling in packed taverns and inns, such as *Carousing Peasants* (fig. 4). The humorous physical exchange between the sitters, the characteristics of the tavern, and the slight elevation and remove that the viewer is offered from the scene are all elements we find in Greenwood's work, showing his close attention to Ostade's work. In his exploration of the play between light and dark, the slightly tilted and elevated perspective of the scene, and the presentation of space, Greenwood's attention to Dutch techniques is as apparent as his attention to a longstanding Dutch genre-scene subject in *Sea Captains*. Hogarth's *A Midnight Modern Conversation* was popular throughout the British empire by the 1750s, printed

Figure 4. Carousing Peasants, Adriaen van Ostade, c. 1630, oil on panel. (The Norton Simon Foundation, F.1972.14.P)

on ceramics, listed in British Caribbean inventories as hanging in homes, and advertised in newspapers as available for purchase. Greenwood took this British visual culture and integrated its broadly disseminated form and iconography of empire with Dutch formal precedents available in Surinam through bilateral shipping with Amsterdam. Within these intermixed influences he inserted the visual and social cultures of Surinam, creating a canvas that illustrates his personal travel, his attention to his surroundings, and his development as an artist.

Hogarth's print pictures processes of exchange across empire through material culture in the Chinese form and decoration of the punch bowl; the punch within the bowl made from rum, sugar, and citrus; the tobacco being smoked; and the newspapers providing shipping and trade information. *A Midnight Modern Conversation* was also rooted in a Dutch tradition of seventeenth-century genre paintings of merry companies and tavern scenes, replicating the humor and moral messages of these canvases. Greenwood's painting escalates the presentation of material exchange beyond Hogarth, saturating the canvas with trade goods with diverse geographical origins surprisingly collected in a Surinam inn. Amid Greenwood's vast assemblage of items spilled, broken, or otherwise overtopped, the central punch bowl of Hogarth's print has multiplied into four vessels of various sizes, painted to resemble Chinese export porcelain. There is no ladle from earlier in the evening to suggest that the bowl functioned as a center bowl would in a London tavern; instead, drinking vessels are passed among participants in the more common colonial practice.[26] Wine on the floor, candleholders, tobacco, the tall case clock, and the mirror on the rear wall of the room, as well as the enslaved persons framing the scene, were all brought by Dutch, French, Spanish, and English shipping to Paramaribo.[27] Traveling goods are integrated with the abundant punch, existing in great quantities in Surinam, where its ingredients originated and from where they were shipped to satisfy English and Dutch appetites for the beverage. The two locally produced raw sugar loaves behind the counter underscore the purpose of the colony and further point to the agricultural system beyond the port city, their dark forms standing behind one of the enslaved figures, waiting for him to blend them into punch.

This canvas also accurately represents the material culture of an Atlantic tavern located in a Caribbean port city. Large Caribbean taverns often had both public and private drinking rooms on their first and second floors, maintaining as few as two and as many as ten drinking rooms in addition to sleeping quarters. These drinking rooms included bar rooms or built-in bars of the type seen in Greenwood's painting, which were caged to protect the owner's investments in both the liquor and barmen. Inventories of well-stocked Caribbean taverns include the furnishings found in Greenwood's picture and more. In the 1735 inventory of a Jamaica tavern, for instance, drinking rooms were furnished with not only tables and chairs but also looking glasses and prints, twelve mezzotints, and twenty-three paintings scattered throughout the establishment's ten rooms. A clock was located in the "bar room," perhaps to serve as a more direct reminder of the hour to patrons. Similar to what Greenwood pictures in his Surinam tavern, the Jamaican tavern's inventory also named a workforce of eighteen male and female enslaved Africans.[28]

Proprietors of taverns built spaces where patrons could conduct their business, communicating through transatlantic networks and receiving news from travelers, friends, and newspapers. Shipping and price lists were often tacked on the walls, as may be illustrated by the barely visible handwriting on the rear wall in Greenwood's canvas. By 1750 these commercial spaces included sports clubs, hair salons, painting and tracing studios, and reading rooms. Taverns periodically served as temporary housing not only for artists but also for their studios and may have been known to Atlantic travelers as places where portraits could be commissioned and painted. Even if Greenwood was not regularly painting in this tavern, it is likely that he frequented one or more of these establishments to cultivate relationships with patrons.

Whether working at a remote plantation or in a Paramaribo tavern, Greenwood lived at the intersection of empires during his residence in Surinam. Even as he painted New England sea captains in the Dutch West Indies, he shrewdly balanced his own interests and local circumstances with his patrons' agendas, integrating divergent cultural influences in a commissioned canvas ultimately picturing professional identity. Often called on as an interpreter between Dutch, French, and English parties, Greenwood in his Surinam memorandum book also charted translations between language groups in Surinam, including "English," "Dutch," "Negro," "Indian," and "Caribbee Indian," not only transcribing words for concepts such as "a fish caught at sea" or "a Spanish lady" but also describing unfamiliar objects for which he knew no English equivalents, including "a large snake worship'd by the Negroes of the Guedal nation" or a "hog in armor."[29] For Greenwood, life in Surinam was characterized by translation, both linguistic and visual.

Even painting merchant-captains from his New England home required turning the many languages that he was absorbing into a single satisfactory picture that could be understood when transferred to a wall in the patron's office in Rhode Island. In his ability to translate between Dutch and English artistic precedents and Surinamese influences, while painting a picture that represented the colony's pervading slave system but could also be viewed as a self-promotional canvas commissioned by Rhode Island merchants, Greenwood demonstrated his growing sophistication as a portraitist moving throughout and working within the British Atlantic. Through consideration of cultural context and the artist's experience, this painting can be understood as more than an imitative satire after Hogarth: as a delicate integration of both local influences and imperial experiences.

Notes

1. Greenwood, Diaries, 1752–1758. For earlier scholarship on Greenwood, see Burroughs, *John Greenwood in America*. Greenwood's second and fourth memoranda books are housed at the New-York Historical Society; the first, also from his time in Surinam and referenced in the second, is at present unlocated, as is the third, from his time in the Netherlands.

2. Greenwood, Diaries, 1752–1758. Greenwood's note regarding Tarton's frames is in-

side the front cover of the volume. For the list of plantations visited, see ibid., 1–2; and for his list of portraits painted, ibid., 174–75.

3. On Greenwood and the shift in portrait painting in the British North American colonies around 1750, see Miles, "Portrait in America," 28–68.

4. Art historians who have touched on the significance of the Atlantic in this period have largely divided along the lines of geographical subspecialty. This has been particularly visible in scholarship on Copley, including Barratt's *John Singleton Copley in America* and Neff's *John Singleton Copley in England,* notably published in the same year (1995). On itinerancy in early American art, see Jaffee, *New Nation of Goods,* esp. 1–46; and Benes and Benes, *Itinerancy in New England and New York.*

5. Bancroft, *Natural History of Guiana,* 350.

6. Nassy, *Essai historique,* 37–45.

7. Price and Price, *Stedman's Surinam,* 126. See also Stedman, *Narrative of a Five Years Expedition;* this edition is based on Stedman's 1790 manuscript, which was heavily edited prior to its publication in 1796 by Stedman.

8. Stedman, *Narrative of a Five Years Expedition,* 129.

9. Ibid., 18.

10. *Boston Evening Post,* 30 May 1752. The excerpt continues: "A few days after, a Duel was fought here between one Mr. Crawford, a Scotchman, and a Dutchman, both officers in this place, Wherein the former was run through the body, since which the later absconds, tho' the Governor makes strict search after him, and demands him dead or alive."

11. Price and Price, *Stedman's Surinam,* xiv. See also Parrish, "Embodying African Knowledge," 258.

12. Significantly, Stedman also indirectly addresses the unlikely possibility that these figures are themselves drunk when describing his first interaction with his ultimate wife in "Surinam marriage," Joanna: "She put a bottle of Madeira wine, water, and some very fine fruit on the table, and explained in the best manner she was able, by gesticulation and broken accounts, that her *massera* with all the family were gone to his plantation to stay a few days upon business, and that she was left behind to receive an English captain whom she supposed to be me. I signified that I was Captain Stedman and then filled her a tumbler of wine, which she would not accept without the greatest persuasion, it being almost unprecedented in this country to see a Negro slave, either male or female, eat or drink in the presence of a European." Stedman, *Narrative of a Five Years Expedition,* 18.

13. Wild, "Old Jenckes Picture."

14. The portraits of Wanton and Hopkins are the fifty-first and fifty-second paintings listed in Greenwood's inventory of portraits painted while in Surinam. Assuming roughly twenty-three pictures per year, they would have been painted in about 1755. On 5 August 1754 the *New-York Mercury* ran the following notice: "Saturday left captain Vardil arrived here in 28 Days from Surinam, and acquaints us that he sailed from thence in Company with the Capts. Hopkins and Johnston, the former for Rhode-Island, and the latter for New-London: He left the following Vessels at Surinam, viz. Malcome from Halifax, Smith from Boston; Goddard, Hawney, Topham, Nichols, Awl, and Benjamin and William Wanton from Rh-Island, Low from Philadelphia, and a Ship from London, bound for Philadelphia also."

15. Postma and Enthoven, *Riches from Atlantic Commerce,* 311. Between 1750 and 1759,

501 British North American and Caribbean ships landed at Paramaribo, or 50.1 percent of the 1,017 ships arriving at the port.

16. *New-York Mercury,* 7 November 1757. The advertisement announced: "Wednesday last Captain Augustine Lawrance came in from Surinam, in 29 Days; where he left the Captains Buckmaster, Owens, Morris, Hopkins, James Hopkins, earl, and two of the Name of Wanton, belonging to Rhode-Island; Frasier, Thompson, Ash, Hoskins, and Ingrham of Boston; with Moore and Chester of New-London."

17. Postma and Enthoven, *Riches from Atlantic Commerce,* 294–302.

18. Joseph Wanton to Nicholas Brown & Company, 4 August 1764, Brown University Steering Committee on Slavery & Justice, Repository of Historical Documents, John Carter Brown Library, accessed 14 May 2017, http://library.brown.edu/cds/catalog/catalog .php?verb=render&colid=17&id=115764409477769.

19. This was Hopkins's first voyage to Africa, and at the time he had no experience on a slave-trading vessel. During the fifteen-month trip he lost 109 of 196 slaves on board. Joseph and William Wanton to Nicholas Brown & Company, 13 August 1764, Brown University Steering Committee on Slavery & Justice, Repository of Historical Documents, John Carter Brown Library, accessed 14 May 2017, http://library.brown.edu/cds/catalog/ catalog.php?verb=render&colid=17&id=115764064293220.

20. Copley and Pelham, *Letters and Papers,* 81.

21. The art historians David Bindman, Charles Ford, and Helen Weston assert that the work "suggests graphically the louche society of the slave traders, where drunken carousing was the principal form of sociability, while Africans, represented by [four] servants, minister to their needs." "Africa and the Slave Trade," 226–28. An American art textbook edited by Angela Miller et al., *American Encounters,* also discusses the painting as an expression of the artist's "comedic disdain" for his subjects, contrasting their indecorum with the black slaves' bodily comportment.

22. Ogée, "Flesh of Theory," 71–72.

23. Ogée, "From Text to Image," 14–20. Hogarth's depiction of the many stages of boozy abandon amused the subjects of *A Midnight Modern Conversation,* as illustrated by the quick use of this image to decorate punch bowls.

24. Greenwood, Diaries, 1752–1758, 47.

25. Ibid., 56–57.

26. Harvey, "Ritual Encounters," 181–91. We can imagine the drinker at the left of the table finding the scene in which he is painted at the bottom of his punch bowl, uncovering Hogarth's scene gulp by gulp.

27. Postma and Enthoven. *Riches from Atlantic Commerce,* 307.

28. See Hancock and McDonald, *Public Drinking in the Early Modern World.* On the expansion of taverns in the Atlantic world around 1750, see xvi–xvii. See also Probate Inventory of William White, Tavernkeeper, 31 January 1736, as reproduced in ibid., 27–44, 240.

29. Greenwood, Diaries, 1752–1758, 10.

Works Cited

Bancroft, Edward. *An Essay on the Natural History of Guiana, in South America.* London: T. Becket & P. A. De Hondt, 1769.

Barratt, Carrie Rebora. *John Singleton Copley in America.* New York: Metropolitan Museum of Art, 1995.

Benes, Peter, and Jane Montague Benes, eds. *Itinerancy in New England and New York.* Annual Proceedings of the Dublin Seminar for New England Folklife, no. 9. Boston: Boston University Press, 1986.

Bindman, David, Charles Ford, and Helen Weston. "Africa and the Slave Trade." In *The Image of the Black in Western Art, Volume III: From the "Age of Discovery" to the Age of Abolition, Part 3: The Eighteenth Century,* edited by David Bindman and Henry Louis Gates Jr., 207–40. Cambridge, MA: Belknap Press of Harvard University Press, 2011.

Burroughs, Alan. *John Greenwood in America, 1745–1752.* Andover, MA: Addison Gallery of American Art, Phillips Academy, 1943.

Copley, John Singleton, and Henry Pelham. *Letters and Papers of John Singleton Copley and Henry Pelham, 1739–1776.* New York: Kennedy Graphics, 1970.

Greenwood, John. Diaries, 1752–1758, 1763–1765. Manuscript Collection, New-York Historical Society.

Hancock, David, and Michelle McDonald, eds. *Public Drinking in the Early Modern World: Voices from the Tavern, 1500–1800.* Vol. 4, *America.* London: Pickering & Chatto, 2011.

Harvey, Karen. "Ritual Encounters: Punch Parties and Masculinity in the Eighteenth Century." *Past and Present* 214, no. 1 (2012): 165–203.

Jaffee, David. *A New Nation of Goods: The Material Culture of Early America.* Philadelphia: University of Pennsylvania Press, 2011.

Lugo-Ortiz, Agnes, and Angela Rosenthal, eds. *Slave Portraiture in the Atlantic World.* New York: Cambridge University Press, 2013.

Miles, Ellen G. "The Portrait in America, 1750–1776." In *American Colonial Portraits, 1700–1776,* edited by Richard H. Saunders and Ellen G. Miles, 28–76. Washington, DC: Smithsonian Institution Press for the National Portrait Gallery, 1987.

Miller, Angela L., Janet C. Berlo, Bryan Wolf, and Jennifer L. Roberts, eds. *American Encounters: Art, History, and Cultural Identity.* New York: Pearson, 2008.

Nassy, David de Ishak Cohen. *Essai historique sur la colonie de Surinam.* Paramaribo, 1788.

Neff, Emily Ballew. *John Singleton Copley in England.* Houston: Museum of Fine Arts in association with Merrell Holberton Publishers, London, 1995.

Ogée, Frédéric. "The Flesh of Theory: The Erotics of Hogarth's Lines." In *The Other Hogarth: Aesthetics of Difference,* edited by Bernadette Fort and Angela Rosenthal, 62–75. Princeton, NJ: Princeton University Press, 2001.

———. "From Text to Image: William Hogarth and the Emergence of a Visual Culture in Eighteenth-Century England." In *Hogarth: Representing Nature's Machines,* edited by Frédéric Ogée, Peter Wagner, and David Bindman, 3–22. Manchester: Manchester University Press, 2001.

Parrish, Susan Scott. "Embodying African Knowledge in Colonial Surinam: Two William

Blake Engravings in Stedman's 1796 Narrative." In *Slave Portraiture in the Atlantic World*, edited by Agnes Lugo-Ortiz and Angela Rosenthal, 257–82. Cambridge: Cambridge University Press, 2013.

Postma, Johannes, and Victor Enthoven, eds. *Riches from Atlantic Commerce: Dutch Transatlantic Trade and Shipping, 1585–1817.* Leiden: Brill, 2003.

Price, Richard, and Sally Price. *Stedman's Surinam: Life in an Eighteenth-Century Slave Society.* Baltimore: Johns Hopkins University Press, 1992.

Stedman, John Gabriel. *Narrative of a Five Years Expedition against the Revolted Negroes of Surinam.* Edited by Richard Price and Sally Price. Baltimore: Johns Hopkins University Press, 1988.

Wild, Edward A. "The Old Jenckes Picture." *Sea Captains Carousing in Surinam* curatorial file, St. Louis Art Museum, St. Louis, MO.

IV

Dramatic Politics

Introduction

BONNIE GORDON

The Beggar's Opera premiered on 29 January 1728. John Gay's ballad opera satirized Italian opera and offered an eighteenth-century mash-up of sounds from Italian opera buffa, Handel's most popular arias, the Scottish folk tradition, and more. The satirical slam on aristocratic culture and what we would understand as high art went global very quickly and was adapted as far away as Jamaica and New York, with individual tunes making their way to taverns in the American colonies. The piece is of course well known to scholars of the eighteenth century, and modern audiences may know it through its reincarnation by Kurt Weill and Bertolt Brecht as *The Threepenny Opera*. This characteristic creation, with its global reach, multimedia production, cross-generic relationships, and ability to incite sympathetic responses in audiences, captures the issues brought forth by the four essays in this section entitled "Dramatic Politics."

The four essays in the section cover a Spanish novelist's satire of preaching, an Italian marriage drama, the resonances of the American Revolution in a famous Mozart opera, and the spatial metaphors of sympathy that run through various literatures. The immense popularity of the ballad opera reminds us that performance mattered differently in the eighteenth century, the era just before the cult of the genius and the autonomous subject, and in its dramatizing of real people and real events it reminds us that the line between performance and life was almost impossible to draw. And the mixing of popular songs with drama suggests a generic fluidity that characterizes the works discussed by each of the authors in this section. The piece feels emblematic of a field of inquiry that these essays enact: historical performance studies. The authors expand our notion of performance and do away with seemingly artificial distinctions between performance and text and between kinds of texts. They point up that the eighteenth century was global in the literal and metaphoric senses of the word and that to understand the eighteenth century is always to balance between a homogenized long century and specific local works, knowledges, and structures.

The section begins with Pierpaolo Polzonetti's "Mozart and the American Revolution," which demonstrates immediately that performance could not be bound by emergent nation-states and that just as tunes from *The Beggar's Opera* made it to Virginia, so too did the American Revolution have aesthetic consequences on the Continent. Polzonetti offers a rich intertextual reading of Mozart's latest and most famous operas, *The Marriage of Figaro, Don Giovanni,* and *Così fan tutte.* He shows the impact of American Revolutionary ideals on Mozart's Vienna, particularly as they played out on the operatic stage.

While Polzonetti writes about the migration of ideas from Europe to the Americas, Adrienne Ward shows readers that performance must be taken seriously as a system for transmitting knowledge and culture and social norms. In "The Drama of Marriage in Eighteenth-Century Venice," her close reading of *La locandiera* reveals the play as deeply tied to the crisis in marriage culture that spread through Italy over the long eighteenth century. The play performs the marriage plot, theorizes male violence, and stages contemporary moral dilemmas.

The third essay, by Jennifer Reed, "Performances of Suffering and the Stagecraft of Sympathy," does a remarkable job of unpacking the peculiarly eighteenth-century notions of sympathy and suffering on which the reception of all of these performances depended. Opera, drama, and other creative expressions worked because of a historically specific sympathetic resonance between audience and performer. As is well known in scholarly circles, Enlightenment philosophers were fascinated by sympathy; it was a fascination that some have argued ultimately led to the human-rights claims that undergirded the revolutions that swept across the globe. Reed writes not about the reach of sympathy, as has often been done, but rather about the limits of sympathy. She focuses especially on ocular and spatial metaphors and on the figure of the spectacle.

The section concludes with an essay that highlights text as a performative space and that listens carefully to the inherent orality of the eighteenth-century written word. Casey Erikson, in "The Aesthetics of Excess: Rococo Vestiges of *Tartuffe* in Isla's *Father Gerundio*," reads *The History of the Famed Preacher, Father Gerundio de Campazas, alias Zotes,* by the Jesuit writer José Francisco de Isla, as delivering a hyperbolic and satiric critique of preaching. Isla uses a rococo aesthetic to enhance a growing critique of theological excess and excessive preaching. The novel uses the ornamental gestures and stylistic gestures it puts on display to emphasize the subversive and destabilizing potential of overzealous discourse. Isla deliberately challenges readers' generic expectations and questions the power of the Catholic Church.

Taken together, these essays remind readers that the work of performance often lies between the written text and the embodied experience; they explore the active interstitial space between the novelistic representation of a preaching style and the musical enactment of revolutionary sentiments. To return to *The Beggar's Opera*, the staying power of a production animated by popular songs rests in its embodiment of the uncanny ability of performances of all kinds to challenge the worlds they inhabit.

Mozart and the American Revolution

PIERPAOLO POLZONETTI

The American Revolution had a substantial impact on Italian opera in the late eighteenth century. At that time, Italian opera was the leading international genre of public entertainment, comparable to the twentieth-century American movie industry. Ideas about Revolutionary America inspired many late-eighteenth-century European opera composers, including Pasquale Anfossi, Carl Ditters von Dittersdorf, Alessandro Guglielmi, Friedrich Gestewitz, Joseph Haydn, Niccolò Piccinni, Giovanni Paisiello, and last but not least, Wolfgang Amadeus Mozart. Nonetheless, the relevance of the American Revolution for our understanding of this repertory has passed unnoticed. This inattention is owing in part to a Eurocentric bias that affects historiography and criticism of the so-called Viennese school, which is also referred to as the classical style in music. Eurocentric criticism has been rather inflexible when dealing with Mozart, Haydn, and Beethoven, the three most revered composers in the Western canon active in Vienna while the city was the capital of the Holy Roman Empire. Traces of the reception of the American Revolution in late-eighteenth-century opera often have been interpreted as prophecies of the French Revolution, even for works composed before 1789, regardless of the conflicting ideological positions of the two revolutionary movements. This bias has produced highly problematic interpretations of the political ideology informing Mozart's operas. The cause for this confusion is also the lack of explicit references in eighteenth-century operas to revolutionary ideas of any kind, which makes it difficult for us to determine whether a work is revolutionary at all and, if it is, which revolutionary ideology it alludes to or is inspired by. During Mozart's time, performing artists, especially opera librettists, composers, and singers, were reluctant to express their political views openly because their works were publicly disseminated in theaters assiduously attended by the social and political establishment on which they depended. Detecting and interpreting operas with a revolutionary ideology composed between the American Revolution and the French calls for a rigorous method of historical contextualization based on the analysis of a web of different kinds of evidence, including personal experiences of playwrights, librettists, composers, and actor-singers; information about revolutionary America shared by artists and opera audiences; purely musical topoi and their meanings; the use and subversion of operatic conventions; and so on. In this essay I will show how ideas generated in or alluding to Revolutionary America penetrated the operatic culture of Mozart's Vienna. I will do so by taking into account the presence of American themes in the Viennese theatrical culture of Mozart's time and focusing on the three comic operas that Mozart wrote in collaboration with his favorite librettist, Lorenzo Da Ponte.

Da Ponte and the American Dream

Lorenzo Da Ponte died in Manhattan, New York, on 17 August 1838. He had spent the last third of his adventurous life in America. In his late American autobiography, the *Compendium of the Life of Lorenzo Da Ponte* (1807), he claims that he immigrated because America appeared to him a hopeful political alternative to less liberal European regimes: "I felt a sympathetic affection for the Americans. I had, besides, suffered so much in aristocratic republics [Venice], and monarchical governments, that I pleased myself with the hope of finding happiness in a country which I thought free."[1]

In the fateful year 1776, while still a professor of literature and rhetoric at the Seminary School of Treviso, in the Republic of Venice, Da Ponte wrote fourteen poetical compositions in Italian and Latin informed by ideas and themes recurrent in European literature about Revolutionary America.[2] The first poem is on the popular theme of a Native American man discussing how people have abandoned the pursuit of happiness by increasing societal regulations. The second poem discusses the role of human laws in the pursuit of happiness given that "the desire for happiness is the same in every man." The fifth is introduced by the headline "whether happiness is proportioned to the distribution of goods: societal norms divide these goods unequally among men, therefore they made happiness not equally possible among men." Finally, the seventh discusses the notion that "Man, free in nature, becomes slave under the law and therefore laws have made human happiness less attainable." Venetian censorship reacted sternly. As Da Ponte recorded, the senators banned him from teaching in any college, seminary, or university of the republic. He recollected, "I bowed my head and I put my hands and my handkerchief on my mouth not to laugh." As his academic career ended, his career as a librettist began, reaching its apex in 1783, when he was appointed poet to the court theater in Vienna, a city that was then experiencing an extraordinarily rich and enlightened season in theatrical and literary culture.[3] Da Ponte's responsibilities in Vienna were not only to compose new works but also to translate plays and libretti from French, edit and adapt Italian libretti, and judge which literary works might be successful. In short, he had to keep up with the latest trends. That same year he met Mozart, who had been working in Vienna since 1781.

America in Viennese Theatrical Culture

The operas of Da Ponte and Mozart were part of a fertile theatrical culture in which values and ideas intersected and circulated among actors playing similar roles in different operas, as well as librettists revising previous works and adapting them to local taste. Mozart's particular participation in this culture demonstrates the dissemination, through opera, of ideas inspired by the American Revolution.

An exemplary case is the Viennese version of a Neapolitan musical comedy titled *La quacquera spiritosa* (The witty Quaker girl), by Guglielmi, performed at the Court Theater during the summer of 1790.[4] In form, plot, character, and subversion of stereotypical roles, the opera pushes conventional boundaries. Da Ponte prepared its Viennese adaptation. Luise Villeneuve, who six months earlier interpreted the first Dorabella in Mozart and Da Ponte's *Così fan tutte,* now played the title role of the American Quaker woman. The opera was produced as a pasticcio, meaning that new pieces were commissioned from various leading composers, including Giovanni Paisiello, Giuseppe Gazzaniga, Domenico Cimarosa, Franz Xavier Süssmayr, Haydn, and Mozart. The plot is bizarre, as Karl Zinzendorf noted in his diary after he attended the opera in Vienna: "implausible plot, but nice music."[5] A young American Quaker woman is sent to Italy against her will by her father to marry an old and wealthy Italian count. Once in Italy, however, she falls in love with the count's servant Tognino. Like Minnie with Dick Johnson in Giacomo Puccini's *La fanciulla del West,* the tough American woman protects her lover from bullies. She also proposes marriage to him at gunpoint, forcing the poor lad to serenade her with an aria in which he compares himself to Dido and his American lady to Aeneas. The inversion of gender roles is implied by the name of the Quaker woman, Vertunna, derived from the name of the Roman god of seasonal change, Vertumnus. As Ovid recounts in the *Metamorphoses* (14.623–771), Vertumnus changed himself into a woman to seduce the misanthropic nymph Pomona, imitating Jove's sex change into Diana to seduce the nymph Callisto (2.401–35). Vertunna also breaks the boundaries of the system of role types dominating the world of Italian comic opera, which was inherited from the *commedia dell'arte* tradition—roughly, the comic, or *buffo* (singing, speaking, and acting in a lowbrow style), the *mezzo carattere* (middlebrow style), and the *serio* (highbrow style).[6] Vertunna, similar to other American characters in operas of this time, does not sing in a style that is confined to a specific type and rhetorical level but continually shifts, mixes, and crosses styles, blurring social boundaries. This is especially clear in a new scene written for the Viennese production consisting of an orchestrated recitative by Mozart, followed by an aria composed by Cimarosa. The orchestrated or accompanied recitative, also called *obbligato,* is a kind of recitative reserved for solemn moments and typically characterized by a high rhetorical level. This piece gives dignity and status to Vertunna, despite the rather plain lines she sings. The music is also void of hyperbolic *seria* traits, making it sound like a sincere statement, not a parody. Mozart's accompanied recitative is remarkable for its equilibrium in a no-genre land in which Vertunna, apart from the words she sings, frees her identity through music by disentangling it from conventional types.[7] Through musical means she is able to convey concepts that would have been hard to express through words in the Italian libretto, not only because the libretto, unlike the score, was carefully monitored by state censors but also because the Italian text was not easy for non-Italian audiences to understand.

The National Court Theater inaugurated its relatively progressive activity fifteen years before its production of *La quacquera spiritosa.* The presentation of works in Vienna based on American subjects increased with the establishment of this theater in 1776, intended by Joseph II as "an instrument of social policy . . . shaped by enlightenment ideology," as Dorothea Link puts it.[8] The National Court Theater offered several plays and operas set in America, such as Joseph Marius Babo's Singspiel *Das Winterquartier in Amerika,* which premiered in Vienna in September 1786, and Nicolas-Sébastien Roch Chamfort's *La jeune indienne,* which bore the title *Die junge Indianerinn,* for which Haydn wrote his Symphony No. 49 as incidental music.[9]

The most successful opera based on an American subject offered at the National Court Theater was Paisiello's *Le gare generose,* set in Boston. This Neapolitan comic opera was revised for Vienna in 1786 and ran from September of that year to December 1787.[10] *Le gare* promotes the notion, very much in line with the American Enlightenment, that the acquisition of financial security is necessary for the pursuit of individual freedom and happiness. Money, which had always had a negative connotation in the Western aristocratic worldview, became now an instrument of virtue and nobility.[11] The idea of prosperity and independent wealth became strongly linked to the new American social and political model.[12] One of the protagonists, Gelinda, was interpreted by Nancy Storace, the first Susanna in Mozart's *Le nozze di Figaro*.

Figaro *and the Unjust Taxation*

Le nozze di Figaro premiered in Vienna, also at the National Court Theater, on 1 May 1786.[13] This opera has often been labeled either as a prophecy of the "wrong" revolution or as a conservative and antirevolutionary work. Martha Nussbaum's program notes of a performance I attended in 2015 at the Lyric Opera theater in Chicago open with this statement: "Officially *The Marriage of Figaro* (1786) is based on Beaumarchais's radical comedy of 1778, a savage indictment of feudalism that was quickly seen as a precursor of the French Revolution."[14] Similarly, Tim Carter aptly summarizes the critical tradition on *Le nozze* by noting that Figaro "has been handed down to history [as] the revolutionary *before* the [French] Revolution" (emphasis added).[15] Conversely, Nicholas Till's use of the Marxist theory of class struggle to interpret Mozart's operas leads him to conclude that "both Beaumarchais's play," on which the opera libretto of *Le nozze* is based, "and Mozart's and Da Ponte's opera are unrevolutionary, even conservative, works: evidence of a modest desire to transform existing social relationships."[16] Till quotes the writings on freedom and equality of Christoph Wieland, an acquaintance of Mozart's and a supporter of the American cause, only to dismiss him for having a "limited bourgeois understanding of these potentially explosive concepts."[17] Wieland's writings, in fact, are consistent with the ideology of the American Revolution, though in stark contrast to later socialistic revolutions, which Beaumarchais, Mozart, and Da Ponte did not care about or fiercely opposed. As Wieland writes, "By equality I do not understand the right of absolute equality, which overthrows all distinctions in civil society between classes and estates, between rich and poor, educated and raw; but only, that every citizen of the state shall be without exception equal before the law."[18] This ideology, shaped by American values on the freedom of the individual more than by class struggles and social concerns, also informs *The Marriage of Figaro*.

Da Ponte's libretto is, as explicitly stated on the title page and in the preface, an adaptation of the French *Le mariage de Figaro*. It recounts a single "day of madness" (*la folle journée*) in the palace of Count Almaviva. The Count intends to reinstate his *droit du seigneur* over his wife's maidservant Susanna. Susanna and her bridegroom-to-be, Figaro, however, will outwit the Count with the help of other allies, as well as of the Count's wife, Rosina, who married Count Almaviva in the prequel play and opera, *The Barber of Seville*. The idea of setting Beaumarchais's play as an opera was not Da Ponte's but Mozart's. On this matter, the librettist is forthcoming. As John Rice has pointed out, "Da Ponte, in his memoirs, generally credited himself with good ideas when he felt that he could get away with it." Crediting Mozart in this case, therefore, "is particularly remarkable, because we find this attribution in a passage designed mostly to reflect well on Da Ponte himself."[19] As the librettist recounts, "The immensity of [Mozart's] genius needed a vast, multiform, sublime subject" (io concepii facilmente che la immensità del suo genio domandava un soggetto esteso, multiforme, sublime). As he recollects, Mozart "one day asked me if I could easily set Beaumarchais's comedy *The Marriage of Figaro* as a drama."[20]

Why Mozart would think that this comedy was a "vast, multiform, and sublime subject" will always remain a puzzle to readers of Beaumarchais's play or Da Ponte's libretto unless we take into account the broad historical context in which these texts were first written and disseminated. I believe that Mozart connected this comedy and its author to imagery about America as it was represented in contemporary art circulating at the time in Europe. The paintings of Benjamin West, John Trumbull, and John Singleton Copley, for example, often depict battles and heroes of America in stormy landscapes. In German literature, Friedrich Maximilian Klinger's 1776 drama *Sturm und Drang*, set in America during the Revolutionary War, gave its name to a whole protoromantic artistic movement devoted to the idea of the sublime.[21] In other words, the comedy itself was not necessarily a "vast, multiform, sublime subject," but the ideas inspiring and informing this dramatic work had these attributes.

We can also assume, considering Mozart's association with Freemasonry, that he had direct exposure to ideas coming from America through the Masonic lodges, couched in their typically sublime and solemn rhetoric. Nicholas Till is well aware of Mozart's possible engagement in the vibrant political debates in Viennese coffeehouses, such as the Cafe Stierbock, which he describes as "a popular masonic haunt, where in 1785 a reception was held for Lafayette, the French hero of the American Revolution."[22] At least two of Mozart's Masonic acquaintances, Johann Georg Adam Foster and

Wieland himself, were active in the dissemination of ideas from Revolutionary America.[23] Mozart had contacts with the Freemasons of the Neuf Sœurs between 1777 and 1778. Benjamin Franklin became the Grand Master of that lodge two years later. Mozart might have met him in Paris. In fact his father, Leopold, wrote to him on 6 April 1778 from Salzburg: "Schreib mir, ob Frankreich den Krieg den Engelländern wirk: erkläret hat?—nun wirst du den americaner Minister H: Dr: Francklin sehen. Frankreich erkennt die 13 Amerikanischen Provinzen für ohnabhängig und hat mit ihnen tracktaten geschlossen" (Write me whether France has really declared war on the English—now you will see the American minister Mister Dr. Franklin. France recognizes the thirteen American colonies as independent and has entered into several treatises with them).[24] In January 1787, a Masonic acquaintance of Mozart's, Count Joseph Emanuel Canal, took him to attend a performance of Paisiello's *Le gare generose.*[25] To flesh out the Masonic connections, the pants role Cherubino, first interpreted at her debut by the Austrian soprano Dorothea Bussani, was apparently inspired by the cross-dressing Chevalier d'Eon, a Freemason who played an important role in the secret operations in support of the American War of Independence. Beaumarchais referred to the chevalier's cross-dressing repeatedly in his correspondence.[26]

Beaumarchais himself wrote both *The Barber of Seville* and *The Marriage of Figaro* while he was supporting the cause of the American Revolution during the late 1770s. His militant role in the revolution at the time of the composition of the first two plays of the Figaro trilogy has never escaped the attention of Beaumarchais scholars.[27] The most important document is his pamphlet in defense of the American Revolution, *Observations sur le Mémoire justificatif de la cour de Londres,* published in 1779 and internationally disseminated.[28] In this document Beaumarchais pretends to act as the herald of King Louis XVI by explaining on his behalf that it was not the fault of the French monarchy that the Americans rebelled against the English central government. Using this pretext, he lists and in turn glorifies the key events of the American Revolution, such as the Stamp Act, the Boston Tea Party, the Boston Massacre, and the War of Independence.[29] Beaumarchais portrays the American Revolution as a civil war within British society rather than as a territorial confrontation between nations. This is particularly evident in the case of the two most explosive issues in Revolutionary rhetoric of the time, unjust taxation and fair trials: "The fact is that the vehement protest of the colonies about the right not to be taxed without representation, and the right to be judged by their peers in the form of juries had found so many supporters in England that it kept and still keeps the nation divided on a subject so relevant to the civil rights of every English citizen."[30] The latter right, to a trial by a jury of their peers, has a central role in *Le nozze di Figaro,* as apparent in the repeated staged trials against Figaro, Cherubino, and the Countess in the course of the opera. The opera is repeatedly turned into a cause célèbre during a time when famous trials were both a form of entertainment and an arena of explosive political activism.[31]

Unjust taxation was even more important because, as Beaumarchais recognizes, "the right not to be taxed without representation" triggered the revolution, carried on by "English citizens" against the tyrannical regime of their own fatherland. What was at stake was not so much a tax break as the abolition of feudal oppression. The entire plot of *The Marriage of Figaro* revolves around stratagems to avoid that most emblematic form of tyrannical taxation, the *jus primae noctis,* or *droit du seigneur.*

At the beginning of Mozart's opera, Susanna tells Figaro that the Count regrets having abolished the infamous right of the feudal lord to have sex with any woman under his domain and reveals that she is his first designated victim. As she leaves the stage, Figaro first vents his outrage in the second scene during a simple recitative, called *secco* (accompanied only by bass and keyboard). This simple recitative, however, shares traits with the more exalted form of recitative, the orchestrated, or *obbligato,* recitative, typically accompanied by the orchestra and reserved for solemn moments. This kind of recitative often introduces and interpolates the vocal line with foregrounded expressive melodic and rhythmic gestures. As in an *obbligato,* in Figaro's *secco* recitative the instrumental bass line presents a foregrounded melodic gesture later recapped in the aria. It is a menacing descending melody that begins with an incisive dactylic rhythmic cell (long-short-short). Figaro's bass voice shares the register of this bass line, resulting in a melody that represents his internalized voice, as if he is already ruminating on his "taxing" problem. Figaro congratulates his master with bitter irony ("Bravo signor padrone!") and acknowledges that finally his eyes have been opened to the true nature of power: "Now I begin to understand the mystery and to see clearly what your plot is about."

In his first solo aria, the cavatina "Se vuol ballare," Figaro continues to address his master directly, as if confronting him.[32] In eighteenth-century opera, the cavatina (the first aria sung by a character) works as a visiting card, defining personality and intent. Unlike typical cavatinas, this piece is a complex and fairly long aria in two tempos. The first section of Figaro's aria is a moderately paced minuet, marked "Allegretto." In Mozart's time the minuet was perceived as "the epitome of choreographic elegance and refinement," as Allanbrook describes it, and, by its associations with the aristocracy it had become the representative dance of the ancien régime.[33]

The first two stanzas of evenly accented five-syllable lines (*quinari*) are accompanied first by the plucking of strings (Mozart notated "pizzicato" under each string part), evoking a guitar, the instrument Figaro threatens to play in order to make the Count dance: "If you want to dance, little Mr. Count, I will play a little guitar for you. If you want to join my school, I will teach you the somersault" (Se vuol ballare, / Signor Contino / Il chitarrino / Le suonerò. // Se vuol venire / Ne la mia scola / La capriola / Le insegnerò). The choice of instrument denotes both the culture of Spain, where the opera is set, and Figaro's social status.[34] Mozart first repeats the first two lines, putting an emphasis on the second repetition in his autograph by underlining it to indicate that it needs to be delivered with more emphasis. He then upsets the simple repetitive rhythm of these lines by repeating them and inserting the affirmative exclamation "sì!" (yes!) after the last line of the first stanza: "Le suonerò, *sì!*" Figaro's *sì* exclamation spikes higher and higher at each repetition, giving it emphasis and realistic dramatic expressivity. The inserted syllable also causes a disruption of the poetical rhythm by stretching Da Ponte's *quinario* into an irregular six-syllable line (*senario*). It is as if Figaro is tripping the Count during his dance lesson. Mozart repeats this line to better convey Figaro's rousing anger. Immediately afterwards, the violin plays a fast and nervous figuration based on a rapid alternation of two adjacent notes.

This two-note elemental melodic figuration is significantly stated as the first theme of the overture. It is the first thematic material we hear in the entire opera. Mozart alerts us to the fact that this thematic idea is essential to the drama. We understand this programmatic move when in "Se vuol ballare" it becomes associated with Figaro's growing rage against the "unjust taxation." The same stormy figuration continues throughout the second stanza, which, like the first, ends the repetition of its last line with the insertion of the word *sì*. As the storm rages more violently, the two-note nervous figuration, now transposed higher, reaches the climactic point of ascending scales, each encompassing an octave, while the score prescribes a continuous alternation of loud and soft dynamics (*forte* and *piano*). The tempestuous music coincides with Figaro's resolution, as he sings "saprò" (I will know how). He is then restrained by the realization that it would be wiser to think it through and come up with an effective and less impulsive strategy, which will consist in dissembling. Similar to Beaumarchais's role in the American

Revolution, Figaro decides to engage in a cold war rather than in an open confrontation. Now he no longer addresses the Count, but himself, as an aside: "But slow down, I will be better able to uncover his secret plot by dissembling" (Ma piano / Meglio ogni arcano / Dissimulando / Scoprir potrò).

For the final stanza of the aria Da Ponte wrote six more lines of the same length and rhythm he had used for the previous stanzas (*quinari*). Mozart, however, set this second section of Figaro's aria in a very different way. He increased the pace from *allegretto* to *presto,* as was customary in multisectional buffo arias. The choice of the tempo indications may suggest not only pace but also something about the affect or mood conveyed in these sections. *Allegretto* literally means "not too happy," an indication of restrained will and action, while *presto* means "quick" but is also an exclamation used as a hastening imperative, an incitation to immediate action ("hurry!"). Even more significantly, Mozart shifted the rhythm and meter from the initial triple-meter minuet to a duple meter contradance (also referred to as *contraddanza, contredanse,* or "country dance").

The contradance, which originated in England, was a more athletic, lower-class dance than the minuet. Whether this dance rhythm was able to evoke the spirit of middle-class English people living in America is hard to determine, but as Allanbrook points out, the dance shares salient rhythmic traits with the Virginia reel.[35] The dance historian Kate Van Winkle Keller documents the practice of dancing reels in Revolutionary America, including at a dance party in 1791 in a fort in Ohio to honor General George Washington. She cites an example in duple meter, like the one in the second part of Mozart's cavatina, published in a late-eighteenth-century collection of reels.[36] Mozart had a deep knowledge of national dances, as his scoring of the fandango in *Le nozze* shows. His inclusion of this dance scene in the opera, notwithstanding the emperor's ban on performing dance in opera, is in itself an indication of how much he valued dance and its power to convey meaning without words.[37] The fandango was often described in the eighteenth-century sources as a New World dance imported to America by captive Africans from Guinea, as Dalrymple reported in his 1774 travelogue. This dance spread in a wide area including today's Mexico, the Caribbean, Puerto Rico, and the Dominican Republic. Beaumarchais himself, during his trip to Spain in 1764, wrote that the fandango could have originated from dances of African American slaves, comparing it to the African American calenda.[38]

A passionate and knowledgeable social dancer for most of his life, Mozart knew how to dance minuets and contradances and was aware of their

"The Air Balloon" contredanse

Figaro's contredanse

L'ar - te scher-men - do, l'ar - te a - do - pran - do

Figure 1. Mozart's *Le nozze di Figaro,* act 1, Figaro's cavatina no. 3, section B, set as a contredanse, mm. 64–45, voice part; compared with the contredanse "The Air Balloon," in *Thompson's Compleat Collection of 200 Favourite Country Dances,* vol. 5, p. 37, transposed here from A major to F major.

social function and meaning. In August 1770 he wrote from Bologna to his sister that his only source of entertainment in what he called a "sleep land" (*Schlafland*) was dancing "English marches" (*englischen Schritten,* meaning contradances in duple meter).[39] Mozart practiced at least the three main types of social dances of the time: the minuet, associated with the upper class; the German dance, or *Deutsche,* which was the most humble; and the contradance, which was the most inclusive dance type.[40] Contradances were published in periodicals and collections marketed to aspirational middle classes, for whom social dance might provide the opportunity to make the right connection or find a good match. One publication of this kind was *Thompson's Compleat Collection of 200 Favourite Country Dances.* In the last volume, among the dances for the year 1785 is one entitled "The Air Balloon," whose initial rhythmic pattern corresponds to Figaro's contradance in the *presto* section of his cavatina (fig. 1). This is a rare instance in the Thompsons' anthology of a contradance featuring a basic pattern joining a dactylic rhythmic cell (long-short-short) with a spondaic (long-long), recalling the cello melodic line at the beginning of Figaro's recitative before the cavatina. It is significant that its title evokes an icon of progress, the aerostatic balloon, whose first flights during these years were shocking the world and even inspiring science-fiction literature in which journeys to utopian worlds in the moon were imagined to take place aboard a flying balloon, as in Daniel Moore's *Account of . . . the Passage to the Moon in a Flying Machine Called an Air Balloon* (1785).[41]

In the contradance section, Figaro plans his course of action against the regime: "Deploying and using my art like a sword, now poking and now joking I will overthrow every plot" (L'arte schermendo, / L'arte adoprando / Di qua pungendo / Di la scherzando / Tutte le macchine / Rovescerò). In "l'arte schermendo," the verb is derived from the noun *scherma* (fencing), suggesting that thought (the ruminating at the beginning of the recitative based on the same rhythmic cell) has turned into militant action. After the final stanza, Da Ponte prescribed a *da capo*, or return of the first section, by writing down the initial four lines of the aria. Mozart followed his librettist's indication at first, in a shortened, written-down *da capo*, but surprisingly, he ended the aria with an incisive orchestral coda: the duple meter and *presto* tempo of the second section returns, giving the last word to the country dance.

Figaro and Susanna will deliver a decisive blow to the Count's plot to exert his unjust sexual taxation thanks to a sudden procurement of money, the necessary tool to secure his and his bride's liberty. This is similar to what happens in *Le gare generose*, in which the slave Gelinda acquires her freedom and unites with her groom thanks to the acquisition of money. (Let us keep in mind that this character was interpreted by Nancy Storace, the actress who played Susanna.) In act 3, scene 4, of *Le nozze*, Figaro is finally free to follow his heart and marry Susanna when an old, rich lady, Marcellina, waives Figaro's contractual obligation to marry her if he was unable to repay her loan of two thousand pezzi duri. The term *pezzi duri* in the Italian libretto is a translation of *piastres fortes* in act 3, scene 15, of Beaumarchais's *Le mariage de Figaro*. In the late eighteenth century, this Spanish currency flowed from Mexico to the rest of the world, making the city of Seville a wealthy banking center.[42] At the end of the century, the currency was still used to pay ransoms for the European prisoners of North African pirates.[43] This simple detail gives an idea of how the Spanish setting of the opera was not necessarily and exclusively "exotic" (as it would be for *Carmen*) or distant to avoid censorship (as the Boston location in Verdi's *Un ballo in maschera* would be) but resonant with the contemporary global economy and politics.[44] Similarly, the financial operations described in *Le gare generose* involve the exchange of capital from a bank located in Cadiz, Spain, to a bank in Halifax, Nova Scotia, which was the British headquarters during the American Revolution and thus enabled relatively secure financial exchanges with the rest of Europe.

The scene in which Figaro acquires freedom from his contractual obligation starts with the magistrate Don Curzio repeating the verdict reached—"Either marry her or pay her back" (O pagarla o sposarla)—in act 3, scene 4. Figaro reverts immediately to another stratagem: he tells Marcellina that he cannot marry her without the permission of his lost parents and recounts how as a baby he was stolen by pirates and found with his gold, precious stones, and fancy garments. Figaro's fanciful story resonates with popular literature about pirates and world travels, such as Pietro Chiari's novels based on American subjects, also central in the plot of *Le gare generose,* in which Gelinda loses her capital and freedom after being abducted by pirates.[45] To prove his respectful lineage, Figaro shows a spatula-shaped tattoo on his arm. The spatula insignia identifies him with the medical guild and therefore marks him as belonging to the wealthy middle class of professionals. As Jessica Waldoff points out, "The recognition scene marks a crucial reversal of the plot," and it is significant indeed that this scene, according to the singer Michael Kelly (the first Don Curzio and Basilio), was Mozart's favorite in the entire opera.[46] Stefano Castelvecchi argues that the excessive repetition of the lines "sua madre?" and "suo padre?" (his mother?, his father?) by the incredulous characters taking part in this funny and moving sextet can be understood as a parody of the sentimental style.[47] I suspect that this ensemble was, in fact, a parody of the recognition scene in Marmontel and Grétry's sentimental opera *Le huron,* in which the protagonist, a Native American, discovers that he is a French gentleman, which makes him eligible to marry the French lady he loves. At this happy discovery, all the other characters on stage, including his lost noble parents, repeat the same lines over and over: "Il a les traits de son père," "Il a les yeux de sa mère."[48] In the scene of *Le nozze* that follows the recognition of Figaro as the long-lost Rafaello, Figaro's parents, Marcellina and Dr. Bartolo, throw money to their lost and found son, while Figaro rejoices and embraces his newfound father and mother, as well as his bride, Susanna. The rapid flux of their exultant recitative is arrested suddenly by a spontaneous two-measure quartet sung a cappella, with Figaro indulging in a moment of Schadenfreude: "Signor Count shall die at my rejoicing" (E schiatti il signor conte al gioir mio). This short passage constitutes one of the rare cases in which a radical political statement absent from the French literary source was added to the libretto: in act 3, scene 19, of *Le mariage* the four characters simply resolve to make haste ("Courons, courons").

The short, four-part statement on "E schiatti il signor conte al gioir mio" introduces a strong cadence in Bb major, which moves away from the F major of the sextet and is itself followed by a harmonic non sequitur in the C-major recitative and aria of the Countess, "Dove sono i bei momenti." The key of Bb major comes back in the following duettino, "Sull'aria." This harmonic link works as a subliminal bridge reinforcing the alliance of Countess Rosina to Figaro's extended family. The Bb-C pairing is also one of the series of harmonic couplings of a flat key followed by a sharp key throughout *Le nozze* and identified by Daniel Heartz as inspired by Paisiello's *Barber*, for which Mozart had a great admiration. Paisiello's opera had premiered at the National Theater in 1783 and was still playing in 1786 in alternation with *Le nozze.*[49]

In the duettino "Sull'aria" (no. 21 in the score) Susanna writes and repeats the words that Rosina tells her to write.[50] The poetical lines Rosina suggests are an invitation for the Count to a rendezvous with Susanna, which will be an ambush allowing the Countess to catch her husband in the act of committing adultery. In this scene Susanna is not merely serving as the Countess's secretary; she enacts the Countess's persona. The Countess dictates the letter, but she does so pretending to be Susanna, who writes the letter so that the Count will recognize her own handwriting and signature. Susanna's and Rosina's authorial personae become exchangeable to the targeted reader (the Count), just as the voices of their dramatis personae become exchangeable to the targeted listeners (the audience). Susanna repeats not only the words Rosina dictates but also her melodic phrases, until the two women sing together in parallel thirds when commenting that the Count will certainly understand the message of the letter. This exchange lessens differences and strengthens the bond between them. It is Rosina who initiates the road to equality by putting in Susanna's pen poetical lines and imagery of a very high stylistic register ("soave," "zeffiretto," "spirerà"). Only three eight-syllable lines (*ottonari*) suffice to convey the message about the appointment, an incisive statement, as in a seria aria from a heroic opera by Metastasio: "Che soave zeffiretto / Verso sera spirerà, / Sotto i pini del boschetto" (What a gentle zephyr will be drifting this evening under the grove's pines).

Mozart allows that soft breeze to blow on everybody and everything, counterpointing supremely light, legato, wave-shaped arpeggios in the winds with soft, ascending, middle-register arpeggios in the violins. In its supreme, transformative lightness this piece is comparable to the flight to the utopian world of the moon in the first act of Haydn's *Il mondo della luna* (1777), in which servants are crowned emperors. It is also similar to invocations and evocations of the moon in the first scenes of both Haydn's and Paisiello's versions of this opera, the latter of which played at the National Court Theater in December 1786. Here too, understood only in terms of the plot, the scene is nothing more than a deception, but the music tells a different story: it invites us to forget about the practical purpose of the letter in *Le nozze di Figaro* or of the moon charade in *Il mondo della luna* and takes us on a liberating journey that, even if only temporary or imagined, remains nevertheless enlightening in every sense of the word. As in Haydn's moon flight, the music of Mozart's duet is conceived to defeat gravity, erasing or subverting hierarchies.[51]

Mozart often conveys ideas by purely musical means and does so in a way that transcends dramatic and historical contexts. The best example of this is the scene in which Mozart's letter duet is played to inmates in Frank Darabont's 1994 film *The Shawshank Redemption*. The ex-banker Andy Dufresne (played by Tim Robbins), who is serving a life sentence, gains the privilege of working in the administrative office. As boxes of books and records that he has ordered for his fellow inmates arrive in the office prison, he locks a guard in the bathroom and uses the loudspeaker to blast the duettino to the entire prison community. The film's narrator—Red, interpreted by Morgan Freeman—explains to us that the heroic deed of playing Mozart's music to the inmates "pissed the warden off somethin' awful." We understand the warden's anger when we see the effect of Mozart's music on the inmates. Their faces suddenly take on expressions of peace and thoughtful dignity, and their gestures convey a temporary release: we see them in the act of looking up to the speakers and therefore raising their heads. Regardless of the words and the plot, the music has the power to make them feel free and equal, even if just for a few minutes. As Red explains:

> I have no idea to this day what those two Italian ladies were singing about. Truth is, I don't wanna know. Some things are best left unsaid. I like to think they were singing about something so beautiful it can't be expressed in words, and makes your heart ache because of it. I tell you those voices soared, higher and farther than anybody in a grey place dares to dream. It was like some beautiful bird flapped into our drab little cage and made those walls dissolve away. And for the briefest of moments, every last man at Shawshank felt free.[52]

During the age of the American Revolution the ability to convey ideas independently from the words in the libretto was essential, not only because opera makers were operating in a culture of limited freedom but also because Italian opera was designed to be accessible to non-Italian-speaking audiences. Another resource at hand was the pervading intertextuality of opera culture. This was generated in part by what I have called *hyperplots,* points of intersection and interference between different operas resulting from the superimposition of similar dramatic elements, as well as by the recurring presence of the same actors in different operas playing similar roles, which results in the overlapping and conflation of dramatis personae.[53] We have seen the case of Nancy Storace playing both Gelinda and Susanna, two characters who, in part by providing money, free their future husbands. Similarly, the buffo bass singer Francesco Benucci, after interpreting the role of the gun-toting, aristocrat-threatening American Quaker in Pasquale Anfossi's *L'americana in Olanda* (Venice, 1778), went on to sing the roles of the servant Figaro in *Le nozze* and the servant Leporello in Da Ponte and Mozart's *Don Giovanni*. In both operas Benucci's servants launch into pronouncements against their masters, especially in their respective cavatinas, "Se vuol ballare signor contino" and "Notte e giorno faticar," in which he complains about "working night and day shifts."[54]

Don Giovanni *and the Critique of Aristocracy*

Don Giovanni, which premiered in Prague on 29 October 1787, presents an even stronger critique of corrupted aristocracy than *Le nozze*. In the former, there is no final reconciliation. It is therefore even more understandable that *Don Giovanni,* like *Le nozze,* has been interpreted as a prophecy of the French Revolution. In his *New Yorker* review of the 2015 Metropolitan Opera production, Richard Brody claims that *Don Giovanni* is "a wild and ironic harbinger of the French Revolution" and concludes: "Mozart and Da Ponte are saying, in effect, that the feudal continent's reigning Don Giovannis are above the law. . . . Two years later came the French Revolution."[55] Once again, to contextualize this opera correctly we need to look at the American Revolution as its more direct point of reference.

The opening ensemble, the *introduzione,* starts with the servant Leporello complaining not only about his heavy workload ("Notte e giorno faticar") but also about his subordinate status, expressing his desire to live like a gentleman and no longer a servant ("voglio fare il gentiluomo / e non voglio più servir"). After all, his aristocratic master does not act with nobility and therefore does not deserve to be a gentleman. Immediately after this, in fact, Don Giovanni enters pursued by Donna Anna, whom he has just sexually assaulted. She leaves as her father, the Commendatore, comes to her rescue. The old man challenges Don Giovanni to a duel. The *introduzione* ends with Don Giovanni killing Donna Anna's father. In the following scene Leporello congratulates his master: "Bravo! Two noble deeds: raping the daughter and killing the father!"[56]

The killing of the father is the most shocking event in the *introduzione* (the sexual assault does not happen on stage). The sight of blood is not what audiences would expect in a comic opera, but Mozart was not the first to adopt this tragic gambit. It is well known that the librettist Giovanni Bertati adopted it for his own version of *Don Giovanni,* set to music by Gazzaniga and premiered on 5 February 1787.[57] What has escaped scholars' attention is that Bertati also represented parricide in his opera buffa *L'orfanella americana,* premiered in Venice with music by Pasquale Anfossi also in 1787.[58] Similarities between the two operas are relevant because *L'orfanella americana* was the only opera of the time to represent the conflict between loyalist and rebellious British soldiers on American soil, which served as an indirect but obvious reference to the War of Independence. The opera stages the violent death of an Indian chief (like the Commendatore, a military commander) and the father of the gentle Native American girl Zeda (hence the title *The American Orphan*). Zeda's father is mortally wounded by the villain of the opera, a greedy and lustful English general named Hestord. In the *introduzione,* Hestord urges his men, "Kill, exterminate these American beasts!" (Ammazzate trucidate queste bestie americane). The old father dies peacefully after securing the union between his daughter Zeda and the rebellious English soldier Bentley. At this point his daughter enters and finds the bloody corpse of her father, crying, "Padre . . . mio padre . . . oh cielo . . . quel sangue," with the words *padre* (father) and *sangue* (blood) repeated to increase their dramatic effect. This scene is analogous to act 1, scene 3, of Mozart's *Don Giovanni,* in which Donna Anna, at the sight of the bloody corpse of her own father cries, "quel *sangue* . . ." and "*padre* mio . . . *padre* amato" (emphasis added). The similarity between the two operas revolves exclusively around the death of the father, which is also present in other literary works representing Revolutionary America, such as Klinger's *Sturm und Drang.* Here a character appropriately named Wild tells his beloved American woman Caroline that he would strangle her father to possess her and then kisses her in ecstasy.[59] In *Prodigals and Pilgrims: The American Revolution against Patriarchal Authority,* Jay Fliegelman documents the pervasive use of antipatriarchal rhetoric during the American Revolution.[60] Antipatriarchal stances are present in most of the operas representing America during the period of the American Revolution, including *La quacquera spiritosa,* in which, as we have seen, the daughter disobeys her father. However, in *Don Giovanni* and in *L'orfanella americana* parricide is represented with ambivalent connotations: it is both horrifying and exhilarating, tragic and comic. For both Donna Anna and Zeda the suppression of the father severs a strong affective family bond but strengthens the new bond with a freely chosen lover. The death of the father works as an ambivalent allegory of the painful suppression and joyful renewal of political authority through the breaking of national affiliation with the natural fatherland.

There is one more piece of evidence embedded in the discourse about the American Revolution that situates the politics of *Don Giovanni* in its historical context. Giacomo Casanova, the famous womanizer, was present in the opera house during the premiere of *Don Giovanni* in Prague. Da Ponte had written his libretto also to rebuke Casanova, with whom he had had a stormy relationship that lasted many years. Ten years earlier Casanova had served as a secret agent against the circulation of American Revolutionary ideas in Venice shortly after Da Ponte was exiled for promoting the idealized concept of Native American "good savages" inspired by Rousseau. In his article "Considerazioni politico-filosofiche . . . ad uso del popolo inglese" (Political-philosophical reflections . . . for the benefit of the English people), Casanova claimed that aristocracy was the perfect form of government and warned, "It would have been deplorable if the King and his ministers had not used all the force against the insurgents in the American colonies." Casanova admitted that things had gone badly in America for the English monarchy but said that at least, thanks to the use of force to violently suppress the revolt, the honor of the king had been preserved. In the same article, Casanova insisted on the necessity for aristocracies and monarchies to exert censorship and limit freedom of expression.[61]

After attending the performance of *Don Giovanni*, Casanova was probably fuming. He immediately set to work to propose editorial changes to the libretto. In the extant fragments of Casanova's version, Leporello defends Don Giovanni by accusing women of being solely responsible for his master's misbehavior: "It is all the fault of the female sex that charms his soul and his heart. Wretched female sex! Source of pain!" (La colpa è tutta quanta / Di quel femmineo sesso / Che l'anima gli incanta / E [che] gli incanta il cor. / O sesso traditor! / Sorgente di dolor!).[62] Casanova felt that Don Giovanni, like himself, was not a predator but a victim of women's seductive power. His own memoir, the *Histoire de ma vie*, reads like a catalog of sexual conquests in which it is often hard to tell who is the conquered and who is the conqueror. Casanova knew that Don Giovanni's story was not only about sex. In late-eighteenth-century culture, especially in the culture of opera buffa, sexuality and politics were intimately interlinked. What could not be addressed in the representation of the public sphere was represented in the intimate and domestic sphere. Sexual abuse in *Don Giovanni* is exposed and denounced not only for its "sinful" cause, which is the lustful desire to possess others regardless of their will, but also for its "criminal" effect, which is the abuse of power over fellow human beings. Casanova's editing of some excerpts of the original libretto appears to have been informed by a political agenda. First, he puts more emphasis on the cause (transferring the guilt to women's power to seduce) than on the effect (eliding his deceit and abuse of women). Second, Casanova's Leporello shows a more reverent attitude toward his master than in Mozart and Da Ponte's version. He becomes a faithful servant, and his rebellious attitude has been tamed. In short, Casanova in his manuscript revision of Da Ponte's libretto made a futile attempt to reestablish old power hierarchies and relations, both sexual and social.

Così fan tutte *and Franklin's War against Mesmerism*

Così fan tutte (1790) is one of the most radical eighteenth-century operas when it comes to representing politics through sexuality. Political readings of the opera tend to privilege either a Marxist approach based on the principle that social and political tensions are ingrained in every human activity, or a symbolic approach as related, again, to the French Revolution.[63] However, in Mozart's time informed readers would hardly have missed the reference to political events in the opera that in fact antedated the 1789 revolution. Revolving around a test of fidelity (two young men seducing each other's sweethearts) and representing a mock mesmeric cure, the opera alluded to a notorious adultery scandal involving Beaumarchais and a banker, Guillaume Kornman, cofounder and sponsor of the French mesmeric society.[64] The confrontation between the two started in 1781 and culminated in a public pamphlets war in 1787, at a time when Antonio Salieri, an acquaintance and supporter of Da Ponte and Mozart, was living and collaborating with Beaumarchais.[65] The playwright attacked the banker and defended his unfaithful wife, who had been locked in a prison for prostitutes, revealing that Kornman had encouraged his wife's lover and created opportunities for the couple's illicit encounters, probably as a test in "animal magnetism" (to use a technical mesmeric term). It is very likely that the early unusual spelling of the name of the character Guglielmo as "Guilelmo" in the original libretto and in Mozart's autograph alluded to Guillaume Kornman.[66]

Mozart may even have met the real-life Guillaume who inspired his character in *Così*. In 1778 Leopold Mozart wrote from Salzburg to his son in Paris asking him to bring music scores and his book on violin playing (*Violinschule*) to "Messieurs Korman [*sic*] etc.: Banquiers."[67] Although Leopold did not say so, it is possible that the intention was to obtain favors, possibly a loan, thanks to their mutual acquaintance, Dr. Mesmer himself, for whom in the late 1760s the twelve-year-old Mozart had played piano and organized the performance of his one-act Singspiel *Bastien und Bastienne* at

Mesmer's own villa.[68] The Mozarts maintained a cordial relationship with the Mesmers for a while, but by the time of *Così fan tutte* Mozart had lost contact with them. After the doctor moved to Paris in 1778, Kornman and his lawyer Nicolas Bergasse appropriated mesmerism, which escaped Anton Mesmer's control and became heavily politicized. It is in fact revealing that, among other things, Kornman's lawyer criticized Beaumarchais's conduct as a spy and a smuggler of weapons in support of American revolutionaries.[69]

By representing this scandal and debunking mesmerism in the opera, Da Ponte, in line with Beaumarchais, opposed the ideology of oppressive medicalization of sexuality promoted by the French mesmerists. Through the satire on mesmeric practices, Mozart and Da Ponte allied with Benjamin Franklin, who publicly denounced mesmerism as a dangerous quack science.[70] Similarly, Thomas Jefferson noted in his journal on 5 February 1785 that mesmerism was "an imputation of so grave nature as would bear an action at law in America," and he rejoiced when it was debunked by Franklin in his scientific report for the French Royal Commission investigating the activities of the French mesmerists. The reason Franklin and Jefferson waged war against mesmerism was that at least in France it had degenerated into a radical mechanistic psychology limiting individual free will.[71] As such it was the very antipodes of the ideology informing the American Revolution.

American Symbols in The Magic Flute

The Magic Flute (1791), Mozart's last opera, based on a libretto by Emanuel Schikaneder, could be interpreted as an opera that also disseminated and was inspired by ideas distinctive of or shared by the American Enlightenment. We have seen that many of Mozart's Masonic brothers whom he met in person were activists in the American Revolution, including Benjamin Franklin. Let us hope that future commentators on this opera will consider this approach. I will conclude with something less complicated and more concrete, the reference in this opera to a popular American theme as circulating in opera and literature during the Revolutionary era: the representation of the myth of the Native American.

In 1772, Niccolò Piccinni composed his second opera based on an American theme, *L'americano*, which was performed in Vienna later the same year. The opera is about a young Native American from California brought to Europe, where he encounters and questions European fashions, customs, and laws.[72] The bird-catcher Papageno in *The Magic Flute* shares

Figure 2. Papageno, engraving dated 1794, color version of the black-and-white engraving first published in the original libretto by Emanuel Schikaneder, *Die Zauberflöte: Eine große Oper in zwei Aufzügen* (1791), as well as in the piano vocal score by Mozart, *Die Zauberflöte: Eine große Oper in zwei Aufzügen für Clavier oder Pianoforte von W. A. Mozart* (1793). (Reproduced with permission)

salient traits of the stereotypical Native American "good savage," with feathers on his head and a free spirit in his heart. Early iconography of Mozart's final opera shows that Papageno, who was first interpreted by the librettist Schikaneder himself, dressed in what could have been easily mistaken for a Native American costume (fig. 2).[73]

The final union of Papagena and Papageno recalls the union and love duet, innocent but charged with positive sexual energy, between Piccinni's Californian man and a simple shepherdess whom he prefers to a European aristocratic lady who wants him as a "serving knight." Here the family nucleus is reestablished, but its foundations are built anew. The music of the love duet opening the second part of *L'americano* creates a serene, idealized, natural soundscape in which birdcalls are reproduced by violins rather than by the more realistic birdlike sound of flutes. The young California man and the European shepherdess compare their love and their singing to the love songs of larks, nightingales, and swallows. The parallels with Papageno's bird songs and whistles and his final duet are hard to miss. Piccinni's first opera based on an American subject, *I napoletani in America* (1768), similarly represents a middle-class Neapolitan woman who marries a Native American man. She does so after escaping an abusive relationship in her fatherland and eventually becoming the governor of an imagined American province. This comic opera was composed as the first news of the rebellion of the American colonies appeared in the leading Italian gazette for international news, the *Gazzetta estera*, reporting on a meeting of "prosperous citizens under the Liberty Tree in Boston," making an oath "that the day that sees America bend to slavery be the last of their existence." That same gazette also reported sympathetically on the assertion of the Sons of Liberty against the "unnatural" principle of taxation without representation.[74]

By the time of *The Magic Flute* the American Revolution had been in the ears of opera audiences for more than twenty years, which means for Mozart's entire adult life. When Mozart died on 5 December 1791, what we now conceptualize as the French Revolution was still running its course: the Terror had not yet begun, King Louis XVI and Queen Marie Antoinette had not been guillotined, not even arrested. The American Revolution, on the other hand, had already made history and inspired more than a dozen operas. Mozart's operas, and possibly some of his instrumental music as well, served as powerful reminders to their original audiences of the American Revolution, perceived then as one of the most radical and innovative movements in the history of humankind.

Notes

This essay is a substantial revision and expansion of the last chapter of my book *Italian Opera in the Age of the American Revolution* (Cambridge: Cambridge University Press, 2011), 308–30. I am grateful to Vicki Cooper for granting permission to use material from this book and to my assistant Lesley Sullivan for her help during the last months of research on this topic.

1. Da Ponte, *Storia compendiosa,* 12–15.

2. The poems are published in the appendix to Marchesan, *Della vita e delle opere di Lorenzo Da Ponte,* 372–430.

3. Da Ponte, *Memorie,* 43–45. On this episode in the context of the tense climate in Venice during the era of the American Revolution see Del Negro, *Il mito americano,* 253–54. See also Hodges, *Lorenzo Da Ponte,* 22–25.

4. [Da Ponte after Palomba], *La quacquera spiritosa.* Link, *National Court Theatre,* 156 (calendar of opera shows in Vienna's theaters), shows *La quacquera* on 13 and 15 August 1790. For a thorough account of this opera and its Viennese production, see Polzonetti, *Italian Opera,* 281–307.

5. Diary of Count Karl Zinzendorf, 1783–92, quoted in Link, *National Court Theatre,* 359: "*La quacquera spiritosa:* sujet incroyable, mais musique jolie."

6. A more nuanced and thorough account of the system of roles in eighteenth-century opera buffa is offered by Cicali, "Roles and Acting."

7. The recitative, inserted in the Viennese manuscript score A-Wn, KT 370, is not listed in the Köchel catalog and has not been included in the complete-works edition, but was printed in facsimile in Weinmann, "Zur Mozart-Bibliographie." The recitative is also reproduced and analyzed in Edge, "Attributing Mozart"; and Polzonetti, *Italian Opera,* 301–7.

8. Link, *National Court Theatre,* 1.

9. Sisman, "Haydn's Theater Symphonies," 332–33. On Babo's *Das Winterquartier in Amerika,* see Adam, *Germany and the Americas,* 1045.

10. Link, *National Court Theatre,* 5–96.

11. On the importance of financial and economical discourse in *Le gare generose,* Mary Hunter has done pioneering work. See especially her "Bourgeois Values in Opera Buffa in 1780s Vienna." For a different interpretation of *Le gare* as an opera inspired by the American Revolution, see Polzonetti, *Italian Opera,* 247–68.

12. Arendt, *On Revolution,* 13. Mozart's awareness of the new idea of the pursuit of happiness as a promise for democracy and prosperity has been hypothesized by Michael Stürmer in "Mozart oder Die Suche nach dem Glück."

13. Da Ponte, *Le nozze di Figaro,* title page.

14. Nussbaum, "*Marriage of Figaro,*" 35. This Chicago production featured Adam Plachetka as Figaro, Christiane Karg as Susanna, and Luca Pisaroni as the Count; it was stage directed by Barbara Gaines and conducted by Henrik Nánási.

15. Carter, *W. A. Mozart,* 37.

16. Till, *Mozart and the Enlightenment,* 145–46.

17. Ibid., 146.

18. Quoted in ibid., 146. On Wieland and the American Revolution, see Dippel, *Germany and the American Revolution*, 26–27, 76, 230, 332.

19. Rice, *Mozart on the Stage*, 66.

20. Da Ponte, *Memorie*, 105.

21. Oberhuber, "Amerikanische Kunst im Zeitalter von Haydn und Mozart."

22. Till, *Mozart and the Enlightenment*, 93–94.

23. See the recurrence of these names in Nettl, *Mozart and Masonry*, and Catherine Thomson, *Masonic Thread in Mozart*.

24. Leopold Mozart, *Mozart Briefe und Aufzeichnungen, Gesamtausgabe*, 2:337, no. 444. Leopold is inquiring about a Franco-American treaty signed in February 1778 together with a second treaty regulating commerce between the two nations.

25. Bramani, *Mozart massone e rivoluzionario*, 48, 66; Deutsch, *Mozart*, 284.

26. Bramani, *Mozart*, 94. For Beaumarchais's letters to Charles Gravier, Count of Vergennes, written in 1775, see Beaumarchais, *For the Good of Mankind*, 63–66.

27. For a concise account of the historical context of the composition of the literary sources for *Le mariage de Figaro*, see Coward, introduction. One of the earliest modern studies on Beaumarchais' active role in the American Revolution is Kite, *Beaumarchais and the War of American Independence*. Many other studies followed, the most comprehensive being Antoinette Shewmake's introduction and critical apparatus for Beaumarchais, *For the Good of Mankind*. Specifically on *Le mariage de Figaro* and the ideology of the American Revolution, see Morton and Spinelli, *Beaumarchais and the American Revolution*, 64, 178, 329.

28. The pamphlet appears in translation in Beaumarchais, *For the Good of Mankind*, 349–77, from which I quote.

29. Beaumarchais, *Observations*, in *For the Good of Mankind*, par. 21: "Did France's intrigue of perfidy inspire the vigorous efforts of a people driven towards independence by tyranny, when the English ships were so proudly sent back to Europe? Did France incite the English obstinately to send them back to America, and the Americans obstinately to refuse them and burn their cargoes?"

30. Ibid., par. 30.

31. Maza, *Private Lives and Public Affairs*.

32. The term *cavatina* does not appear in the first edition of the libretto, but it appears in Mozart's autograph score, *Le nozze di Figaro K. 492*, 1:53.

33. Allanbrook, *Rhythmic Gesture in Mozart*, 33–35; see also 79–82 for the identification of the dance rhythmic gestures in "Se vuol ballare."

34. Da Ponte, *Le nozze di Figaro*, act 1, scene 2. For the score, the reader may want to consult the most commercially available edition of Mozart, *The Marriage of Figaro (Le nozze di Figaro) in Full Score*, 41–47. Interestingly, Susanna plays the guitar too, using it to accompany Cherubino's song "Voi che sapete" (*Le nozze*, act 2, scene 2). The guitar belongs to Countess Rosina (as she commands Susanna to "prendi la mia chitarra e l'accompagna"), but Rosina, as we learn in the prequel, *The Barber of Seville*, was in fact a middle-class woman who became a countess by marrying Count Almaviva.

35. Allanbrook, *Rhythmic Gesture in Mozart*, 55, 81.

36. Van Winkle Keller, *Dance and Its Music in America*, 65. The example is from an

eighteenth-century anthology, *A Selection of Scots Reels or Country Dances* (London: Preston, c. 1778–87).

37. For an in-depth study of the fascinating and complicated issue of the fandango scene in the act-3 finale of *Le nozze di Figaro,* performed at the premiere and two more times by professional dancers plus Benucci (Figaro) and then cut, see Link, "Fandango Scene in Mozart's *Le nozze di Figaro."* Link concludes that the fandango scene is "the point of sharpest confrontation between the two competing males, Figaro and the Count" (92).

38. Dalrymple, *Travels through Spain and Portugal,* 51. Craig H. Russell quotes Dalrymple and other modern sources to document the American origins of the fandango in his critical commentary to *Santiago de Murcia's "Códice Saldívar no. 4,"* 1:50–51. Beaumarchais's report on the fandango is quoted and discussed in Charnon-Deutsch, *Spanish Gypsy,* 50. I am grateful to Tekla Babyak for calling my attention to this and other evidence pointing to the American identity of the fandango. She did so during a lively and productive discussion at the end of my presentation at the colloquium series of the music department of the University of California, Davis, on 19 October 2015.

39. Mozart to his sister, Nannerl, 4 August 1770, in Leopold Mozart, *Mozart Briefe und Aufzeichnungen, Gesamtausgabe,* 1:378, no. 202: "Meine einzige Lustbarkeit besteht darmalen in englischen Schritten, und Capriol und spaccatmachen. Italien ist ein Schlafland! es schlafert einem immer! Addio leb wohl!"

40. Lyndmayr-Brandl, "Dances," 134.

41. *Thompson's Compleat Collection of 200 Favourite Country Dances,* 5:37. On sciencefiction and utopian literature inspired by the Montgolfiers' early flying experiments and its connection with the imaginary of the American Revolution, see Polzonetti, *Italian Opera,* 98.

42. On 10 June 1786 one could read in the leading Italian newspaper, the *Gazzetta Universale:* "Everybody knows that the Asian market is open to every nation through the exchange of pezzi duri, many of which are lost every year in China, Japan, Persia, and Hindustan. The central bank of Mexico has coined more than 18 and a half million pezzi duri last year. . . . In Seville everybody can see how much wealth and affluence comes from those mines that for the last three centuries have provided enough metal to sustain such an unlimited circulation of cash." A similar report appeared in the *Gazzetta Universale* on 10 July 1787.

43. Bono, *Lumi e corsari,* 235.

44. On *Un ballo in maschera,* see Rosen, "Tale of Five Cities."

45. Pietro Chiari's *La donna che non si trova* (1762), *L'americana raminga* (1763), and *La corsara francese* (1781) belong to this genre. For a critical and historical account of these works, see Buccini, *Americas in Italian Literature and Culture,* 63–67.

46. Waldoff, *Recognitions in Mozart's Operas,* 11.

47. Castelvecchi, "Sentimental and Antisentimental," 7–11.

48. Marmontel, *Le huron,* act 1, scene 6.

49. Heartz, "Constructing *Le nozze di Figaro,"* 148–50; Link, *National Court Theatre,* 87, 94.

50. The title "Canzonetta sull'aria" does not appear in the original edition of the libretto (p. 70), but it appears in the autograph sketch of the Bibliotheca Mozartiana der Internationalen Stiftung Mozarteum Salzburg, KV 492, facsimile in Mozart, *Le nozze di*

Figaro K. 492, 3:85. Here Mozart notates, above the inserted line for the Contessa, "canzonetta sull'aria," the indication "dettando a Sus[anna]" (dictating to Susanna), and above Susanna's part the indication "scrivendo" (writing).

51. On this opera and other operas representing imaginary worlds on the moon as a metaphor for America, see the first two chapters of Polzonetti, *Italian Opera.*

52. For two differing interpretations of this duet in Darabont's film, see Hunter, "Opera in Film"; and Chua, "Listening to the Self." For my own observations on this duet as represented in the film I am grateful to my students at Notre Dame and to my imprisoned students at the Westville Correctional Facility, where I taught a semester-long class entitled "Opera and Ideas" and discussed this scene again on 21 April 2017.

53. Polzonetti, "Opera as Process," 17.

54. An account of Benucci's success in Vienna and his creative role in Mozart's operas is offered by Heartz, "Constructing *Le nozze di Figaro*," 134–35.

55. Brody, "Revelations of *Don Giovanni.*"

56. Da Ponte, *Il dissoluto punito o sia il D. Giovanni,* act 1, scene 2: "Bravo! / Due imprese leggiadre! / Sforzar la figlia ed ammazzare il padre!" A similar critique of nobility as a prerogative of aristocracy occurs later when Don Giovanni seduces a farmer's bride, the farm girl Zerlina, by reassuring her that "nobility has honesty imprinted in its eyes" (la nobiltà / ha dipinta negli occhi l'onestà). The affair also concludes with a scene of deplorable sexual violence, act 1, scene 9.

57. Bertati, *Don Giovanni, o sia il convitato di pietra.* Theatrical and operatic versions of the myth of Don Giovanni are documented in several studies, including Russell, *Don Juan Legend,* and Pirrotta, *Don Giovanni's Progress.*

58. In 1790 Bertati's libretto was set anew by Friedrich Christoph Gestewitz in Dresden.

59. Klinger, *Sturm und Drang,* act 2, scene 4.

60. See also Duncan, *Lovers, Parricides, and Highwaymen,* showing that the whole literary movement of the Sturm und Drang was affected by imagery of parricide and antipatriarchalism.

61. Politropo Pantaxeno Selvaggio [Giangiacomo Casanova], "Considerazioni politico-filosofiche sull'Antica Aristocrazia Romana a esempio a tutte le nazioni che voliono mantenersi libere: Ad uso del popolo inglese," *Opuscoli miscellanei,* April 1780, quoted in Del Negro, *Il mito americano,* 127–28. On Casanova's position against the American Revolution, see also ibid., 82, 101, 121.

62. Macchia, "Casanova e il *Don Giovanni* di Mozart." The quotation from Casanova's revision of act 2, scene 9, is on 158. The relationship between Casanova and Da Ponte emerges from the librettist's autobiography, *Memorie,* as translated by Abbott, 232–39.

63. For an example of a Marxist political reading, see Charles Ford, *Così;* for the interpretation of the opera as symbolically relating to the French Revolution, see Natošević, "*Così fan tutte.*"

64. Polzonetti, "Mesmerizing Adultery."

65. Da Ponte's first libretto of *Così* was in fact intended for Salieri. Salieri abandoned the project after beginning the composition of the opera. See Brown and Rice, "Salieri's *Così fan tutte.*"

66. Da Ponte, *Così fan tutte*. On the autograph, see Tyson, *Mozart*, 185.

67. Leopold Mozart, *Mozart Briefe und Aufzeichnungen, Gesamtausgabe*, 2:413, no. 467.

68. Solomon, *Mozart*, 74, claims that *Bastien und Bastienne* was composed in accordance with the tastes and ideological proclivities of Mesmer and his guests.

69. Polzonetti, "Mesmerizing Adultery," 263–64.

70. Benjamin Franklin, *Report of Dr. Benjamin Franklin, and Other Commissioners*.

71. Jefferson, *Papers of Thomas Jefferson*, 7:635. On Franklin's and Jefferson's opposition to mesmerism, see Darnton, *Mesmerism and the End of the Enlightenment*, 62–66. Darnton also documents that notwithstanding the opposition of Jefferson and Franklin, mesmerism eventually came to America thanks to the zeal of George Bush, an early American mesmerist. A sharp reading of *Così fan tutte* in relation to contemporary mechanistic psychology is offered by Lütteken, "Negating Opera through Opera."

72. On this opera see Polzonetti, *Italian Opera*, 170–201.

73. The illustration by Ignaz Alberti representing this character as first interpreted by the author of the libretto, Emanuel Schikaneder, in Mozart, *Die Zauberflöte* (1791), is similar to the cover illustration of one of the early piano vocal scores of the opera, Mozart, *Die Zauberflöte* (1793).

74. *Gazzetta estera*, no. 1 (April 1767–March 1768), "prefazione"; no. 32 (10 November 1767); no. 45 (9 February 1768). On the early journalistic reports of the American Revolution in Italy, see Venturi, *End of the Old Regime in Europe*, 407–9.

Works Cited

Adam, Thomas, ed. *Germany and the Americas: Culture, Politics, and History, a Multidisciplinary Encyclopedia*. Santa Barbara, CA: ACB-CLIO, 2005.

Allanbrook, Wye Jamison. *Rhythmic Gesture in Mozart: "Le Nozze di Figaro" and "Don Giovanni."* Chicago: University of Chicago Press, 1983.

Arendt, Hannah. *On Revolution*. With a new introduction by Jonathan Shell. New York: Penguin, 2006.

Babo, Joseph Marius. *Das Winterquartier in Amerika: Ein Originallustspiel in einem Auszug*. Vienna: Logenmeister, 1778.

Beaumarchais, Pierre-Augustin Caron de. *For the Good of Mankind: Pierre-Augustin Caron de Beaumarchais Political Correspondence Relative to the American Revolution*. Compiled, edited, and translated by Antoinette Shewmake. Lanham, MD: University Press of America, 1987.

———. *Observations sur le Mémoire justificatif de la cour de Londres*. London and Philadelphia: Et se trouve par-tout, 1779.

Bertati, Giovanni. "Don Giovanni, o sia il convitato di pietra." A metatheatrical act inserted in *Il capriccio drammatico, rappresentazione per musica di Giovanni Bertati, per la seconda opera da rappresentarsi nel Teatro Giustiniani di S. Moisè il carnovale dell'anno 1787*, 31–71. Venice: Casali, 1787.

———. *L'orfanella americana, commedia per musica in quattro atti di Giovanni Bertati da rappresentarsi nel Teatro di S. Moisè per la prima opera dell'autunno 1787.* Venice: Casali, 1787.

Bono, Salvatore. *Lumi e corsari: Europa e Maghreb nel Settecento.* Perugia: Morlacchi, 2005.

Bramani, Lidia. *Mozart massone e rivoluzionario.* Milan: Mondadori, 2005.

Brody, Richard. "The Revelations of *Don Giovanni* at the MET." *New Yorker,* 17 February 2015.

Brown, Bruce Allan, and John Rice. "Salieri's *Così fan tutte.*" *Cambridge Opera Journal* 8, no. 1 (1996): 17–43.

Buccini, Stefania. *The Americas in Italian Literature and Culture: 1700–1825.* Translated by Rosanna Giammarco. University Park, PA: Pennsylvania State University Press, 1997.

Carter, Tim. *W. A. Mozart: "Le nozze di Figaro."* Cambridge: Cambridge University Press, 1987.

Castelvecchi, Stefano. "Sentimental and Antisentimental in *Le nozze di Figaro.*" *Journal of the American Musicological Society* 53, no. 1 (2000): 1–24.

Charnon-Deutsch, Lou. *The Spanish Gypsy: The History of a European Obsession.* University Park: Pennsylvania State University Press, 2004.

Chua, Daniel K. L. "Listening to the Self: *The Shawshank Redemption* and the Technology of Music." *Nineteenth-Century Music* 34, no. 2 (2011): 341–55.

Cicali, Gianni. "Roles and Acting." In *The Cambridge Companion to Eighteenth-Century Opera,* edited by Anthony R. DelDonna and Pierpaolo Polzonetti, 85–98. Cambridge: Cambridge University Press, 2009.

Coward, David. Introduction to *The Figaro Trilogy,* by Pierre-Augustin Caron de Beaumarchais, vi–xv. Translated by David Coward. Oxford: Oxford University Press, 2003.

Dalrymple, William. *Travels through Spain and Portugal in 1774 with a Short Account of the Spanish Expeditions against Algiers in 1775.* London: Almon, 1777.

Da Ponte, Lorenzo. *Così fan tutte o sia la scuola degli amanti, dramma giocoso in due atti da rappresentarsi nel teatro di corte l'anno 1790.* Vienna: Società Tipografica, 1790.

———. *Il dissoluto punito o sia il D. Giovanni: Dramma giocoso in due atti da rappresentarsi nel teatro di Praga l'anno 1787.* Prague: Schoenfeld, 1787.

———. *Memorie.* In *Memorie e libretti mozartiani,* 1–396. 7th ed. Milan: Garzanti, 2006. Translated by Elizabeth Abbott as *The Memoirs of Lorenzo Da Ponte* (New York: Dover, [1967]).

———. *Le nozze di Figaro, commedia per musica tratta dal francesce in quattro atti, da rappresentarsi nel Teatro di Corte l'anno 1786.* Vienna: Giuseppe Nob. De Kurzbeck, 1786.

———. *Storia compendiosa della vita di Lorenzo Da Ponte scritta da lui medesimo / Compendium of the Life of Lorenzo Da Ponte Written by Himself.* Bilingual ed. New York: Riley, 1807.

[Da Ponte, Lorenzo, after Giuseppe Palomba]. *La quacquera spiritosa, comedia per musica in due atti da rappresentarsi nel Real Teatro di Corte l'anno 1790: La musica è del Signor Pietro Guglielmi Maestro di Cappella Napoletano.* Vienna: Società Tipografica, 1790.

Darnton, Robert. *Mesmerism and the End of the Enlightenment in France.* Cambridge, MA: Harvard University Press, 1968.

Del Negro, Piero. *Il mito americano nella Venezia del '700.* Padua: Liviana, 1986.

Deutsch, Otto Erich. *Mozart: A Documentary Biography.* Translated by Eric Bloom, Peter Branscombe, and Jeremy Noble. Stanford, CA: Stanford University Press, 1965.

Dippel, Horst. *Germany and the American Revolution (1770–1800): A Sociohistorical Investigation of Late Eighteenth-Century Political Thinking.* Translated by Bernhard U. Uhlendorf. Foreword by Robert R. Palmer. Wiesbaden: Franz Steiner, 1978.

Duncan, Bruce. *Lovers, Parricides, and Highwaymen: Aspects of Sturm und Drang Drama.* Rochester, NY: Camden House, 1999.

Edge, Dexter. "Attributing Mozart, (i): Three Accompanied Recitatives." *Cambridge Opera Journal* 13, no. 3 (2001): 197–237.

Fliegelman, Jay. *Prodigals and Pilgrims: The American Revolution Against Patriarchal Authority, 1750–1800.* Cambridge: Cambridge University Press, 1982.

Ford, Charles. *"Cosi": Sexual Politics in Mozart's Operas.* Manchester: Manchester University Press, 1991.

Franklin, Benjamin. *Report of Dr. Benjamin Franklin, and Other Commissioners, Charged by the King of France, with the Examination of the Animal Magnetism, as Now Practised at Paris.* Translated from the French by the Royal Society of Medicine. London: Johnson, 1785.

Heartz, Daniel. "Constructing *Le nozze di Figaro.*" In *Mozart's Operas,* edited by Thomas Bauman, 133–55. Berkeley and Los Angeles: University of California Press, 1990.

Hodges, Sheila. *Lorenzo Da Ponte: The Life and Times of Mozart's Librettist.* Madison: University of Wisconsin Press, 2002.

Hunter, Mary. "Bourgeois Values in Opera Buffa in 1780s Vienna." In *Opera Buffa in Mozart's Vienna,* edited by Mary Hunter and James Webster, 170–85. Cambridge: Cambridge University Press, 1997.

———. "Opera in Film: Sentiment and Wit, Feeling and Knowing—*The Shawshank Redemption* and *Prizzi's Honor.*" In *Between Opera and Cinema,* edited by Joe Jeongwon and Theresa M. Rose, 93–119. New York: Routledge, 2002.

Jefferson, Thomas. *The Papers of Thomas Jefferson.* Edited by Julian P. Boyd et al. 60 vols. to date. Princeton, NJ: Princeton University Press, 1950–.

Kite, Elizabeth Sarah. *Beaumarchais and the War of American Independence.* Foreword by James M. Beck. Boston: R. G. Badger, [1918].

Klinger, Friedrich Maximillian. *Sturm und Drang: Ein Schauspiel.* 1776. Reprint, Stuttgart: Philipp Reclam, 1970. Available in English in *Five Plays of the Sturm und Drang,* translated by Betty Senk Waterhouse, 145–90. Lanham, MD: University Press of America, 1986.

Link, Dorothea. "The Fandango Scene in Mozart's *Le nozze di Figaro.*" *Journal of the Royal Musical Association* 133, no. 1 (2008): 69–92.

———. *The National Court Theatre in Mozart's Vienna: Sources and Documents, 1783–1792.* New York: Oxford University Press, 1998.

Lütteken, Laurenz. "Negating Opera through Opera: *Così fan tutte* and the Reverse of the Enlightenment." *Eighteenth-Century Music* 6, no. 2 (2009): 229–41.

Lyndmayr-Brandl, Andrea. "Dances." In *The Cambridge Mozart Encyclopedia,* edited by Cliff Eisen and Simon P. Keefe, 133–36. Cambridge: Cambridge University Press, 2006.

Macchia, Giovanni. "Casanova e il *Don Giovanni* di Mozart." In *Tra Don Giovanni e Don Rodrigo: Scenari settecenteschi*, 147–64. 3rd ed. Milan: Adelphi, 1989.

Marchesan, Angelo. *Della vita e delle opere di Lorenzo Da Ponte, con aggiunta della famosa accademia poetica per la quale dovette esulare da Venezia e d'altri versi inediti.* Treviso: Turrazza, 1898.

Marmontel, Jean François. *Le huron, comédie en deux actes et en vers, mêlée d'ariettes, représentée pour la première fois par les Comédiens Italiens Ordinaires du Roi, le 20 août 1768.* Paris: Merlin, 1770.

Maza, Sarah. *Private Lives and Public Affairs: The Causes Célèbres of Prerevolutionary France.* Berkeley and Los Angeles: University of California Press, 1993.

Morton, Brian N., and Donald C. Spinelli. *Beaumarchais and the American Revolution.* Lanham, MD: Lexington Books, 2003.

Mozart, Leopold, et al. *Mozart Briefe und Aufzeichnungen, Gesamtausgabe.* Edited by Wilhelm A. Bauer, Otto Erich Deutsch, and Joseph Heinz. 7 vols. Kassel: Bärenreiter, 1962–78.

Mozart, Wolfgang Amadeus. *The Marriage of Figaro (Le nozze di Figaro) in Full Score.* Mineola, NY: Dover, 1979.

———. *Le nozze di Figaro K. 492: Facsimile of the Autograph Score.* 3 vols. Los Altos, CA: Packard Humanities Institute; Kassel: Bärenreiter, 2007.

———. *Die Zauberflöte: Eine große Oper in zwei Aufzügen.* Vienna: Alberti, 1791.

———. *Die Zauberflöte: Eine große Oper in zwei Aufzügen für Clavier oder Pianoforte von W. A. Mozart.* Berlin: Hummel, 1793.

Natošević, Constanze. *"Così fan tutte": Mozart, die Liebe und die Revolution von 1789.* Kassel: Bärenreiter, 2003.

Nettl, Paul. *Mozart and Masonry.* New York: Dorset, 1957.

Nussbaum, Martha C. "*The Marriage of Figaro:* Craziness, Reciprocity, Love." Program notes in *Lyric 2015/16 Season: Mozart The Marriage of Figaro,* 26 September–24 October 2015, 35–37.

Oberhuber, Konrad. "Amerikanische Kunst im Zeitalter von Haydn und Mozart." In *Mozart: Experiment Aufklärung im Wien des Ausgehenden 18. Jahrhunderts,* edited by Herbert Lachmayer, 273–82. Vienna: Da Ponte Institute; Ostfildern: Cantz, 2006.

Pirrotta, Nino. *Don Giovanni's Progress: A Rake Goes to the Opera.* Translated by Harris Saunders. New York: Marsilio, 1994.

Polzonetti, Pierpaolo. *Italian Opera in the Age of the American Revolution.* Cambridge: Cambridge University Press, 2011.

———. "Mesmerizing Adultery: *Così fan tutte* and the Kornman Scandal." *Cambridge Opera Journal* 14, no. 3 (2002): 263–96.

———. "Opera as Process." In *The Cambrige Companion to Eighteenth-Century Opera,* edited by Anthony R. DelDonna and Pierpaolo Polzonetti, 3–23. Cambridge: Cambridge University Press, 2009.

Porta, Nunziato. *L'americana in Olanda, dramma giocoso per musica in due atti di Nunziato Porta da rappresentarsi nel nobil Teatro di San Samuele l'autunno dell'anno 1778.* Venice: Fenzo, 1778.

Rice, John A. *Mozart on the Stage.* Cambridge: Cambridge University Press, 2009.

Rosen, David. "A Tale of Five Cities: The Peregrinations of Somma's and Verdi's *Gustavo III* (and *Una vendetta in dominò* and *Un ballo in maschera*) at the Hands of the Neapolitan and Roman Censorship." *Verdi Forum* 26–27 (1999–2000): 53–66.

Russell, Charles C. *The Don Juan Legend before Mozart.* Ann Arbor: University of Michigan Press, 1993.

Russell, Craig H., ed. *Santiago de Murcia's "Códice Saldívar no. 4,": A Treasury of Secular Guitar Music from Baroque Mexico.* 2 vols. Urbana: University of Illinois Press, 1995.

Shewmake, Antoinette. Introduction to *For the Good of Mankind: Pierre-Augustin Caron de Beaumarchais Political Correspondence Relative to the American Revolution*, compiled, edited, and translated by Antoinette Shewmake, 1–58. Lanham, MD: University Press of America, 1987.

Sisman, Elaine R. "Haydn's Theater Symphonies." *Journal of the American Musicological Society* 43, no. 2 (1990): 292–352.

Solomon, Maynard. *Mozart: A Life.* New York: HarperCollins, 1995.

Stürmer, Michal. "Mozart oder Die Suche nach dem Glück." *Frankfurter Allgemeine-Magazin* 614 (6 December 1991): 24–33.

Thompson's Compleat Collection of 200 Favourite Country Dances Perform'd at Court, Bath, Tunbridge & All Public Assemblies with Proper Figures or Directions to Each Tune, Set for the Violin, German-Flute, & Hautboy. 5 vols. London: Printed for Saml. Ann & Peter Thompson, 1762–80.

Thomson, Catherine. *The Masonic Thread in Mozart.* London: Lawrence & Wishart, 1977.

Till, Nicholas. *Mozart and the Enlightenment: Truth, Virtue and Beauty in Mozart's Operas.* New York: Norton, 1992.

Tyson, Alan. *Mozart: Studies of the Autograph Scores.* Cambridge, MA: Harvard University Press, 1987.

Van Winkle Keller, Kate. *Dance and Its Music in America, 1528–1789.* Hillsdale, NY: Pendragon, 2007.

Venturi, Franco. *The End of the Old Regime in Europe, 1768–1776: The First Crisis.* Translated by R. Burr Lichtfield. Princeton, NJ: Princeton University Press, 1989.

Waldoff, Jessica. *Recognitions in Mozart's Operas.* New York: Oxford University Press, 2006.

Warburton, Ernest, ed. *The Librettos of Mozart.* 7 vols. New York: Garland, 1992.

Weinmann, Alexander. "Zur Mozart-Bibliographie." *Wiener Figaro* 47 (1980): 6–7.

The Drama of Marriage in Eighteenth-Century Venice

Carlo Goldoni's *La locandiera*

ADRIENNE WARD

This essay proposes a new reading of Carlo Goldoni's beloved comedy *La locandiera,* written and first performed at the Teatro Sant'Angelo in Venice in 1752. As its title implies, the protagonist is a female innkeeper. Her captivating qualities (she is named Mirandolina, after all), the guesthouse-bordello analogy, and Venice's reputation for fun and games certainly support associations with the erotic, a theatrical mainstay.[1] Goldoni's play can be appreciated in another context, however: that of the eighteenth-century Venetian marital crisis, when confusion and conflicts over marriage regulation came to a head.[2]

Interpreting *La locandiera* against the background of Venetian marriage culture adds a new facet to criticism that has largely focused on the comedy's socioeconomic valence.[3] The canonical view equates Mirandolina's psychological triumph over the Cavaliere to the new hegemony of the bourgeois class and its value system: single-minded dedication to clear vision, honest work, and market gain.[4] Considering the comedy in light of matrimonial institutions and practices yields additional insights, however. It reveals the play's pointed commentary on the difficult dynamics of family formation. It shows the extent to which multiple sectors were constrained and both sexes afflicted by reductive class dogma and stifling social parameters. The marriage context grays the traditional reading whereby one socioeconomic cohort neatly dominates another, and one sex vanquishes its competitor.

Recent critics who cite marriage in *La locandiera* continue to relate it to the comedy's promotion of the merchant ethos. Roberto Alonge, for example, remarks that "Mirandolina's refusal to marry really means [that she can] avoid the role of wife and the damnation of maternity, both of which would compete for time she could use to realize herself in her work, in the running of the guesthouse."[5] Similarly, Luigi Lunari discusses the hypothetical marriage between Mirandolina and any one of her three patrician patron-suitors. The distance she keeps from them is not intended to prevent contamination of the superior rank (a concern normally associated with that same rank) but instead emphasizes their being unworthy of the benefits of her social role and status (a perspective her own class increasingly espoused). According to Lunari, Mirandolina's antimarriage stance translates into the bourgeois's confident rejection of the nobility.[6] Such assessments are astute and consistent with Silvana Seidel Menchi's alert to not underestimate the role that class and class ambition played in early modern marriage formation.[7] In this context, the customarily aspiring bourgeois who forswears ascendant social mobility makes a bold statement.

But Mirandolina expresses dismay with much more than the vanity of her social superiors. In varying ways, she and all the characters in the play struggle with a system that oppresses the individual subject, especially in terms of marital relations. Both sexes, together with all the social classes—noble, bourgeois, and *popolo*—seek greater freedom to control life status; more reliable, principled marriage commitment; and domestic security and satisfaction. As everyone knows, these "life enhancements" figured in the promise of the antiaristocratic and capitalist regime gaining momentum in eighteenth-century Europe. New modes did not take hold easily, however, and the Venetian Republic presented uniquely complex impediments to change. *La locandiera* gives poignant voice to the struggle. Goldoni seems to sympathize with Venetians of all ranks in his articulation of the resistance to and adaptation around explicit local marital and gender paradigms.

On the surface, *La locandiera* does not appear to take up substantive concerns regarding marriage.[8] But in fact it engages rather intensively with key issues pertinent to the Venetian scene in this period: a troubling decline in marriages, especially in sanctioned patrician unions; a rise in unorthodox marriages; and an increase in suits for separation and divorce. The play, and more specifically relations between Mirandolina and the single men surrounding her, dramatize many of the conditions that were both cause and consequence of the marriage dilemma.

Let us begin with a brief summary of the plot. The action takes place at an inn in Florence. The proprietor, the witty and vivacious Mirandolina, has inherited the inn from her recently deceased father. Often the aristocratic patrons of the inn fall under her spell, and the play opens with an exchange between two such noblemen, the Marquis di Forlipopoli and the Count d'Albafiorita. Both admit they're taken with the innkeeper and will vie for her. The impoverished Marquis claims he'll win her with the repute attached to his prestigious title; the Count, newly ennobled, will attract her with plentiful gifts, proof of his financial well-being. Then a new guest arrives, the Cavaliere di Ripafratta. He is a nobleman as well, but he differs from the Count and Marquis insofar as he claims to disdain all women. Mirandolina, in one of her famous monologues, states that she will never marry and also notes that she's accustomed to male adoration. Thus she swears she will break through the Cavaliere's aversion and mounts a clever campaign to trick him into falling for her. As she works her ruse, her servant Fabrizio frets, reminding her from time to time of her obligation to her deceased father, who on his deathbed decreed that she should marry him. Mirandolina's plan to thwart the Cavaliere succeeds, but the minute he is fully taken in by her charms, she turns on him, ridiculing his weakness. When he responds with rage, Mirandolina realizes she's gone too far. She quickly discloses to all present that she will marry Fabrizio. The Count and the Marquis toast to her upcoming nuptials, while the Cavaliere leaves the inn in disgrace.

La locandiera spotlights the idea of Mirandolina's marriage from the very beginning, in this exchange between the Count and Marquis in the play's first scene:

Marchese: A proposito di camerieri: vi è quel cameriere che ha nome Fabrizio: mi piace poco. Parmi che *La locandiera* lo guardi assai di buon occhio.

Conte: Può essere che lo voglia sposare. Non sarebbe cosa mal fatta. Sono sei mesi che è morto il di lei padre. *Una giovane sola alla testa di una locanda si troverà imbrogliata.* Per me, se si marita, le ho promesso trecento scudi.

Marchese: Se si mariterà, io sono il suo protettore, e farò io ... E so io quello che farò.

Conte: Venite qui: facciamola da buoni amici. Diamole trecento scudi per uno. (1.1)

(*Marquis:* Speaking of servants ... there's that servant named Fabrizio. I don't like him much. It looks like the mistress has really taken a liking to him.

Count: Maybe she wants to marry him. It wouldn't be a bad idea. It's been six months since her father died. *A young woman alone running an inn will get into trouble.* For my account, if she marries, I've promised her three hundred scudi.

Marquis: If she gets married, I'm the one who looks out for her, and I'll give her ... well, that's my business, I know what I'll do.

Count: What do you say to this? Let's pitch in together as friends. We'll each
  give her three hundred scudi.)[9]

This short dialogue compresses several crucial aspects pertaining to marriage. It emphasizes Mirandolina's fatherless state and thus the perception of
her vulnerability. It underscores the importance of dowries, the prevalence
of the public gaze and ensuing judgment, and male rivalry. However, the
men's competition to expedite Mirandolina's marriage is predicated on her
decision to wed in the first place. The conversation between the Count and
Marquis, which ends on their dual hypotheses ("if she marries . . ."), points
to the essential question running parallel to, if not superseding, curiosity
about the outcome of her seduction game: will Mirandolina take a husband,
and what consequences await her decision?

As a nubile woman unsupervised by a paternal authority figure, Mirandolina constitutes an especially charged, volatile social element. Even with
fathers present, unmarried daughters of a certain age embodied the nexus of
several potential instabilities, risks to domestic and communal order. They
could compromise family honor, disrupt estate succession, confuse relations
between families, and stain community morality.

Mirandolina's father's recent death increases the sense of urgency. The
passing of a paterfamilias typically heralded the marriage of children (sons
first and foremost) to safeguard family patrimony and assure familial stability.[10] Women lacking a father or paternal stand-in further destabilized the
usual male-centered marriage transaction, in which two fathers, or a father
and a son-in-law, contracted the union.[11] Mirandolina exists in a familial
vacuum: she has no father, mother, aunt, uncle, sibling, or maidservant to
advise her. Fabrizio highlights her isolation in act 3, scene 14: "siete una
giovane sola, senza padre, senza madre, senza nessuno. Se foste maritata,
non andrebbe così" (you are a young woman alone, without father, without
mother, without anyone. If you were married, these things [referring to the
Cavaliere's aggression] wouldn't happen). Mirandolina is entirely her own
counsel and spokesperson, and thus the complex of relationships and hierarchies requisite for sound social equilibrium depends entirely on her.

In addition, she stands at the helm of a thriving business enterprise.[12]
As such she constitutes a doubly desirable property. Formerly working at
her father's side, she now calls attention to the absence of a male merchant-
manager. Among nonaristocratic populations, "marriage was in large measure an economic relationship, no matter how [spouses] felt about the people
they married. The norm was . . . the 'two-person career.' When a spouse

died, a job opening was created. . . . The widow or widower remarried to fill the opening, or a son and daughter took over and almost simultaneously acquired a mate."[13] Marriage for nonnoblemen also usually marked economic independence (i.e., legal emancipation), and here Mirandolina's allure acquires further meaning. Eighteenth-century Venetian society largely adhered to the stem-family tradition, transferring family patrimony from generation to generation through only one son at a time.[14] Noninheriting sons thus had greater obstacles to marriage and would have coveted women like Mirandolina as heiresses to substantial means.[15] Beatrice Gottlieb states that "it was the dream of non-inheriting sons to marry heiresses and, as a result, hook into just such a [well-to-do woman's] stem-family household."[16]

When Mirandolina says in her first monologue that all the men who visit her inn fall in love with her and fawn over her and that very many even bring up marriage, we can well imagine the attraction.[17] "Se avessi sposati tutti quelli che hanno detto volermi, oh avrei pure tanti mariti!" (If I'd married all the men who have said they loved me, I'd have a boatload of husbands!), she exclaims (1.9). But she declares that she has no interest in marrying. In the same speech she states:

> *Mirandolina:* A maritarmi non ci penso nemmeno; non ho bisogno di nessuno; vivo onestamente, e godo la mia libertà. Tratto con tutti, ma non m'innamoro mai di nessuno. (1.9)

> (*Mirandolina:* I don't even think about getting married. I don't need anyone. I live honestly, and I enjoy my freedom. I chitchat with them all, but I never fall in love, not with one.)

Why is Mirandolina opposed? First, she does not require the financial support. When the Count and the Marquis offer her dowry money after her marriage to Fabrizio is announced, she says she doesn't need it (3.18). Likewise, she states that she does not need love. It is important to note that Mirandolina references love only in the derogatory terms common to the Goldonian critique of the debauched aristocratic world of *galanteria* (gallantry, libertinism). She calls the men who court her "spasimanti" (simpering romantics), "cascamorti" (players, casanovas), and "uomini effeminati" (wimps, sissies) (1.9, 1.15). She gives no sign of desire for an intimate mate, for personal affection, or for consensual companionate tenderness.[18]

What Mirandolina apparently also does not wish for, though she voices this only indirectly, are the constraints and oppression of marriage. A relatively new body of scholarship is thickening descriptions of the lived marriage experience and domestic violence that plagued so many Settecento households.[19] In eighteenth-century Venice, a woman's aversion to matrimony could easily have stemmed from fears of being neglected and sequestered in the house, watching her assets be squandered by a profligate mate or, worse, suffering verbal and physical spousal abuse.[20]

These types of complaints filled growing piles of petitions for separation in the Venetian ecclesiastical court. Venetian wives, not husbands, brought the overwhelming majority of separation and annulment suits in the seventeenth and eighteenth centuries. The prominent reason given by plaintiffs was *criminale maritale barbarie* (criminal conjugal cruelty) or *tirannia maritale* (marital tyranny)—verbal, bodily, and psychological abuse—by spouses.[21] *La locandiera* shows us this savage side of man when the Cavaliere discovers he's been duped and sees Mirandolina showing preference for Fabrizio. He flies into a jealous fury that provokes real anxiety in the innkeeper, the only sign of vulnerability in a woman who otherwise controls herself and everyone and everything around her.

The Cavaliere's potential for rage glimmers long before the final scenes of act 3. Early on in the seduction scene (2.4), as Mirandolina entices him with her charms, stage directions dictate that he behave "con qualche passione" (with some intensity), and become "alterato" (anxious, worked up). Later he speaks "con affanno" (under stress) and "con imperio" (imperiously) (2.8). Act 2 ends on his violent gesture provoked when others see him ministering to the fainted Mirandolina: "He hurls a vase to the ground, and it breaks near the Count and Marquis, and he exits furiously" (2.19; getta il vaso in terra, e lo rompe verso il Conte ed il Marchese, e parte furiosamente).

The drama peaks in act 3 with the Cavaliere's full-blown anger, which also accrues in stages. In act 3, scene 14, he knocks at Mirandolina's door and demands to see her, whereupon she puts him off. In scenes 15 and 16 he returns, knocking more vehemently and trying to force the door open: "si sente che la sforza" (one hears him forcing it). He matches his physical efforts with verbal threats: "Apritemi, giuro al cielo" (Open up, I swear to God) and "Aprimi o la getto a basso" (You open up or I'll knock it down). Once he enters, he sputters at Fabrizio, who tries to forestall him: "Va' via, briccone, che ti rompo il cranio" (3.16; Get out of here, scoundrel, or I'll break your skull). As the Count goads him, his ire swells and he grabs a sword to challenge the Count (3.17). Stage directions indicate his amassing fury—first "alterato" (upset), then "irato" (irate).

Finally, Mirandolina administers her coup de grâce. Pretending to defend the Cavaliere, she states to all that though she tried to get him to love her,

her words, tears, even her fainting, had no effect. The Cavaliere at last comprehends the fraud perpetrated on him. He wants to flee, but Mirandolina dares him to prove he is not in love—and thus jealous—by witnessing then and there her marriage to Fabrizio: "In presenza di questi Cavalieri, vo' dar la mano di sposa [a voi, caro Fabrizio]" (In front of these noblemen, I want to give my hand in marriage [to you, dear Fabrizio]). At this point the Cavaliere erupts. Addressing Mirandolina, he switches from the formal *voi* to the informal *tu,* a clear expression of disrespect and contempt:

> *Cavaliere:* Sì, maledetta, spòsati a chi tu vuoi. So che tu m'ingannasti; so che trionfi dentro di te medesima d'avermi avvilito, e vedo sin dove vuoi cimentare la mia tolleranza. Meriteresti ch'io pagassi gl'inganni tuoi con un pugnale nel seno; meriteresti ch'io ti strapassi il cuore, e lo recassi in mostra alle femmine lusinghiere, alle femmine ingannatrici. Ma ciò sarebbe un doppiamente avvilirmi. (3.18)

> (*Cavaliere:* Go ahead, damned woman, marry whoever you want. I know you tricked me, I know that inside you're celebrating having brought me down so low, I see how far you push my limits. You deserve a knife in your chest as payback; I ought to rip your heart out and parade it in front of all women players, women cheats. But that would be a double insult to me.)

After cursing her flattery, tears, and lies, he concludes:

> *Cavaliere:* Tu mi hai fatto conoscere qual infausto potere abbia su noi il tuo sesso, e . . . che per vincerlo non basta, no, disprezzarlo, ma ci conviene fuggirlo. (*parte*) (3.18)

> (*Cavaliere:* You've taught me what sick power your sex has over us, and . . . that to overcome it it's not enough to despise it, one has to run from it. [*exits*])

Staging the Cavaliere's unleashed temper certainly had its antecedents. One might recall other famous performing tyrants, such as Polifonte in Scipione Maffei's tragedy *Merope* (first performed in 1713), Artabano in Metastasio's opera seria *Artaserse* (1730), or Mahomet in the eponymous Voltairean tragedy (1736). But a scene of male fury in a domestic environment would also have evoked the despotic Venetian husbands cited in increasing lawsuits brought by wives. To be successful in their separation suits, Venetian women had to prove life-threatening physical punishment meted out by their spouses.[22] The image of an enraged, avenging husband pounding on a household door further recalls the enduring metaphor of family as political microcosm. In the case of *La Serenissma,* such a scene clashed directly with "the dominant understanding of Venetian self-fashioning, [where] tyranni-cal rule was an abuse of authority and constituted the antithesis of republi-can ideals, which placed public welfare, stability, and . . . freedom . . . at the centre of political behavior."²³

Theatricalizing male violence in the eighteenth century had yet further significance. Evoking a larger discourse on the ideal of the polished, civi-lized man (opposed to his crude, rustic counterpart, unable to modulate his passions), it underscored the tie between honor and public image. The Cavaliere becomes most unhinged when he realizes he has been seen by others. Daniela Hacke's discussion of husband-on-wife assault emphasizes the high degree of public visibility of family life in Venetian neighborhoods. The household, she remarks, "was not yet a private and intimate sphere and marital discord was the object of public evaluation."²⁴ What is more, as important as wifely obedience was, marital discord was usually viewed as a failing of the husband to properly control his domain.²⁵ It cast doubt on his alleged natural superiority. On the legal narratives she examines, Hacke remarks that "the escalation of household disputes was commonly interpreted as the husband's loss of temper and good sense. Wife-beating husbands are portrayed as furious and as having given up prudence and wisdom, overpowered by their emotions."²⁶ The theater audience as witness to the Cavaliere's irrational behavior was not so far from those neighbors, family members, and friends whose testimony about other accused male persecutors proved so decisive in separation suits.²⁷ In addition, over the course of the eighteenth century, Venetian intellectual and political circles— predominantly male domains—grew in their sympathy and assistance to women subjugated by cruel husbands.²⁸ With the Cavaliere on display, as it were, Mirandolina observes him as well. In front of such an example of undesirable, unfit husband material, surely she is vindicated in her distrust of the marital arrangement.

Even without the specter of a ferocious husband, Mirandolina's dis-missal of marriage would have resonated with growing desires for indi-vidual autonomy with respect to one's life status. Volker Hunecke notes the general rule that while titled Venetian parents, and more broadly, the fam-ily's political and economic policy, determined *whom* a child would marry, those same young men and women had a say as to *whether* to marry. Pa-trician wills and testaments from nearer the end of the century reveal in-creasing freedom granted to daughters. Family patriarchs progressively con-sidered "the possibility that daughters would choose neither marriage nor convent, but rather . . . lay spinsterhood, and made arrangements for their secure futures in this case as well."[29] Hunecke concedes, however, that this freedom extended more often to children of the nobility, whereas the situation of the third and fourth estates (the *ceto medio* and the *popolo*) more readily imposed marriage on offspring.[30] Anne Schutte's trenchant study on early modern forced monachization contests such freedom granted to aristocratic youth. Given enormous pressures to carefully manage the inheritance stream, eighteenth-century patrician patriarchs asserted full control over the destinies of all their offspring.[31] In either case, Mirandolina and others in her *ceto medio* would have been constrained in this regard. Her repudiation of marriage is all the more incisive and premonitory. She is *emancipata* (legally independent) in a juridical, economic sense and seems to want to match that condition with freedom from the obligation to form a family.

Mirandolina's dalliance with the Cavaliere can be interpreted in yet another way, and here the drama might have packed its biggest punch for audiences, women spectators above all. The heroine's game comprises a provocative inverse dramatization of seduction and breach of promise, one of the most prevalent and infamous allegations brought to canon and civil courts.[32] Women were the most frequent claimants, often accusing higher-ranking men of sexual attentions and/or verbal statements of marital intent, followed by the *promessa disattesa* (broken promise). One quarter of seventeenth-century Venetian seduction-and-breach-of-promise cases were brought by fatherless women, more evidence still of the difficulties faced by daughters without a paternal presence.[33] Mirandolina's remark cited above clearly alludes to her personal awareness of her own susceptibility: "If I'd married all the men who have said they loved me, I'd have a boatload of husbands!" (1.9). But she turns the pattern on its head. After insinuating a deeply felt affinity with the Cavaliere, on which he begins to entertain future happiness, she decisively reneges.[34] While in her thrall, the Cavaliere tells Mirandolina that she deserves a king's love ("Voi meritereste l'amore di un Re") and can order him around as she wishes ("potete dispor di me con autorità")—but she cuts short his reveries and tramples his devotion (3.6).

The tension of the marriage promise impacts Fabrizio in a more definitive way. He has been promised Mirandolina's hand in actual terms, by her father, and he suffers the anxiety of the pledge awaiting fulfillment. Fabrizio's situation comprises another subdrama within the marriage context, hinging on the inherent stress of the betrothal period. Agreed-upon nuptials could be thwarted in multiple ways, leading to breach-of-promise claims.[35] Fabrizio has a lot to lose. To put it another way, wedding Mirandolina is an upwardly mobile move by which he, of all the men, stands to gain the most.[36]

The play figures the Cavaliere as Mirandolina's potential spouse in additional ways. When other characters engage him regarding his misogyny, the conversation quickly turns to wives. The Cavaliere's antagonistic attitude toward love and women and the notion of matrimony are frequently linked.[37] First, in this dialogue with the Count and the Marquis:

> *Conte:* Non siete mai stato innamorato?
> *Cavaliere:* Mai, né mai lo sarò. Hanno fatto il diavolo per darmi moglie, né mai l'ho voluto.
> *Marchese:* Ma siete unico della vostra casa: non volete pensare alla successione?
> *Cavaliere:* Ci ho pensato più volte, ma quando considero che per avere figliuoli mi converrebbe soffrire una donna, mi passa subito la volontà. (1.4)

> (*Count:* Haven't you ever been in love?
> *Cavaliere:* Never, and I never will be. They've gone crazy trying to give me a wife, and I've never wanted one.
> *Marquis:* But you're the only family descendant—don't you think about succession?
> *Cavaliere:* I've thought about it a lot, but when I consider that to have children I would have to suffer a wife, the desire quickly passes.)

When the Cavaliere learns that a wealthy old friend of his has died in Siena, leaving an only child, a daughter, and that friends there are pressing for his marriage to the well-to-do young heiress, he exhorts:

> *Cavaliere:* Non s'affatichino per me, che non ne voglio saper nulla. Lo sanno pure, che io non voglio donne per i piedi. . . . Moglie a me! Piuttosto una febbre quartana. (1.11)

> (*Cavaliere:* They mustn't exert themselves for me, I don't want anything to do with it. And they know I don't want women in my way. . . . Me, with a wife! Better a case of malaria.)

A short while later, in their first exchange, Mirandolina discloses her own repugnance toward marriage and asks the Cavaliere if he is married:

> *Mirandolina:* . . . ho avuto delle buone occasioni; eppure non ho mai voluto maritarmi, perché stimo infinitamente la mia libertà.
> *Cavaliere:* Oh sí, la libertà è un gran tesoro.
> *Mirandolina:* E tanti la perdono scioccamente.
> *Cavaliere:* So ben io quel che faccio. Alla larga!

Mirandolina: Ha moglie V.S. illustrissima?
Cavaliere: Il cielo me ne liberi. Non voglio donne. (1.15)

(*Mirandolina:* . . . I've had some good offers; and yet I never wanted to
   marry, because I infinitely value my freedom.
Cavaliere: Oh yes, freedom is a great treasure.
Mirandolina: And so many foolishly lose it.
Cavaliere: Not me, I know what I'm doing. Keep it far from me!
Mirandolina: Does your lordship have a wife?
Cavaliere: Heaven help me. I don't want women.)

The conflation of women with wives and the Cavaliere's obstinate rejection
of them would surely have recalled those cohorts of Venetian men who were
not marrying, either because of family or class financial agendas or because
of personal choice (where, as will be seen, class belonging had a strong influence, mainly in the case of the patriciate). As mentioned above, the desire
to preserve patrimony led many Venetian families to permit only one official marriage per generation.[38] Ancient antiuxorial sentiment lived on in
the local belief, shared among patrician men especially, that marriage was
a heavy yoke that prevented the full exercise and enjoyment of one's rights
and responsibilities as a *nobiluomo*.[39]

   Here it will be useful to open a parenthesis on the Venetian governing
system. The legendary exclusivity of the patriciate limited membership to
families descended from the "original" founding lineages. Authenticity was
reified in the *Libro d'Oro* (Golden book), which listed the names of the qualified families. Only male representatives from these houses, or *casati*, were
eligible to sit on the Great Council, the most important state body insofar
as it alone both produced candidates for all governing posts and voted them
into place. Membership in the patriciate therefore necessitated focused
political involvement, and having to tend to a wife and the tasks accruing
to the head of household was thought to compromise the glory that could
come only from total dedication to public affairs.[40]

   One statistic asserts that 66 percent of marriageable Venetian noblemen
remained single in the eighteenth century.[41] One in ten patricians did not
marry until age of forty, and widowers did not remarry, even when the first
marriage had produced no male progeny.[42] Visitors to Venice remarked on
the disinclination to marry among patrician men, and the number of *fraterna*, or households shared by a married man, his wife, and his offspring,
and all the husband's unwed brothers.[43] But were the scruples imputed above
truly felt? Ideological opposition to marriage for the good of the state might

have been compensatory, for men prohibited from establishing a ménage of their own. In fact, a good number of the surfeit of Venetian bachelors, or "subaltern patriarchs," as Stanley Chojnacki terms them, were involved in irregular marriages, a distressing bane of the times.[44]

It will be easier to understand irregular marriage, as well as to identify where and how *La locandiera* evokes such practices, by first describing the regular matrimonial route prescribed to patricians.[45] Ideal nuptials for a male member of the Venetian patriciate would have respected the demands of three important entities: church, family, and state. Church law required adherence to the Tametsi decree (the reform established by Council of Trent in 1563), which mandated that the couple's local parish priest must preside over the sacrament. It had also been decreed that marriages must be preceded by banns, that there must be witnesses, and that the ceremony must take place inside or in front of the church. The canonical patrician matrimony—a public celebration of the merger of two families—would easily have met all such ecclesiastical obligations. The second necessary approval issued from the families themselves. The scenario described above infers the model situation: that both spouses originated from qualified noble bloodlines and that their respective patriarchs agreed to the union. A peaceful, mutually gratifying (to the families, at least), endogamous marriage would assure longevity of the ideologies and privileges particular to the patrician elite. Lastly, and following quickly upon the second imperative, the state entered the picture, in terms of validating the noble status of the partners and documenting the marriage for civil purposes. The state office known as the Avogaria del Comune discharged this task.

Registration of patrician nuptials facilitated the transfer of patrimony but also served a crucial function for the Venetian governance structure. Recall that only men whose families appeared in the *Libro d'Oro* were eligible for membership in the Great Council, from whose ranks virtually all officeholders (in municipal, regional, mainland territories) were elected. When the Avogaria del Comune guaranteed the credentials of a patrician marriage, their judgment also permitted noble status to pass to offspring. Of course the Venetian patriciate desired its steady repopulation. A thriving number of men in the Great Council meant a strong pool of nominees for leadership positions, as well as a healthy voting base to elect those leaders. The civil stipulations regarding noble marriages thus sustained the political dominance of the ruling class.

On the ground, however, circumstances were not so idyllic. Prevailing conditions, primarily the restriction of marriages to defend family wealth, thwarted the ritual and regulation described above. They further cultivated a tangle of alternative marital scenarios. These in turn threatened the status quo, especially that of patrician hegemony. *La locandiera* spotlights all of these irregular matrimonial realities. In doing so it addresses multiple cohorts across classes and genders, each bound by one or another aspect of the changing socioeconomic landscape.

Consider first the phenomenon of mixed, or interclass, marriage. *La locandiera* foregrounds the *matrimonio dispari* (unequal marriage) in an extraordinary way, when one considers that it contains not one pair of marriageable individuals (man and woman) from the same class. Where most plays and operas of the time featured one or more duos of *innamorati* (lovers) whose homogeneous social station forecasted their eventual nuptials, here the characters are a collection of isolated singletons. Any character's marriage to another of the opposite sex would constitute a mésalliance.

One such potential interclass match is that of Mirandolina with the Marquis. Despite his early conversation with the Count about the possibility that she would marry Fabrizio, the Marquis himself entertains notions of taking her as his wife.[46] Such a union would not have been so far-fetched. For increasing numbers of Venetian patrician men, especially those whose families of origin were down on their financial luck, marriage to a nonnoble woman who came accompanied by a generous dowry and/or income-generating enterprise saved the day. The ready capital wielded by the merchant sector reinforced, when it didn't rescue, the standing of aristocratic *casati* (family clans) rich in provenance but poor in cash. Acute social awareness of which families were more and less solvent is attested to by Giacomo Nani's 1750 division of the "corpo aristocratico di Venezia" (aristocratic sector of Venice) into five distinct ranks based on economic standing.[47] Marriages even between families of different levels in this hierarchy could be perceived as quasi-exogamous, and the least distance traversed, the better. The Marquis's presumed location at the bottom of the financial ranking thus makes his union with Mirandolina the most imaginable among the play's potential noble-bourgeois matchups.[48]

For different reasons, however, the Cavaliere might have figured as a likely marital candidate for the innkeeper. Like the Marquis and the Count, he hails from the nobility, but according to contemporary heraldic classifications, he would have ranked notably lower than them and just above the noble-nonnoble dividing line.[49] Focusing solely on nomenclature (and again, since bridging shorter versus larger gaps in social station was less socially disturbing), he could have seemed the most feasible husband for someone of Mirandolina's rank. Alonge notes the Cavaliere's desirability from yet another perspective: he possesses attributes lacking in each of the other noble protagonists: wealth (missing in the Marquis) and lineage (missing in the Count).[50] Were Mirandolina to aspire to marry up, the Cavaliere appears the most advantageous mate. *La locandiera* certainly reminds audiences of ambitious nonnoblewomen, represented by the two overtly gold-digger actresses, Ortensia and Dejanira.

Outsider marriage was a ubiquitous trend across all eighteenth-century Europe. In Venice, unions between nobles and nonnoble brides rose from 25 percent of the total of patrician nuptials in 1775 (a percentage that had remained constant since the mid-seventeenth century) to 50 percent at the century's end.[51] Still, these new, blended families continued to be controversial, especially in a state founded on such assiduously coded ruling privilege. Those patrician men who sought to marry *in regola* (officially, in accordance with the rules) had to submit the marriage to special validation procedures if they wanted noble standing transferred to their children. The system implemented by the Avogaria del Comune, the Venetian state entity charged with legitimizing mésalliances, required that prospective nonnoble brides undergo the *prova di nobiltà* (nobility test).[52] Passing this exam ensured that progeny would acquire the titled father's noble rank. Among the requirements, applicant brides had to verify the total absence of *arti meccaniche* (manual labor) in their families going back several generations.

Mirandolina, so often on stage with bedsheets, soups, or iron in hand, would not have passed the test. In fact, the comedy shines a bright light on Mirandolina's hands. In act 2 the expression *fatto colle mie mani* (made with my hands) or variants thereof appear six times in a five-scene sequence (2.2–2.6). In one scene alone (2.4), that wherein the innkeeper tempts the Cavaliere with the refinements of her cooking, her hands are cited three times. The sexual insinuation is plain, but in addition, one of the first scenes in the play to feature Mirandolina's hands alludes obliquely to marriage. Midway through act 1, Mirandolina slyly mimics the nuptial gesture with the Cavaliere, after condoning another of his outbursts against men who succumb to the fairer sex:

> *Mirandolina:* Guardi che debolezza! innamorarsi subito di una donna.
> *Cavaliere:* Questa io non l'ho mai potuta capire.
> *Mirandolina:* Bella fortezza! Bella virilità!
> *Cavaliere:* Debolezze! Miserie umane!

Mirandolina: Questo è il vero pensare degli uomini. Signor Cavaliere, mi
porga la mano.
Cavaliere: Perché volete ch'io vi porga la mano?
Mirandolina: Favorisca, si degni, osservi, son pulita.
Cavaliere: Ecco la mano.
Mirandolina: Questa è la prima volta che ho l'onore d'aver per la mano un
uomo che pensa veramente da uomo. (*Cavaliere ritira la mano*)
Cavaliere: Via, basta così. (1.15)

(*Mirandolina:* What weakness! Falling in love on the spot with a woman!
Cavaliere: I've never been able to understand that.
*Mirandolina:*Talk about being a man! That's real manning up right there!
Cavaliere: Pussies! Weak-minded losers!
Mirandolina: Yes, this is how real men think. Sir, give me your hand.
Cavaliere: Why do you want my hand?
Mirandolina: Please, go ahead, see, I'm being proper.
Cavaliere: Here is my hand.
*Mirandolina:*This is the first time I've had the honor of holding the hand
of a man who actually thinks like a man. [*Cavaliere pulls his hand back*]
Cavaliere: Stop now, that's enough.)

Mirandolina's request that the Cavaliere give her his hand echoes the numerous instances in coeval theater works where the solicited or proffered hand constitutes *amore in pegno* ("pledged love," i.e., a promise of future marriage). "La mano porgimi / D'amore in pegno" (Give me your hand / As a sign of pledged love), sings one of many protagonists in serious and comic operas alike.[53]

Were the Cavaliere to wed Mirandolina, he would offend the sensibilities of many old-school Venetian patricians staunchly opposed to the contamination of the family bloodline by a *femmina di vil condizione* (woman of low class or status). Returning to the seduction scenes of act 2, one finds this disruptive aspect of the mésalliance foregrounded in the following exchange:

Cavaliere: Voi siete la prima donna di questo mondo con cui ho avuto la
sofferenza di trattar con piacere.
Mirandolina: Le dirò, signor Cavaliere; non già ch'io meriti niente; ma *alle
volte si danno questi sangui che s'incontrano. Questa simpatia, questo
genio si dà anche fra persone che non si conoscono.* Anch'io provo per lei
quello che non ho sentito per alcun altro. (2.4)
(*Cavaliere:* You are the first woman in my life whose company is actually
a pleasure.

Mirandolina: Let me tell you, Sir Cavaliere, and not that I am at all worthy, but *sometimes one blood mixes well with another. This mutual feeling, this liking, occurs even between people who don't know each other well.* I too feel something for you that I've never felt for any other man.)[54]

Critics for whom the marriage between Mirandolina and any of her social betters is impossible point to the innkeeper's tense awareness of, indeed her frustration with, the fact that Venetian protocols forbid any of the noblemen from proposing nuptials.[55] Assuming such tension, Mirandolina's actions and remarks jab all the more at the minefield surrounding marital propriety and class rank.

The more likely future relationship for the two protagonists is that of concubinage.[56] Essentially practicing consensual, or common-law, marriage, Venetian men and women at all social levels cohabited without the sanction of church or state. Doing so allowed for a certain degree of sexual and domestic convenience, if not stability, while sidestepping religious and civil constraints. Venetian *nobiluomini* who lived in a quasi-married state with women of inferior status engaged in "elite concubinage, [which] involved a man of high status keeping (*tenere a sua posta*) a woman of humble condition."[57] Alexander Cowan notes: "Lay concubinage was a generally accepted phenomenon in early modern Venice. Male patricians of all ages created households and brought up families with women from a broad social spectrum. They were able to do so because . . . many of the older criteria for household-formation remained deeply rooted. . . . Individuals of both sexes and all levels of society were willing to accept that if a man and a woman cohabited and had children, this constituted a legitimate household."[58] What's more, for a man (and, indirectly, his family of origin) concubinage "solved many problems."[59] Aside from dependable companionship, it allowed personal choice in one's mate, as well as the chance to establish one's own household, away from the *fraterna* and bothersome family interference. Unmarried domestic partnerships evaded, if only superficially, the problems harped on in the cultural discourse on the tyranny of marriage. Finally, the relationship could be easily undone, minus the difficulties of religious and state procedures for separation or divorce.

Discrete conditions governed concubinal relationships in the case of patrician men. While their illegitimate sons were denied noble status, Venetian law allowed their daughters to reenter patrician networks through marriage to bona fide *nobiluomini.*[60] These daughters could then give birth to sons—

grandsons to the original cohabiting patrician man—who, when they came of age, would be permitted a place in the Great Council. But here again, the ease with which a consensual marriage could be upturned meant that it could quickly fall victim to family politics. A patrician might abandon his live-in partner once she had begotten the valuable requisite daughter(s) or if the opportunity arose for marriage to a *nobildonna* with the proper ceremony. Concubines were the least significant element in the familial equation and could be cast aside with little thought.

Cohabiting couples may have had steadier and more enduring family arrangements if they sought religious sanction through the institution of secret marriage.[61] The *matrimonio segreto* (secret marriage) option secured church blessing but avoided public, that is, state and legal, recognition of the union. Keeping the marriage out of civil records protected the family assets from incursion by anyone outside those designated by the patriarch. At the same time, the secret marriage erased the scandal of "living in sin," gave confessional peace of mind, and safeguarded the process of noble title transfer described above. As long as partners refrained from making material claims on family patrimony, both concubinal situations and secret marriages were tolerated, and on occasion even encouraged. They were a "widely recognized, if irregular, phenomenon."[62]

Returning to the play, Mirandolina and the Cavaliere evince the potential for the elite concubinal relationship (with or without the shield of secret marriage). In fact, the lexicon surrounding the custom referenced the concubine as a *donna libera* (free woman), understood to be "at the free disposition of her partner and none other." A woman thus labeled differed from a *donna del mondo* (woman of the world), namely, a prostitute, and concubines enjoyed higher status than the latter.[63] Mirandolina's repeated entreaties for freedom (*libertà*) bring this dimension into view.

Needless to say, and despite their avowed compensatory aspects, this patchwork of marriage forms and domestic understandings created formidable problems for the Venetian state. Neither of the two primary unorthodox behaviors—partnering with a woman but flouting official marital regulations or dug-in bachelorhood—augured well for the republic's governance. Men who followed either path came under fire for "defraud[ing] the Patria of their succession."[64] The Venetian elite opposed to aggregations (periodic ennoblements of subpatrician groups) as a remedy for increasing membership in the Great Council especially deplored the renunciation of proper matrimony by nobles of the sword. Recall that when the Marquis hears that the Cavaliere has no interest in marrying, the first thing he asks is whether he's not worried about succession (1.4).

Mirandolina states in her first-act monologue, "La nobiltà non fa per me" (The nobility is not for me) (1.9). And yet, as the Cavaliere falls harder and harder for her charms, *La locandiera* dangles before its audience either a glaring mésalliance or the tricky business of concubinage. Mirandolina's reference to the meeting of two bloods and her earlier simulation of marriage with the Cavaliere highlight the omnipresence of marital pressures (for and against), as well as the polemics surrounding marriage regulation, especially given the chaotic dynamics of interclass movement.

Of course, as all lovers of the play know, Mirandolina ends up marrying Fabrizio, the servant selected for her by her father. Critics entertaining the idea of a feminist strain in the play often interpret this ending as her capitulation, even her defeat: the fun is over, the ludic moment ends, Mirandolina's temporary power ceases. The father's will intones from beyond the grave, and woman is enclosed once again in patriarchy and a "gray bourgeois existence."[65] Other critics see her marriage to Fabrizio as a deliberate choice that she knows will guarantee her a certain level of control, given his lower social status.[66] But these readings continue to focus on Mirandolina's *election* to marry and undervalue the idea that she is *driven* to it: her marriage to Fabrizio comes about only as an expedient to shelter her from the aggression of the enraged Cavaliere; otherwise her procrastination might have gone on for who knows how long. In any case, theirs will not be the prescriptive conjugal relationship.

When she finally accedes, and Fabrizio seizes his moment to play hard to get, Mirandolina commands him to give her his hand. Goldoni's comedies are famous for ending on a redemptive note, with wayward characters voicing the lessons they have learned. Here, at just the moment when she sounds as if she might be repenting and welcoming the reformative propensity of marriage, Mirandolina undermines such expectations, repeating the exact phrase—"so io quel che farò"—uttered by the Marquis in his early exchange with the Count.

Mirandolina: Zitto, signori, zitto. È andato via, e se non torna, e se la cosa mi passa così, posso dire di essere fortunata. Pur troppo, poverino, mi è riuscito d'innamorarlo e mi son messa ad un brutto rischio. Non ne vo' saper altro. Fabrizio, vien' qui, caro, dammi la mano.
Fabrizio: La mano? Piano un poco, signora. Vi dilettate d'innamorar la gente in questa maniera, e credete ch'io vi voglia sposare?

Mirandolina: Eh via, pazzo! È stato uno scherzo, una bizzarria, un punti-glio. Ero fanciulla, non aveva nessuno che mi comandasse. Quando sarò maritata, so io quel che farò.
Fabrizio: Che cosa farete? (3.19)

(*Mirandolina:* Quiet, everybody, quiet down. [The Cavaliere's] departed, and if he doesn't come back, and I get out of this okay, I can call myself lucky. Poor guy, I managed to hook him and I put myself at a big risk. Let's not talk about it any more. Fabrizio, come here, give me your hand.
Fabrizio: My hand? Slow down there, ma'am. You play games with people like this and then think I want to marry you?
Mirandolina: Oh go on, you goof! It was a joke, a crazy scheme, done for silly spite. I was a girl, and had no one to command me. Once I am married, I'll know how to manage things [*so io quel che farò*].
Fabrizio: How will you manage things?)

The Marquis had resorted to this expression when he realized he could not match the cash dowry gift flaunted by the Count:

Conte: Per me, se si marita, le ho promesso trecento scudi.
Marchese: Se si mariterà, io sono il suo protettore, e farò io. . . . E *so io quello che farò.*

(*Count:* For my account, if she marries, I've promised her three hundred scudi.
Marquis: If she gets married, . . . I'll give her . . . well, that's my business, *I know what I'll do.*)

His remark, uttered to cover the void behind his noble facade, paradoxically throws it into relief. Such unmasking is paralleled when Mirandolina uses the same line and gives the lie to any outward suggestion that she will defer to and obey her future husband. It doesn't help that Fabrizio seems as clueless as ever about who she is.

La locandiera derives its drama from an increasingly complex Venetian matrimonial scene. The very star of the Venetian premiere, Maddalena Raffi Marliani, had suffered her own marital woes, exemplifying yet again the porosity between Goldoni's stage fictions ("Theater") and their environs ("World"). Mirandolina's antipathy toward marriage may have paralleled Marliani's own life circumstance. Married to the actor and *capocomico* Giuseppe Marliani of the Medebach troupe, Marliani reputedly separated from him and the acting profession for six years when he proved incorrigibly adulterous.[67] The Mirandolina role fell to her just at the moment of her return to both theater and husband, a reunion possibly marked with dubious hopes regarding her mate. In fact, Giuseppe Marliani (stage role Brighella) played the part of Fabrizio, adding still more metabiographical resonance to the comedy performance.[68]

Even if audiences heard Marliani in Mirandolina's praise of the joys of single life, the antimarriage declamations should also be heard as echoing the concerns of a much larger collective. As early as the beginning of the seventeenth century, women had begun to voice distinct critiques of local matrimonial systems. In Venice, Moderata Fonte (1555–92) and Lucrezia Marinella (c. 1571–1653) were among the most vocal protesters.[69] The French legacy counted Madame de Montpensier (1627–93) and Madame de La Fayette (1634–93), with La Fayette's followers among women expressing distrust of, if not outright opposition to, practices attending marriage and impacting wives.[70] In England, Richardson's novel *Clarissa* had just been published (1748), with a French translation issued in 1751, one year before *La locandiera*'s premiere.[71] Literate Venetian theatergoers had likely at least heard of, if not consumed, the bestselling story of a young, upper-middle-class woman persecuted by familial feuding and politics, whose overriding desire is to avoid marriage in order to live a life of peace and virtue.

It is ironic that to escape from male violence Mirandolina enters an institution itself associated with high levels of male aggression. Absent the Cavaliere's outburst, she might never have taken a husband, and she would not have been an anomaly in her Venetian setting. Single women heading their own households, widowed and unmarried, outnumbered single men two to one.[72] Mirandolina evaded a real danger in the Cavaliere, and the play suggests that she is assured to have a position of control and power even as she marries. She will surely not be inscribed within what one historian calls the "distinctly female form of subjection," that of wifely status.[73] Mirandolina's independence inverts the "secular ideology of household hierarchy [and] the principle of patriarchal rule and obedience."[74]

Similarly, the Cavaliere models a lesson for men in the audience, but not simply to wise up about duplicitous women, as Goldoni warns in his preface.[75] The final scenes show the ugliness of male passion untethered and the terror it could inspire in women. *La locandiera* proposes that men, and especially those who might become Venetian leaders, should moderate their appetites and reactions. Greater equanimity renders a man less vulnerable to womanly attractions. And should one be so charmed, a level-headed nature would permit more discernment and possibly a more peaceable family life.

It is impossible to know exactly what the men and women sitting in the *palchetti* of the Teatro Sant'Angelo thought about watching and experiencing *La locandiera*. Lunari points out that eighteenth-century stage offerings reproduced, not the pioneering thought of elites, but rather modes and values that had fully permeated a large population.[76] Tiziana Plebani reminds us of both the reflective and the instructive nature of Goldoni's theater: it staged the stressful situations young people lived every day and simultaneously modeled how one was to respond in those situations. Theater operated as a "life manual" of sorts.[77] David Wiles's notion that the eighteenth century still allowed for active, collective audience engagement invites the idea that this play connected with—or even created—a community or communities among married and unmarried Venetians of multiple social stations. These groups would have experienced "cathartic liberation seeing their . . . anxieties articulated on stage, and . . . liberation in the shared recognition of those anxieties."[78]

La locandiera most likely occasioned multiple communities. Men might have been chastened by the Cavaliere's performance of male barbarity but just as likely convinced that wives, of any stripe, were to be avoided. Women might have been inspired to seek more rigorously a form of personal happiness that dispensed with marriage. Surely Mirandolina's multiple calls for *libertà* conjure a wish in this direction.[79] Patricians in the theater must have sensed the fissures in their dominance, beset as it was on so many marriage-related fronts. The play's intensive presentation of these vulnerabilities may explain its relatively poor reception. In sharp contradiction to Goldoni's glowing recollection of its success (written more than thirty years later in his memoirs), *La locandiera* actually ran only four nights. The prima donna Teodora Raffi, presumably feeling edged out by the new soubrette Marliani, forced her husband, and head of the Medebach company, to close the play. Raffi ordered the revival of the *comédie larmoyante Pamela*, in which she had had the feature role. *La locandiera* did not enjoy wide appeal until the mid-nineteenth century.[80]

Disturbances on the marriage front would only intensify as the century wore on. In England in 1753, a clampdown on clandestine marriages led to the Hardwicke Marriage Act, which mandated banns, a church ceremony, and—the biggest shift in policy—parental consent.[81] In France, a liberal divorce law was enacted in 1792, only to be repealed ten years later.[82] In Germany, the very periodical piece that sparked Immanuel Kant's famous 1784 essay "What is Enlightenment?" debated jurisdictionalism in the context of marriage.[83]

In Venice, a civil summit was called in 1782 seeking to quell the chaos around marriage, especially the too-frequent appeal for its dissolution. The resulting 1788 legislation did not bode well for wives. Women's separation and annulment suits were subjected to increasingly stringent proofs to make sure they weren't motivated by spurious reasons (i.e., scandalously desiring to be free of marriage shackles). Pending and victorious litigants were equally distrusted, with retroactive investigation to identify women engaged in *irregolar condotta* (suspicious conduct). Church and public opinion was able to slow to some extent these authoritarian civil moves, but in general the later century saw new waves of repressive energy unleashed on questions of marriage and divorce.[84]

La locandiera reveals itself as much more than a manifesto for the vitality of one social class over another, or one sex over its rival. Tightly embedded in a fraught marriage culture, it stages the apprehensions, resistance, and coping and retaliatory strategies of men and women across social sectors. Developments in the fifty years following the first performances of *La locandiera* show that the marriage drama it enacted would play on for decades.

Notes

1. The gerund *mirando* derived from the Italian verb *mirare*, which in the Settecento had much the same meaning as it does today. The fourth edition (1729–38) of the *Vocabolario degli Accademici della Crusca* gives the following meanings: "to stare at," "to fix one's gaze upon"; also "to aim toward," "to seek to obtain," and "to admire, to highly regard." The Latin root *mira-* further conveyed the nouns "wonder," "wonderful thing," "prodigy," "surprise," "extraordinary," and "miracle." Thus the attractive Mirandolina might have embodied for her spectators a diminutive "wonder" and something or someone to be attained.

2. The boom in the last thirty-five years in scholarship on early modern marriage includes the important works on the seventeenth- and eighteenth-century Venetian scene by Ambrosini, Chojnacka, Chojnacki, Cowan, Cozzi, De Biase, Hacke, Hunecke, Martini, Plebani, Schutte, and Seidel Menchi.

3. As one might imagine, criticism on *La locandiera* is imposing. In the last century perspectives have evolved from benign views of Mirandolina as a sly but delightful coquette, an entertaining female Don Giovanni emblematic of the charming, playful sides of an eighteenth century oriented around women and gallantry (e.g., Baratto, *"Mondo" e "teatro"*; Momigliano), to analysis focused on the play's socioeconomic and (often Marxist) political significance, especially its promotion of a productive labor class opposed to an exploitative ruling sector (e.g., Baratto, "Nota"; Dazzi; Fido, *Le inquietudini* and *Nuova guida*; Flora). More recent studies acknowledge darker, more complicated and contradictory charges in the comedy. Among the most important of these newer interrogations are Alonge, "Intermezzo" and "Sistema"; Anglani; Crotti, "Chiasmi" and "Fuori

di scena"; and Momo. See Borsellino, Guidotti, Mangini, and Vazzoler for more detailed bibliographies on *Locandiera* and Goldoni criticism.

4. Alonge's analyses offer refreshing and penetrating insights from within this perspective.

5. Alonge, "Sistema," 79.

6. Lunari, 45–46.

7. Seidel Menchi, "I processi matrimoniali," 42–43.

8. Nearly every Goldoni play touches upon issues related to marriage, but some address them more deliberately. These include *La donna di garbo* (1743), *I gemelli veneziani* (1745), *La buona moglie* (1749), *Il cavaliere e la dama* (1749), *La famiglia dell'antiquario* (1750), *Pamela nubile* (1750), *Pamela maritata* (1751), *La moglie saggia* (1752), and *La trilogia della villeggiatura* (1761).

9. Emphasis added. All translations are mine unless otherwise indicated.

10. Gottlieb, *Family*, 60.

11. Ibid., 62–63.

12. In act 2, scene 2, the Cavaliere praises the quality of the locanda; Mirandolina remarks in act 2, scene 4, on her numerous and able staff and the excellence of their service.

13. Gottlieb, *Family*, 54. Also Hacke, 104, and Chojnacka.

14. Davis, 62–74; Hunecke, *Patriziato*, 148–52; Pomata; Schutte, *Force*, 54–57.

15. Often these women remained in their parental home, into which the new husband moved. Such an arrangement was known in France as a "son-in-law marriage" (*mariage à gendre*). Gottlieb, *Family*, 15–18.

16. Ibid., 15.

17. The adverb *anche* (even), used here as an intensive to stress the difference between the two comparative terms (mere courting versus proposing marriage) emphasizes the difference between marriage-minded men and others.

18. The degree to which apparently "progressive" countries like England embraced this more "modern" mode of marital relationship is still debated. Most scholars note that Italian states in the eighteenth century still had a limited conception and acceptance of marriage as companionate partnership. Schutte, *Force*, 82–88. See also Plebani; and Seidel Menchi, "I processi matrimoniali" and *Marriage in Europe*.

19. Dolan, Gowing, Hacke, Trouille. For family and usually paternal violence perpetrated on children to push them into either marriage or monachization, see Schutte, *Force*, 144–46, 155–58.

20. Schutte questions the "blanket assertion" by other scholars that well-born women "were restricted to their home and one or two adjacent contrade." "Society," 355–57. However, other data suggest that the threat of sequestration was a persistent reality for Venetian women. Even wives who contested their marriages through the proper channels fell victim to it, in circumstances that worsened as time went on. A 1782 law decreed that from the moment a woman initiated a separation or annulment suit, she was to be put immediately in a convent or *conservatorio* (at her husband's expense) until the final ecclesiastical ruling. She was permitted visits only from blood relations or her church lawyer. Positive legal outcomes did not translate to automatic freedom from the husband's authority. Only wives granted marriage annulment (*divorzio proprio*) were free to

remarry, but these were the minority of cases. Most winning plaintiffs gained separation (*divorzio semplice*), under which they still remained under the husband's control and were often constrained to live in such a way as to be easily monitored. See, generally, Cozzi, "Note."

21. Cozzi, "Note," 279. "Asprezza e crudeltà de' mariti" (husbands' harshness and cruelty) reads the official phrasing of one of four reasons stipulated as grounds for separation by a group of special experts called in by the Council of X to consult on marriage legislation in the difficult 1780s. (The others were taking religious vows, committing adultery, and falling from the faith.) Ibid., 303. De Biase lists the justifications stated by plaintiffs suing for separation (for those suits that reached sentence) in eighteenth-century Venice. Physical violence perpetrated by the husband appears more frequently than any other infraction. The official terms used in the suits include *sevizie, mali trattamenti, pericolo vita, ingiurie, violenze,* and *odio capitale.* "Problemi," 158–60. On the definition and instances of *odio capitale* (capital hate), see Hacke, 125–30; and Lombardi, "L'odio capitale."

22. Hacke, 129.

23. Ibid., 8.

24. Ibid., 139. Hacke cites the abusive husband who gagged his wife to prevent those outside the home from hearing him beat her and thereby preclude witnesses. Ibid., 127. See also Schutte, "Society," 365–66, on city and neighborhood environments putting family behavior on view.

25. On the obedience imperative for Italian wives in the eighteenth century, see Guerci.

26. Hacke, 129.

27. Ibid., 74–85, 139–43.

28. Cozzi, "Note," 280–84.

29. Hunecke, *Patriziato,* 157.

30. Ibid., 152–57.

31. Schutte, *Force,* 52–57.

32. Some scholars note that accusations of "promessa disattesa" decreased significantly after the Council of Trent's 1563 Tametsi ruling, which pronounced marriages valid only if the local parish priest was present when a couple exchanged the sacramental vows. But breach-of-promise cases persisted into the eighteenth century, if in lesser numbers. La Rocca outlines a case in 1772, and Cozzi cites provisions addressing the problem in Venice and Naples as late as 1779–80. La Rocca; Cozzi, "Note," 279. Also see Lombardi, *Matrimoni.* An indirect indication that "seduction-and-breach-of-promise" claims must have been made in the latter half of the Settecento is provided by Luca De Biase. Venetian annulment suits that cite as their justification "difetto del proprio parrocco" (absence of the local parish priest) reveal that couples continued to flout the Tametsi regulation and to make the nuptial commitment on their own. Such acts would have been more susceptible to disagreements on the nature or existence of obligation incurred by either party. The "difetto del proprio parroco" explanation appears as late as 1766. "Problemi," 159–61.

33. Hacke, 53–54.

34. The Cavaliere typically expresses his dilemma in terms of his future, whether in

a conditional sense, that is, who he might become or what he would do based on having met Mirandolina, or in a literal sense, as in what he or Mirandolina will actually do in a successive moment. Dialogue that pivots on a conditional future for the Cavaliere includes statements such as this line whispered to Mirandolina during the seduction scene: "Non vorrei che voi mi faceste mutar natura" (2.4; I wouldn't want you to make me change my ways); and "Io non sarei così" (2.6; I would not be like that [boastful and boorish like the Marquis]). In the latter case the hypothetical condition is unspoken but no less conveyed: "I would not be like [the Marquis] if, instead of him, you were to take me as lover/husband." The Cavaliere's unresolved future revolves particularly around whether he will resume his original travel plan or stay on at the locanda for a longer period. He repeatedly raises his intention to continue to Livorno, in tension with his desire to remain near Mirandolina (2.1, 2.3, 2.9, and 2.16).

35. Gottlieb, *Family,* 76–79; Hunecke, *Patriziato,* 140.

36. Alonge, "Sistema," 74–76.

37. Alonge points out that the Cavaliere is not a misogynist but rather opposed to longer-term love relationships with women. He's amenable to momentary flings but not committed partnerships. Ibid., 80.

38. In noble families that limited marriage to only one son, the one least apt for a successful political career (thus not necessarily the firstborn) was often chosen to be the *sposo di casa,* the "collective family's husband." In compensation for his sacrifice (of freedom, liberty) for the welfare of the family at large, this son would commonly receive a slightly greater portion of family assets or inheritance. Hunecke, *Patriziato,* 151; see also Gottlieb, *Family,* 60.

39. Hunecke, *Patriziato,* 146–57. On the history of antimarriage or antiuxorial convictions, see Cozzi, "Note," 287–88, 298, and D'Elia.

40. Hunecke, *Patriziato,* 148.

41. Davis, 72. Davis is citing research by Ernst Rodenwaldt (1954), based on data Hunecke characterizes as very dubious but that nonetheless have been accepted by many scholars since. "Matrimonio," 298. Hunecke sees a more accurate picture in Beltrami, which notes minimal changes in marriage rates going back to the late sixteenth century. *Patriziato,* 157. The perception of fewer marriages in the Venetian patriciate across the eighteenth century results from the actual decline in the official, civil registration of marriages. If this waning was offset by a rise in "irregular" noble marriages, that is, domestic relationships not formally registered with the republic's Avogaria del Comune, then technically the Venetian marriage rate did not diminish as drastically as imagined. In any case, fewer sanctioned nuptials and more unconventional unions posed a problem for authorities and society at large.

42. Hunecke, *Patriziato,* 153.

43. Ibid., 147–48.

44. Chojnacki, 244.

45. Ambrosini, 429–31; Cowan, "Patricians" and *Marriage;* Cozzi, "Padri"; De Biase, *Amore* and "Vincoli"; Gottlieb, "Meaning"; Hacke; Lombardi, "Fidanzamenti" and *Matrimoni;* Martini; Schutte, "Society."

46. The Marquis professes his admiration and affection for Mirandolina more openly than the other nobles, and in act 1, scene 8, he confesses to her directly that if only he

had the financial security of the Count, he would marry her. His admission sparks her monologue in the very next scene, where she rails against male admirers, marriage, and men in general.

47. Hunecke, *Patriziato,* 60–71, 419; Hunecke, "Matrimonio," 289–91.

48. Comparini's study of mixed marriage in Goldoni's plays offers a spectrum of least to most censured social combinations. In her schema, a Cavaliere-Mirandolina wedding match would have been highly problematic, based on his age (not yet elderly) and financial vigor.

49. Genta.

50. Alonge, "Sistema," 88–87.

51. Cowan, *Marriage;* Hunecke, "Matrimonio," 318.

52. Cowan, *Marriage;* Hunecke, "Matrimonio." Traditional gauges of noble essence depended on family (blood) ancestry, expressed in quantitative terms. Note, for example, the Tuscan injunction that a nobleman's prospective wife be a *donna quartata,* meaning that all four of her grandparents had patrician status. Bizzocchi, 123.

53. Act 1, scene 3, of Giovanni Bertati's libretto for the dramma giocoso *La villanella rapita.* The phrase (and one can assume the gesture) occurs also in various works by Zeno and Metastasio.

54. Emphasis added.

55. Alonge, "Sistema," 74; Baratto, *"Mondo" e "teatro,"* 133–34.

56. On concubinage in eighteenth-century Venice, see Cowan, "Patricians" and *Marriage;* Cozzi, "Padri"; and Martini.

57. Schutte, "Society," 370–72.

58. Cowan, "Patricians," 289.

59. Ibid., 290.

60. The process for such was complicated, however, requiring that the patrician father retroactively seek the *prova di nobiltà* for his concubine in order to marry her in accordance with patrician provisions. See Cowan, "Patricians" and *Marriage.*

61. Cowan, "Patricians," 277; Plebani, 265–87.

62. Cowan, "Patricians," 278.

63. Ibid., 279.

64. Hunecke, *Patriziato,* 147. Also Davis, 121–22.

65. Fioretti, 109.

66. Momo, 104; Sala di Felice, 82–83. Lunari sees her consciously choosing to avoid the fate of other Goldoni characters who married up, that is, dodging subservience and abuse (45).

67. *Enciclopedia dello Spettacolo,* s.v. "Marliani."

68. Some also compare the fictional conflict between the Cavaliere and Mirandolina to the tense relations between Goldoni and Marliani. She had become his protégée, but their rapport eventually grew tense, especially once he decided to end his affiliation with the Vendramin management and the Medebach troupe. Herry, "Goldoni and 'Teodora'"; Lunari, 15–17; Sala di Felice.

69. Fonte; Marinella. Arcangela Tarabotti (1604–52), also Venetian, wrote similarly about the tyranny enacted on women obliged to join religious orders in *La semplicità ingannata (Paternal Tyranny)* (1654).

70. On La Fayette's novels see DeJean.

71. The first Italian translation did not emerge until the 1780s, with *L'istoria di Miss Clarissa Harlove, lettere inglesi.*

72. Hacke, 25. Ambrosini, 424–29, points out the difficulties for single women ("lay spinsters") at this time. Hacke notes that sometimes unmarried women joined with married women informally separated from their husbands to make new households, sharing expenses and enjoying companionship. Also see Chojnacka.

73. Sommerville, 174.

74. Hacke, 89.

75. Goldoni, *La locandiera,* 779–80.

76. Lunari, 29–30.

77. Plebani, 122–25.

78. Wiles, 4–5. Wiles talks about premodern theater performance as a social event, and spectatorship and audience response "in terms of group processes rather than . . . the cognitive processes of individual spectators" more common to later time periods. Ibid., 14.

79. Interestingly, Schutte notes a surprising occurrence of what she calls a "language of liberty" in court documents pleading for the release from vows for men and women religious precisely at midcentury. This rhetoric stands out because while "the language of liberty would appear to be integral to the discourse of involuntary monachization," it rarely appears. Schutte connects this sudden profreedom rhetoric to a fledgling Italian affirmation of adolescents' personal choice as to life vocation. *Force,* 255, 262. De Biase identifies the 1750s as a crucible period for the conjugal chaos of the later Settecento. Since separation and divorce suits took a long time to process and resolve (and many didn't even reach sentencing), their proliferation in the 1770s, 1780s, and 1790s points back to dissatisfactions arising much earlier in time; he asserts that the midcentury, precisely the timing of *La locandiera,* was an essential moment for changes in attitudes, values, and mores. "Problemi," 153.

80. Pedretti.

81. Scholars continue to debate the causes and consequences of the Hardwicke Act. See Outhwaite; Parker; and Probert, "Common Law Marriage" and *Marriage Law.*

82. Copley, Desan, Phillips, Traer.

83. The Reverend Johann Friedrich Zöllner's piece in the *Berlinische Monatsschrift* was responding in turn to an essay by one of the paper's editors, Johann Erich Beister, entitled "Proposal, not to engage the clergy any longer when marriages are conducted" (April 1783).

84. Cozzi, "Note."

Works Cited

Alonge, Roberto. "Intermezzo metodologico: Luchino Visconti, primo critico goldoniano." In *Goldoni il libertino: Eros, violenza, morte,* 88–101. Rome: Laterza, 2010.
———. "Il sistema di Mirandolina." In *Goldoni dalla commedia dell'arte al dramma borghese,* 55–93. Milan: Garzanti, 2004.

Adrienne Ward

Adrienne Ward

Adrienne Ward

Adrienne Ward

Adrienne Ward

Adrienne Ward

Adrienne Ward

Adrienne Ward

Adrienne Ward

Adrienne Ward

Adrienne Ward

Adrienne Ward

Adrienne Ward

Adrienne Ward

Ambrosini, Federica. "Toward a Social History of Women in Venice." In *Venice Reconsidered,* edited by John Martin and Dennis Romano, 420–41. Baltimore: Johns Hopkins University Press, 2000.

Anglani, Bartolo. *Goldoni: Il mercato, la scena, l'utopia.* Naples: Liguori, 1983.

Baratto, Mario. *"Mondo" e "teatro" nella poetica di Goldoni.* Venice, 1957.

———. "Nota sulla *Locandiera.*" *Studi goldoniani* 5 (1979): 115–23.

Beltrami, Daniele. *Storia della popolazione di Venezia dalla fine del secolo XVI alla caduta della Repubblica.* Padua: CEDAM, 1954.

Biester, Johann Erich. "Vorschlag, die Geistlichen nicht mehr bei Vollziehung der Ehen zu bemühen." *Berlinische Monatsschrift* 2 (1783): 265–75.

Bizzocchi, Roberto. *In famiglia.* Rome: Laterza, 2001.

Borsellino, Nino, ed. *L'interpretazione goldoniana: Critica e messinscena.* Rome: Officina, 1982.

Chojnacka, Monica. *Working Women of Early Modern Venice.* Baltimore: Johns Hopkins University Press, 2001.

Chojnacki, Stanley. "Subaltern Patriarchs: Patrician Bachelors." In *Women and Men in Renaissance Venice,* 244–56. Baltimore: Johns Hopkins University Press, 2000.

Comparini, Lucie. "L'Amour sous contrat: Alliances et mésalliances dans le théâtre de Carlo Goldoni." *Revue des études italiennes* 40 (1994): 107–24.

Copley, A. R. H. *Sexual Moralities in France, 1780–1980.* London: Routledge, 1989.

Cowan, Alexander. *Marriage, Manners and Mobility in Early Modern Venice.* Aldershot: Ashgate, 2007.

———. "Patricians and Partners in Early Modern Venice." In *Medieval and Renaissance Venice,* edited by Ellen E. Kittell and Thomas F. Madden, 276–93. Urbana: University of Illinois Press, 1999.

Cozzi, Gaetano. "Note e documenti sulla questione del 'divorzio' a Venezia (1782–1788)." *Annali dell'Istituto Storico Italo-Germanico di Trento* 7 (1981–82): 275–360.

———. "Padri, figli e matrimoni clandestini." *La cultura* 14 (1976): 169–213.

Crotti, Ilaria. "I chiasmi teatrali della *Locandiera.*" *Problemi di critica goldoniana* 11 (2002): 169–227.

———. "'Fuori di scena io non so fingere': Mirandolina e le altre." In *Selvagge e angeliche: Personaggi femminili della tradizione letteraria italiana,* edited by Tatiana Crivelli, 125–39. Leonforte: Insula, 2007.

———. "Margini del viaggio: Tra Marivaux e Goldoni." *Annali d'Italianistica* 21 (2003): 137–59.

Davis, James Cushman. *The Decline of the Venetian Nobility as a Ruling Class.* Baltimore: Johns Hopkins University Press, 1962.

Dazzi, Manlio. *Carlo Goldoni e la sua poetica sociale.* Turin: Einaudi, 1957.

De Biase, Luca. *Amore di stato.* Palermo: Sellerio, 1992.

———. "Problemi ed osservazioni sul 'divorzio' nel patriziato veneziano del XVIII: Un'analisi storica seriale." *Atti dell'Istituto Veneto di scienze morali, arti, lettere* 140 (1981–82): 143–62.

———. "Vincoli nuziali ed extra-matrimoniali nel patriziato veneziano in epoca goldoniana: I sentimenti, gli interessi." *Studi trentini di scienze storiche* 61, no. 4 (1982): 319–67.

DeJean, Joan. *Tender Geographies.* New York: Columbia University Press, 1991.

D'Elia, Anthony F. *The Renaissance of Marriage in Fifteenth-Century Italy.* Cambridge, MA: Harvard University Press, 2004.

Desan, Suzanne. *The Family on Trial in Eighteenth-Century France.* Berkeley: University of California Press, 2004.

Dolan, Frances E. *Marriage and Violence: The Early Modern Legacy.* Philadelphia: University of Pennsylvania Press, 2008.

Enciclopedia dello Spettacolo. Vol. 7. Edited by Silvio D'Amico. Rome: Le Maschere, 1954.

Fido, Franco. *Le inquietudini di Goldoni.* Genoa: Costa & Nolan, 1995.

———. *Nuova guida a Goldoni.* Turin: Einaudi, 2000.

Fioretti, Daniele. "Il matrimonio nella commedia di Goldoni." *Problemi di critica goldoniana* 16 (2009): 106–10.

Flora, Francesco. "Il *Feudatario* e gli ordini sociali nel teatro di Goldoni." In *Atti del Convegno Internazionale di Studi Goldoniani, Promosso Dal Comune di Venezia, dall'Istituto Veneto di Scienze, Lettere Ed Arti, e Dalla Fondazione Giorgio Cini Venezia, 28 Settembre–1 Ottobre 1957,* special issue in 2 vols., edited by Vittorio Branca and Nicola Mangini, *Studi goldoniani* 2 (1960): 618–78.

Fonte, Moderata. *Il merito delle donne.* Edited by Adriana Chemello. Mirano: Eidos, 1988.

Genta, Enrico. "Titoli nobiliari." In *Enciclopedia del diritto,* 44:674–84. Varese: Giuffrè, 1992.

Goldoni, Carlo. *La locandiera.* In *Tutte le opere,* edited by Giuseppe Ortolani, 4:773–858. Turin: Einaudi, 1935–56.

———. *Memoirs of Carlo Goldoni.* Edited by W. A. Drake. Translated by John Black. New York: Knopf, 1926.

Gottlieb, Beatrice. *The Family in the Western World from the Black Death to the Industrial Age.* New York: Oxford University Press, 1993.

———. "The Meaning of Clandestine Marriage." In *Family and Sexuality in French History,* edited by Roberto Wheaton and Tamara K. Hareven, 49–83. Philadelphia: University of Pennsylvania Press, 1980.

Gowing, Laura. *Domestic Dangers: Women, Words, and Sex in Early Modern London.* Oxford: Oxford University Press, 1996.

Guerci, Luciano. *La sposa obbediente.* Turin: Tirrenia, 1988.

Guidotti, Angela. "La locandiera." In *Encyclopedia of Italian Literary Studies,* edited by Gaetana Marrone, 871–72. New York: Routledge, 2007.

Hacke, Daniela. *Women, Sex, and Marriage in Early Modern Venice.* Aldershot: Ashgate, 2004.

Herry, Ginette. "De Teodora à Maddalena." *Les cahiers (Comédie francaise)* 6, no. 6 (1993): 15–27.

———. "Goldoni e la Marliani." *Studi goldoniani* 8 (1988): 137–58.

Hunecke, Volker. "Matrimonio e demografia del patriziato veneto (secc. xvii–xviii)." *Studi veneziani* 21 (1999): 269–319.

———. *Il patriziato veneziano alla fine della repubblica.* Tubingen: Jouvence, 1995.

La Fayette, Marie-Madeleine Pioche de la Vergne, comtesse de. *La Princesse de Clèves.* 1678.

———. *Zayde.* 1670.

La Rocca, Chiara. "Interessi famigliari e libero consenso nella Livorno del Settecento." In *I processi matrimoniali degli archivi ecclesiastici italiani,* edited by Silvana Seidel Menchi and Diego Quaglioni, vol. 2, *Matrimoni in dubbio,* 529–50. Bologna: Mulino, 2001.

Lombardi, Daniela. "Fidanzamenti e matrimoni dal Concilio di Trento alle riforme settecentesche." In *Storia del matrimonio,* edited by Michela De Giorgio and Christiane Klapisch-Zuber, 215–50. Rome: Laterza, 1996.

———. *Matrimoni di antico regime.* Bologna: Mulino, 2001.

———. "L'odio capitale, ovvero l'incompatibilità di carattere." In *I processi matrimoniali degli archivi ecclesiastici italiani,* edited by Silvana Seidel Menchi and Diego Quaglioni, vol. 1, *Coniugi nemici: La separazione in Italia dal XII al XVIII secolo,* 335–50. Bologna: Mulino, 2000.

Lunari, Luigi. Introduction to *La locandiera,* edited by Carlo Pedretti, 13–46. Milan: Rizzoli, 1976.

Mangini, Nicola. *Bibliografia goldoniana (1908–1957).* Venice: Istituto per la Collaborazione Culturale, 1961.

Marinella, Lucrezia. *Nobiltà et eccellenza delle donne co' difetti et mancamenti degli uomoni.* Venice: Ciotti, 1601.

Martini, Gabriele. "La donna veneziana del '600. Tra sessualità legittima ed illegittima: Alcune riflessioni sul concubinato." *Atti dell'Istituto Veneto di scienze morali, arti, lettere* 145 (1986–87): 301–39.

Momigliano, Attilio. *Saggi goldoniani.* Edited by Vittore Branca. Venice: Istituto per la Collaborazione Culturale, 1968.

Momo, Arnaldo. *La carriera delle maschere nel teatro di Goldoni, Chiari, Gozzi.* Venice: Marsilio, 1992.

Montpensier, Anne-Marie-Louise d'Orléans, duchesse de. *Against Marriage.* Edited and translated by Joan DeJean. Chicago: University of Chicago Press, 2002.

Nicastro, Guido. *Goldoni e il teatro del secondo Settecento.* Bari: Laterza, 1979.

Outhwaite, R. B. *Marriage and Society.* London: Europa, 1981.

Parker, Stephen. *Informal Marriage, Cohabitation and the Law, 1750–1989.* New York: St. Martin's, 1990.

Pedretti, Carlo. "La fortuna della *Locandiera.*" In *La locandiera,* edited by Carlo Pedretti, 47–50. Milan: Rizzoli, 1976.

Phillips, Roderick. *Family Breakdown in Late Eighteenth-Century France.* Oxford: Oxford University Press, 1980.

Plebani, Tiziana. *Un secolo di sentimenti.* Venice: Istituto Veneto di Scienze, Lettere ed Arti, 2012.

Pomata, Gianna. "Family and Gender." In *Early Modern Italy,* edited by John Marino, 69–86. Oxford: Oxford University Press, 2002.

Probert, Rebecca. "Common Law Marriage: Myths and Misunderstandings." *Child and Family Law Quarterly* 20, no. 1 (2008): 1–22.

———. *Marriage Law and Practice in the Long Eighteenth Century: A Reassessment.* Cambridge: Cambridge University Press, 2009.

Richardson, Samuel. *Clarissa.* London, 1748.

Sala di Felice, Elena. "Goldoni e gli attori: Una relazione di imprescindibile reciprocità." *Quaderns d'Italià* 2 (1997): 47–85.

Schutte, Anne Jacobson. *By Force and Fear.* Ithaca, NY: Cornell University Press, 2011.

———. "Society and the Sexes in the Venetian Republic." In *A Companion to Venetian History,* edited by Eric Dursteler, 353–77. Leiden: Brill, 2013.

Seidel Menchi, Silvana. "I processi matrimoniali come fonte storica." In *I processi matrimoniali degli archivi ecclesiastici italiani,* edited by Silvana Seidel Menchi and Diego Quaglioni, vol. 1, *Coniugi nemici: La separazione in Italia dal XII al XVIII secolo,* 15–94. Bologna: Mulino, 2000.

———, ed. *Marriage in Europe, 1400–1800.* Toronto: University of Toronto Press, 2016.

Seidel Menchi, Silvana, and Diego Quaglioni, eds. *I processi matrimoniali degli archivi ecclesiastici italiani.* 4 vols. Bologna: Mulino, 2000–2006.

Sommerville, Margaret. *Sex and Subjection.* London: St. Martin's, 1995.

Tarabotti, Arcangela. *Paternal Tyranny.* Edited and translated by Letizia Panizza. Chicago: University of Chicago Press, 2004. Originally published as *La semplicità ingannata* (Leiden, 1654).

Traer, James. *Marriage and the Family in Eighteenth-Century France.* Ithaca, NY: Cornell University Press, 1980.

Trouille, Mary. *Wife Abuse in Eighteenth Century France.* Oxford: Voltaire Foundation, 2009.

Vazzoler, Franco. "Qualche osservazione in margine agli *Atti* del Convegno di Venezia." In *Tra libro e scena: Carlo Goldoni,* edited by Carmelo Alberti and Ginette Herry, 212–15. Venice: Cardo, 1996.

Wiles, David. *Theatre and Citizenship.* Cambridge: Cambridge University Press, 2011.

Zöllner, Johann Friedrich. "Ist es rathsam, das Ehebündniß ferner durch die Religion zu sancieren?" *Berlinische Monatsschrift* 2 (1783): 508–17.

Performances of Suffering and the Stagecraft of Sympathy

JENNIFER REED

In the mid- to late eighteenth century, the so-called Age of Sensibility, questions of how individuals were to relate to one another in civil society were increasingly theorized. Jonathan Lamb posits that these questions—questions of sympathy—arise in situations of "comparative powerlessness in which the function and tendency of social roles is no longer directly apparent to those who fill them."[1] His analysis persuasively describes the postfeudal, post-Reformation landscape of the eighteenth century, in which the rise of mercantile capitalism and revolutionary politics caused significant upheaval in social interactions. Enlightenment philosophers thought and wrote a great deal about sympathy, questioning the circumstances and conditions under which someone might care for another or act on his behalf. This culminated in what Lynn Hunt calls "the sudden crystallization of human rights claims at the end of the eighteenth century"[2] The rise of the novel can be seen as a broad cultural reflex to this newly galvanized concern with identifying with others.

I contend that although theories of sympathy in the eighteenth century are rightly characterized as primarily spectatorial, the emphasis that falls on ocular centricity fails to consider the importance of space and of spatial metaphorics. The literature and philosophy of the period conflates ocular metaphorics and spatial metaphorics in its thinking about sympathy, but they are nonetheless distinct. Attention to these spatial metaphorics gives particular insight into where the limits of sympathy can be found and what images of containment and incursion tell us about the conditions required for sympathetic engagement. A consideration of how sympathy works in space is particularly important in that supposedly ideal sphere of sympathetic engagement: the theatrical space. I will explore the figure of the spectacle often invoked to illustrate sympathetic engagement in eighteenth-century philosophy and unpack the often overlooked components of stagecraft—theatrical technologies and spatial considerations—to identify their importance in facilitating sympathy. I argue here that eighteenth-century theories and representations of sympathy required that the spaces of suffering and spectation be distinct but that there also be some measured reciprocity between the two. I will be arguing that theatrical spaces and technologies are used in the eighteenth century to think through these requirements of successful sympathy. I will consider Laurence Sterne, the English novelist who helped define the sentimental in fiction, and Henry Fielding, the dramatist who in his final work presented his dying body as an object of sympathy.

The centrality of the metaphor of the theater has become a commonplace in discussions of sympathy. As Jonathan Lamb writes, theater "has been supplying metaphors and illustrations for the discussion of sympathy" throughout its exploration in seventeenth- and eighteenth-century philosophy.[3] To elaborate, Lamb articulates a quick review, beginning with Descartes's soul, perched on the pineal gland and surveying the representations of the passions clustered below it. In this example, it is worth noting that it is the observer who is elevated, not those figures that represent the players: the passions. Lamb also considers Hume's theater of the mind and finally the carefully tuned performance that Smith's victim must give in order to win the approval of a skeptical audience.[4] However, it is the technologies employed by the theatrical space itself that seem most interesting in terms of exploring the somatic and spatial relationships that permit sympathy or in which sympathy fails. A performance of suffering that successfully elicits sympathy pays close attention to where the limits of sympathy are to be found—these limits often have spatial properties—and navigates these limits using careful stagecraft.

In *The Theory of Moral Sentiments* Smith begins his discussion of sympathy with the seminal example of "our brother upon the rack" and describes the change of place that successful sympathizing necessitates. Smith concludes that it is "by the imagination [that] we place ourselves in his situation . . . we enter as it were into his body, and become in some measure the same person with him."[5] We should consider the implications of the spatial metaphorics of moving "into" the body of another, set up by the rather theatrical technology of the rack, which elevates the object of suffering and distances him from the spectator.

On the next page, Smith turns to another example of the spectator and the object of his sympathy in which the experience is, once again, mediated by a specific technology, as well as by space and elevation. "The mob," Smith tells us, "when they are gazing at a dancer on the slack rope, naturally writhe and twist and balance their own bodies, as they see him do, and as they feel that they themselves must do if in his situation."[6] The crowd is alive to the particularities of the dancer's experience on the rope as they gaze upwards. They have "moved into his body" so successfully that they find their own bodies performing simulations of his acrobatics in unconscious sympathetic identification. Commentators often focus on the example of the rack to the exclusion of the rope-dancing performance, but the example of the rope-dancer is crucial to cementing the link Smith seeks to make between the kind of suffering that elicits sympathy and performance. The other prefatory examples Smith invokes are "beggars in the street" and limbs at which "strokes" are "aimed," but neither beggar nor endangered limb is described as performing.[7] It is in the image of the rope-dancer that Smith explicitly unites performance, physical peril, and rendered sympathy, and I claim that the discrete spaces of performance and spectation are crucial to its effectiveness.

I would like to introduce one more consideration in Smith's discussion of sympathy and performance: the danger for the spectator in sympathizing and the necessity of protecting oneself against the potential ravages of over-sympathizing. In *The Theory of Moral Sentiments* he observes that

> we often struggle to keep down our sympathy with the sorrow of others. Whenever we are not under the observation of the sufferer, we endeavour, for our own sake, to suppress it as much as we can. When we attend to the representation of a tragedy, we struggle against that sympathetic sorrow which the entertainment inspires as long as we can, and we give way to it at last only when we can no longer avoid it: we even then endeavour to cover our concern from the company. If we shed any tears, we carefully conceal them, and are afraid, lest the spectators, not entering into this excessive tenderness, should regard it as effeminacy and weakness.[8]

There is an important sense in which to sympathize with a suffering other is dangerous to the subject who sympathizes. The space of the theater is used here to illustrate the way that the spectator resists "enter[ing] into . . . [the] excessive tenderness" caused by the spectacle. Instead of easy passage between the space of spectation and the space of performed suffering, Smith observes that the spectator feels the need to "conceal" and fear any perception of sympathizing. If the spectator sympathizes, the spaces of suffering and spectation bleed into one another and the spectator becomes, in the midst of the other spectators, a spectacle himself and takes measures to hide that spectacle from those who "regard" him.

The concern about oversympathizing, and about the effect of oversympathizing, is expressed again in the context of the theater in this episode, published in the *Savanna-la-Mar Gazette* in Westmoreland Parish, Jamaica, in 1788:

> The following extraordinary effect of Sympathy, or extra-transfer of Pas-
> sions, was had from a Young Lady of veracity, who lately visited this Par-
> ish, from Scotland, and who was an eye-witness to the scene; . . . In the
> autumn of 1785, during the Leith races, when Mrs. Siddons, at Edinburgh,
> performed the part of Belvidera, in Otway's Tragedy of Venice Preserved,
> a Miss G——— . . . who had for the week engaged the stage-box, a Young
> Lady of such amiable manners and exquisite sentiments that she passed
> under the name of the Sentimental Beauty, had her passions so wrought up
> towards the catastrophe, that when Belvidera (Mrs. S.) came in frantic, after
> the execution scene, turning her eyes to the box and fixing them on Miss
> G———, she instantly caught the passion, pulled off first one shoe, then the
> other, and threw them upon the stage. She was instantly forced into a sedan
> chair—the windows of which she broke; she was then carried home . . .
> [but] the phrenzy, or inflammation, had taken too fast hold of her brain,
> and she died in 48 hours after.[9]

This episode offers an ominous warning of the consequences of entering too completely into the "excessive tenderness" evoked in the theatrical space. The danger for Miss G——— appears when Mrs. Siddons "fix[es]" her eyes on her and the two share "passion" that quickly kills Miss G———. Miss G———'s relative isolation in the stage-box makes her more susceptible to "catching" sympathy for Mrs. Siddons in addition. The stage-box separates Miss G——— from her fellow audience members, who recall Smith's imaginary spectator to himself and cause him to "suppress" his sympathy, thus protecting himself from accusations of "effeminacy," "weakness," and perhaps the more serious condition contracted by Miss G——— via sympathy. The stage-box further endangers Miss G——— by placing her in easy view of Mrs. Siddons as she performs Belvidera's suffering. In Smith's example of the dangers of oversympathizing, the tragedy is used as an example of a situation in which the spectator is "not under the observation of the sufferer." However, Miss G———'s position in the stage-box lays her open to the observation of Mrs. Siddons, embodying the suffering of Belvidera. Miss G——— responds by instinctively creating a connection between her own space and the space of the stage, pulling off her shoes and throwing them onto the stage. Both of these examples suggest that limits must be imposed on the sympathy rendered by the audience member and that those limits might be found in maintaining separate spaces of suffering and of sympathizing.

With these illustrations as points of reference, I now turn to Fielding's *Journal of a Voyage to Lisbon.* We find the language of ropes, pullies, and general stage equipment replicated here in what is arguably the most wrenching scene in the *Journal,* and the scene seemingly most deserving of sympathy. In this scene, Fielding describes his "entrance" to the *Queen of Portugal,* the boat on which he will make his journey.[10] However, Fielding does not elicit sympathy from those observers who were present, and his performance of suffering fails to summon the sympathetic response desired. I argue that this is the result of a failure of attention to concerns of stagecraft.

The deterioration of Fielding's condition necessitates boarding the ship via a "chair" "hoisted . . . with pullies," in which the dramatist himself becomes the spectacle.[11] Fielding describes the cruelty of his reception on board: "Upon my entrance into the boat, I presented a spectacle of the highest horror. The total loss of limbs was apparent to all who saw me, and my face contained marks of a most diseased state, if not of death itself. In this condition, I ran the gaunt-lope (so, I think, I may justly call it) through rows of sailors and watermen, few of whom failed of paying their compliments to me, by all manner of insults and jests on my misery."[12]

Fielding's suffering, far from enlisting a sympathetic move "into" his body, provokes a reaction that, in his words, "leads the mind into a train of very uncomfortable and melancholy thoughts."[13] Unlike the supple dancer's use of ropes as an instrument to showcase physical dexterity and ability, Fielding's elevation in the course of being winched aboard merely serves to demonstrate his "total loss of limbs" and the "marks of a most diseased state, if not of death itself."[14]

Here, Fielding seems to present all the necessary particulars of "spectacle": his elevation for consideration, his exhibition of a picture of undeniable suffering, and a "mob" available for spectation. He would seem to be a clear candidate for sympathetic identification, which, as Lamb points out, "most easily figures as a theatre."[15] However, sympathy is denied him. The elevation that provides a suitable spectacle for the communication of sympathy in the case of the rack and the slack rope, in Smith's examples, provides instead something more like an Artaudian theater of cruelty in Fielding's experience. Surely it is not the case that merely the grotesquerie of the spectacle Fielding presents excludes him from the economies of sympathy. After all, to return to Smith's paradigm, concerns such as the grotesque state of the body should not be sufficient to bar sympathetic identification. Smith notes, in *The Theory of Moral Sentiments:* "Persons of delicate fibres . . . complain that in looking on the sores and ulcers which are exposed by beggars in the streets they are apt to feel an itching or uneasy sensation in the corre-spondent part of their own bodies."[16] It is my contention that Fielding's body pushes the limits of sympathy, not in visual terms but in spatial ones. Field-ing violates the terms of stagecraft and breaks something like "the fourth wall," pushing into the space required between sufferer and spectator. Sym-pathy is an exchange predicated on distance between parties.

In Fielding's account of boarding the ship, we can see him making tex-tual corrections in reassigning his body to the upper regions of the scene. Fielding is winched above the crowd of sailors, who use the opportunity of his elevation to mock his appearance. However, his description works to re-assign and reverse positions of high and low in order to recover for himself the altitude of higher class and moral superiority. "It may be said," Fielding reflects caustically, "that this barbarous custom [of mockery] is peculiar to the English, and of them only to the lowest degree . . . and never shows itself in men who are polish'd and refin'd."[17] Here, he not only banishes his tor-mentors to the "lowest degree" of society but also hierarchizes their comic aesthetic—parody and jest—as the lowest form of comedy. Fielding, a mas-ter of low comedy himself, could find it convenient to take the high ground here and discriminate further between high and low on this basis.

On his boarding the ship, even though Fielding uses the technologies of the spectacle and of stage equipment, the spatial model breaks down be-cause he "ran the gaunt-lope . . . *through* rows of sailors and watermen."[18] He doesn't allow the spectators the space that is required to see sympathy as travel and not contagion. He doesn't allow them the position of observa-tion comfortably occupied by Smith's impartial spectator. Instead he swings toward them like the bowling ball he physically resembles, and the "rows" of sailors and watermen become the pins endangered by his encroachment.

Fielding had himself figured material roundness as an image of the dis-tended or inflated self, which fails to engage sympathetically. In *Tom Jones* Fielding writes: "Poor Jones was one of the best-natured fellows alive, and had all that weakness which is called compassion, and which distinguishes this imperfect character from that noble firmness of mind which rolls a man, as it were, within himself, and, like a polished bowl, enables him to run through the world without being once stopped by the calamities which hap-pen to others."[19] Here, the symbolic logic of the round figure, rolled "within himself" and "run[ing] through the world," conjures disgust not only for Fielding's grotesque body but for the preoccupation of self connoted by the image. Fielding seems to "run through the world" and runs "the gaunt-lope" directly into the crowd of sailors, breaking down the distinction between

Figure 1. A Sphere, projecting against a plane, James Gillray, 1792. (Beinecke Rare Book and Manuscript Library, Yale University)

the space of suffering and the space of spectation, endangering the sailors physically and emotionally with the contagion of disease and of sympathy.

The stifling effect of this lack of distance is illustrated by a body that resembles Fielding's in James Gillray's 1792 cartoon *A Sphere, projecting against a plane* (fig. 1). It depicts two well-known public figures of the late eighteenth century: William Pitt, the Tory prime minister, and Albinia Hobart, a society hostess. Gillray's image seems, at first, to present us with a fairly simple visual joke of fat and thin, something of a staple in graphic satire. But a closer look at the cartoon shows that its vectors are more subtle and rich than this. Its subject, on further examination, seems to be the failure of reciprocity and correct social relationships. Although the two figures face each other and in fact press against each other, neither physicality permits meaningful contact. Neither the globular Hobart, imprisoned in the sphere, nor the painfully thin Pitt, hands planted in his pockets, can interact with the other. As Gillray's inscription states, emphasizing the Euclidean basis of the joke, the plane, "when applied ever so closely to a sphere, can only touch its Superficies, without being able to enter it." The ability of sympathy to enable "ent[ry] into" the body of the other, as Smith puts it, is frustrated here by the opposing bodies that push up against each other while maintaining discrete spaces highlighted by their opposite body types.

In terms of the translation across space required by technicians of sympathy like Adam Smith, we should consider a further technology of sympathy: the map. Gillray's title invokes the action of projecting a sphere onto a plane, or stereographic projection, which is a basic tenet of mapping. Stereographic projection was employed first by the ancient Egyptians and then the ancient Greeks, when one of its most important uses was the mapping of celestial charts. We can see that failure to go a step beyond oneself is a failure of the body, but also a failure of mapping and of correctly projecting oneself onto the world or the universe. In Gillray's cartoon neither figure's proportions translate onto the other's; they do not transfer. At first the failure of sympathy seems to result only from the failure of the figure imprisoned in the sphere. However, the figure of the plane, Pitt, who stares straight ahead and whose hands are tightly fixed in his pockets, also has a kind of physicality that resists exchange. The sphere's projection in Gillray's cartoon is one that pushes fruitlessly against something impermeable rather than one that, as in stereographic projection, translates one set of dimensions onto another kind of body. The bodies that Gillray presents, though, already to some extent monstrous, do not keep the requisite distance from each other to permit successful sympathetic exchange. Also note that the sphere, Hobart, is rolled, not just in herself, but on top of a small stage or platform, another example of an attempt and failure of the use of stagecraft for the solicitation of sympathy.

Proceeding from Fielding's failed attempt at sympathy as he swings through the crowd of unsympathetic sailors, we find another scene of literary bowling, and a more successful but perhaps equally problematic instantiation, of soliciting sympathy in Laurence Sterne's *Tristram Shandy*. In the novel, Tristram's Uncle Toby, wounded at the siege of Namur in the Nine Years' War, uses the Shandys' bowling green for the staging area of his reenacted sieges. His reenactments from the war are a coping mechanism that allows him to process the trauma of his injury. Where Fielding comes to embody the destructive technologies of bowling, specifically the object of the ball itself, Sterne's characters remove these technologies and replace them with imagined human interactions. Fielding's text makes objects of people, and Fielding becomes a kind of projectile dangerously invading the space of the spectatorial crowd below. Conversely, Sterne's text peoples and humanizes those arenas meant for objects in the recovery of the bowling green for the site of a performance of Toby's traumatic experience. While a reenactment of war might seem far from humanizing, the status of Toby and his faithful manservant Trim's reenactments as therapeutic replications of previous violence lends them a character much more like the technologies that permit sympathy, and they become both spectacle and theater, in which sympathetic identifications take place. We learn that Trim had "often cried at his master's sufferings, but never shed a tear at his own."[20] Furthermore, Toby describes to Walter Shandy "that infinite delight, in particular, which has attended my sieges in my bowling green, has arose within me, and I hope in the corporal too, from the consciousness we both had, that in carrying them on, we were answering the great ends of our creation."[21] Uncle Toby's description invokes shared consciousness with another, which the creation of particular, delineated space permits and which a performance of suffering within that space facilitates.

The key to the reconstruction of Toby and Trim's fortifications is proportion. The fortifications themselves can be read as an attempt to rebuild the borders between fragile selves and cruel projectiles—cannonballs such as Fielding figures when he swings in among the sailors who reject him so robustly—but it is particularly interesting that these fortifications have themselves been miniaturized, have been drawn in to narrower proportions. In order to successfully solicit sympathy, Smith counsels, "we must look at ourselves . . . with the same eyes with which we look at others: we must imagine ourselves not the actors, but the spectators of our own conduct."[22] As Lynn Festa observes, in Smith's example, "the man on the rack is . . . weighing how much he can rightfully expect the witness to grasp and moderating his cries accordingly."[23] It seems to me not coincidental that Festa employs the language of "weighing" and measuring how much suffering has successfully traversed the border between the actor and the spectator. The spatial is always at work in the allocation of sympathy.

Toby and Trim's careful weighing, measuring, and mapping seems to be an exercise in practicing this moderation of scale in the performance of suffering. In fact, Toby undertakes the study of the "environs" of Namur, which begins with his careful study of a map of Namur and concludes with the erection of his fortifications, so that he will be able to present his painful experience to the host of "fresh friends and fresh enquirers" in a measured and reserved way.[24] These friends and enquirers are the spectators, by one remove, of his injury at Namur and of his performance of it during his convalescence. Toby hopes to become "so far master of his subject, as to be able to talk upon it without emotion."[25] He sees this as an important part of his recovery, and we might see it as an equally crucial part of the solicitation of sympathy from the stream of well-wishers supplied by his well-meaning brother. Toby's grasp of the material conditions of the scene of his injury better equip him to present those conditions orally, in measured language, and performatively, in miniaturized siegeworks.

Toby's careful attention to the spatial dynamics that permit sympathy recalls the anecdote of Uncle Toby and the fly in *Tristram Shandy*. As Tristram relates it, Toby releases an "over-grown" fly that had "tormented him cruelly all dinner-time" from his cupped hand and through the sash window that he opens for the purpose, telling it, "'Go,—go poor devil . . . I'll not hurt a hair of thy head. The world is surely wide enough to hold both thee and me."[26] While this episode is typically read as an example of Toby's great love for his fellow creatures and his sensitivity to suffering, I would like to draw attention to the emphasis on the ability to release the fly from its disagreeable confinement that attends Toby's solicitousness. When Toby opens the window to release the fly, it is the correct regulation of space—qualified access to "the wid(th)" of the world—which Toby cites as his reason for sympathizing with its plight. Tristram, who witnessed this as a boy of ten, recalls that Toby's "harmony of movement, attuned by mercy" found "a passage to my heart," which imprinted a "lesson of universal good-will." This attention to proportion and space in the exercise of sympathy rehearses the importance of separation between the spectator and the object of sympathy.

The performances that facilitate sympathy are a kind of work. Like work, they attend to process and motion rather than to objects. Likewise, rather than being a spontaneous moment of connection, sympathetic connection is always a kind of work, which functions through the spectacle and the correct deployment of space and spatial metaphorics. These technologies of theater are part of a larger category of technologies of sympathy, which are necessary because they recapture some of the stability of the border, or spectatorial distance, between sufferer and spectator. They facilitate entry into another's situation precisely because those that are successful reimpose the border between the sufferer and the onlooker and create the kind of spatial model that is required for the protosympathetic respondent to enter into a sympathetic exchange. Perhaps what is most notable about how models of sympathy were brokered in the eighteenth-century understanding is the broad-based interdisciplinarity with which they were approached. Cross-pollination between theater and moral philosophy, theaters of war and theaters of drama, literature, travel narrative, and graphic satire, allowed eighteenth-century thinkers to approach the problem of sympathy through a lens that encompassed a multiplicity of disciplines.

Notes

1. Lamb, *Evolution of Sympathy*, 1.
2. Hunt, *Inventing Human Rights*, 20.
3. Lamb, *Evolution of Sympathy*, 35.
4. Ibid.
5. Smith, *Theory of Moral Sentiments*, 4.
6. Ibid., 5.
7. Ibid.
8. Ibid., 184.
9. *Savanna-la-Mar Gazette*, 15 July 1788, 3.
10. Fielding, *Journal*, 23.
11. Ibid.
12. Ibid.
13. Ibid.
14. Ibid.
15. Lamb, *Evolution of Sympathy*, 35.
16. Smith, *Theory of Moral Sentiments*, 12.
17. Fielding, *Journal*, 23.
18. Ibid., emphasis added.
19. Fielding, *Tom Jones*, 668.
20. Sterne, *Tristram Shandy*, 517.
21. Ibid., 416.
22. Ibid., 257.
23. Festa, *Sentimental Figures*, 30.
24. Sterne, *Tristram Shandy*, 75, 74.
25. Ibid., 79.
26. Ibid., 124.

Works Cited

Artaud, Antonin. *The Theater and Its Double*. Translated by Mary Caroline Richards. New York: Grove, 1958.

Festa, Lynn. *Sentimental Figures of Empire in Eighteenth-Century Britain and France.* Baltimore: Johns Hopkins University Press, 2006.

Fielding, Henry. *The History of Tom Jones, A Foundling.* London: Penguin Classics, 2005.

———. *The Journal of a Voyage to Lisbon.* 2nd ed. London: Penguin Books, 1996.

Hume, David. *A Treatise of Human Nature.* Oxford: Oxford University Press, 2000.

Hunt, Lynn. *Inventing Human Rights: A History.* New York: Norton, 2008.

Keymer, Thomas. Introduction to *The Journal of a Voyage to Lisbon,* by Henry Fielding. 2nd ed. London: Penguin Books, 1996.

Lamb, Jonathan. *The Evolution of Sympathy in the Long Eighteenth Century.* London: Pickering & Chatto, 2009.

Paulson, Ronald, and Thomas Lockwood, eds. *Henry Fielding: The Critical Heritage.* London: Routledge & Kegan Paul, 1969.

Smith, Adam. *The Theory of Moral Sentiments.* New York: Cambridge University Press, 2002.

Sterne, Laurence. *The Life and Opinions of Tristram Shandy, Gentleman.* London: Penguin Books, 2003.

The Aesthetics of Excess

Rococo Vestiges of *Tartuffe* in Isla's *Father Gerundio*

CASEY R. ERIKSEN

Taking an occasional pinch of snuff, the narrator of the *History of the Famed Preacher, Father Gerundio de Campazas, alias Zotes* (1758, 1768) invites his reader to view the rhetorical excesses of the fictional preachers of his age. In his widely celebrated and heatedly contested novel, the Jesuit writer José Francisco de Isla presents a hyperbolic, satirical, and indeed scathing critique of the preaching practices of his day. Father Gerundio and his mentor, Father Blas, convey not only a caricature of ornamented, illogical discourse but an ideology of excess that privileges performance and stylized distortion over fidelity to theological principles. Father Gerundio in particular emerges as a disconcertingly problematic figure; he is a fool, educated by the supposed experts of his age, who achieves material success and broad acclaim for his ability to ignite, perplex, and inspire the masses with his pyrotechnic rhetoric. When one turns an eye to content, however, it becomes apparent that the sermons lack critical depth, theological accuracy, or sound academic reasoning. The stylized, visual discourse privileges the decorative qualities of language, and the narrative reveals the dangerous misapplication of both theological doctrine and reason itself.

Isla situates himself within a broader tradition of writers, including Juvenal, Molière, and Cervantes, who used hyperbole and satire to reveal the hypocrisies and contradictions of their age. Though critics have explored the aesthetic characteristics of Father Gerundio's rhetoric to some degree, the aims of this essay are to approach Isla's novel through a comparative lens and to suggest that these rococo features contain vestiges of Molière's *Tartuffe*. Such a comparison provides a valuable approach to better inform critical readings of *Father Gerundio*.

In his prologue, Isla invokes the figure of Tartuffe to provide a discursive and aesthetic frame in which to discuss the protagonist as well as church predication generally: "Y ya que te has suavizado un poquitico, hablemos en confianza. ¿Hay por ventura en el mundo, ni aun en la Iglesia de Dios, estado alguno tan santo, tan serio ni tan elevado donde no se encuentren algunos individuos ridículos, exóticos, y extravagantes? . . . Y si algún satírico o algún cómico quiere corregirlas haciendo visible y como de bulto su ridiculez, ya en la sátira, ya en el teatro, ¿no se vale siempre de algún nombre fingido y por lo común estrafalario? . . . Pero dime, ¿ha habido hasta ahora en él alguno que se llamase *Tartufa*? Y con todo eso, el bellaco de Molière . . . da una carga cerrada a los hipócritas de todas profesiones." (Let us speak with a more friendly freedom. Is there then in the world, or even in the church of God, any order of men so serious, so elevated, or so holy, that there are not to be found in it many most ridiculous, absurd, and extravagant individuals? . . . And if any satirist or comic poet endeavors to correct them, does he not always avail himself of a feigned name, and for the most part a whimsical or slovenly one? . . . But tell me; was there ever in the world a man called *Tartuffe*? And yet that rogue of a Molière . . . lays about him so unmercifully on the hypocrites of all professions.)[1]

This invocation points toward a way of reading *Father Gerundio* and recognizes the discursive potential of the world's Gerundios to destabilize readers' expectations, as well as institutions of power such as the Catholic Church. Isla's narrative, then, proposes to laugh away tired practices and to cast idle theological training out of existence, specifically by drawing attention to the scathing humor and dangers of rhetorical excess. Irony and satire drive the author's commentary; through hyperbole, false modesty, pun, and ornamented rhetoric, Isla envelops the sermons in a rococo aesthetic consistent with the *Tartuffe* model.

Before discussing rhetorical and aesthetic similarities in detail, I should first define the bounds of such a comparison. Isla does not merely reproduce the figure of Tartuffe in his novel; rather, he employs irony and excess to convey the florid language, gestures, and allure of verbal seduction that also are characteristics of Molière. In her chapter discussing the meaning of irony, Claire Colebrook reminds her reader that "irony is a type of speech act, but it is one that also opens up the question of a theory of meaning (the relation between language in the world). . . . Irony plays between 'we' (who see) and a limited point of view, whether this is a linguistic, social, or visual limit."[2] The notion of irony as a speech act—set in relation to a broader society—comes to the fore in *Father Gerundio;* Isla consistently casts Gerundio's vanity and sonorous, adorned sermons in an ironic mode. Rebecca Haidt has shown that sound associations, Latinisms, and adornment convey not merely a baroque aesthetic meant to confuse and persuade audiences but also a discourse closely attuned to rococo sensibilities. Haidt writes in

Seduction and Sacrilege that Father Gerundio "possesses an agglomeration of sounds that, through their excess, convey the sense that details and surface decoration can overwhelm. . . . Decorations of Gerundian preaching are cultivated [and] lavish. . . . His obsession with decorating the *exordio* (or introduction), does not serve to generate an aura of monarchical grandeur or of sacred mystery, but rather cultivates audiences' vanity and their sense of wonder at his prodigious verbalizations."[3]

Like Tartuffe, Father Gerundio appeals to listeners' narcissism through the use of ostentatious platitudes and, at the same time, confuses his audience with illogical lines of reasoning. Through misapplication of reason and obscure allusions, Father Gerundio deploys sermons that are in the end self-serving. Father Gerundio's public, illiterate and provincial, was effectively suited for what Haidt describes as an act of winning the crowd: "'*Galantear*' is invoked precisely in *Fray Gerundio* to denote the link between appearance and display . . . we see a link between Gerundian rhetoric's tendency toward a valorization of excessive ornamentation over reason, and a *galan's* valorization of dress and movement over example."[4] The connection between stylized gesture and its rhetorical effect is at the heart of both *Tartuffe* and *Father Gerundio.* Although Molière writes a comedy set for the stage, and Isla, a social commentary against ineffective preaching, both authors utilize physical gesture and rhetorical excess to emphasize the deceptive, dangerous qualities of language.

Both works recognize the seductive power of verbal artifice, which in the case of *Father Gerundio* results in a systematic desecration of Church doctrine. For Isla, Father Gerundio is not only a satirical and deceptive figure but, more explicitly, a ridiculous and scandalous manipulator of sacred texts. The misapplication of rhetorical prowess, as such, holds theological implications. According to Haidt, "Preachers who manipulate their audiences through seductive effects—such as sounds that will please listeners' hearing . . . not only misrepresent sacred teachings, but also *teach* listeners the wrong way to 'hear the word of God.'"[5]

Isla situates such a critique within the broader frame of the historical controversies of his age; the ostentatious sacrilege described in the novel reveals Isla's contribution to heated contemporary debates between Jesuits and Jansenists. José Luis Abellán writes that the divisions lay primarily in "polemics surrounding divine Grace and predestination. To defend the rights of the individual against authority and the spirit against moral Probabilism, Cornelius Jansen put forth his *Augustinus*. . . . His five propositions were declared heretical in the papal bull *Cum occasione* (1653) given by Innocent

X."⁶ Jesuits viewed Jansenist doctrine as at odds with Augustinian teachings, specifically as it related to free will and grace. Points of contention involved Jansenist theological training, as well as the practice of preaching in rural areas. Jansenists sought to reaffirm the political and theological authority of bishops and often preached their platforms in the provinces to bolster support among illiterate audiences. The Jesuits and the papacy viewed the Jansenists as poorly trained, and heated transnational debates ensued throughout religious communities and beyond. The 1713 bull *Unigenitus* eventually condemned Jansenist propositions as "ill-sounding, offensive to pious ears, scandalous, pernicious, rash, injurious to the Church and its practices, contumelious to Church and State . . . blasphemous, suspected and savouring of heresy, [and] favouring heretics."⁷ Isla, I hasten to repeat, was a Jesuit.

One should note the emphasis placed on the aural, didactic element associated with ineffective preaching: it was precisely this quality that made the Jansenist sermons so dangerous in rural communities. Joel Saugnieux remarks that "Christianity is essentially a religion of speech. . . . The preacher speaks, but it is God that instructs. . . . The sermon is comparable to the Eucharistic Host; it constitutes the favored nourishment of the soul."⁸ To cite Saint Augustine, "Our daily bread on this earth is the word of God, which is always proclaimed to the churches."⁹ According to this approximation, to misrepresent theological doctrine through convoluted, illogical predication would constitute no less than blasphemy. Tartuffe projects a posture of divine authority to gain influence over Orgon and his mother. Through ornamented rhetoric, gesture, and misapplication of theological discourse, Father Gerundio similarly misrepresents doctrine for his own ends.

It is useful to consider specific textual examples from both sources, beginning with the functions of gesture in both works. As Gerundio delivers his extravagant sermons, he animates his listeners through signs of hyperbolic pageantry: "Levantóse, pues, con bizarrísimo denuedo, volvió a hacerse cargo de todo el auditorio con grave y majestuoso despejo, tremoló sucesivamente sus dos pañuelos, primero el de color, con que se sonó en seco, y después el blanco, que pasó por la cara *ad pompam et ostentationem;* entonó su Alabado con voz gutural y hueca. Persignóse espurriendo bien la mano derecha . . . y dio principio a su sermón de esta manera." (Behold then; now he raises himself with the boldest grace; the audience is again observed by him with a graver and more majestic look; his two handkerchiefs successfully 'mock the air with idle state.' The gayly-coloured one is applied to the clear trumpet of his nose, and the immaculate one passed-round his angelic face *ad pompam* and *ostentationem;* he thunders out his 'For ever *praised, etc'* in a guttural and hollow voice; he crosses himself with an extended hand . . . and began his sermon in this manner.)[10] Such extravagance and luxury explicitly destabilize notions of religious humility, since the religious are expected to take a vow of poverty. As Carmen Martín Gaite points out, priority given to image over actual content underscores a propensity to "hide, through moving surfaces of changing decoration, the very emptiness of people."[11]

Father Gerundio is indeed poorly trained; ironically, he learned his oratory skills from the most celebrated and ridiculous of preachers, Father Blas. This successful "expert" and mentor is also of the disposition that applauds gesture and luxury in the pulpit. As Father Gerundio prepares to deliver one of his sermons, he dons colorful handkerchiefs and consults Father Blas for advice concerning whether he should wear spectacles: "Se rió mucho de su ofrecimiento, diciéndole que los anteojos en un mozo . . . era la cosa más ridícula del mundo, y que así los hombres de juicio como los bellacos hacían gran burla de aquella afectación." ([But Father Blas] laughed heartily at this proposition, telling him that spectacles on a young man . . . was the most ridiculous thing in the world, and that men of sober judgment as well as wicked ways would ridicule the affectation.)[12] Blas, from experience, of course recognizes the utility of fashionable appearances, demonstrating that ostentation can indeed yield material profit in the form of fine linen, tobacco, money, and other trifles.

When one reads *Tartuffe* and *Father Gerundio* comparatively, a similar discursive strategy emerges; a form of rhetorical alchemy occurs in which vices are passed as virtues. Seductive discourse is thus engaged to claim influence over others. In act 3, scene 3, of *Tartuffe*, the impostor uses deliberately ambiguous speech to attempt to seduce Elmire. He collapses the sacred and the profane, couching his carnal desires in theological language; at the same time, his hand placement and gestures reveal his true intentions:

> *Tartuffe:* I've prayed with all my power —
> But prayed in vain, until this happy hour.
>
> . . . .
>
> About the constant visits you are paid
> Were prompted not by any mean emotion,
> But rather by a pure and deep emotion,
> A fervent zeal . . .
>
> *Elmire:* No need for explanation.
> Your sole concern, I'm sure, was my salvation.

Tartuffe: (*Taking Elmire's hand and pressing her fingertips*)
Quite so; and such great fervor do I feel . . .

Elmire: Ooh! Please! You're pinching!

Tartuffe: 'Twas from excess of zeal.
I never meant to cause you pain, I swear.
I'd rather . . .
(*Places hand on Elmire's knee*)[13]

Note here the misapplication of religious rhetoric in service of an earthly, erotic seduction. The words "fervor" (*ferveur*) and "zeal" (*zèle*), coupled with Tartuffe's desirous grasps, underpin the irony of the scene and expose the materiality of his true goals.

Nevertheless, not all rhetorical seduction need be restricted solely to the erotic or sensual. As María Teresa Hurtado de Mendoza Zabalgoitia and Ramiro Jesús Sandoval suggest, "El erotismo está constantemente cambiando, dependiendo de factores sociales, culturales y personales, donde— hoy en día—la mercadotecnia tiene una influencia importante. El erotismo puede manifestarse de varias formas como: conductas auto-eróticas, conductas heterosexuales, conductas homosexuales, fantasías sexuales, estímulos visuales, y la búsqueda de nuevas formas de disfrute y satisfacción sexual." (Eroticism is constantly changing, depending on social, cultural, and personal factors, in which today marketing holds an important influence. Eroticism can manifest in several ways: autoerotic behavior, heterosexual behavior, homosexual behavior, sexual fantasies, visual stimuli, and the search for new forms of enjoyment and sexual satisfaction.)[14] Though there is doubtless a sexual dimension to the erotic, the visual, aggrandized quality of Isla's rhetoric takes many forms and is central to Isla's invocation of religious reform.

In both *Tartuffe* and *Father Gerundio* one consistently recalls an attempt to engage listeners' desire for wish-fulfillment—telling people what they most want to hear—in order to achieve self-serving, material goals. In one instance, Father Gerundio seeks advice to develop an effective funeral sermon. Father Blas offers some guidance but nevertheless confuses virtue and vice: "Pues, ¿hay más que bautizar esos vicios con el nombre de virtudes? Y cátalo todo compuesto. Di que ninguno le excedió en la condensación, que pocos le igualaron en el ingenio, que a nadie concedió ventajas en lo penetrativo. . . . Ves ahí desfigurados sus vicios y vestidos a la moda, en traje de virtudes morales." (What is there more than to christen his vices with the name of virtues, and thy business is done. Say that no one exceeded him in condescension, that few equalled him in ingenuity, that he was outdone by nobody in penetration. . . . There thou hast his vices metamorphosed at once, and fashionably clothed in the garb of moral virtues.)[15] Albeit hyperbolic and humorous, the notion of "dressing up" hypocrisy reframes and celebrates both preachers' behavior. Yet again excess takes priority over humility, and Gerundio and Blas lead audiences to accept false declarations.

In *Tartuffe*, a similar rhetorical posture exists in act 3, scene 6, in which the antagonist assumes a coded, ornamented discourse of false modesty to gain material goods. Damis has already approached his father in an effort to persuade him about Tartuffe's intentions. Here, Orgon confronts Tartuffe to attempt to determine the truth:

> *Orgon:* Can it be true, this dreadful thing I hear?
>
> *Tartuffe:* Yes, Brother, I'm a wicked man, I fear:
> A wretched sinner, all depraved and twisted,
> The greatest villain that has ever existed.
> My life's one heap of crimes, which grows each minute;
> There's naught but foulness and corruption in it;
> And I perceive that Heaven, outraged by me,
> Has chosen this occasion to mortify me.
> Charge me with any deed you wish to name,
> I'll not defend myself, but take the blame.
>
> . . . .
>
> *Orgon: (To Damis)*
> You deceitful boy, how dare you try
> To stain his purity with so foul a lie?[16]

In this moment of dramatic irony, Tartuffe assumes the posture of a pious, humble penitent. Orgon interprets Tartuffe's hyperbolic, false modesty as further proof of his humility and true devotion. It would seem that Orgon is to this point incapable of viewing Tartuffe as otherwise; the latter even chooses not to defend himself—to "turn the other cheek," as found in the book of Matthew. Ironically, this feigned piety affords Tartuffe even greater influence in the household. Orgon thereafter dismisses his son, embraces Tartuffe, and offers him his inheritance. In this way, a rhetoric of stylized double-talk both destabilizes and reconfigures power relations within the family. It need not be emphasized that the family stands in, of course, for broader social and political structures.

In the case of *Father Gerundio,* John H. R. Polt calls attention to the novel as a vehicle for social commentary: "Isla, who might have criticized rhetorical and intellectual abuses in any number of ways, did choose to do so by means of a novel. His message concerns the real world, and an aspect of the real world which was very important to him; but it is conveyed through fiction, through deliberate falsehood."[17] Through the direct intervention of Isla's narrator (to take a snuff of tobacco, for example), the reader is reminded that he or she is indeed reading a literary account that bears upon the larger historical and political context of the age. Russell P. Sebold points out specifically that *Father Gerundio* is a novel that operates within the Cervantine vein: "Isla's profoundest literary insight was his awareness of the Cervantian synthesis. But his insight was strictly intellectual [in] the neoclassical interpretation of the *Quixote* as pure satire. Satire could not leave the hero on the poetic mountain peaks of Amadís, and the age of Luzán was too myopic to see the tragicomic hilltops of Don Quixote. . . . Isla felt a satirical hero had to be an assemblage of all that was ridiculous in all heroes. This technique would achieve the same synthesis of universal imitation and historical truth, but on the ground level of history, rather than on a middle ground."[18] According to Sebold, Isla engages *Don Quixote* and at the same time develops character through an extensive process of note-taking, using aspects of historical source figures as the basis of his own social commentary.[19]

Comparative approaches to the eighteenth century such as the rereading of *Father Gerundio* in dialogue with *Tartuffe,* cast in relief to historical circumstances, offer fruitful possibilities for new approximations to Isla's novel. Through this comparative approach, the study moves beyond existing readings on aesthetic characteristics alone to open new interpretative approaches across literary traditions. Like Molière, Isla renders preaching styles in an exaggerated fashion and creates a satirical send-up of rhetorical excess. This posture is so valuable because through satire and humor Isla can more effectively convey his criticism in a compelling manner. On satire and humor, José Enrique Martínez Fernández summarizes that "José Francisco de Isla construye un personaje ficticio, fray Gerundio de Campazas, predicador extravagante, con el fin de ridiculizar y corregir a los predicadores culterano-conceptistas de la época que desde el pulpito vertían toda clase de insensateces basándose en una erudición llena de citas latinas y de conceptos hueros, de atrevidos y estúpidos silogismos, de correspondencias absurdas, de equívocos y agudezas." (José Francisco de Isla constructs a fictitious character, Father Gerundio de Campazas, an extravagant preacher, in order to ridicule and correct the *culterano-conceptista* preachers of the age, who from the pulpit spewed all manner of follies, based on an erudition full of Latin quotes, empty concepts, daring and meaningless syllogisms, absurd correspondences, misconceptions, and wit.)[20] Like Molière, Isla engages satire with an eye toward social reform. It is useful to recall that satire often involves the use of irony and exaggeration to draw attention to contemporary social or political circumstances so as to suggest an alternative solution by means of a negative example. This brand of social criticism is indeed at work in Isla's novel, and such a rhetorical posture situates Isla alongside Cervantes and Molière in a broader literary tradition of satirical writing. In its moment, Isla's satire negotiated an important issue that held theological implications. Irony and satire provided an effective mode of commentary on important contemporary circumstances.

This essay has argued that Isla appropriates *Tartuffe* in the narration of his own rhetorical and theological critique. Like *Tartuffe*, *Father Gerundio* conveys a rococo aesthetic—chiefly through hyperbolic argumentation, ornamented gesture, and stylized rhetoric—to emphasize the potential that luxurious discourse possesses to destabilize. Both men manipulate their audiences through ostentatious speech and behavior. This comparative approach is both relevant and utilitarian, as it provides a discursive framework in which to broaden contemporary debates surrounding Isla's critique of theological excess. Looking broadly across genres and centuries, we are invited to consider the ways in which a *Tartuffe* model better informs the scope of Isla's satire. His criticism, although wildly humorous and masterful, holds important religious implications given that Isla exposes the dangers of inadequate seminary preparation and illogical lines of rhetoric. Like Horace and Cervantes, Isla reaffirms to readers that a narrative that is both useful and entertaining will resonate more concretely in the mind. As a call for comprehensive theological reform, *Father Gerundio* draws attention to the consequences of Jansenist-style predication, immortalizing its greatest champion and laughing him into the pages of historical and cultural memory.

Notes

1. Spanish from Isla, *Fray Gerundio* (1995), 112; English from Isla, *Father Gerundio* (1772), 23, 25.
2. Colebrook, *Irony*, 15, 17.
3. Haidt, *Seduction and Sacrilege*, 46, 47.
4. Ibid., 72.
5. Ibid., 49.
6. Abellán, "El jansenismo español," 30.

7. Blakeney, *Popery*, 76.

8. Saugnieux, *Les jansénistes*, 23, 34.

9. Astell, *Eating Beauty*, 75.

10. Spanish from Isla, *Fray Gerundio* (1995), 80; English from Isla, *Father Gerundio* (1772), 79.

11. Martín Gaite, *Usos amorosos*, 48.

12. Spanish from Isla, *Fray Gerundio* (1995), 76; English from Isla, *Father Gerundio* (1772), 71.

13. Molière, *Tartuffe*, 239.

14. Hurtado de Mendoza Zabalgoitia and Sandoval, "La construcción del erotismo masculino y femenino," 60.

15. Spanish from Isla, *Fray Gerundio* (1995), 95; English from Isla, *Father Gerundio* (1772), 252.

16. Molière, *Tartuffe*, 243.

17. Polt, "Ironic Narrator," 373.

18. Sebold, "Naturalistic Tendencies," 312; see also Alter, *Partial Magic*, chap. 4.

19. Sebold provides a pertinent discussion of character development, satire, and additional imaginative possibilities of *Father Gerundio* in further detail. "Naturalistic Tendencies," 310–11.

20. Martínez Fernández, "Burla, sátira, y humor," 117.

Works Cited

Abellán, José Luis. "El jansenismo español y la renovación de la predicación en el Padre Isla." *Revista de la Universidad Complutense* 1 (1981): 30–41.

Alter, Robert. *Partial Magic: The Novel as a Self-Conscious Genre.* Berkeley: University of California Press, 1975.

Astell, Ann W. *Eating Beauty: The Eucharist and the Spiritual Arts of the Middle Ages.* Ithaca, NY: Cornell University Press, 2006.

Blakeney, Richard P. *Popery in its Social Aspect.* Stockbridge, MA: Hard Press Editions, 2012.

Colebrook, Claire. *Irony in the Work of Philosophy.* Omaha: University of Nebraska Press, 2002.

Haidt, Rebecca. *Seduction and Sacrilege: Rhetorical Power in "Fray Gerundio de Campazas."* Cranbury, NJ: Associated University Presses, 2002.

Hurtado de Mendoza Zabalgoitia, Maria Teresa, and Ramiro Jesús Sandoval. "La construcción del erotismo masculino y femenino." *Revista Rayuela* 2 (2011): 60–64.

Isla, José Francisco de. *Historia del famoso predicador Fray Gerundio de Campazas, alias Zotes.* Ed. Russell P. Sebold. 4 vols. Madrid: Clásicos Castellanos, 1964.

———. *Historia del famoso predicador Fray Gerundio de Campazas, alias Zotes.* Ed. Enrique Rodríguez Cepeda. Madrid: Cátedra, 1995.

———. *The History of the Famous Preacher, Friar Gerund de Campazas: Translated from the Spanish.* London: T. Davies, 1772.

Martínez Fernández, José Enrique. "Burla, sátira, y humor en *Fray Gerundio de Cam-*

pazas: Huellas de la comicidad carnavalesca." *Epos: Revista de filología* 15 (1999): 175–97.

Martín Gaite, Carmen. *Usos amorosos del dieciocho en España.* Barcelona: Anagrama, 1987.

Molière. *Tartuffe.* Trans. Richard Wilbur. New York: Harcourt Brace, 1997.

Polt, John H. R. "The Ironic Narrator in the Novel: Isla." *Studies in Eighteenth Century Culture* 9 (1979): 371–85.

Saugnieux, Joel. *Les jansénistes et le renouveau de la prédication dans l'Espagne du XVIIe siècle.* Lyon: Impr. de la Université de Lyon, 1976.

Sebold, Russell P. "Naturalistic Tendencies and the Descent of the Hero in Isla's *Fra Gerundio.*" *Hispania* 41 (1958): 308–14.

About MapScholar

JAMES P. AMBUSKE AND CAROL GUARNIERI

The essays in this collection are accompanied by "The Digital Eighteenth Centuries," a digital atlas created on the MapScholar platform. You can find the site by visiting http://www.mapscholar.org/18th. MapScholar is an NEH- and ACLS-funded digital platform for geospatial visualization with a special emphasis on historical cartography. S. Max Edelson, an associate professor of history at the University of Virginia, and William A. Ferster, an assistant research professor in the Curry School of Education and director of visualization for the Sciences, Humanities & Arts Technology Initiative (SHANTI) at UVA, created MapScholar to provide scholars with a tool to build digital atlases of historical maps. Its origins lay in solving a vexing problem in the dissemination of academic research centered on complex imagery: how to overcome publisher-imposed restrictions on the number of images that appear in traditional print monographs. MapScholar allows authors to overcome these limitations and display the full range of their image-based research.

MapScholar is more than just a program to display geo-referenced or geo-rectified maps: it enables authors to build digital interpretative frameworks around them. In this sense, MapScholar embodies the eighteenth century's interdisciplinary nature. It permits users to bring different forms of knowledge and knowledge production together to annotate maps with text, aggregated data, KML-shapefiles, and external media. As the essays in this volume demonstrate, eighteenth-century women and men wrote and imagined their worlds beyond the narrowly assigned borders that we use to define our respective disciplines today. MapScholar encourages similar intellectual collaboration across fields. As free, open-source software, it allows experts in the humanities and computer sciences to pursue a variety of research questions and then build better versions of the tool to answer them. The companion MapScholar site for this collection of essays demonstrates, not the culmination of the program's capabilities, but one possible way to expand each essay's scope and audience. On page 2 of this site, you will find a how-to guide that will help you navigate the atlas and enhance your consumption of the essays in this book. We also encourage you to visit www.mapscholar.org for examples of other MapScholar sites and to view a copy of the developer's guide.

Contributors

JAMES P. AMBUSKE received his PhD in history from the University of Virginia in 2016. He is a historian of the American Revolution with particular interests in Scotland and America in the late eighteenth century. A former Georgian Papers Programme Fellow, James is currently the Farmer Postdoctoral Fellow in Digital Humanities at the University of Virginia School of Law Library, where he codirects the Scottish Court of Session Records Digital Archive Project and the 1828 Catalogue Collection Project.

KATELYN D. CRAWFORD is William Cary Hulsey Curator of American Art at th Birmingham Museum of Art. She was previously Assistant Curator of American Art at the Nelson-Atkins Museum of Art in Kansas City, Missouri. She completed her doctorate in the history of art and architecture at the University of Virginia in 2017. Her dissertation, "Transient Painters, Traveling Canvases: Portraiture and Mobility in the British Atlantic, 1750–1780," received research support from the Henry Luce Foundation/ American Council of Learned Societies and the Smithsonian American Art Museum.

CARRIE B. DOUGLASS is Professor of Anthropology at the University of Virginia. She is the author of *Bulls, Bullfighting and Spanish Identities* (Arizona, 1997) and coeditor of *Barren States: The Population "Implosion" in Europe* (Bloomsbury, 2005). In 2008 she was a fellow at the International Center for Jefferson Studies, at Monticello, where she began research on her current project on Thomas Jefferson and equine culture in eighteenth-century Virginia.

CASEY R. ERIKSEN is Visiting Assistant Professor of Hispanic Studies at Shenandoah University. He has published articles and chapters with *Prosopopeya: Revista de crítica contemporánea*, the Universitat de València, and elsewhere. He has also collaborated with Enrique Peláez Malagón (Universitat de València) in a comparative examination of poetry and religious iconography. Eriksen has been awarded the Tibor Wlassics Dante Research Fellowship and received other research support from the Buckner W. Clay

Endowment for the Humanities at the University of Virginia and from the Mellon Foundation.

DAVID T. GIES is Commonwealth Professor of Spanish at the University of Virginia. He has published sixteen books, including *Theatre and Politics in Nineteenth-Century Spain: Juan de Grimaldi as Impresario and Government Agent* (Cambridge, 1988), *The Theatre in Nineteenth-Century Spain* (Cambridge, 1994), *The Cambridge Companion to Modern Spanish Culture* (1999), *The Cambridge History of Spanish Literature* (2004), *The Cambridge History of Theatre in Spain* (coedited, 2012), and *Eros y amistad* (Barcelona, 2016). Author of more than 100 articles and 130 scholarly book reviews, he edits *Dieciocho,* a journal dedicated to the study of the Spanish Enlightenment. In 2007 he was named Encomienda de Número de la Orden de Isabel la Católica by His Majesty Juan Carlos, king of Spain. In 2013 he was elected president of the Asociación Internacional de Hispanistas.

BONNIE GORDON is Associate Professor of Music at the University of Virginia. Her books include *Monteverdi's Unruly Women* (Cambridge, 2004) and a cross-cultural volume of essays coedited with Martha Feldman, *The Courtesan's Arts* (Oxford, 2006). She has also published on Thomas Jefferson's sounds, contemporary female singers, and castrati. She is currently working on two book projects: *Voice Machines: The Castrato, The Cat Piano and Other Strange Sounds* and *Jefferson's Ear.* Her honors include a National Endowment for the Humanities Fellowship and the Robert Lehman Visiting Professorship at Villa I Tatti, The Harvard University Center for Italian Renaissance Studies.

CAROL GUARNIERI is a PhD candidate in the Department of English at the University of Virginia, where she is completing her dissertation project, "Creole Constitutions: Subjecthood and the Early Novel in the British Caribbean."

RUTH HILL is Professor of Spanish and Andrew W. Mellon Chair in the Humanities at Vanderbilt University. She teaches courses in the history of early modern science, critical race studies, and Latin American and US literature and culture. She is the author of *Sceptres and Sciences in the Spains* (Liverpool, 2000), *Hierarchy, Commerce, and Fraud in Bourbon Spanish America* (Vanderbilt, 2005), and numerous scholarly essays. She edited a special number of the *Journal of Spanish Cultural Studies* entitled "Categories and Crossings: Critical Race Studies and the Spanish World" (2009).

LOUIS P. NELSON is Professor of Architectural History and Associate Provost for Outreach at the University of Virginia. He is the author of *American Sanctuary: Understanding Sacred Spaces* (Indiana, 2006); *The Beauty of Holiness: Anglicanism and Architecture in Colonial South Carolina* (North Carolina, 2008), the 2010 SESAH Best Book of the Year; and, with Maurie McInnis, *Shaping the Body Politic: Art and Political Formation in Early America* (Virginia, 2011). His current research engages the spaces of enslavement in West Africa and in the Americas, working to document and interpret the buildings and landscapes that shaped the transatlantic slave trade.

ANDREW O'SHAUGHNESSY is Vice President of Monticello, Saunders Director of the Robert H. Smith International Center for Jefferson Studies at the Thomas Jefferson Foundation, and Professor of History at the University of Virginia. His most recent book, *The Men Who Lost America: British Leadership, the American Revolution and the Fate of the Empire* (Yale, 2013), received eight national awards, including the New York Historical Society American History Book Prize, the George Washington Book Prize, and The Society of Military History Book Prize. He is also the author of *An Empire Divided: The American Revolution and the British Caribbean* (Pennsylvania, 2000). He is a coeditor of *Old World, New World: America and Europe in the Age of Jefferson* (Virginia, 2010), part of the Jeffersonian America series. A Fellow of the Royal Historical Society, he is an editor of the *Journal of American History* and the *Journal of the Early Republic*.

BRAD PASANEK is Associate Professor in the Department of English of the University of Virginia. He is the author of *Metaphors of Mind: An Eighteenth-Century Dictionary* (Johns Hopkins, 2015). He has directed several digital projects, including a digital variorum edition of Thomas Jefferson's *Notes on the State of Virginia*, "The Mind is a Metaphor" database, "18thConnect," and "Hands on Literature."

MICHAEL PICKARD is Assistant Professor of English at Millsaps College. He has published in *Studies in Romanticism* and *The Helen Burns Poetry Anthology: New Voices*. He is currently writing a book about Eudora Welty.

PIERPAOLO POLZONETTI, Professor of Musicology at the University of California, Davis, specializes in opera and eighteenth-century music and culture. He is the author of *Italian Opera in the Age of the American Revolution* (Cambridge, 2011) and a coeditor of the *Cambridge Companion to*

Eighteenth-Century Opera. He is the recipient of the Lewis Lockwood book award and the H. Colin Slim and Albert Einstein article awards, all conferred by the American Musicological Society. His research has been funded by the Earhart Foundation, the American Council for Learned Societies, and the National Endowment for the Humanities.

JENNIFER REED is the Florence Levy Kay Fellow in Eighteenth-Century Studies at Brandeis University. Her work has been published in *Caribbeana: The Journal of the Early Caribbean Society* and the *Journal of Popular Culture,* and she has work forthcoming in *Making Humanities Matter,* part of the Debates in Digital Humanities series of the University of Minnesota Press.

SOPHIA ROSENFELD is Walter H. Annenberg Professor of History at the University of Pennsylvania. She is the author of *A Revolution in Language: The Problem of Signs in Late Eighteenth-Century France* (Stanford, 2001) and *Common Sense: A Political History* (Harvard, 2014), which won the Mark Lynton History Prize and the Society for the History of the Early American Republic Book Prize. She also coedits the journal *Modern Intellectual History.* She has held fellowships from the Guggenheim Foundation, the School of Social Science at the Institute for Advanced Studies, the Mellon Foundation, the Remarque Institute at NYU, and the American Council of Learned Societies.

MARY D. SHERIFF was the W. R. Kenan Jr. Distinguished Professor of Art History at the University of North Carolina at Chapel Hill. The author of numerous books, including *J.-H. Fragonard: Art and Eroticism* (Chicago, 1990), *The Exceptional Woman: Elisabeth Vigée-Lebrun and the Cultural Politics of Art* (Chicago, 1996), *Moved by Love: Inspired Artists and Deviant Women in Eighteenth-Century France* (Chicago, 2004), and *Antoine Watteau: Perspectives on the Artist and the Culture of His Time* (Delaware, 2006), she also edited several collections of essays and was a Guggenheim Fellow.

PATRICIA MEYER SPACKS is Edgar F. Shannon Professor Emerita at the University of Virginia. Past president of the Modern Language Association, she is the author of more than a dozen books, including *The Female Imagination* (Knopf, 1975), *Gossip* (Knopf, 1985), *Desire and Truth* (Chicago, 1990), *Boredom* (Chicago, 1995), *Novel Beginnings* (Yale, 2006), and *On Rereading* (Harvard, 2011).

CYNTHIA WALL is Professor of English at the University of Virginia. She is the author of *The Literary and Cultural Spaces of Restoration London* (Cambridge, 1998) and *The Prose of Things: Transformations of Description in the Eighteenth Century* (Chicago, 2005), honorable mention for the James Russell Lowell Prize. She is an editor of works by Alexander Pope, Daniel Defoe, and John Bunyan. She has been awarded fellowships from the American Council of Learned Societies and the National Endowment for the Humanities. Her current book project is *Grammars of Approach: Landscape, Narrative, and the Linguistic Picturesque.*

ADRIENNE WARD is Associate Professor of Italian at the University of Virginia. Her area of specialty is seventeenth- and eighteenth-century Italian literature, with a focus on theater production and culture, as well as the role and treatment of gender in literary works of the early modern period. Her publications include *Pagodas in Play: China on the Eighteenth-Century Italian Opera Stage* (Bucknell, 2010) and articles in *Theatre Journal, Literature Compass, Problemi di critica goldoniana, Italica,* and *Quaderni d'Italianistica.*

CHAD WELLMON is Associate Professor of German Studies at the University of Virginia. He is the author of *Becoming Human: Romantic Anthropology and the Embodiment of Freedom* (Pennsylvania State, 2010) and *Organizing Enlightenment: Information Overload and the Invention of the Modern Research University* (Johns Hopkins, 2015), as well as numerous essays in journals such as *Representations, Eighteenth Century Theory and Interpretation, Hedgehog Review, Eighteenth-Century Studies,* the *Goethe Yearbook,* and *Studies in Romanticism.* He is also coeditor of *The Rise of the Research University: A Sourcebook.*

RICHARD WILL is Associate Professor in the McIntire Department of Music at the University of Virginia. He specializes in classical, folk, and roots music of America and Europe. He is the author of *The Characteristic Symphony in the Age of Haydn and Beethoven* (Cambridge, 2002) and coeditor of *Engaging Haydn: Culture, Context, and Criticism* (Cambridge, 2012). He has also published essays on the symphony, the orchestra, opera, religious music, and folk music in a variety of journals and collections. Currently he is working on a new book, *Don Giovanni Live: Performance, Media, and the Progress of a Modern Myth.*

Index

Price, Richard, 183
print culture, 11, 16, 27, 31
printing history, 12; British, 40–48; German, 14–35, 36n14
publicness, 15; public sphere, 14, 33, 35, 37n47, 219
Puccini, Giacomo, 204; *La fanciulla del West,* 204
puechel/puchuele/puchivel/pucheula, 74, 75, 76, 78, 80, 81, 90n4
puntees, 127

Quakers, 204, 217

race: black, 72–91; *blanqueamiento* (whitening of humans), 5, 72, 74, 76, 78, 79, 82, 86, 89, 90n4; hybridity, 87–88; hypodescent, 73; *morisca* (black female quadroon), 83, 84; mulatto, 72, 74, 75, 76, 82–85, 87, 90–91n7; Negrophobia, 84, 86; *ochavón/ochavóna,* 76, 78, 83; octoroon, 70, 72, 74, 75, 76, 79, 80, 83, 84; one-drop rule, 73; *puechel/puchuele/puchivel/puchuela,* 74, 75, 76, 78, 80, 81, 90n4; quadroon, 80–85; 72, 74–76, 80–85; quintroon, 82–83; *torna-atrás* ("throwback"), 84–85; white, 72–91
Raffi, Teodora, 253
Ramírez de Carrión, Manuel, 77–78, 91n9; *Maravillas de naturaleza,* 77
Randolph, Col. Thomas Mann, 111, 112, 113
Randolphs, 104
Rapin, Paul de, 44, 47; *The History of England,* 44, 47
reading public, 15, 16, 18, 33
reception piece, 152, 162, 164, 174
Réceuil Julienne (painting exhibition), 170
Regency France, 169, 170; government, 171
Rembrandt van Rijn, 189
requinterona, 83
rice, 120
Rice, John A., 207
Richardson, Richard, 111, 118n40
Richardson, Samuel, 252; *Clarissa,* 252, French translation, 252; *Pamela,* 63, as *comédie larmoyante,* 253
Richetti, John, 56

Rivington family, 43
Roberts, Justin, 121, 123
Roberts, Justin, 121, 123, 138, 139, 140
rococo aesthetic, 148, 149, 152, 164, 200, 276, 277, 284
Rolfe, Thomas, 105
romance, 51, 59
Rousseau, Jean-Jacques, 36n15, 219
royalty (English), 57, 97, 99
Russia, 54, 55

Sadeler, Jan (elder), 156, 157; *The Story of the Family of Seth,* 157, 159
Saint-Pierre, Bernardin de, 173; *Paul et Virginie,* 173
Salieri, Antonio, 220, 227n65
salta-atrás, 75, 84, 89
Sandoval, Ramiro Jesús, 281
Sarazin, Jacques, 173; *Magdalen,* 173
satire, 159, 170, 186, 192, 199–200, 221, 270, 274, 276–78, 283–84
satyrs, 148, 157, 158
Saugnieux, Joel, 279
Scherping, J., 178
Schikaneder, Emanuel, 221, 222, 223
Schmidt, James, 16, 18, 36n15
Scotland, 44, 57, 267; Edinburgh, 44, 47, 267
Schutte, Anne Jacobson, 241, 259n79
Scott, Katie, 162–63
Scudéry, Madeleine de, 154; *Clélie,* 154; *Carte de Tendre,* 154, 156, 159, 160
Sebold, Russell P., 283
Second Anglo-Dutch War, 181
Seidel Menchi, Silvana, 234
Seminary School of Treviso, 203
sensibility, 264
Shakespeare, William, 41; *First Folio of William Shakespeare,* 41; *Othello,* 73
Shangri-la, 174
sirens, 155, 163–64, 166, 168, 174
Siskin, Clifford, 19–20
slavery, 69–71, 95, 101, 120–38, 147, 178, 180–86, 191–92, 211, 213, 223
slaves: burial, 126; executions, 128–29, 131; music and dance, 126; punishment, 128–31; rape, 130–31, 138; surveillance, 131–34, 137, 138; torture, 128–31; villages, 123–27, 133, 134, 136, 137, 138

War of the Spanish Succession, 61; Battle
of Blenheim, 62
Washington, George, 107, 110, 112, 117n10,
117n21, 211
Waterson, William, 111
Watson, Davy, 108–9
Watteau, Jean-Antoine, 147–48, 151–54,
157, 160, 162–74; *Allegory of Spring*, 163;
Départ des comediens Italiens en 1697,
170; *Départ pour les Isles*, 170–72, 174;
Pèlerinage à l'île de Cythère, 147, 152,
153, 171, 173–74
Wayles, Elizabeth, 106
Wayles, John, 117n15, 118n40
Wayles, Martha, 106, 117n15
Wednesday Society (Friends of the En-
lightenment), 24, 25, 31, 32, 33
Weill, Kurt, *The Threepenny Opera*, 199
Welch, Saunders, *An Essay on the Office
of the Constable*, 46
West, Ann, 113
West, Benjamin, 207
white (race), 72–91

Wieland, Christoph, 206, 208; *Der
Teutsche Merkur*, 30
Wild, Edward A., 183
Wiles, David, 253
Williams, Cynric, 132, 139, 140
Wilson, David, 47
Wolff, Christian, 37n44
women, 51, 52, 55, 57, 59, 60, 61, 62, 63,
219–20, 233–59; in business, 236
Wood, John, 135, 136; *A Series of Plans for
Cottages or Habitations of the Laborer
either in Husbandry or the Mechanic
Arts*, 135, 136
Wordsworth, William, *Ode on Intima-
tions of Immortality*, 64
Wythe, George, 112

Zedlitz, Karl A. Freiherr von, 25, 26
Zöllner, Johann Friedrich, 16, 18, 21, 22,
24, 32, 36, 259n83; "Is it wise to no
longer sanction marriage through religion?," 18, 21, 22, 24